An Introduction to ANSYS® Fluent® 2019

John E. Matsson, Ph.D., P.E.

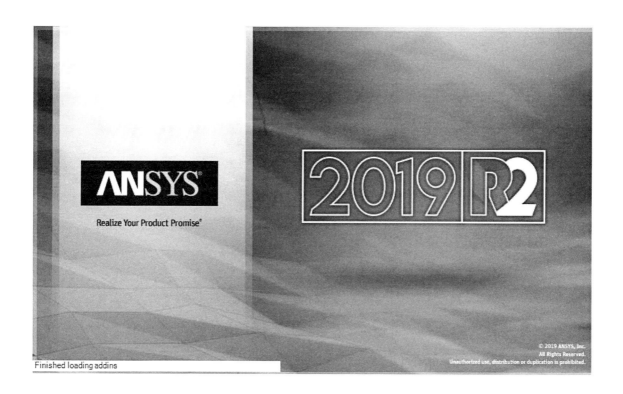

SDC
PUBLICATIONS

SDC Publications
P.O. Box 1334
Mission, KS 66222
913-262-2664
www.SDCpublications.com
Publisher: Stephen Schroff

ISBN-13: 978-1-63057-330-0
ISBN-10: 1-63057-330-2

Printed and bound in the United States of America.

Acknowledgements

I would like to thank Stephen Schroff of SDC Publications for his help in preparing this book for publication.

About the Author

Dr. John Matsson is a Professor of Engineering and Chair of the Engineering Department at Oral Roberts University in Tulsa, Oklahoma. He earned M.S. and Ph.D. degrees from the Royal Institute of Technology in Stockholm, Sweden, in 1988 and 1994, respectively, and completed postdoctoral work at the Norwegian University of Science and Technology in Trondheim, Norway. His teaching areas include Finite Element Methods, Fluid Mechanics, Manufacturing Processes, and Principles of Design. He is a member of the American Society of Mechanical Engineers ASME Mid-Continent Section. Please contact the author jmatsson@oru.edu with any comments, questions, or suggestions on this book.

Notes:

TABLE OF CONTENTS

Notes:

CHAPTER 1. INTRODUCTION

A. ANSYS Workbench

ANSYS Workbench is an integrated simulation platform that includes a wide range of systems in the toolbox including analysis systems, component systems, custom systems, and design exploration, see Table 1.1.

Analysis Systems	Component Systems	Custom Systems	Design Exploration
Design Assessment	ACP (Post)	FSI: Fluid Flow (CFX) > Static Structural	Direct Optimization
Eigenvalue Buckling	ACP (Pre)	FSI: Fluid Flow (FLUENT) > Static Structural	Parameters Correlation
Electric	Autodyn	Pre-Stress Modal	Response Surface
Explicit Dynamics	BladeGen	Random Vibration	Response Surface Optimization
Fluid Flow (CFX)	CFX	Response Spectrum	ROM Builder
Fluid Flow (Fluent)	Engineering Data	Thermal-Stress	Six Sigma Analysis
Harmonic Acoustics	External Data		
Harmonic Response	External Model		
IC Engine (Fluent)	Fluent		
IC Engine (Forte)	Fluent (with Fluent Meshing)		
Magnetostatic	Forte		
Modal	Geometry		
Modal Acoustics	Mechanical APDL		
Random Vibration	Mechanical Model		
Response Spectrum	Mesh		
Rigid Dynamics	Microsoft Office Excel		
Static Acoustics	Performance Map		
Static Structural	Results		
Steady-State Thermal	System Coupling		
Thermal-Electric	Turbo Setup		
Topology Optimization	Turbo Grid		
Transient Structural	Vista AFD		
Transient Thermal	Vista CCD		
TurbomachineryFluid Flow	Vista CPD		
	Vista RTD		

Table 1.1 Available systems in ANSYS Workbench Toolbox

ANSYS Workbench also has a Project Schematic where the details for the process of execution of the different analysis systems are available. These details of each analysis system in the project schematic include Engineering Data, Geometry, Model, Setup, Solution and Results. Furthermore, properties of schematics are available for user input.

B. ANSYS DesignModeler

The geometry for the Fluid Flow (Fluent) flow study project can be created either in DesignModeler or alternatively using SpaceClaim. DesignModeler is a parametric modeler designed to draw 2D sketches and model 3D CAD parts. ANSYS DesignModeler has nine different toolbars as listed in Table 1.2.

Toolbars
Active Plane/Sketch toolbar
Display toolbar
Feature toolbar
File toolbar
Graphics Options toolbar
Menus toolbar
Rotation Modes toolbar
Selection toolbar
Undo/Redo toolbar

Table 1.2 Toolbars in ANSYS DesignModeler

Moreover, the Sketching Toolboxes in DesignModeler include Draw, Modify, Dimensions, Constraints and Settings as shown in Table 1.3.

Constraints	Dimensions	Draw	Modify	Settings
Auto Constraints	Angle	Arc by 3 Points	Chamfer	Grid
Coincident	Animate	Arc by Center	Copy	Major Grid Spacing
Concentric	Diameter	Arc by Tangent	Corner	Minor-Steps per Major
Equal Distance	Display	Circle	Cut	Snaps per Minor
Equal Length	Edit	Circle by 3 Tangents	Drag	
Equal Radius	General	Construction Point	Duplicate	
Fixed	Horizontal	Construction Point at Intersection	Extend	
Horizontal	Length/Distance	Ellipse	Fillet	
Midpoint	Move	Line	Move	
Parallel	Radius	Line by 2 Tangents	Offset	
Perpendicular	Semi-Automatic	Oval	Paste	
Symmetry	Vertical	Polygon	Replicate	
Tangent		Polyline	Spline Edit	
Vertical		Rectangle	Split	
		Rectangle by 3 Points	Trim	
		Spline		
		Tangent Line		

Table 1.3 Sketching Toolboxes in ANSYS DesignModeler

C. ANSYS Meshing

ANSYS Meshing produces the mesh using Mesh Methods and Mesh Controls as shown in Tables 1.4 and Table 1.5.

Hexahedral Meshing	Tetrahedral Meshing	Surface Meshing
Cut cell Cartesian	ANSYS CFX-Mesh	Default quad, quad/tri or tri
General Sweep	Patch conforming	Uniform quad or quad tri
Hex-dominant	Patch independent	
MultiZone		
Thin Sweep		

Table 1.4 Mesh methods in ANSYS Meshing

Global Mesh Control	Local Mesh Control
Curvature-based refinement settings	Automatic Contact Detection
Element midside node settings	Body, face, edge curvature-based refinement
Inflation settings	Body, face, edge, vertex sizings
Physics preference settings	Body, face, edge, vertex sphere of influence
Pinch (defeaturing) settings	Body mesh method controls
Proximity-based refinement settings	Body of Influence
Quality settings	Contact Sizing
Relevance settings	Gap tool
Rigid-body behavior settings	Inflation controls
Smoothing settings	Mapped-face meshing controls
Transition/growth settings	Match mesh controls
	Pinch controls
	Solver-based refinement controls
	Virtual topologies

Table 1.5 Mesh controls in ANSYS Meshing

D. ANSYS Fluent

ANSYS Fluent is a computational fluid dynamics software package that is written in the C language. Fluent has numerous capabilities for simulations as shown in Table 1.6.

Fluent Capabilities
2D Planar flows, Axisymmetric flows, Axisymmetric flows with swirl, 3D Flows
Acoustics
Cavitation flows
Chemical species mixing and reaction
Compressible flows, Incompressible flows
Forced heat transfer, Mixed convection heat transfer, Natural heat transfer
Free surface flows
Ideal gases, Real gases
Inviscid flows, Laminar flows, Turbulent flows
Lumped Parameter Models
Melting and Solidification
Multiphase flows
Newtonian flows, Non-Newtonian flows
Porous media
Steady flows, Time-dependent flows

Table 1.6 Some of the capabilities for ANSYS Fluent

There are eleven add on modules available in ANSYS as shown in Table 0.7.

Fluent Add on Modules
Adjoint Solver
Dual-Potential MSMD Battery Model
Fiber Model
Fuel Cell and Electrolysis Model
Macroscopic Particle Model
MHD Model
PEM Fuel Cell Model
Population Balance Model
Single-Potential Battery Model
SOFC Model with Unresolved Electrolyte
Reduced Order Model

Table 1.7 Add on modules for ANSYS Fluent

The user interface of Fluent includes the Outline View and the Task Page. The Outline View includes Setup, Solution, Results and Parameters & Customization, see Table 1.8. The different categories and variables available in setup, solution and results are shown in Tables 1.9-1.12.

Setup	Solution	Results	Parameters & Customization
Boundary Conditions	Calculation Activities	Animations	Custom Field Functions
Cell Zone Conditions	Cell Registers	Graphics	Parameters
Dynamic Mesh	Controls	Plots	User Defined Functions
General	Initialization	Reports	User Defined Memory
Materials	Methods	Scene	User Defined Scalars
Models	Monitors	Surfaces	
Named Expressions	Report Definitions		
Reference Frames	Run Calculation		
Reference Values			

Table 1.8 Outline view options in ANSYS Fluent

Setup Models
Acoustics (Ffowcs-Williams & Hawkings, Wave Equation)
Discrete Phase (Numerics, Parallel, Physical Models, Tracking, UDF)
Electric Potential (Potential Equation)
Energy (Energy Equation)
Heat Exchanger (Dual Cell Model, Macro Model Group, Ungrouped Macro Model)
Multiphase (Eulerian, Mixture, Volume of Fluid, Wet Stream)
Radiation (Discrete Ordinates DO, Discrete Transfer DTRM, P1, Rosseland, Surface to Surface S2S)
Solidification and Melting (Back Diffusion, Solidification/Melting)
Species (Composition PDF Transport, Non-Premixed Combustion, Partially Premixed Combustion, Premixed Combustion, Species Transport)
Structure (Linear Elasticity)
Viscous (Detached Eddy Simulation DES, Inviscid, k-epsilon 2 eqn, k-omega 3 eqn, Laminar, Reynolds Stress 5 eqn, Scale-Adaptive Simulation SAS, Spalart-Allmaras 1 eqn, Transition k-kl-omega 3 eqn, Transition SST 4 eqn)

Table 1.9 Models options in ANSYS Fluent

Setup Reference Values
Area (m2)
Density (kg/m3)
Enthalpy (j/kg)
Length (m)
Pressure (pascal)
Ratio of Specific Heats
Temperature (k)
Velocity (m/s)
Viscosity (kg/m-s)

Table 1.10 Reference values in ANSYS Fluent

Solution	
Calculation Activities	Monitors
Autosave	Convergence Conditions
Execute Commands	Report Files
Cell Register Operations	Report Plots
Solution Animation	Residual

Table 1.11 Calculation activities and monitors options in ANSYS Fluent

Results			
Animations	**Graphics**	**Plots**	**Reports**
Scene Animation	Contours	FFT	Discrete Phase
Solution Animation Playback	Mesh	File	Fluxes
Sweep Surface	Vectors	Histogram	Forces
	Particle Tracks	Interpolated Data	Surface Integrals
	Pathlines	Profile Data	Volume Integrals
	Vectors	XY Plot	

Table 1.12 Animation, graphics, plots and reports options in ANSYS Fluent

The different options that are available for the General Setup are Gravity, Mesh and Solver with the details as shown in Table 1.13.

General		
Gravity	**Mesh**	**Solver**
X (m/s2)	Check	2D Space (Axisymmetric, Axisymmetric Swirl, Planar)
Y (m/s2)	Display…	Time (Steady, Transient)
Z (m/s2)	Report Quality	Type (Density-Based, Pressure-Based)
	Scale…	Velocity Formulation (Absolute, Relative)
	Units…	

Table 1.13 Gravity, mesh and solver options in ANSYS Fluent

The different Solution Methods are shown in Table 1.14.

Solution Methods	
Pressure-Velocity Coupling	**Pressure-Based Solver, Spatial Discretization**
Coupled	Gradient (Green-Gauss Cell Based, Green-Gauss Node Based, Least Squares Cell Based)
PISO	Pressure (Body Force Weighted, Linear, PRESTO!, Second Order, Standard)
SIMPLE	Momentum (First Order Upwind, Power Law, QUICK, Second Order Upwind, Third-Order MUSCL)
SIMPLEC	Energy (First Order Upwind, Power Law, QUICK, Second Order Upwind, Third-Order MUSCL)
	Density-Based Solver, Spatial Discretization
	Gradient (Green-Gauss Cell Based, Green-Gauss Node Based, Least Squares Cell Based)
	Flow (First Order Upwind, Second Order Upwind, Third-Order MUSCL)

Table 1.14 Solution methods options in ANSYS Fluent

E. References

1. ANSYS Fluent Getting Started Guide, Release 19.1, April 2018, ANSYS, Inc.
2. ANSYS FLUENT Theory Guide, Release 15.0, January 2013, ANSYS, Inc.
3. ANSYS Fluent Tutorial Guide, Release 18.0, January 2017, ANSYS, Inc.
4. ANSYS FLUENT User's Guide, Release 15.0, November 2013, ANSYS, Inc.
5. ANSYS Meshing User's Guide, Release 15.0, November 2013, ANSYS, Inc.
6. ANSYS Workbench User's Guide, Release 12.1, November 2009, ANSYS, Inc.
7. DesignModeler User Guide, Release 14.5, October 2012, ANSYS, Inc.

Notes:

Notes:

CHAPTER 2. FLAT PLATE BOUNDARY LAYER

A. Objectives

- Creating Geometry in ANSYS Workbench for ANSYS Fluent Flow Simulation
- Setting up ANSYS Fluent Simulation for Laminar Steady 2D Planar Flow
- Setting up Mesh
- Selecting Boundary Conditions
- Running Calculations
- Using Plots to Visualize Resulting Flow Field
- Compare with Theoretical Solution using Mathematica Code

B. Problem Description

In this chapter, we will use ANSYS Fluent to study the two-dimensional laminar flow on a horizontal flat plate. The inlet velocity for the 1 m long plate is 5 m/s, and we will be using air as the fluid for laminar calculations. We will determine the velocity profiles and plot the profiles. We will start by creating the geometry needed for the simulation.

C. Launching ANSYS Workbench and Selecting Fluent

1. Start by launching ANSYS Workbench. Double click on Fluid Flow (Fluent) that is located under Analysis Systems in Toolbox.

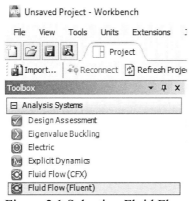

Figure 2.1 Selecting Fluid Flow

D. Launching ANSYS DesignModeler

2. Select Geometry under Project Schematic in ANSYS Workbench. Right-click on Geometry and select Properties. Select 2D Analysis Type under Advanced Geometry Options in Properties of Schematic A2: Geometry. Right-click on Geometry in Project Schematic and select to launch New DesignModeler Geometry. Select Units>>Millimeter as the length unit from the menu in DesignModeler.

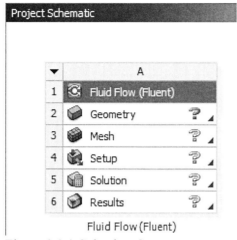

Figure 2.2a) Selecting Geometry

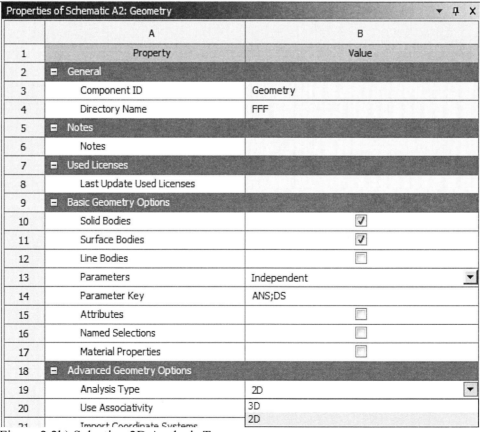

Figure 2.2b) Selecting 2D Analysis Type

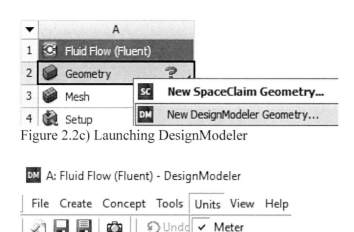

Figure 2.2c) Launching DesignModeler

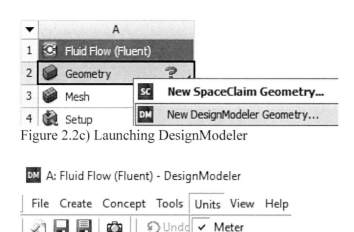

Figure 2.2d) Selecting the length unit

3. Next, we will be creating the geometry in DesignModeler. Select XYPlane from the Tree Outline on the left-hand side in DesignModeler. Select Look at Sketch ⟨icon⟩. Click on the Sketching tab in the Tree Outline and select the Line sketch tool.

   Draw a horizontal line 1,000 mm long from the origin to the right. Make sure you have a *P* at the origin when you start drawing the line. Also, make sure you have an *H* along the line so that it is horizontal and a *C* at the end of the line.

   Select Dimensions within the Sketching options. Click on the line and enter a length of 1,000 mm. Draw a vertical line upward 100 mm long starting at the end point of the first horizontal line. Make sure you have a *P* when starting the line and a *V* indicating a vertical line. Continue with a horizontal line 100 mm long to the left from the origin followed by another vertical line 100 mm long.

   The next line will be horizontal with a length 100 mm starting at the endpoint of the former vertical line and directed to the right. Finally, close the rectangle with a 1,000 mm long horizontal line starting 100 mm above the origin and directed to the right.

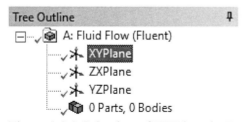

Figure 2.3a) Selection of XYPlane in Tree Outline

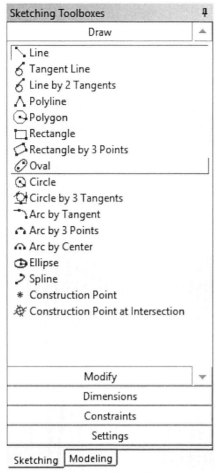

Figure 2.3b) Selection of Line tool

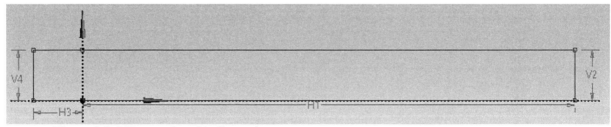

Figure 2.3c) Rectangle with dimensions

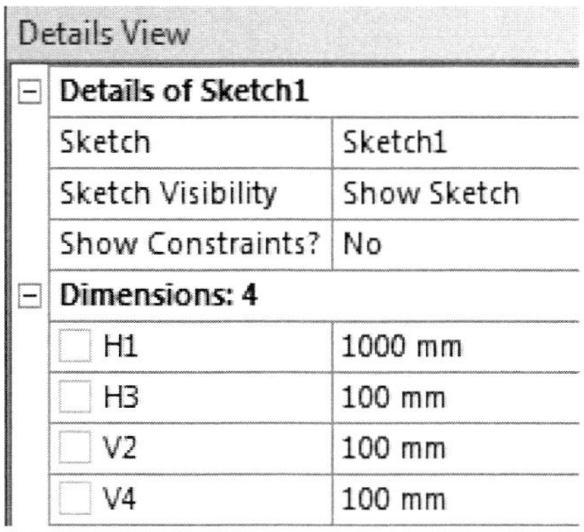

Details View	
Details of Sketch1	
Sketch	Sketch1
Sketch Visibility	Show Sketch
Show Constraints?	No
Dimensions: 4	
H1	1000 mm
H3	100 mm
V2	100 mm
V4	100 mm

Figure 2.3d) Dimensions in Details View

4. Click on the Modeling tab under Sketching Toolboxes. Select Concept>>Surfaces from Sketches in the menu. Control select the six edges of the rectangle as Base Objects and select Apply in Details View. Click on Generate in the toolbar ⌐⫶ Generate. The rectangle turns gray. Right click in the graphics window and select Zoom to Fit and close DesignModeler.

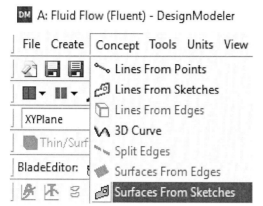

Figure 2.4a) Selecting Surfaces from Sketches

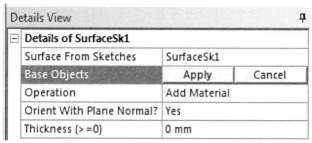

Figure 2.4b) Applying Base Objects

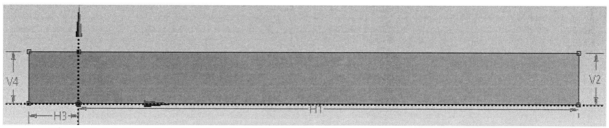

Figure 2.4c) Completed rectangle in DesignModeler

E. Launching ANSYS Meshing

5. We are now going to double click on Mesh under Project Schematic in ANSYS Workbench to open the Meshing window. Select Mesh in the Outline of the Meshing window. Right click and select Generate Mesh. A coarse mesh is created. Select Unit Systems>>Metric (mm, kg, N …) from the bottom of the graphics window.

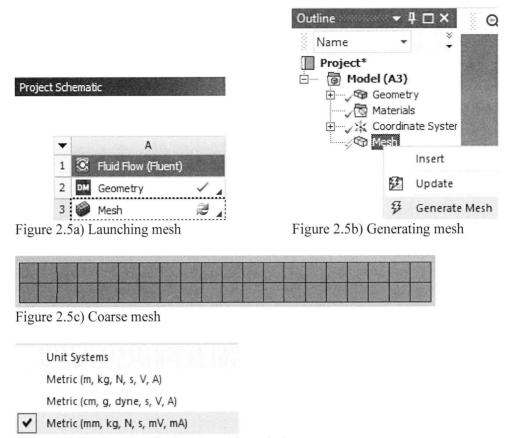

Figure 2.5a) Launching mesh   Figure 2.5b) Generating mesh

Figure 2.5c) Coarse mesh

Figure 2.5d) Selection of units in meshing window

Select Mesh>> Controls>>Face Meshing from the menu. Click on the yellow region next to Geometry under Scope in Details of Face Meshing. Select the rectangle in the graphics window. Click on the Apply button for Geometry in Details of "Face Meshing". Select Mesh>>

Controls>>Sizing from the menu and select Edge .

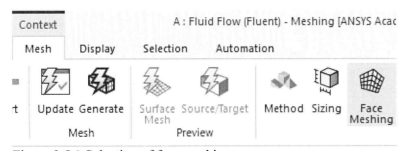

Figure 2.5e) Selection of face meshing   Figure 2.5f) Sizing

Select the upper longer horizontal edge of the rectangle, control select the lower horizontal edges and the vertical edges for a total of 5 edges. Click on Apply for the Geometry in "Details of Edge Sizing". Under Definition in "Details of Edge Sizing", select Element Size as Type, 1.0 mm for Element Size, and Hard as Behavior. Select the following Bias Type - - — —— and enter 12.0 as the Bias Factor.

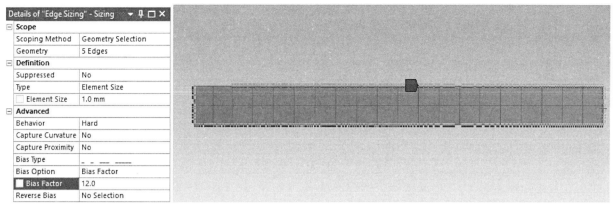

Details of "Edge Sizing" - Sizing ▾ 🖈 □ ×	
⊟ **Scope**	
Scoping Method	Geometry Selection
Geometry	5 Edges
⊟ **Definition**	
Suppressed	No
Type	Element Size
☐ Element Size	1.0 mm
⊟ **Advanced**	
Behavior	Hard
Capture Curvature	No
Capture Proximity	No
Bias Type	_ _ __ ___
Bias Option	Bias Factor
☐ Bias Factor	12.0
Reverse Bias	No Selection

Figure 2.5g) Details of edge sizing for three of the horizontal edges and the vertical edges

Repeat the selection of Mesh>>Controls>>Sizing from the menu once again but this time select the upper horizontal edge to the left of the origin. Enter the same Element Size, Behavior, and Bias Factor but the Bias Type ──── ── - - . Click on Home>>Generate Mesh in the menu and select Mesh in the Outline. The finished mesh is shown in the graphics window.

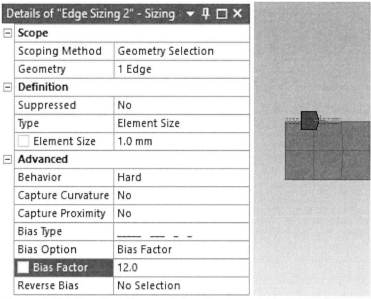

Details of "Edge Sizing 2" - Sizing ▾ 🖈 □ ×	
⊟ **Scope**	
Scoping Method	Geometry Selection
Geometry	1 Edge
⊟ **Definition**	
Suppressed	No
Type	Element Size
☐ Element Size	1.0 mm
⊟ **Advanced**	
Behavior	Hard
Capture Curvature	No
Capture Proximity	No
Bias Type	──── ── - -
Bias Option	Bias Factor
☐ Bias Factor	12.0
Reverse Bias	No Selection

Figure 2.5h) Details of edge sizing for the remaining horizontal edge

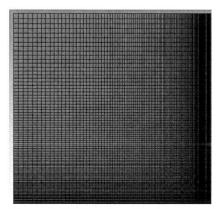

Figure 2.5i) Details of finished mesh

We are now going to rename the edges for the rectangle. Select the left edge of the rectangle, right click and select Create Named Selection. Enter *inlet* as the name and click on the OK button.

Repeat this step for the right vertical edge of the rectangle and enter the name *outlet*. Create a named selection for the lower longer horizontal right edge and call it *wall*. Finally, control-select the remaining three horizontal edges and name them *ideal wall*.

Figure 2.5j) Named selections

Select File>>Export...>>Mesh>>FLUENT Input File>>Export from the menu. Select Save as type: FLUENT Input Files (*.msh). Enter "boundary-layer-mesh" as file name and click on the Save button. Select File>>Save Project from the menu. Name the project "Flat Plate Boundary Layer". Close the ANSYS Meshing window. Right click on Mesh in Project Schematic and select Update.

F. Launching ANSYS Fluent

6. We are now going to double click on Setup under Project Schematic in ANSYS Workbench to open Fluent. Launch the 2D Double Precision solver of Fluent. Check the Double Precision and Parallel as Processing Options. Set the number of Solver Processes equal to the number of cores (in this case there are 8 cores). Click on the plus sign next to Show More Options. Write down the location of the working directory as you will use this information later. Click on the OK button to launch ANSYS Fluent.

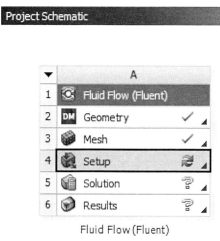

Figure 2.6a) Launching Setup

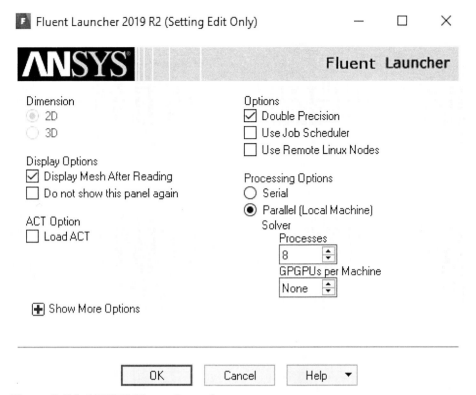

Figure 2.6b) ANSYS Fluent Launcher

```
Console
-----------------------------------------------------------------------
ID     Hostname       Core   O.S.         PID     Vendor
-----------------------------------------------------------------------
n7     DESKTOP-QQG8MCG  8/8  Windows-x64  13360   Intel(R) Core(TM) i7-7820HQ
n6     DESKTOP-QQG8MCG  7/8  Windows-x64  12752   Intel(R) Core(TM) i7-7820HQ
n5     DESKTOP-QQG8MCG  6/8  Windows-x64  4296    Intel(R) Core(TM) i7-7820HQ
n4     DESKTOP-QQG8MCG  5/8  Windows-x64  6872    Intel(R) Core(TM) i7-7820HQ
n3     DESKTOP-QQG8MCG  4/8  Windows-x64  11828   Intel(R) Core(TM) i7-7820HQ
n2     DESKTOP-QQG8MCG  3/8  Windows-x64  3988    Intel(R) Core(TM) i7-7820HQ
n1     DESKTOP-QQG8MCG  2/8  Windows-x64  11900   Intel(R) Core(TM) i7-7820HQ
n0*    DESKTOP-QQG8MCG  1/8  Windows-x64  12944   Intel(R) Core(TM) i7-7820HQ
host   DESKTOP-QQG8MCG       Windows-x64  8968    Intel(R) Core(TM) i7-7820HQ
```

Figure 2.6c) Example of console printout for four cores

7. Check the scale of the mesh by selecting the Scale button under Mesh in General on the Task Page. Make sure that the Domain Extent is correct and close the Scale Mesh window.

Figure 2.7a) Scale Check

27

Figure 2.7b) Scale Mesh

8. Double click on Boundary Conditions under Setup in the Outline View. Double click on *inlet* under Zone on the Task Page. Choose Components as Velocity Specification Method and set the X-Velocity to 5 (m/s). Click on the OK button to close the window. Double click on *ideal_wall* under Zones. Check Specified Shear as Shear Condition and keep zero values for specified shear stress. Click OK to close the window.

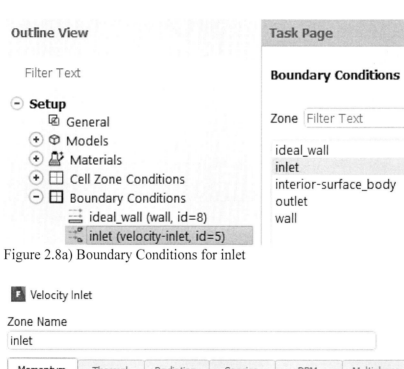

Figure 2.8a) Boundary Conditions for inlet

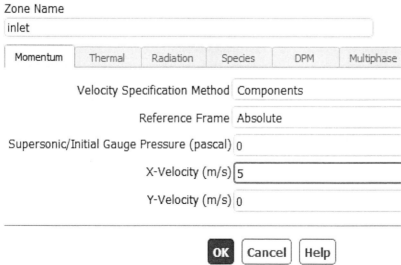

Figure 2.8b) Inlet velocity

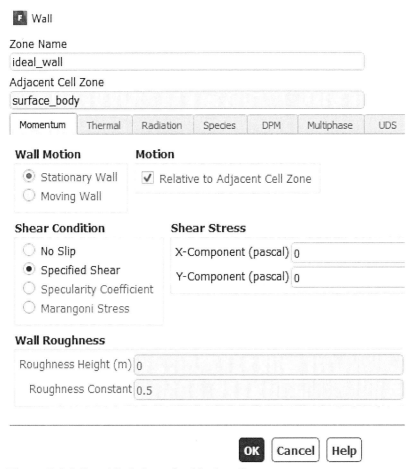

Figure 2.8c) Specified shear for ideal wall

9. Double click on Methods under Solution in the Outline View. Select *Standard* for Pressure and *First Order Upwind* for Momentum. Double click on Reference Values under Setup in the Outline View. Select *Compute from inlet* on the Task Page.

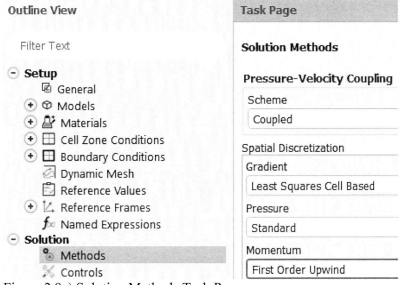

Figure 2.9a) Solution Methods Task Page

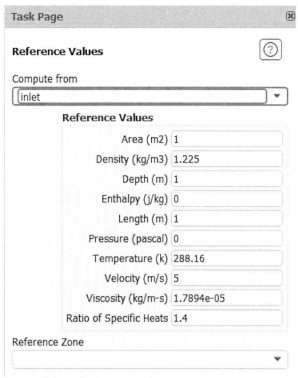

Figure 2.9b) Reference values

10. Double click on Initialization under Solution in the Outline View, select *Standard Initialization*, select *Compute from inlet* and click on the *Initialize* button.

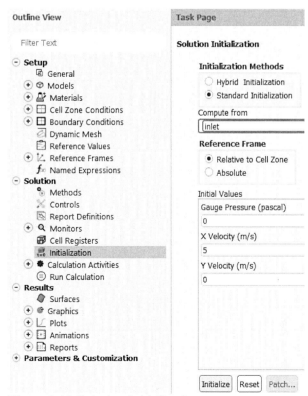

Figure 2.10 Solution Initialization

11. Double click on Monitors under Solution in the Outline View. Double click on Residual under Monitors and enter 1e-9 as *Absolute Criteria* for all Residuals. Click on the OK button to close the window.

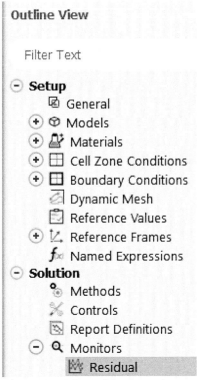

Figure 2.11a) Residual monitors

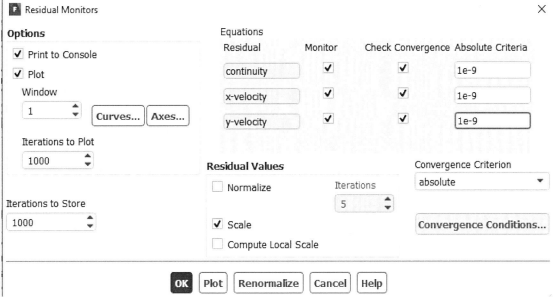

Figure 2.11b) Residual Monitors settings

12. Double click on Run Calculation under Solution and enter 5000 for *Number of Iterations*. Click on the *Calculate* button.

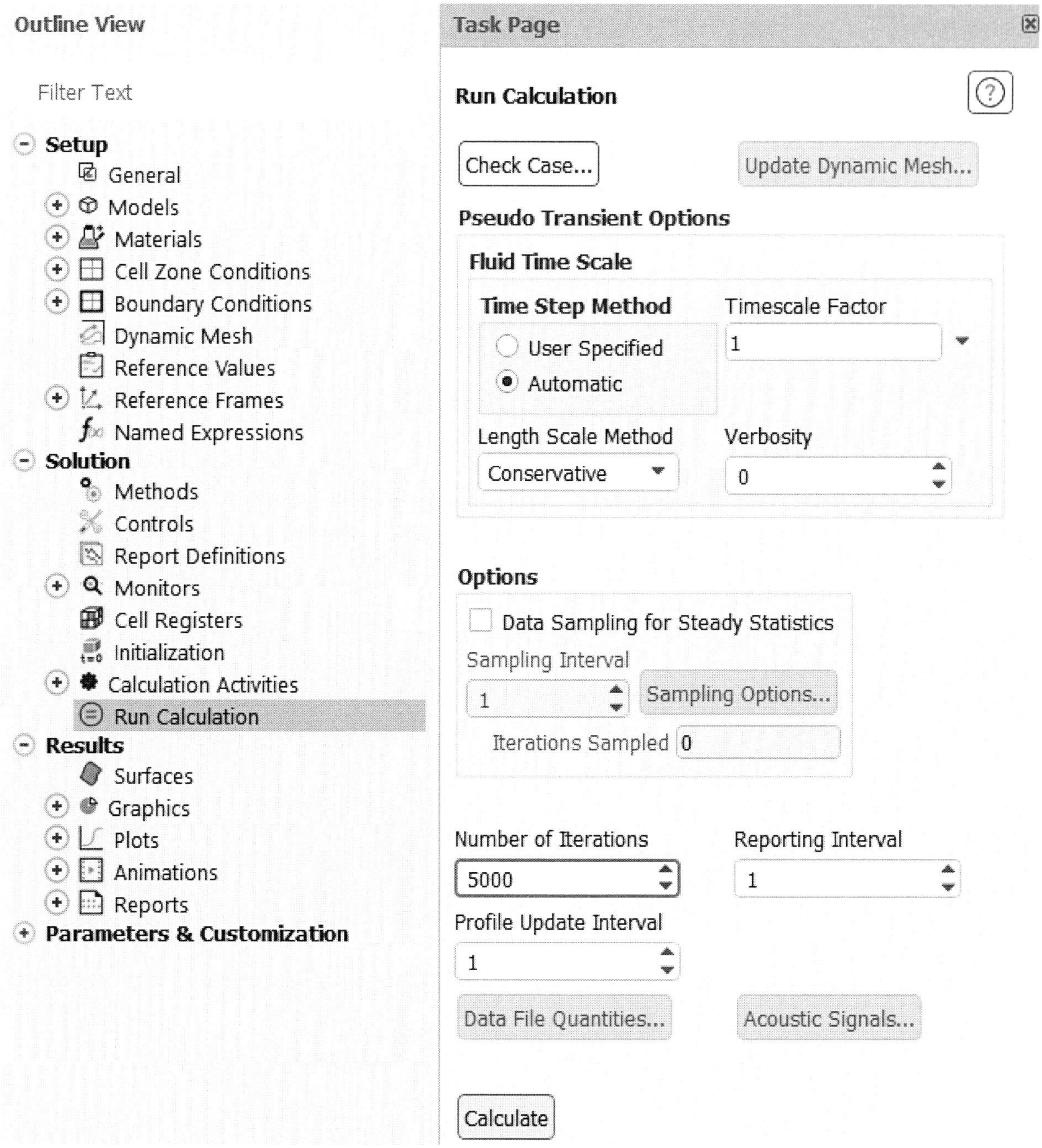

Figure 2.12a) Running the calculations

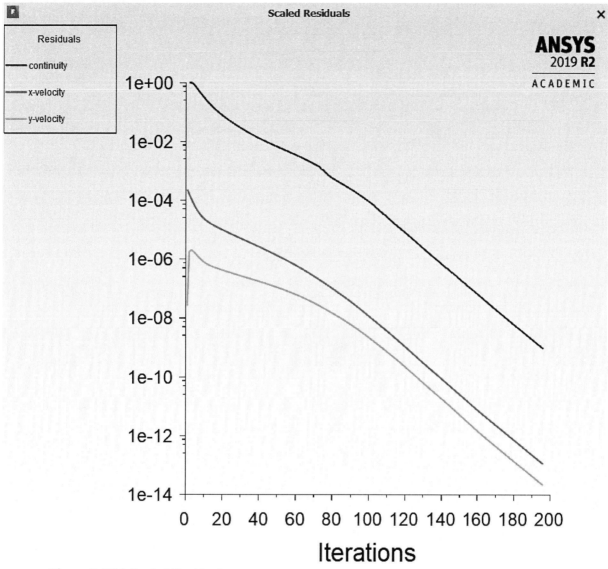

Figure 2.12b) Scaled Residual

G. Post-Processing

13. Select the Results tab in the menu and select Create>>Line/Rake under Surface. Enter 0.2 for x0 (m), 0.2 for x1 (m), 0 for y0 (m), and 0.02 m for y1 (m). Enter x=0.2m for the New Surface Name and click on Create. Repeat this step three more times and create vertical lines at x = 0.4m (length 0.04 m), x=0.6m (length 0.06 m), and x=0.8m (length 0.08 m). Close the window.

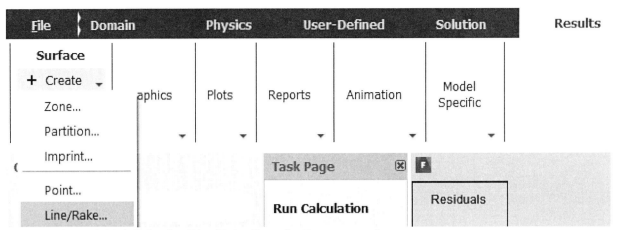

Figure 2.13a) Selecting Line/Rake from the Post-processing menu

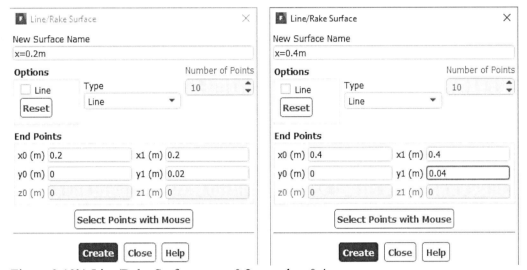

Figure 2.13b) Line/Rake Surfaces at x=0.2 m and x=0.4m

14. Double click on Plots and XY Plot under Results in the Outline View. Uncheck Position on X Axis under Options and check Position on Y Axis. Set Plot Direction for X to 0 and 1 for Y. Select Velocity… and X Velocity as X Axis Function. Select the four surfaces x=0.2m, x=0.4m, x=0.6m, and x=0.8m. Click on the *Axes* button.

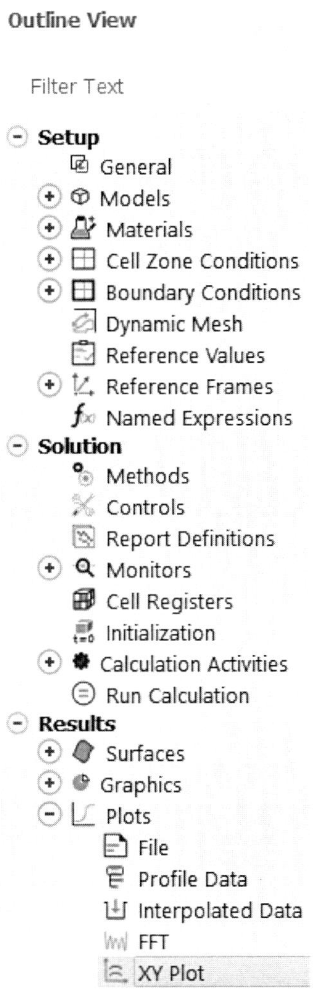

Outline View

Filter Text

- **Setup**
  - 🗐 General
  - ⊕ 🖫 Models
  - ⊕ 🖉 Materials
  - ⊕ ▦ Cell Zone Conditions
  - ⊕ ▦ Boundary Conditions
  - 🖉 Dynamic Mesh
  - 🗎 Reference Values
  - ⊕ 🖉 Reference Frames
  - 𝑓∞ Named Expressions
- **Solution**
  - 🖉 Methods
  - ✂ Controls
  - 🗒 Report Definitions
  - ⊕ 🔍 Monitors
  - 🖩 Cell Registers
  - 🖥 Initialization
  - ⊕ ✿ Calculation Activities
  - ⊖ Run Calculation
- **Results**
  - ⊕ 🖉 Surfaces
  - ⊕ 🖉 Graphics
  - ⊖ 🖉 Plots
    - 🖹 File
    - 🖺 Profile Data
    - ⊔ Interpolated Data
    - 🖂 FFT
    - 🖂 XY Plot

Figure 2.14a) XY Plot setup

🅵 Solution XY Plot

XY Plot Name

xy-plot-1

Options	Plot Direction	Y Axis Function
✔ Node Values	X 0	Direction Vector
☐ Position on X Axis	Y 1	X Axis Function
✔ Position on Y Axis	Z 0	Velocity...
☐ Write to File		X Velocity
☐ Order Points		

File Data [0/0]   ≡ ≡✓ ≡ₓ

Load File...

Free Data

Surfaces Filter Text

outlet
wall
x=0.2m
x=0.4m
x=0.6m
x=0.8m

New Surface ⌄

Save/Plot   Axes...   Curves...   Close   Help

Figure 2.14b) Settings for Solution XY Plot

15. Select the X Axis, uncheck Auto Range under Options, enter 6 for Maximum Range, select general Type under Number Format and set Precision to 0. Click on the Apply button. Select the Y Axis, uncheck the Auto Range, enter 0.01 for Maximum Range, select general Type under Number Format, and click on the Apply button. Close the Axes window.

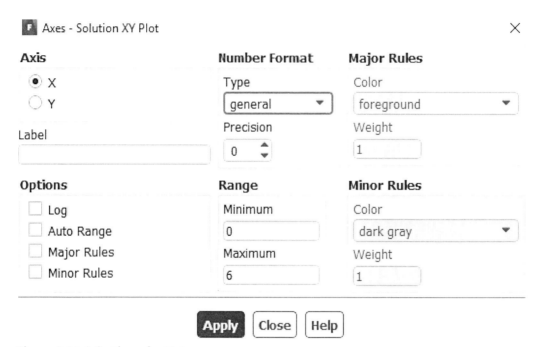

Figure 2.15a) Settings for X Axes

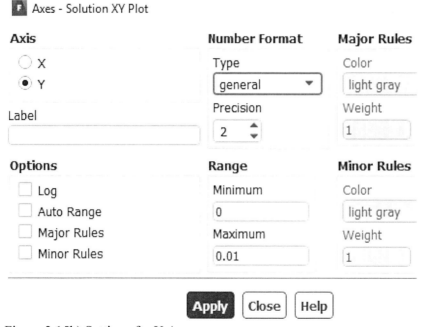

Figure 2.15b) Settings for Y Axes

16. Click on the Curves… button in the Solution XY Plot window. Select the first pattern under Line Style for Curve # 0. Select no Symbol for Marker Style and click on the Apply button.

Next select Curve # 1, select the next available Pattern for Line Style, no Symbol for Marker Style, and click on the Apply button. Continue this pattern of selection with the next two curves # 2 and # 3. Close the Curves – Solution XY Plot window. Click on the Save/Plot button in the Solution XY Plot window.

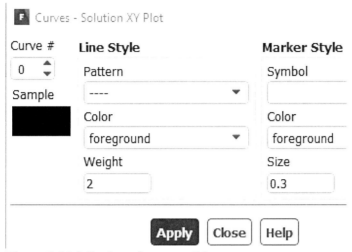

Figure 2.16a) Settings for curve # 0

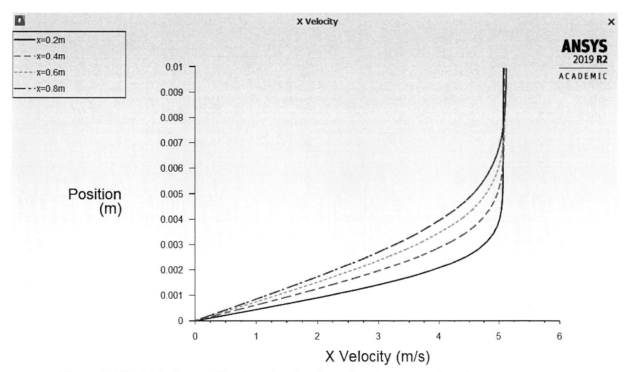

Figure 2.16b) Velocity profiles for a laminar boundary layer on a flat plate

Select the *User Defined* tab in the menu and *Custom*. Select *Operand Field Functions* from the drop-down menu by selecting *Mesh…* and *Y-Coordinate*. Click on *Select* and enter the definition as shown in Figure 2.16e). You need to select *Mesh…* and *X-Coordinate* to complete the definition of the field function. Enter *eta* as *New Function Name*, click on *Define* and close the window.

Repeat this step to create another custom field function. This time, we select *Velocity...* and *X Velocity* as *Field Functions* and click on *Select*. Complete the *Definition* (as shown in Figure 2.16f) and enter *u-divided-by-freestream-velocity* as *New Function Name*, click on *Define* and close the window.

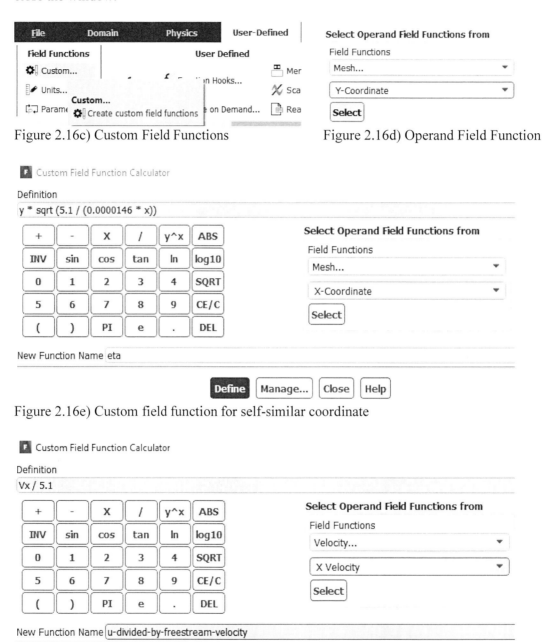

Figure 2.16c) Custom Field Functions   Figure 2.16d) Operand Field Function

Figure 2.16e) Custom field function for self-similar coordinate

Figure 2.16f) Custom field function for non-dimensional velocity

17. Double click on Plots and XY Plot under Results in the Outline View. Set X to 0 and Y to 1 as Plot Direction. Uncheck *Position on X Axis* and *Position on Y Axis* under *Options*. Select *Custom Field Functions* and *eta* for *Y Axis Function* and select *Custom Field Functions* and *u-divided-by-freestream-velocity* for *X Axis Function*.

Place the file "*blasius.dat*" in your working directory. This file can be downloaded from *sdcpublications.com*. See Figure 1.19 for the Mathematica code used to generate the theoretical Blasius velocity profile for laminar boundary layer flow over a flat plate. In this case the working directory is *C*:\Users\John Matsson. Click on *Load File*. Select Files of type: All Files (*) and select the file "*blasius.dat*". Select the four surfaces *x=0.2m, x=0.4m, x=0.6m, x=0.8m* and the loaded file *Theory*. Click on the Axes button.

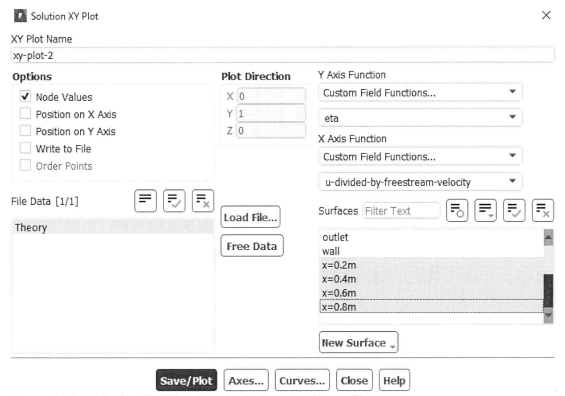

Figure 2.17a) Solution XY Plot for self-similar velocity profiles

Select *Y Axis* in Axes-Solution XY Plot window and uncheck *Auto Range*. Set the *Minimum Range* to 0 and *Maximum Range* to 10. Set Precision to 0 under Number Format. Set the Label to *eta* and click on *Apply*.

Select *X Axis* in Axes-Solution XY Plot window and set the Label to *u/U*. Check the box for *Auto Range*. Set Precision to 1 under Number Format. Click on Apply and close the window. Click on Save/Plot in the Solution XY Plot window. Close the Solution XY Plot window.

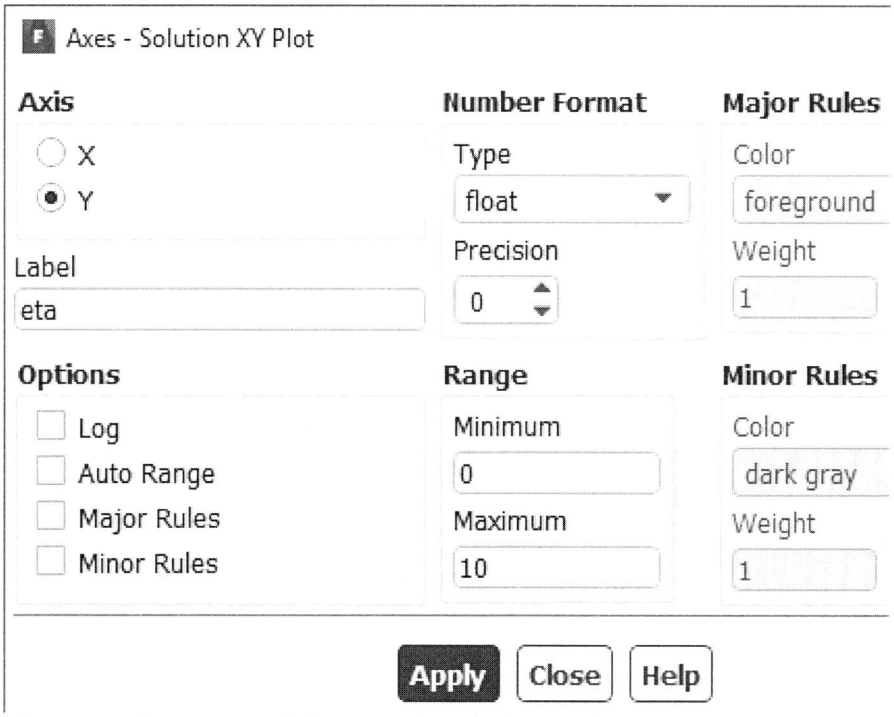

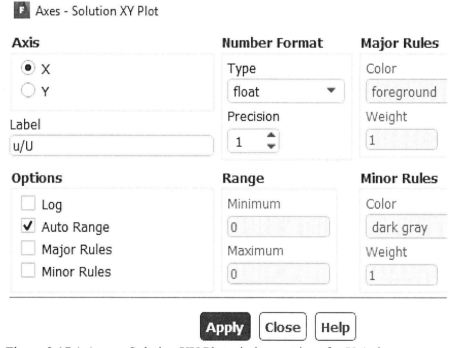

Figure 2.17b) Axes – Solution XY Plot window settings for Y Axis

Figure 2.17c) Axes – Solution XY Plot window settings for X Axis

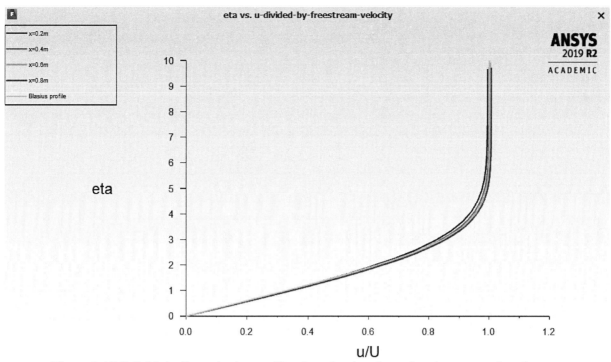

Figure 2.17d) Self-similar velocity profiles for a laminar boundary layer on a flat plate

Select the User Defined tab in the menu and Custom. Select Operand Field Functions from the drop-down menu by selecting Mesh… and X-Coordinate. Click on Select and enter the definition as shown in Figure 2.17e). Enter *re-x* as New Function Name, click on Define and Close the window.

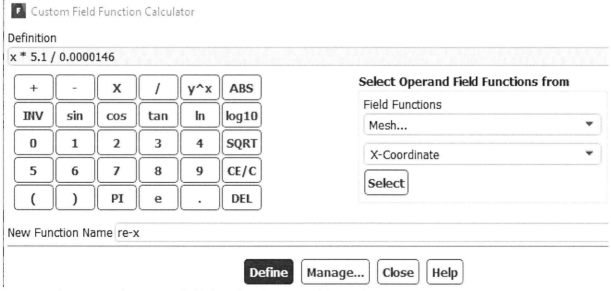

Figure 2.17e) Custom field function for Reynolds number

18. Double click on Plots and XY Plot under Results in the Outline View. Set X to 0 and Y to 1 under Plot Direction. Uncheck Position on X Axis and Position on Y Axis under Options. Select *Wall Fluxes* and *Skin Friction Coefficient* for Y Axis Function and select Custom Field Functions and *re-x* for X Axis Function.

Place the file "*Theoretical Skin Friction Coefficient*" in your working directory. Click on Load File. Select Files of type: All Files (*) and select the file "*Theoretical Skin Friction Coefficient*". Select *wall* under Surfaces and the loaded file Skin Friction under File Data. Click on the Axes button.

Figure 2.18a) Solution XY Plot for skin friction coefficient

Check the X Axis, check the box for Log under Options, enter Re-x as Label, uncheck Auto Range under Options, set Minimum to 100 and Maximum to 1000000. Set Precision to 0 under Number Format and click on Apply.

Check the Y Axis, check the box for Log under Options, enter Cf-x as Label, uncheck Auto Range, set Minimum to 0.001 and Maximum to 0.1, set Precision to 3 and click on Apply. Close the window. Click on Save/Plot in the Solution XY Plot window.

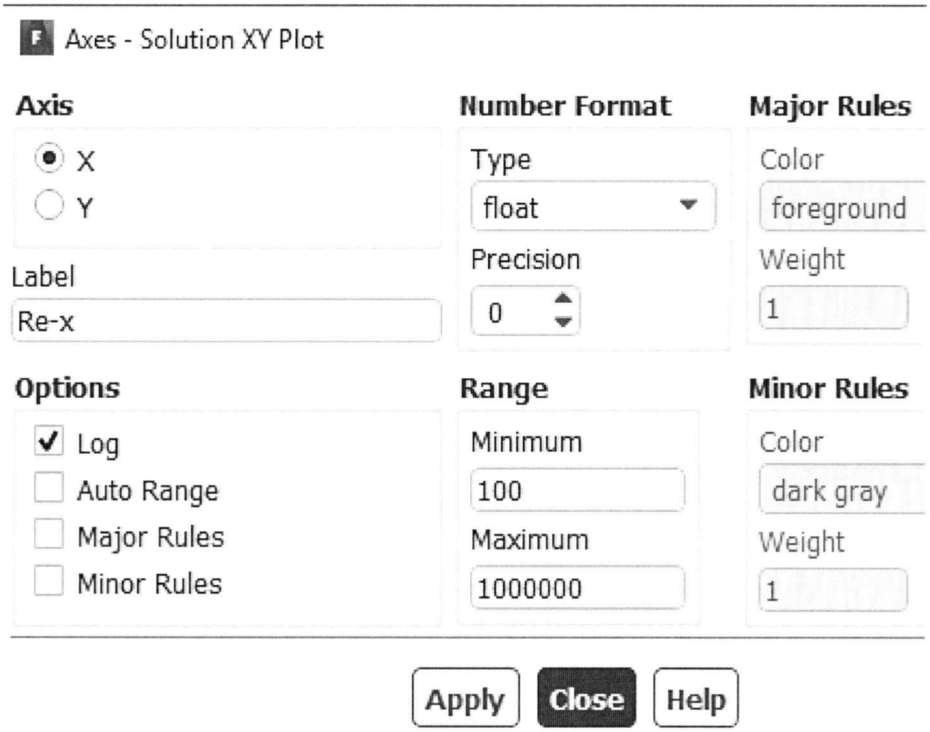

Figure 2.18b) Axes – Solution XY Plot window settings for X Axis

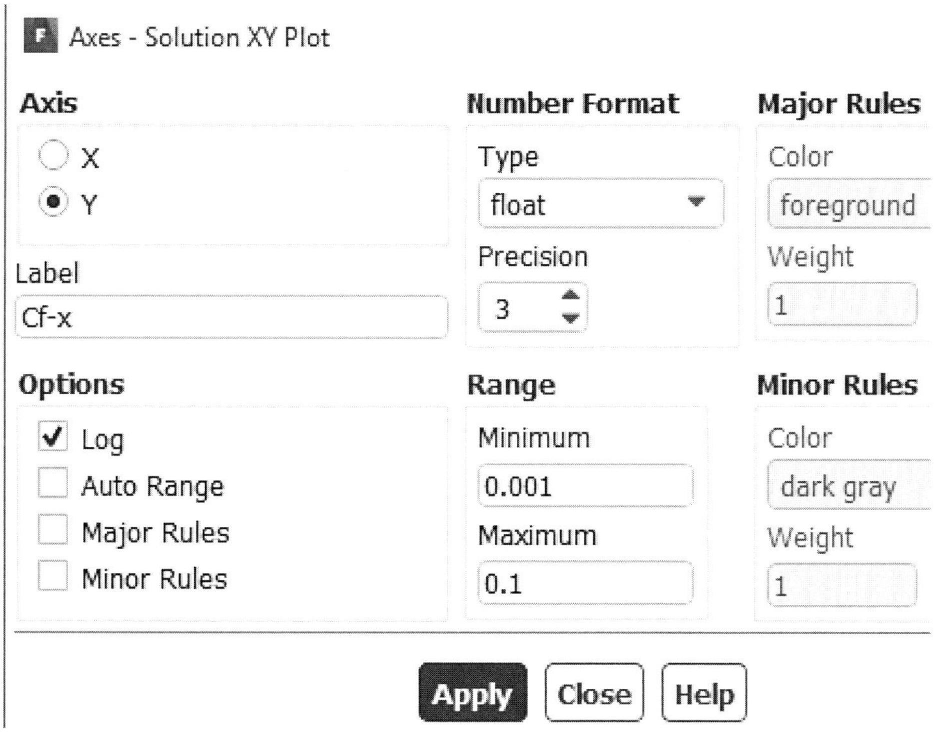

Figure 2.18c) Axes – Solution XY Plot window settings for Y Axis

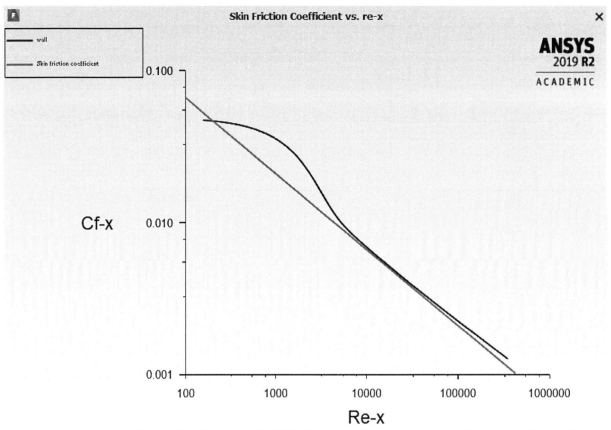

Figure 2.18d) Comparison between ANSYS Fluent and theoretical skin friction coefficient for laminar boundary layer flow on a flat plate

H. Theory

19. In this chapter we have compared ANSYS Fluent velocity profiles with the theoretical Blasius velocity profile for laminar flow on a flat plate. We transformed the wall normal coordinate to a similarity coordinate for comparison. The similarity coordinate is defined by

$$\eta = y\sqrt{\frac{U}{\nu x}} \qquad (2.1)$$

where y (m) is the wall normal coordinate, U (m/s) is the free stream velocity, x (m) is the distance from the start of the wall and ν (m²/s) is the kinematic viscosity of the fluid.

We also used the non-dimensional streamwise velocity u/U where u is the dimensional velocity profile. u/U was plotted versus η for ANSYS Fluent velocity profiles in comparison with the Blasius theoretical profile and they all collapsed on the same curve as per definition of self-similarity. The Blasius boundary layer equation is given by

$$f'''(\eta) + \frac{1}{2}f(\eta)f''(\eta) = 0 \qquad (2.2)$$

with the following boundary conditions

$$f(0) = f'(0) = 0, f'(\infty) = 0 \tag{2.3}$$

The Reynolds number for the flow on a flat plat is defined as

$$Re_x = \frac{Ux}{\nu} \tag{2.4}$$

The boundary layer thickness δ is defined as the distance from the wall to the location where the velocity in the boundary layer has reached 99% of the free stream value. For a laminar boundary-layer we have the following theoretical expression for the variation of the boundary layer with streamwise distance x and Reynolds number Re_x.

$$\delta = \frac{4.91x}{\sqrt{Re_x}} \tag{2.5}$$

The corresponding expression for the boundary layer thickness in a turbulent boundary layer is given by

$$\delta = \frac{0.16x}{Re_x^{1/7}} \tag{2.6}$$

The local skin friction coefficient is defined as the local wall shear stress divided by the dynamic pressure.

$$C_{f,x} = \frac{\tau_w}{\frac{1}{2}\rho U^2} \tag{2.7}$$

The theoretical local friction coefficient for laminar flow is determined by

$$C_{f,x} = \frac{0.664}{\sqrt{Re_x}} \qquad Re_x < 5 \cdot 10^5 \tag{2.8}$$

and for turbulent flow we have the following relation

$$C_{f,x} = \frac{0.027}{Re_x^{1/7}} \qquad 5 \cdot 10^5 < Re_x < 10^7 \tag{2.9}$$

```
sol = NDSolve[{f'''[η] + 0.5 f[η] f''[η] == 0, f[0] == f'[0] == 0, f'[10] == 1}, f, η];
myplot = Plot[f'[η] /. First[sol], {η, 0, 10}, AxesLabel → {"u/U", "η"}];
axisFlip = # /. {x_Line | x_GraphicsComplex :→ MapAt[# ~ Reverse ~ 2 &, x, 1],
     x : (PlotRange → _) :→ x ~ Reverse ~ 2} &;
myplot // axisFlip

SetDirectory["C:\\Users\\jmatsson"];
mylist = Table[{f'[η] /. First[sol], η}, {η, 0, 10, 0.5}];
TableOfValues1 = Prepend[mylist, {""}];
TableOfValues1 = Prepend[TableOfValues1, {"((xy/key/label \"Blasius profile\")"}];
TableOfValues1 = Prepend[TableOfValues1, {""}];
TableOfValues1 = Prepend[TableOfValues1, {"(labels \"X Velocity\" \"η-Coordinate\")"}];
TableOfValues1 = Prepend[TableOfValues1, {"(title \"Theory\")"}];
TableOfValues1 = Append[TableOfValues1, {")"}];
Grid[TableOfValues1]
Export["blasius.dat", TableOfValues1]
```

Figure 2.19 Mathematica code for theoretical Blasius laminar boundary layer

I. References

1. Çengel, Y. A., and Cimbala J.M., Fluid Mechanics Fundamentals and Applications, 1st Edition, McGraw-Hill, 2006.
2. Richards, S., Cimbala, J.M., Martin, K., ANSYS Workbench Tutorial – Boundary Layer on a Flat Plate, Penn State University, 18 May 2010 Revision.
3. Schlichting, H., and Gersten, K., Boundary Layer Theory, 8th Revised and Enlarged Edition, Springer, 2001.
4. White, F. M., Fluid Mechanics, 4th Edition, McGraw-Hill, 1999.

J. Exercises

2.1 Use the results from the ANSYS Fluent simulation in this chapter to determine the boundary layer thickness at the streamwise positions as shown in the table below. Fill in the missing information in the table. U_δ is the velocity of the boundary layer at the distance from the wall equal to the boundary layer thickness and U is the free stream velocity.

x (m)	δ (mm) Fluent	δ (mm) Theory	Percent Difference	U_δ (m/s)	U (m/s)	ν (m^2/s)	Re_x
0.2						0000146	
0.4						0000146	
0.6						0000146	
0.8						0000146	

Table 2.1 Comparison between Fluent and theory for boundary layer thickness

2.2 Change the element size to 2 mm for the mesh and compare the results in XY Plots of the skin friction coefficient versus Reynolds number with the element size 1 mm that was used in this chapter. Compare your results with theory.

2.3 Change the free stream velocity to 3 m/s and create an XY Plot including velocity profiles at $x = 0.1, 0.3, 0.5, 0.7$ and 0.9 m. Create another XY Plot with self-similar velocity profiles for this lower free stream velocity and finally create an XY Plot for the skin friction coefficient versus Reynolds number.

2.4 Use the results from the ANSYS Fluent simulation in Exercise 1.3 to determine the boundary layer thickness at the streamwise positions as shown in the table below. Fill in the missing information in the table. U_δ is the velocity of the boundary layer at the distance from the wall equal to the boundary layer thickness and U is the free stream velocity.

x (m)	δ (mm) Fluent	δ (mm) Theory	Percent Difference	U_δ (m/s)	U (m/s)	ν (m²/s)	Re_x
0.1						0000146	
0.2						0000146	
0.5						0000146	
0.7						0000146	
0.9						0000146	

Table 2.2 Comparison between Fluent and theory for boundary layer thickness

Notes:

CHAPTER 3. FLOW PAST A CYLINDER

A. Objectives

- Using ANSYS Workbench to Model the Cylinder and Mesh
- Inserting Boundary Conditions and Free Stream Velocity
- Running ANSYS Fluent Simulation for Laminar Transient 2D Planar Flow
- Using FFT Analysis, Velocity and Pressure Plots for Visualizations

B. Problem Description

We will study the flow of air past a cylinder and we will analyze the problem using ANSYS Fluent. The diameter of the cylinder is 50 mm and the free stream velocity is 0.06 m/s.

C. Launching ANSYS Workbench and Selecting Fluent

1. Start by launching ANSYS Workbench. Double click on Fluid Flow (Fluent) that is located under Analysis Systems in the Toolbox.

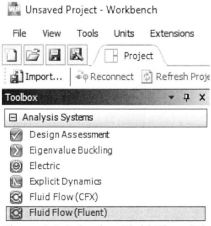

Figure 3.1 Selecting Fluid Flow (Fluent)

D. Launching ANSYS DesignModeler

2. Select Geometry under Project Schematic in ANSYS Workbench. Right-click on Geometry and select Properties. Select 2D Analysis Type under Advanced Geometry Options in Properties of Schematic A2: Geometry. Right-click on Geometry under Project Schematic and select to launch New DesignModeler Geometry. Select Units>>Millimeter as the length unit from the menu in DesignModeler.

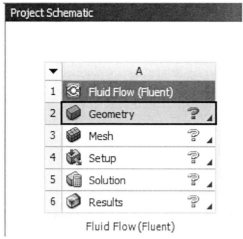

Figure 3.2a) Selecting Geometry

	A	B
	Property	Value
2	⊟ General	
3	Component ID	Geometry
4	Directory Name	FFF
5	⊟ Notes	
6	Notes	
7	⊟ Used Licenses	
8	Last Update Used Licenses	
9	⊟ Basic Geometry Options	
10	Solid Bodies	☑
11	Surface Bodies	☑
12	Line Bodies	☐
13	Parameters	Independent
14	Parameter Key	ANS;DS
15	Attributes	☐
16	Named Selections	☐
17	Material Properties	☐
18	⊟ Advanced Geometry Options	
19	Analysis Type	2D
20	Use Associativity	3D / 2D
21	Import Coordinate Systems	

Properties of Schematic A2: Geometry

Figure 3.2b) Selecting 2D Analysis Type

50

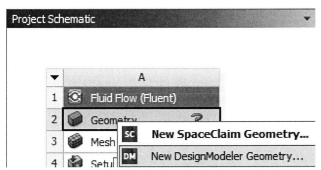

Figure 3.2c) Launching DesignModeler

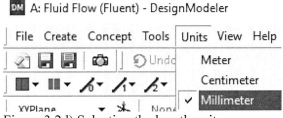

Figure 3.2d) Selecting the length unit

3. Next, we will be creating the geometry for the simulation. Select XYPlane from the Tree Outline on the left-hand side. Select Look at Sketch. Click on the Sketching tab in the Tree Outline, select the Draw tab within the Sketching options, and select the Circle sketch tool.

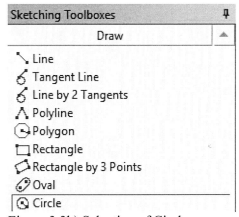

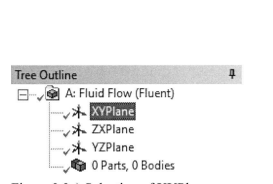

Figure 3.3a) Selection of XYPlane   Figure 3.3b) Selection of Circle

Draw a circle centered at the origin of the coordinate system in the graphics window. Make sure that you move the cursor so that you get the letter *P* in the graphics window indicating that your circle will be centered at the origin. Select the Dimensions tab within the Sketching options and select Diameter. Click on the circle in the graphics window and enter 50 mm for the diameter D1 under Dimensions:1 in Details View.

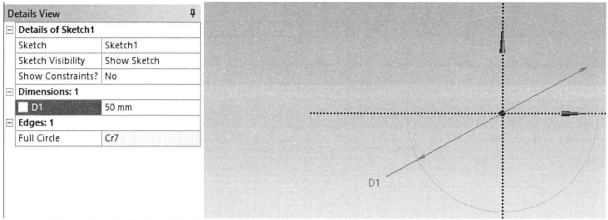

Figure 3.3c) Circle with dimension

Click on the Modeling tab in the Tree Outline and select Concepts>>Surfaces from Sketches from the menu. Click on the circle in the graphics window and select Apply as Base Objects in Details View. Click on Generate. The circle turns gray.

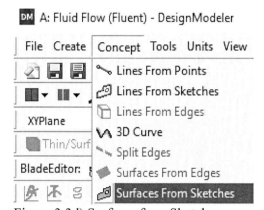

Figure 3.3d) Surfaces from Sketches

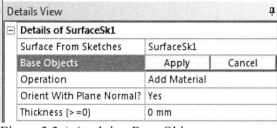

Figure 3.3e) Applying Base Objects

Click on the Modeling tab in the Tree Outline and select the XYPlane. Click on New Sketch . Select Rectangle by 3 Points from the Sketching tools. Zoom out in the graphics window so that the ruler at the bottom of the graphics window is showing 0.00 – 1000.00 (mm). Click anywhere outside of the circle in the upper left corner (2nd quadrant) of the graphics window, followed by clicking anywhere outside of the circle in the lower left corner (3rd quadrant) of the graphics window (make sure you have a V before clicking), and finally click in the right-hand plane outside of the circle (4th quadrant).

Select the Dimensions tab under Sketching Toolboxes, select Horizontal and click on the vertical edges of the rectangle. Enter 1575 mm as the horizontal length of the rectangle. Select the vertical axis and the vertical edge of the rectangle on the left-hand side. Enter 575 mm as the length. Select the Vertical dimensioning tool and click on the horizontal edges of the rectangle. Enter 1250 mm as the vertical length of the rectangle. Click on the horizontal axis and the lower horizontal edge of the rectangle. Enter 625 mm as the length. Right-click in the graphics window and select Zoom to Fit.

Details View	
Details of Sketch2	
Sketch	Sketch2
Sketch Visibility	Show Sketch
Show Constraints?	No
Dimensions: 4	
H2	1575 mm
H3	575 mm
V4	1250 mm
V5	625 mm
Edges: 4	
Line	Ln8
Line	Ln9
Line	Ln10
Line	Ln11

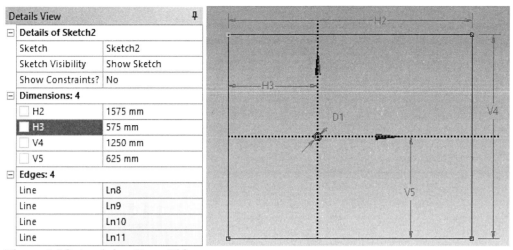

Figure 3.3f) Applying Base Objects

Select Concept>>Surface from Sketches from the menu. Click on Sketch2 in the Tree Outline and select Apply for Base Objects in Details View. Select Operation>>Add Frozen in Details View followed by Generate.

Details View	
Details of SurfaceSk2	
Surface From Sketches	SurfaceSk2
Base Objects	1 Sketch
Operation	Add Frozen
Orient With Plane Normal?	Yes
Thickness (>=0)	0 mm

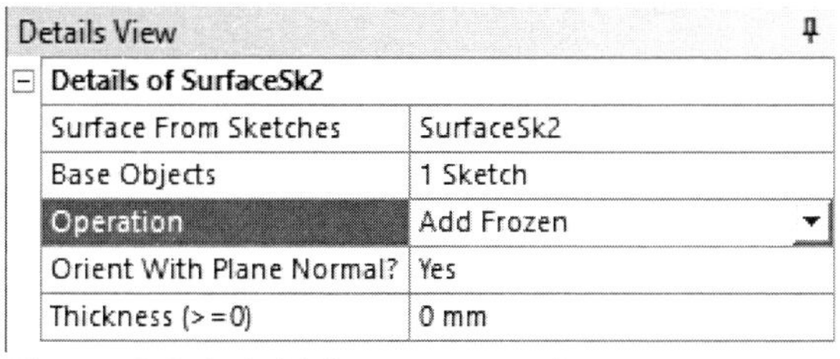

Figure 3.3g) Add frozen operation

Select Create>>Boolean from the menu. Select Subtract Operation from the Details View. Click on the mesh region around the cylinder in the graphics window and click on Apply as Target Bodies. Select the Cylinder as the Tool Body, see Figure 3.3j), and click on Generate.

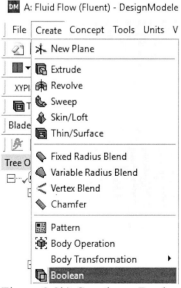

Figure 3.3h) Creating a Boolean

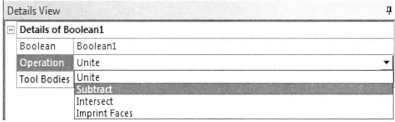

Figure 3.3i) Selecting a subtracting operation

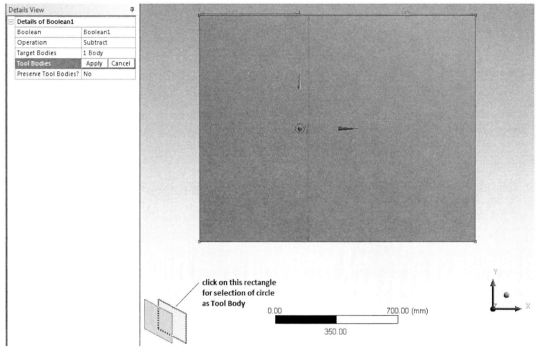

Figure 3.3j) Selecting tool body

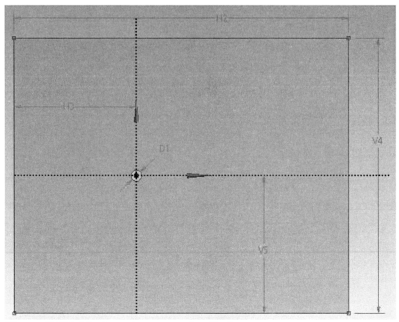

Figure 3.3k) Mesh region around cylinder

4. Select *XYPlane* in the Tree Outline and create a New Sketch 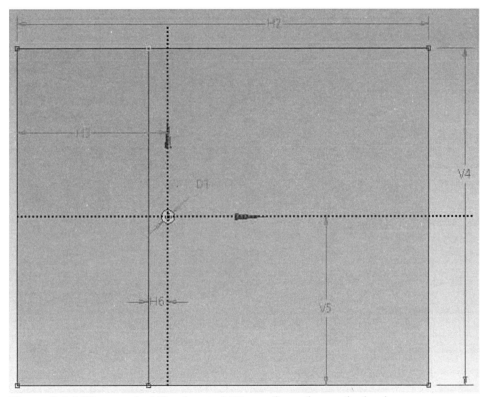 . Select the Sketching tab and select Line under the Draw tab. Draw a vertical line in the mesh region from top to bottom and to the left of the cylinder. Make sure you have a *C* when you start the line, a *V* indicating that the line is vertical and another *C* at the end of the line. The vertical line will intersect the entire mesh region. Position the line 75 mm from the vertical axis.

   Select Concepts>>Lines from Sketches from the menu. Select from the graphics window the newly created vertical line and Apply it as a Base Object in Details View. Click on Generate. Create another sketch in the *XYPlane* with a vertical line 75 mm to the right of the vertical axis and repeat all the different steps as listed above.

   Finally, repeat these steps two more times with one line from left to right intersecting the mesh region and positioned 75 mm above the cylinder and another line positioned 75 mm below the cylinder.

Figure 3.4a) First vertical line located 75 mm from the vertical axis

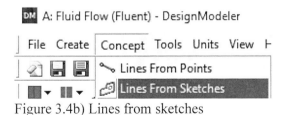

Figure 3.4b) Lines from sketches

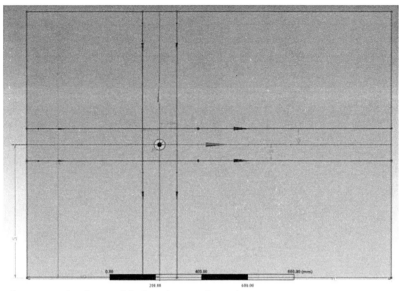

Figure 3.4c) Lines added to the mesh region

Select Tools>>Projection from the menu. Select Edges on Face as type in Details View. Control-select all 12 line-segments for the 4 lines that you have created and Apply as the Edges in the Details View. Select the mesh region and Apply it as the Target under Details View. Click Generate.

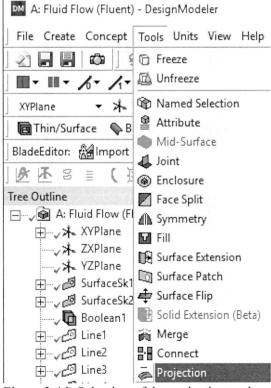

Figure 3.4d) Selection of the projection tool

You should now have 9 different regions for meshing. Select File>>Save Project from the menu and save the project with the name "Cylinder Flow Study". Close DesignModeler.

E. Launching ANSYS Meshing

5. Next, we will be creating the mesh around the cylinder. We are now going to double click on Mesh in Project Schematic to open the Meshing window.

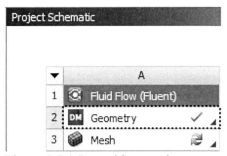

Figure 3.5a) Launching mesh

Select Mesh under Model (A3) in Project under Outline on the left-hand side. Select Mesh>>Controls>>Face Meshing from the menu. Control-select all 9 faces of the mesh. Apply the Geometry under Details of "Face Meshing".

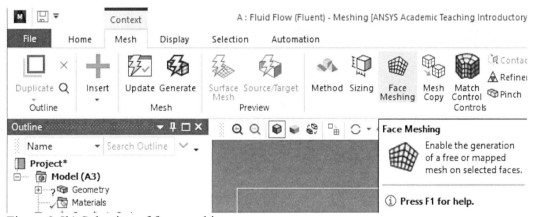

Figure 3.5b) Selection of face meshing

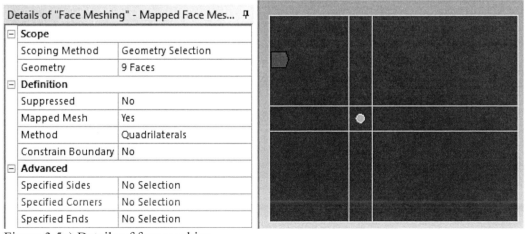

Figure 3.5c) Details of face meshing

Select Mesh>>Controls>>Sizing from the menu, right-click in the graphics window and select Cursor Mode>>Edge. Control-select the three edges to the left and bottom of the mesh region as shown in Figure 3.5d). Apply the Geometry under Details of "Edge Sizing". Select Number of Divisions as Type under Details of "Edge Sizing". Set the Number of Divisions to 100. Set the Behavior to Hard. Select the Bias Type at the top from the drop-down menu. Enter a Bias Factor of 10.

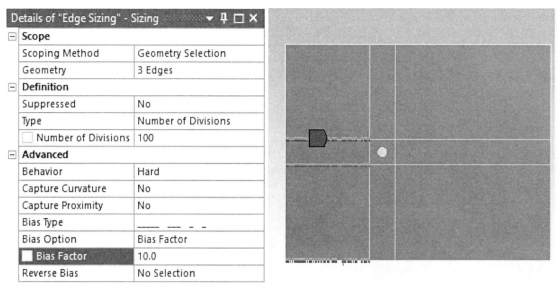

Figure 3.5d) Details for first mesh sizing

Select Mesh>>Controls>>Sizing from the menu. Control-select the three edges to the right and bottom of the mesh region as shown in Figure 3.5e). Apply the Geometry under Details of "Edge Sizing". Select Number of Divisions as Type under Details of "Edge Sizing". Set the Number of Divisions to 150. Set the Behavior to Hard. Select the second Bias Type from the drop-down menu. Enter a Bias Factor of 10.

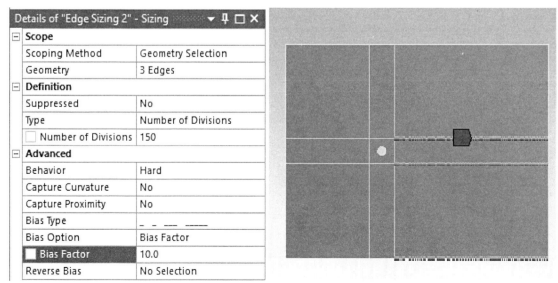

Figure 3.5e) Details for second mesh sizing

Select Mesh>>Controls>>Sizing from the menu. Select the horizontal upper left edge. Apply the Geometry under Details of "Edge Sizing". Select Number of Divisions as Type under Details of "Edge Sizing". Set the Number of Divisions to 100. Set the Behavior to Hard. Select the second Bias Type from the drop-down menu. Enter a Bias Factor of 10, see Figure 3.5f).

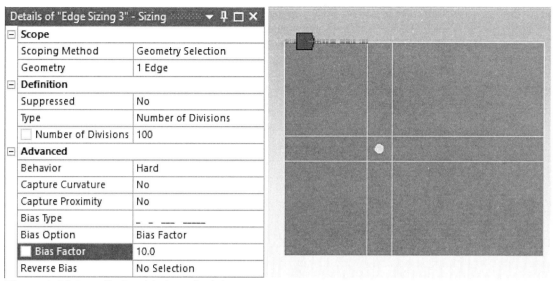

Figure 3.5f) Details for third mesh sizing

Select Mesh>>Controls>>Sizing from the menu. Select the upper horizontal right edge. Apply the Geometry under Details of "Edge Sizing". Select Number of Divisions as Type under Details of "Edge Sizing". Set the Number of Divisions to 150. Set the Behavior to Hard. Select the first Bias Type from the drop-down menu. Enter a Bias Factor of 10, see Figure 3.5g).

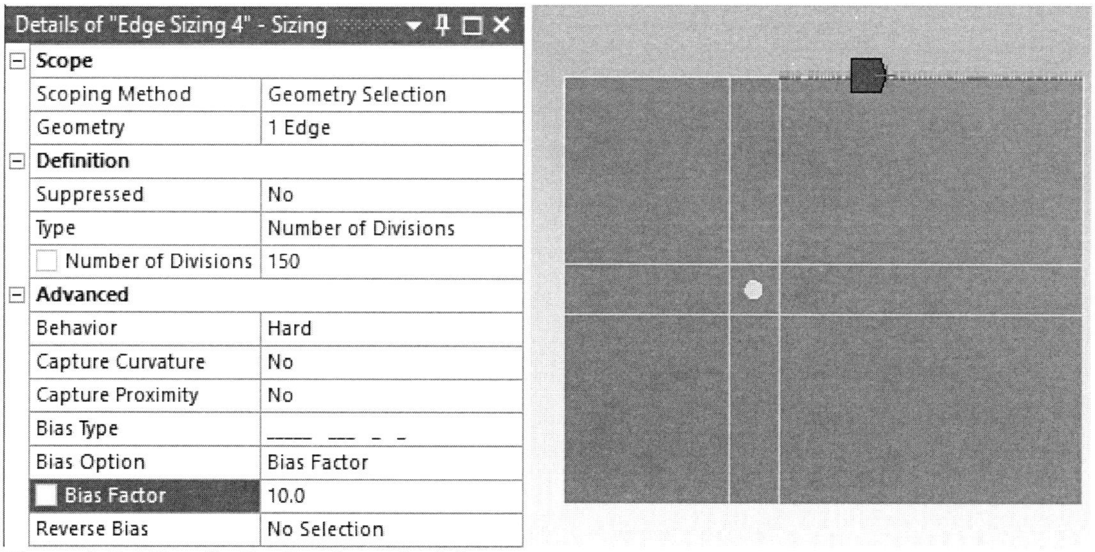

Figure 3.5g) Details for fourth mesh sizing

Select Mesh>>Controls>>Sizing from the menu. Control-select the 8 short edges around the cylinder and on the edges as shown in Figure 3.5h). Apply the Geometry under Details of "Edge Sizing". Select Number of Divisions as Type under Details of "Edge Sizing". Set the number of Divisions to 50. Set the Behavior to Hard.

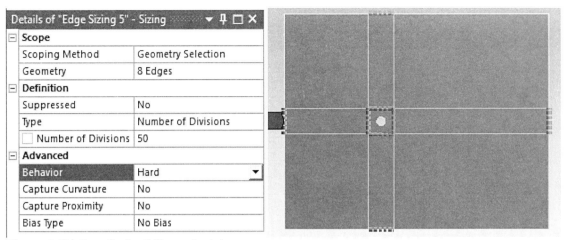

Figure 3.5h) Details for fifth mesh sizing

Select Mesh>>Controls>>Sizing from the menu. Control-select the four edges as shown in Figure 3.5i). Apply the Geometry under Details of "Edge Sizing". Select Number of Divisions as Type under Details of "Edge Sizing". Set the Number of Divisions to 100. Set the Behavior to Hard. Select the first Bias Type from the drop-down menu. Enter a Bias Factor of 20.

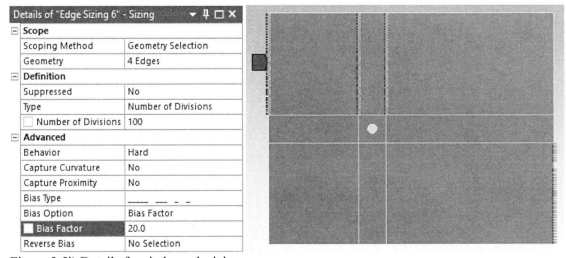

Figure 3.5i) Details for sixth mesh sizing

Select Mesh>>Control>>Sizing from the menu. Control-select the four edges as shown in Figure 3.5j). Apply the Geometry under Details of "Edge Sizing". Select Number of Divisions as Type under Details of "Edge Sizing". Set the Number of Divisions to 100. Set the Behavior to Hard. Select the second Bias Type from the drop-down menu. Enter a Bias Factor of 20.
Right click on Mesh in the tree outline and select Generate Mesh.

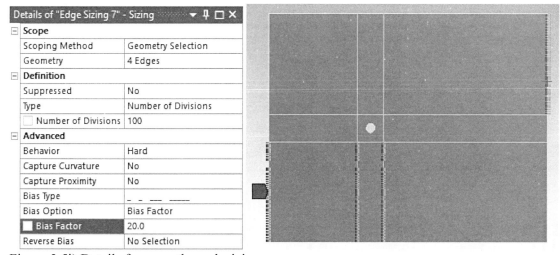

Figure 3.5j) Details for seventh mesh sizing

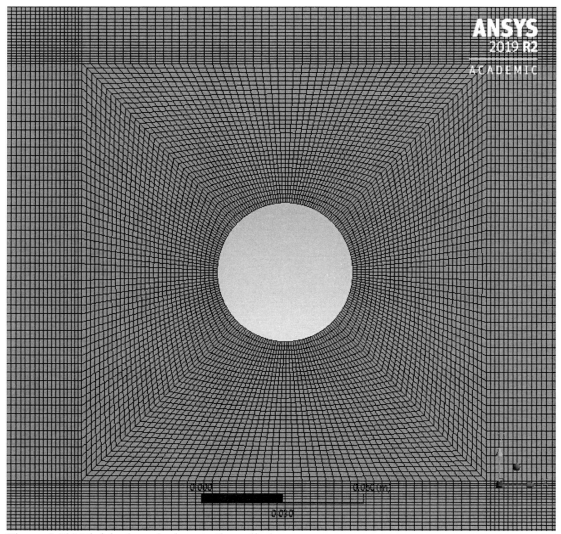

Figure 3.5k) Finished mesh close to the cylinder

CHAPTER 3. FLOW PAST A CYLINDER

6. Select Geometry in the outline. Select the Edge Selection Box ⬚. Control-select the 3 vertical edges on the right-hand side, right click and select Create Named Selection. Name the edges "outlet" and click OK. Name the 3 vertical edges to the left "inlet" and name the edge of the cylinder "cylinder". Name the 6 horizontal edges (3 at the top and 3 at the bottom) "symmetry".

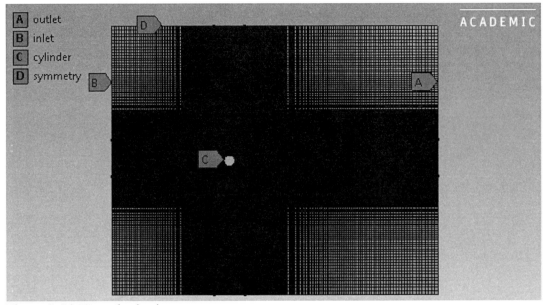

Figure 3.6a) Named selections

Open Geometry in the outline, select Line Body, and select Thermal Fluid as Model Type in Details of "Line Body". In Geometry, right click the Line Body and select Suppress Body.

Details of "Line Body"	▼ ⏚ ☐ ✕
⊞ **Graphics Properties**	
⊟ **Definition**	
☐ Suppressed	Yes
Coordinate System	Default Coordinate System
Cross Section	
Offset Mode	Refresh on Update
Offset Type	Centroid
Model Type	Thermal Fluid
Fluid Cross Area	0. m^2
Fluid Discretization	Upwind/Linear
Reference Frame	Lagrangian
⊟ **Material**	
Assignment	
Fluid/Solid	Defined By Geometry (Solid)
⊞ **Bounding Box**	
⊞ **Properties**	
⊞ **Statistics**	

Figure 3.6b) Details of Line Body

Select File>>Export>>Mesh >>FLUENT Input File>>Export from the menu. Enter the name *cylinder-flow-mesh* and select FLUENT Input Files (*,msh) as Save as Type. Select File>>Save Project… from the menu. Close the meshing window. Right click on Mesh under Project Schematic in ANSYS Workbench and select Update.

F. Launching ANSYS Fluent

7. Double click Setup under Project Schematic in ANSYS Workbench. Check the Options box Double Precision. Select Parallel Processing Options. Select number of Processes equal to the total number of cores. Click on the plus sign next to Show More Options. You can see the location of your working directory. Click OK to launch Fluent. Select Transient Time under General on the Task Page on the left-hand side.

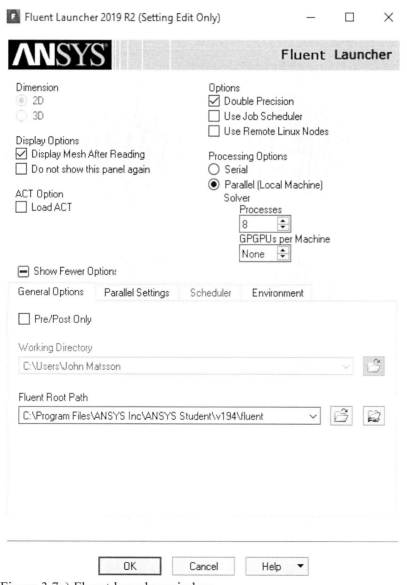

Figure 3.7a) Fluent launcher window

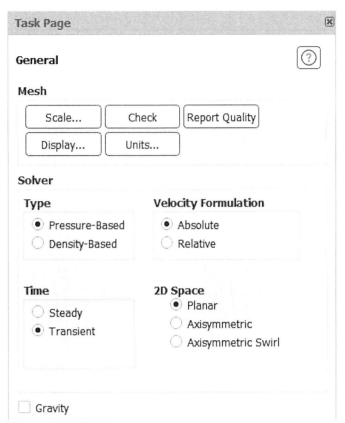

Figure 3.7b) Task page

8. Double-click on Boundary Conditions under Setup in the Outline View. Double click on the inlet Zone on the Task Page. Select Components as Velocity Specification Method. Enter 0.06 m/s as X-Velocity. Click OK to close the Velocity Inlet window.

    Double-click on Methods in the Outline View under Solution. Set the Pressure-Velocity Coupling Scheme to PISO. Uncheck the box for Skewness-Neighbor Coupling. Select Green-Gauss Cell Based Gradient under Spatial Discretization.

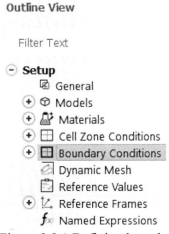

Figure 3.8a) Defining boundary conditions

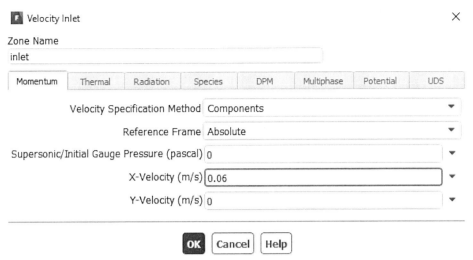

Figure 3.8b) Velocity inlet boundary condition

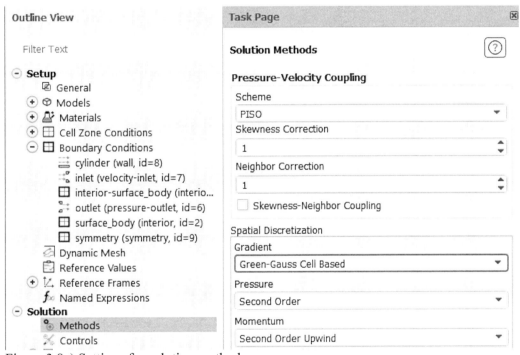

Figure 3.8c) Settings for solution methods

9. Double-click on Initialization in the Outline View under Solution. Enter 0.06 for X-Velocity (m/s). Click on Initialize.

    Double-click on Reference Values under Setup in the Outline View. Select Compute from inlet from the drop-down menu. Set the value for Area (m2) to 0.05 and Length (m) to the same value. Select *solid-surface_body* as Reference Zone.

    Double-click on Report Definitions under Solution in the Outline View. Select New>>Force Report>>Lift… from the drop-down menu. Select cylinder as Wall Zones. Check the boxes for Report File, Report Plot and Print to Console under Create. Click on the OK button to close the Lift Report Definition window. Close the Report Definitions window.

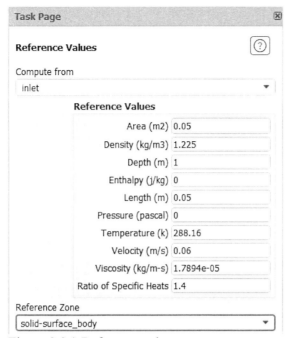

Figure 3.9a) Reference values

Figure 3.9b) New Force Report

Figure 3.9c) Lift report definition

Double-click on Run Calculation under Solution on the left-hand side in the Outline View. Enter 0.2 for the Time Step Size (s) and 600 for number of Time Steps. Enter 30 for Max Iterations/Time Step and click on Calculate.

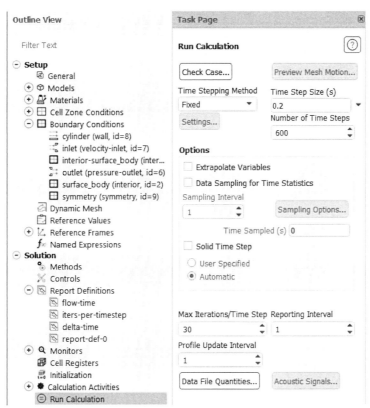

Figure 3.9d) Calculation settings

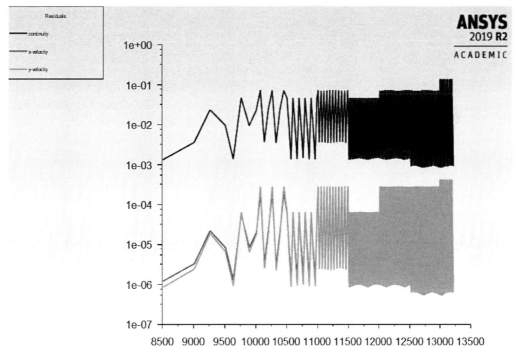

Figure 3.9e) Scaled residuals

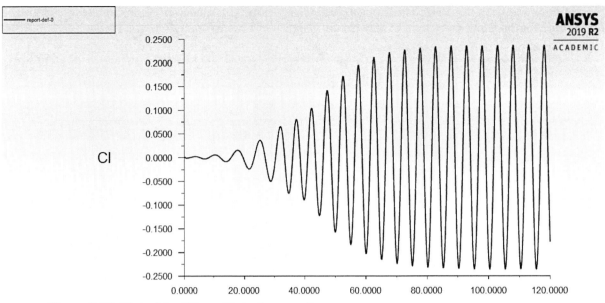

Figure 3.9f) Plot of the lift coefficient versus time

G. Post-Processing

10. Open Plots under Results in the Outline View. Double-click on FFT. Select Load Input File in the Fourier Transform window. Select the file with the name "report-def-0-rfile.out" and click OK. Click on Plot FFT in the Fourier Transform window. Check the box for Write FFT to File under Options in the Fourier Transform window and click on the Write FFT button. Save the file with All Files (*) as file type and the name "fft-data" in the working directory. This file can be opened in Notepad. The power spectral density maximum is at 0.2 Hz.

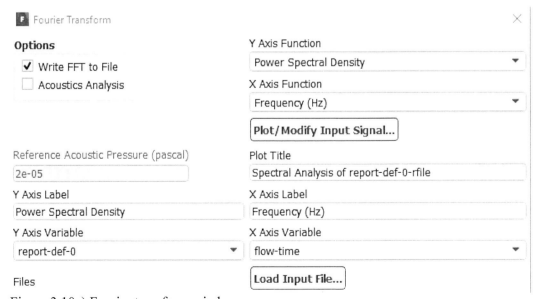

Figure 3.10a) Fourier transform window

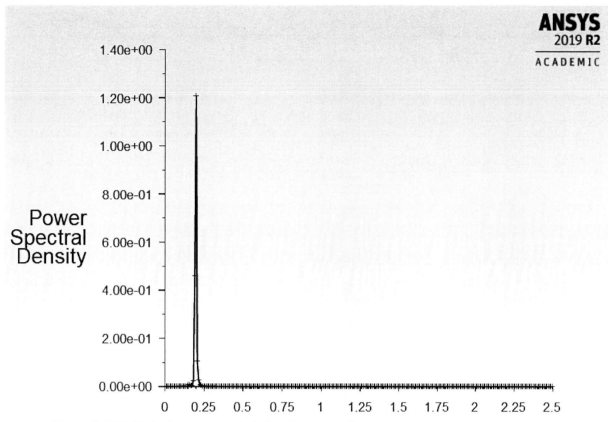

Figure 3.10b) Plot of power spectral density versus frequency

Double-click on Contours in Graphics under Results in the Outline View. Enter *static-pressure* as Contour Name in the Contours window. Select Contours of Pressure… and Static Pressure. Check the box Filled under Options. Select all Surfaces and click on Save/Display.

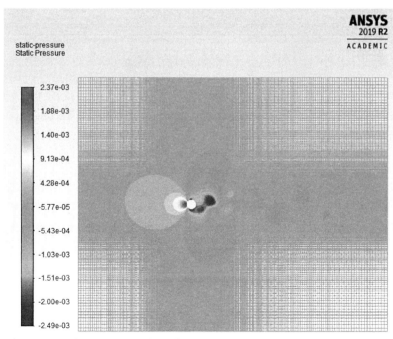

Figure 3.10c) Contours plot of pressure

Select Contours of Velocity and Vorticity Magnitude. Enter vorticity-magnitude as Contour Name in the Contours window. Check the box Filled under Options. Select all surfaces and click on Save/Display.

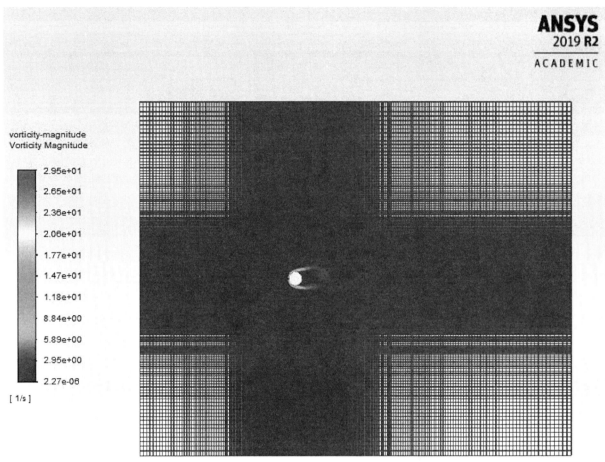

Figure 3.10d) Contour plot of vorticity

Find the coefficient of drag by double-clicking on Reports under Results in the Outline View. Double-click on Forces under Reports. Click Print and write down the value for the total drag coefficient that you have calculated: 1.1509.

H. Theory

11. The drag coefficient from experiments for a smooth cylinder is found using the following curve-fit formula:

$$C_{D,Exp} = 1 + \frac{10}{Re^{2/3}} \qquad 0 \leq Re \leq 250{,}000 \tag{3.1}$$

We determine the Reynolds number for the flow around the cylinder that is defined as

$$Re = Ud/v = 0.06 * 0.050 / 1.5 * 10^{-5} = 200 \tag{3.2}$$

where U is the magnitude of the free stream velocity, d is the diameter of the cylinder, and v is the kinematic viscosity of air at room temperature. The difference between ANSYS Fluent and experiments for the drag coefficient is 11%.

The Strouhal number S is one of the many non-dimensional numbers used in fluid mechanics and based on the oscillation frequency of fluid flows. In this case the Strouhal number is based on the vortex shedding frequency f and can be defined as

$$S = \frac{fd}{U} = \frac{0.2Hz*0.050m}{0.06\,m/s} = 0.167 \tag{3.3}$$

This value of the Strouhal number from ANSYS Fluent can be compared with DNS (Direct Numerical Simulation) results by Henderson[3], see also Williamson and Brown[6]. The difference is 15%.

$$S_{DNS} = 0.2698 - \frac{1.0272}{\sqrt{Re}} = 0.1968 \tag{3.4}$$

I. References

1. Cimbala, J.M., Fluent-Laminar Flow over a cylinder, Penn State University, 29 January 2008.
2. Flow Over a Cylinder, Fluent Inc. [FlowLab 1.2], April 16, 2007.
3. Henderson, R., Nonlinear dynamics and pattern formation in turbulent wake transition, J. of Fluid Mech., 352, (65-112), 1997.
4. Tutorial 6. Flow Past a Circular Cylinder. Fluent Inc. January 17, 2007.
5. Validation 3. Laminar Flow Around a Circular Cylinder, Fluent Inc. September 13, 2002.
6. Williamson, C. H. K., and Brown G.L., A series in $1/\sqrt{Re}$ to represent the Strouhal-Reynolds number relationship of the cylinder wake, Journal of Fluids and Structures, 12, (1073 – 1085), 1998.

J. Exercises

3.1 Rerun the simulation with the same free stream velocity and Reynolds number and the same mesh but use a Time Step Size of 0.25 s and 500 as the Number of Time Steps. Set Max Iterations /Time Step to 30. Determine the drag coefficient and compare with equation (3.1). Determine the Strouhal number and compare with equation (3.4). Include plots of the lift coefficient over time and power spectral density versus frequency.

3.2 Rerun the simulation shown in this chapter for a lower free stream 0.05 m/s but with the same mesh and for the same diameter 0.05 m of the cylinder. Use the same Time Step Size, Number of Time Steps and Max Iterations/Time Step as in this chapter. Determine the Reynolds number. Determine the drag coefficient and compare with equation (3.1). Determine the Strouhal number and compare with equation (3.4). Include plots of the lift coefficient over time and power spectral density versus frequency. Also, include contour plots of static pressure, vorticity and velocity magnitude.

Notes:

CHAPTER 4. FLOW PAST AN AIRFOIL

A. Objectives

- Using ANSYS Workbench to Model the NACA 2412 Airfoil and Mesh
- Inserting Boundary Conditions and Free Stream Velocity
- Running Turbulent Steady 2D Planar ANSYS Fluent Simulations
- Using Velocity and Pressure Plots for Visualizations
- Determine Lift and Drag Coefficients for Zero Angle of Attack

B. Problem Description

The purpose of this simulation is to become familiar with a few basic aerodynamic concepts and terms such as Reynold's number, coefficients of lift, drag, and pressure. We will therefore study the flow of air past the NACA 2412 airfoil and we will analyze the problem using ANSYS Fluent. The chord length of the airfoil is 230 mm, the angle of attack is 0° and the free stream velocity is 12.7 m/s.

Another airfoil shape that has been studied extensively is the Clark-Y airfoil. One of the first measurements of pressure distributions on this airfoil was completed by Jacobs et al.[1], followed by Marchman and Werme[2] and Stern et al. [3] that made low Reynolds number measurements. Warner[4] and Matsson[5] have also determined results from tests of the Clark-Y airfoil. The NACA 2412 airfoil has been tested by Matsson et al.[6].

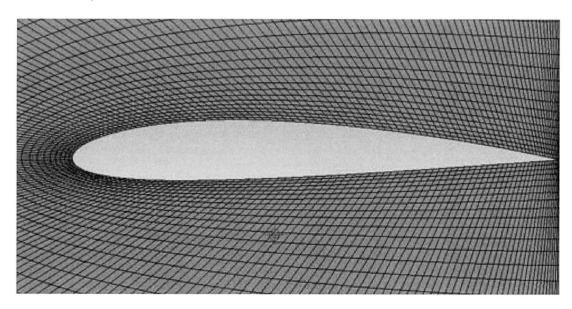

C. Launching ANSYS Workbench and Selecting Fluent

1. Start by launching ANSYS Workbench. Double click on Fluid Flow (Fluent) that is located under Analysis Systems in Toolbox.

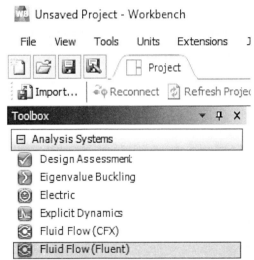

Figure 4.1 Selecting Fluid Flow in ANSYS Workbench

D. Launching ANSYS DesignModeler

2. Right click Geometry and select Properties. In Properties of Schematic A2: Geometry, select Analysis Type 2D under Advanced Geometry Options. Right-click on Geometry in the Project Schematic window and select New DesignModeler Geometry. Select **Units>>Millimeter** from the menu as the desired length unit in the new DesignModeler window.

Select Create>>Point from the menu. We will use the coordinates file *NACA_2412_Airfoil* that is available for download at *sdcpublications.com*. Open the Coordinates File from Details View and click on Generate. Select Look At Face 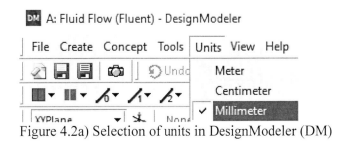 . Select Concept>>Lines From Points in the menu. Right click in the graphics window and select Point Chain. Right click in the graphics window and select Select All. Apply the Point Segments in Details View. Click on Generate. Select Concept>>Surfaces From Edges from the menu. Right click in the graphics window and Select All. Apply Edges in Details View. Click on Generate.

Figure 4.2a) Selection of units in DesignModeler (DM)

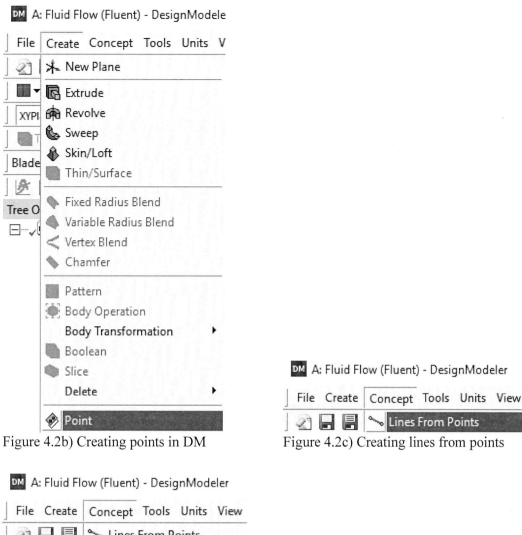

Figure 4.2b) Creating points in DM

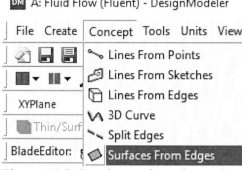

Figure 4.2c) Creating lines from points

Figure 4.2d) Creating surfaces from edges

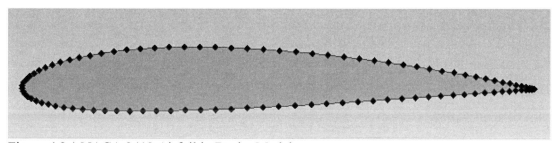

Figure 4.2e) NACA 2412 Airfoil in DesignModeler

3. Next, we will be creating the mesh region around the airfoil. Create a new coordinate system by first clicking on New Plane ![plane icon]. Select Type>>From Coordinates in the Details View. Enter 230 mm for FD11, Point X. Click on Generate. Select the new Plane4 in the tree outline and click on ![sketch icon] to generate a new sketch. Click on the Sketching tab and select Arc by Center from the Draw tab. Click on Look At Face/Plane/Sketch ![look at icon]. Click at the origin of the coordinate system at the trailing edge of the airfoil. Make sure that you see the letter *P* when you move the cursor over the origin of the coordinate system. Next, click on the vertical axis above the origin (make sure you have a *C*) and finally on the vertical axis below the origin (make sure you have a *C* once again), see Figure 4.3b).

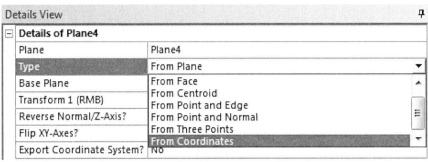

Figure 4.3a) A new plane from coordinates

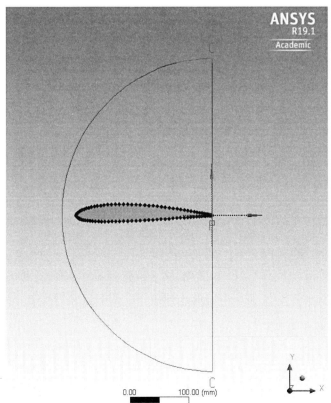

Figure 4.3b) Half-circle around the NACA 2412 airfoil

4. Select Rectangle by 3 Points from the Draw tab. Click at the intersection of the arc and the positive vertical axis, at the intersection between the arc and the negative vertical axis, and finally click in the right-hand side plane. Select Modify and Trim from Sketching Toolboxes. Click on the lines of the rectangle that are aligned with and on top of the vertical axis.

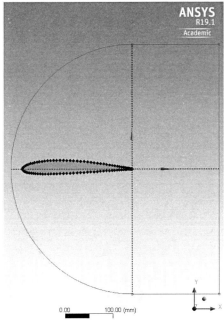

Figure 4.4a) Half-circle and rectangular mesh region around the NACA 2412 airfoil

Select Dimensions under Sketching Toolboxes, select Radius under Dimensions and select the arc in the graphics window. Set the radius of the arc to 2875 mm which gives a ratio of the radius of the arc to the chord length of 12.5. Next, select Horizontal under Dimensions from the Sketching Toolboxes and click on the vertical axis and the vertical edge of the rectangle on the right-hand side. Enter 5750 mm as the length.

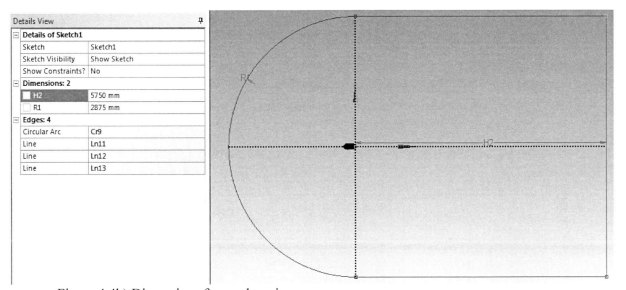

Figure 4.4b) Dimensions for mesh region

Select Concept>>Surface from Sketches. Select Sketch1 under Plane4 in the Tree Outline and Apply as Base Objects in Details View. Select Operation>>Add Frozen in Details View followed by Generate.

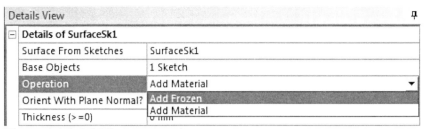

Figure 4.4c) Add frozen operation

5. Select Create>>Boolean from the menu. Select Subtract Operation from the Details View. Click on the mesh region in the graphics window and click on Apply as Target Bodies in Details View. Select the Airfoil as Tool Bodies in Details View and click on Generate, see Figure 4.5c).

Figure 4.5a) Creating a Boolean

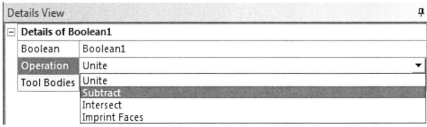

Figure 4.5b) Selecting a subtracting operation

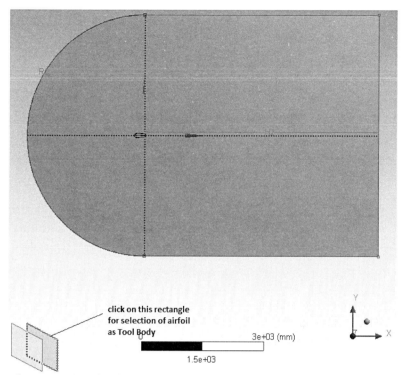

click on this rectangle
for selection of airfoil
as Tool Body

Figure 4.5c) Selection of Tool Body

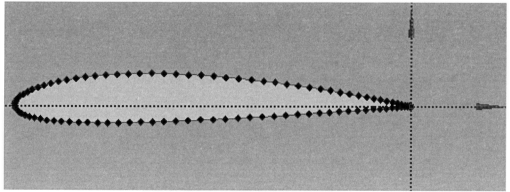

Figure 4.5d) Completed subtraction operation

6. Select Plane 4 in the tree outline and create a new sketch ⬚. Select the Sketching tab and the Line tool under Draw. Draw a line on the vertical axis from top to bottom that intersects the entire mesh region. Select Concepts>>Lines from Sketches from the menu. Select the newly created vertical line and Apply it as a Base Object in the Details View. Click on Generate.

    Repeat this step and create a horizontal line on the horizontal axis for Plane4 that is drawn from left to right and goes through the whole mesh region including the leading and trailing edges of the airfoil. You will need to create a Coincident Constraint using the Sketching Toolbox and inserting the constraint between the new horizontal line and the horizontal axis. It may be helpful to draw the horizontal line a little bit below the horizontal axis and use the constraint to fix the line with the horizontal axis.

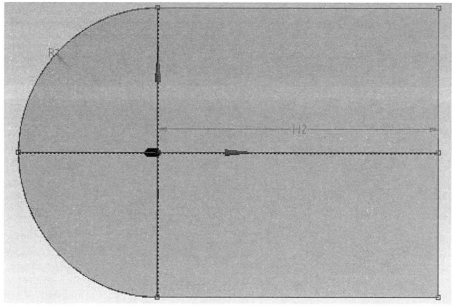

Figure 4.6 Completed vertical and horizontal lines through the mesh region

7.   Select Tools>>Projection from the menu. Select Edges on Face as Type. Control-select both parts of the newly created vertical line and the two parts of the newly created horizontal line and Apply the four Edges in the Details View. Click in the yellow region next to Target in Details View. Select the mesh region around the airfoil and Apply it as the Target under Details View. Click Generate. You should now have four different mesh regions.

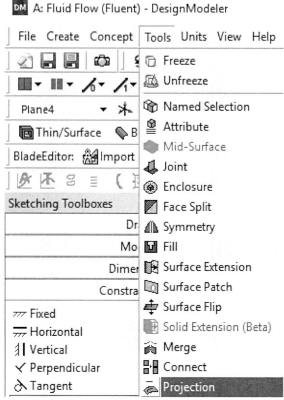

Figure 4.7a) Selection of the projection tool

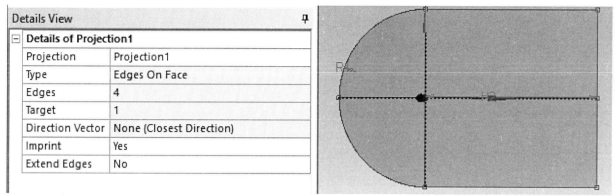

Figure 4.7b) Details view for projection

Click on the plus sign next to 2 Parts, 2 Bodies in the Tree Outline. Right click the Line Body and select Suppress Body. Select File>>Save Project from the menu and save the project with the name "NACA 2412 Airfoil Flow Study". Close DesignModeler.

E. Launching ANSYS Meshing

8. Double click on Mesh under Project Schematic in ANSYS Workbench. Select Mesh in the Outline of the Meshing window and select Mesh>>Controls>>Face Meshing from the menu. Control-select all four faces of the mesh. Apply the Geometry under Details of "Face Meshing".

Figure 4.8a) Selection of face meshing

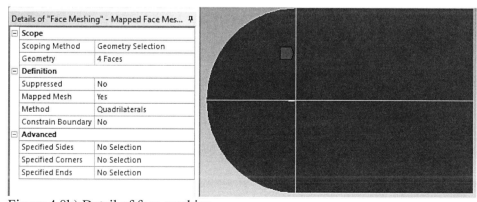

Figure 4.8b) Detail of face meshing

Select Mesh Control>>Sizing and click on the Edge Selection Filter [icon]. Control-select the four edges as shown in Figure 4.8c). Apply the Geometry under Details of "Edge Sizing". Select Number of Divisions as Type under Details of "Edge Sizing". Set the number of Divisions to 50. Set the Behavior as Hard. Select the first Bias Type from the drop-down menu. Enter a Bias Factor of 150.

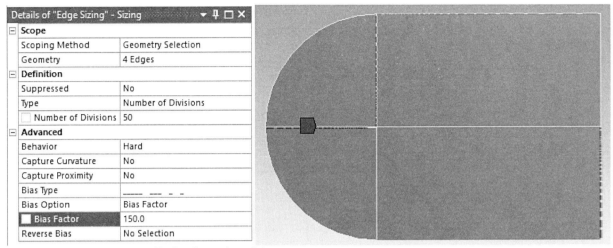

Figure 4.8c) Details for first edge sizing

Create another identical edge sizing but this time select the four remaining straight edges, see Figure 4.8d). Select the same number of divisions 50 and behavior Hard. Select the second Bias Type ‗ ‗ ‗‗ ‗‗‗ from the top from the drop-down menu and the same bias factor of 150.

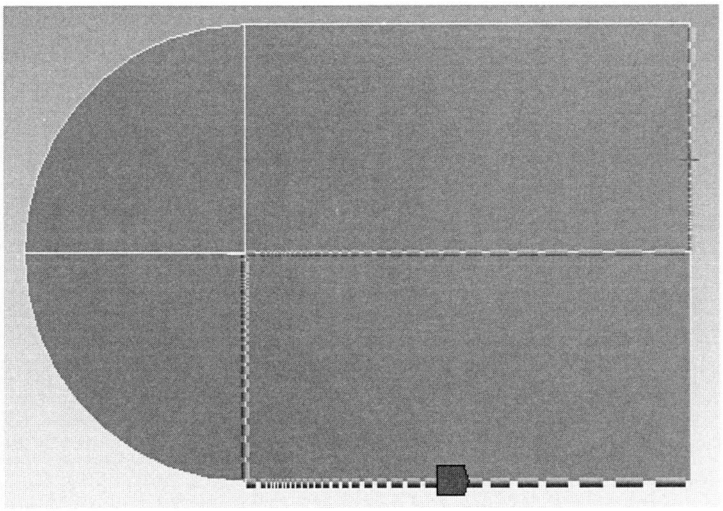

Figure 4.8d) Details for second edge sizing

The final edge sizing will be for the two round edges. Set the Number of Divisions to 100 and Hard behavior. No bias will be used for the round edges. Right click on Mesh in the tree outline and select Generate Mesh.

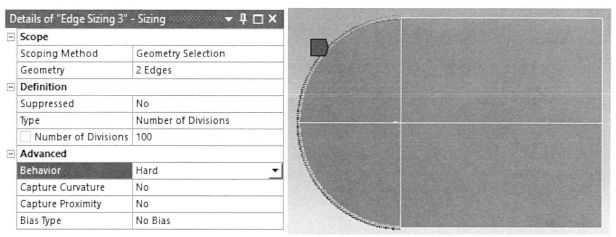

Figure 4.8e) Details of edge sizing for the two round edges

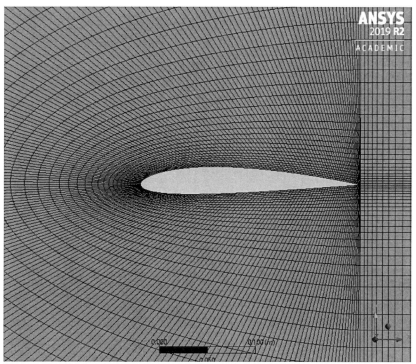

Figure 4.8f) Finished mesh around the airfoil

9. Select Geometry in the Outline. Select the Edge Selection filter ⬚. Control-select the two vertical edges on the right-hand side of the mesh region, right click and select Create Named Selection. Name the edges "outlet" and click OK. Name the two round edges "inlet". Name the horizontal upper and lower edges "symmetry". Save the project. Select File>>Export>>Mesh>>FLUENT Input File>>Export from the menu. Enter "airfoil-flow-mesh" as file name and Save as type: FLUENT Input Files (*.msh). Close the meshing window. Right click on Mesh and select Update in ANSYS Workbench.

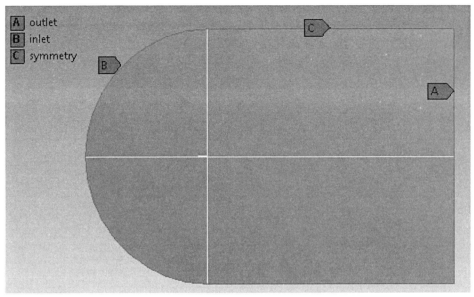

Figure 4.9 Named selections for mesh

F. Launching ANSYS Fluent

10. Double click on Setup under Project Schematic in ANSYS Workbench. Check the Options box Double Precision. Select Parallel Processing Options. Select number of Processes to the same number as the total number of cores for your computer. You can click on the plus sign next to Show More Options and take a note of the location for your working directory. Click OK to launch Fluent.

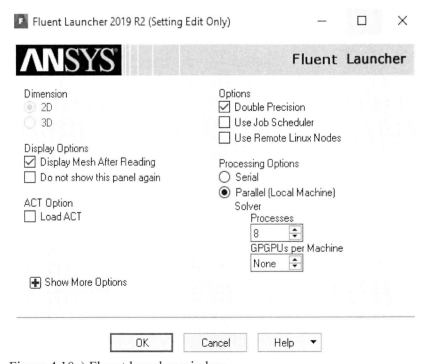

Figure 4.10a) Fluent launcher window

Select the Density-Based Solver under General on the Task Page. Double-click on Models under Setup in Outline View and double click on the Viscous-Laminar model on the Task Page. Select the Spalart-Allmaras (1 eqn) turbulence model. Select OK to close the Viscous Model window.

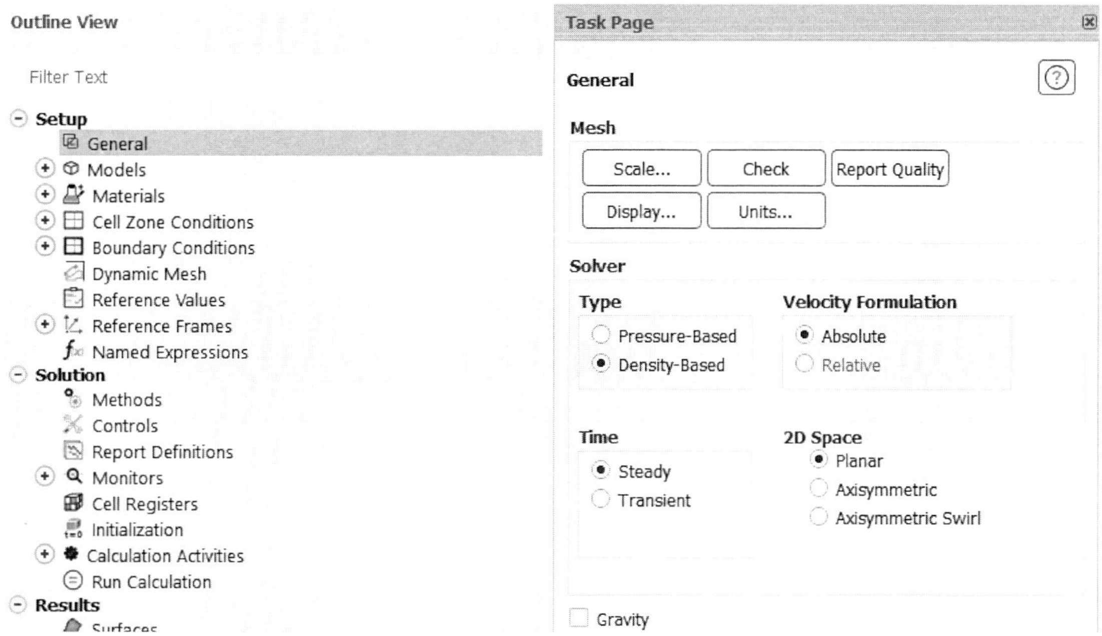

Figure 4.10b) General solution setup

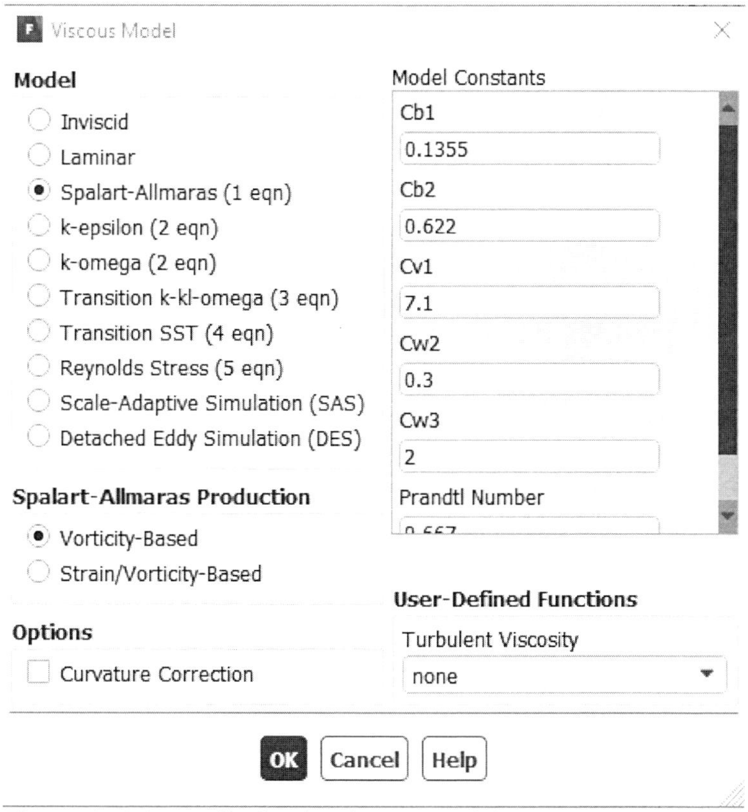

Figure 4.10c) Details for the viscous model

11. Double click on Boundary Conditions under Setup in Outline View. Double click the inlet Zone on the Task Page. Select Components as Velocity Specification Method. Enter 12.7 m/s as X-Velocity (m/s). Click OK to close the Velocity Inlet window.

Figure 4.11 Velocity inlet boundary condition

12. Double click on Monitors under Solution in the Tree. Double click on Residual under Monitor. Change the Convergence Criterion for all four residuals to 1e-8. Click on OK to exit the Residual Monitors window. Double click on Initialization under Solution under the Outline View. Select Standard Initialization as Initialization Method, select Compute from inlet and click on Initialize. Select File>>Save Project from the menu. Double click on Run Calculation under Solution in the Outline View. Set number of Iterations to 10000. Click on Calculate. Click OK when the calculations are complete.

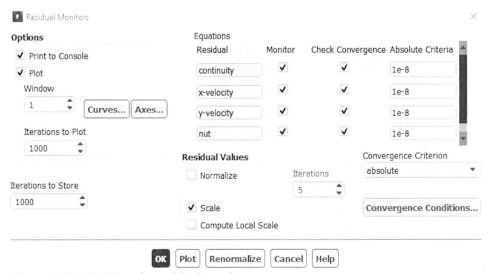

Figure 4.12a) Settings for residual monitors

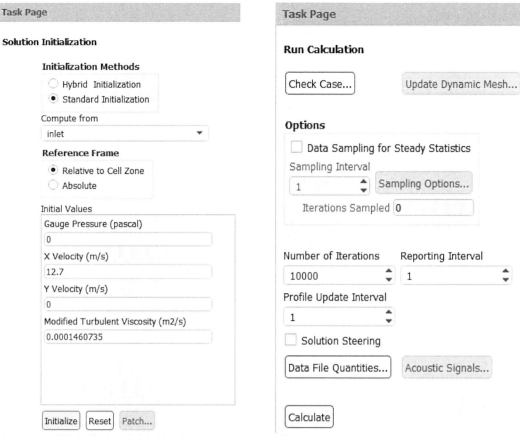

Figure 4.12b) Solution initialization

Figure 4.12c) Running calculations

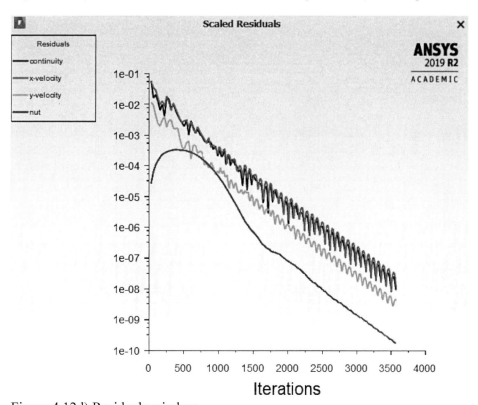

Figure 4.12d) Residuals window

G. Post-Processing

13. Double click on Graphics under Results in the Outline View. Display a plot of pressure contours by double clicking on Contours under Graphics, check the box for Filled under Options, select all Surfaces and select Pressure and Static Pressure under Contours of followed by Save/Display. Create another contour plot for Velocity and Velocity Magnitude.

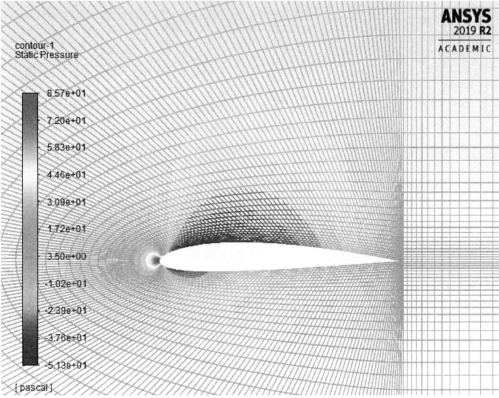

Figure 4.13a) Pressure contours around NACA 2412 airfoil

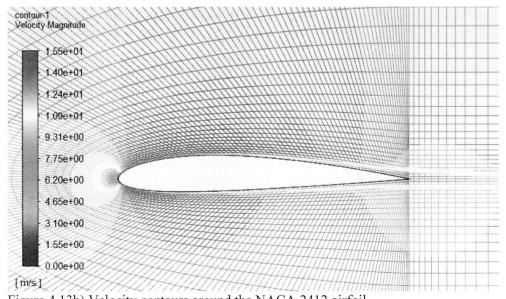

Figure 4.13b) Velocity contours around the NACA 2412 airfoil

14. Double click on Reference Values under Setup in the Outline View. Select Compute from inlet. Enter the value 0.23 for Length (m) which is the chord length and enter the value 12.7 for Velocity (m/s). Enter the value 0.3048 for Depth (m) and 0.070104 for Area (m2).

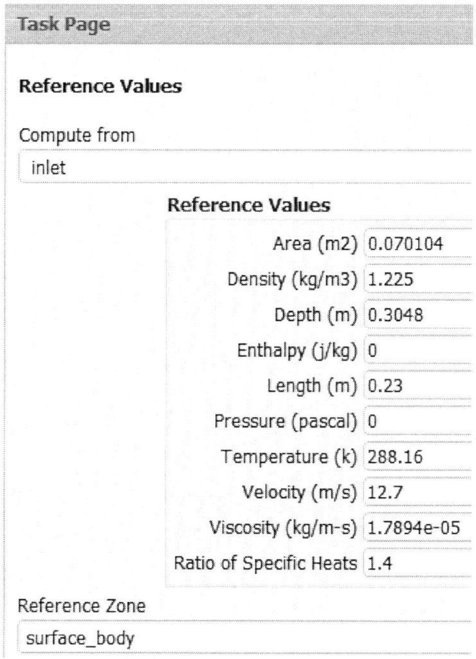

Task Page

Reference Values

Compute from

inlet

Reference Values	
Area (m2)	0.070104
Density (kg/m3)	1.225
Depth (m)	0.3048
Enthalpy (j/kg)	0
Length (m)	0.23
Pressure (pascal)	0
Temperature (k)	288.16
Velocity (m/s)	12.7
Viscosity (kg/m-s)	1.7894e-05
Ratio of Specific Heats	1.4

Reference Zone

surface_body

Figure 4.14a) Reference values

Find the coefficient of drag by double clicking on Reports under Results in the Outline View. Double click on Forces under Reports. Set the Direction Vector in the Force Reports window to 1 for X and 0 for Y. Click Print and write down the value for the total drag coefficient that you have calculated $C_d = 0.017688831$. Repeat this step to find the value for the lift coefficient using 0 for X and 1 for Y for the Direction Vector in the Force Reports window. The value for the lift coefficient is $C_l = 0.19927405$.

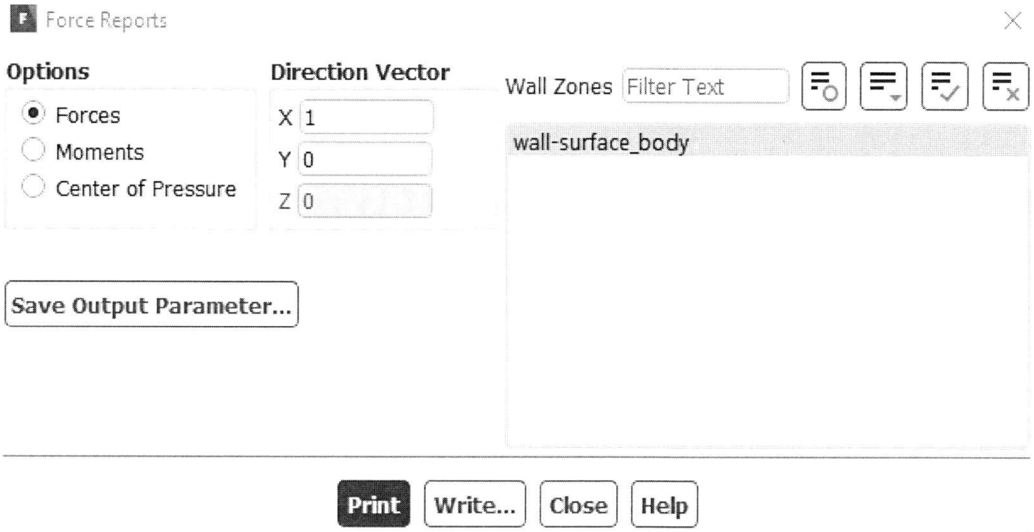

Force Reports

Options
- Forces
- Moments
- Center of Pressure

Direction Vector
- X 1
- Y 0
- Z 0

Wall Zones | Filter Text

wall-surface_body

Save Output Parameter...

Print | Write... | Close | Help

Figure 4.14b) Force reports

Determine the Reynolds number for the flow around an airfoil that is defined as $Re = Uc/v$ where U is the magnitude of the free stream velocity, c is the chord length of the airfoil, and v is the kinematic viscosity of air at room temperature. You will find that $Re = 200,000$. The angle of attack AoA for the flow case that we studied in this chapter was zero degrees.

Open the Mesh by right-clicking on the Mesh in the Project Schematic in ANSYS Workbench and select Edit. Click on the plus sign next to Mesh. Change the values for Number of Divisions for the three different Edge Sizings to 60 and 120 instead of the current values 50 and 100. Right click on Mesh and select Generate Mesh.

Select File>>Export>>Mesh>>FLUENT Input File>>Export from the menu. Save the mesh with the name "fine-airfoil-flow-mesh". Select File>>Close Meshing, right click on Mesh in the Project Schematic in ANSYS Workbench and select Update. Right click on Setup in ANSYS Workbench and select Update. Double click on Setup and reinitialize the solution. Run the calculations. Enter the reference values once again and calculate the drag and lift coefficients.

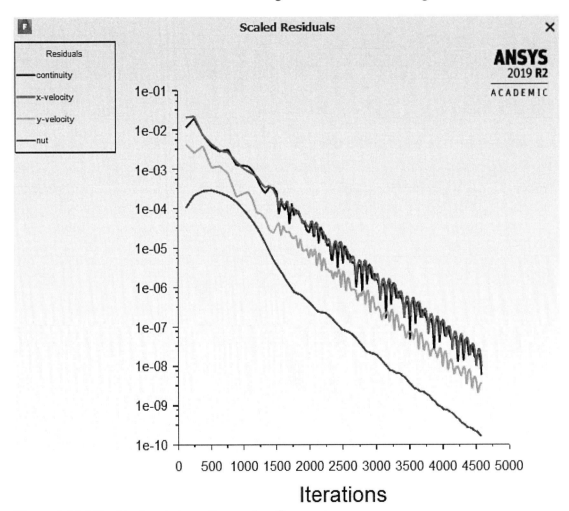

Figure 4.14c) Residuals window after mesh refinement

$Re = 200{,}000$	Unrefined Mesh	Refined Mesh
C_d	0.01769	0.01662
C_l	0.19927	0.20069
Angle of Attack	0	0
Number of Divisions	50, 100	60, 120

Table 4.1 Comparison of drag and lift coefficient for two different mesh sizes

H. Theory

15. The Reynolds number for the flow over an airfoil is determined by

$$Re = \frac{Uc}{v} \tag{4.1}$$

where U (m/s) is the magnitude of the free stream velocity, c (m) is the chord length of the airfoil, and v (m²/s) is the kinematic viscosity of air at room temperature.

The pressure distribution over the airfoil is expressed in non-dimensional form by the pressure coefficient

$$C_p = \frac{p_i - P}{\frac{1}{2}\rho U^2} \tag{4.2}$$

where ρ (kg/m³) is the free stream density and where p_i (Pa) is the surface pressure at location i and p (Pa) is the pressure in the free stream. The pressure coefficient can alternatively be related to the velocity distribution u (m/s) around the airfoil through

$$C_p = 1 - \left(\frac{u}{U}\right)^2 \tag{4.3}$$

The lift and drag coefficients can be determined from

$$C_l = \frac{F_l}{\frac{1}{2}\rho U^2 bc} \tag{4.4}$$

$$C_d = \frac{F_d}{\frac{1}{2}\rho U^2 bc} \tag{4.5}$$

, where F_l and F_d (N) are lift and drag forces and b (m) is the wingspan.

I. References

1. Jacobs E.N., Stack J. and Pinkerton R.M. "Airfoil Pressure Distribution Investigation in the Variable Density Wind Tunnel." NACA Report No. 353, 1930.
2. Marchman III J.F and Werme T.D. "Clark-Y Airfoil Performance at Low Reynolds Numbers." AIAA-84-0052, 1984.
3. Stern F., Muste M., Houser D., Wilson M. and Ghosh S. "Measurement of Pressure Distribution and Forces acting on an Airfoil.", Laboratory Experiment #3, 57:020 Mechanics of Fluids and Transfer Processes (http://css.engineering/uiowa.edu/fluidslab/pdfs/57-020/airfoil.doc)

4. Warner E.P. "Airplane Design: Performance." McGraw-Hill, New York, 1936

5. Matsson J., "A Student Project On Airfoil Performance", Annual Conference & Exposition, Honolulu, Hawaii, 2007.

6. Matsson J., Voth J., McCain C. and McGraw C., "Aerodynamic Performance of the NACA 2412 Airfoil at Low Reynolds Number", ASEE 123rd Annual Conference & Exposition, New Orleans, LA, June 26-29, 2016.

7. Abbott, I.H., Von Doenhoff, A.E., "Theory of Wing Sections: Including a Summary of Airfoil Data", Dover Publications, 1959.

J. Exercises

4.1 Determine contours of pressure and velocity for the flow field around an airfoil with a different NACA number than the one covered in this chapter. Include the corresponding mesh refinement level, number of iterations, refine threshold, number of cells refined, drag coefficient, lift coefficient, Reynolds number and the angle of attack as shown in Table 4.1 for the NACA 2412 airfoil. Include the residuals window after the solution has converged and include a printout of the mesh around the airfoil.

4.2 Continue with Exercise 4.1 using different angles of attack AoA = 2, 4, 6, 8, 10, 12 degrees for the same Reynolds number. For each AoA, refine the mesh until you get a converged solution. Plot the drag and lift coefficients versus AoA and compare with experimental results for the chosen airfoil using data from Abbott and Von Doenhoff[7].

CHAPTER 5. RAYLEIGH-BENARD CONVECTION

A. Objectives

- Using ANSYS Workbench to Create the Mesh for 3D Rayleigh-Bénard Convection
- Inserting Wall Boundary Conditions
- Running Laminar Steady 3D ANSYS Fluent Simulations
- Using Contour Plots for Visualizations
- Compare Results with Neutral Stability Theory

B. Problem Description

Bénard[1] was the first scientist to experimentally study convection in a fluid layer with a free surface heated from below. Rayleigh[2] used linear stability analysis to theoretically explain and study the stability of the fluid motion between horizontal parallel plates with the hotter plate at the bottom. Chandrasekhar[3] completed the linear stability analysis for Rayleigh-Bénard convection and Koschmieder[4] showed the development of the research in this area during the following couple of decades.

There are only a few experiments including Koschmieder and Pallas[5], Hoard et al.[6] and to some extent Matsson[6] that have produced the concentric ring cells in Rayleigh-Bénard convection that according to stability theory should appear with a rigid upper boundary condition. This instability with an upper rigid wall in experiments is very sensitive to the surface roughness and flatness of the upper wall.

In this chapter, we will study Rayleigh-Bénard convection and we will analyze the problem using ANSYS Fluent in 3D. The enclosure is filled with water and the temperature of the cold wall is 296.5 K while the hot wall is at 298 K. The diameter of the enclosure is 100 mm and the depth 4.8 mm.

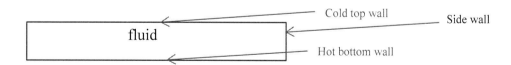

C. Launching ANSYS Workbench and Selecting Fluent

1. Start by launching ANSYS Workbench. Double click on Fluid Flow (Fluent).

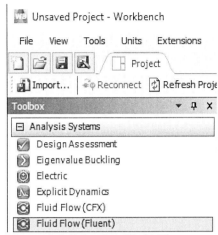

Figure 5.1 Selecting Fluid Flow

D. Launching ANSYS DesignModeler

2. Right-click on Geometry in Project Schematic and select Properties. Select Geometry and 3D Analysis Type under Advanced Geometry Options in Properties of Schematic A2: Geometry. Right click on Geometry and open a New DesignModeler Geometry. Select **Millimeter as the Unit** from the menu in DesignModeler.

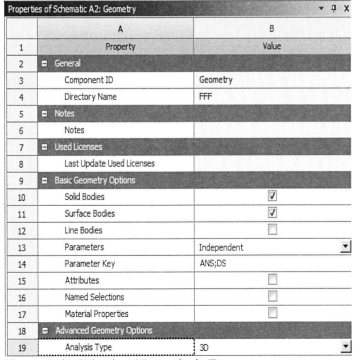

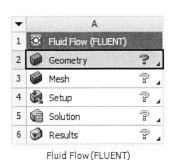

Figure 5.2a) Geometry   Figure 5.2b) Selecting 3D Analysis Type

3. Next, we will be creating the mesh region for the simulation. Select XYPlane from the Tree Outline. Select Look at Sketch 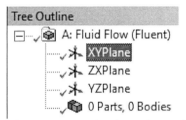. Select the Sketching tab and draw a circle from the origin. Select the Dimensions tab in Sketching Toolboxes. Click on the circle and enter a diameter of 100 mm. Select Create>>Extrude from the menu. Select Sketch1 under XYPlane in the Tree Outline and Apply the sketch as Geometry in Details View. Enter 4.8 mm as FD1, Depth (>0). Click on Generate ⌐≠ Generate and Close DesignModeler.

Figure 5.3a) Selection of XYPlane

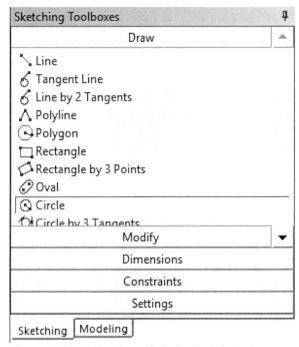

Figure 5.3b) Selection of circle sketch tool

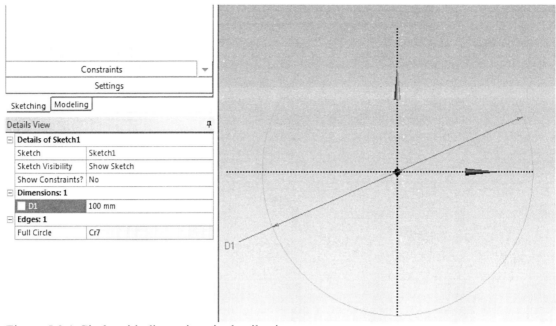

Figure 5.3c) Circle with dimensions in details view

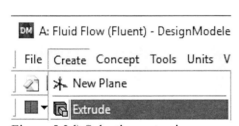

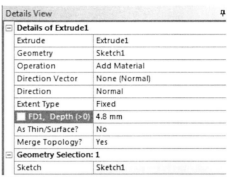

Figure 5.3d) Selecting extrusion   Figure 5.3e) Details of extrusion

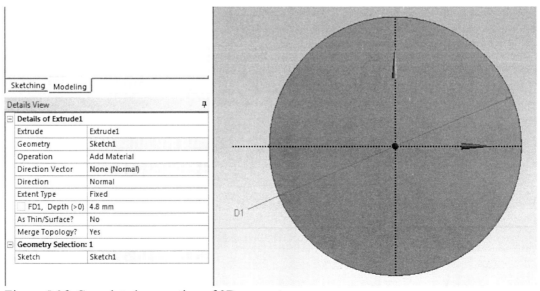

Figure 5.3f) Completed generation of 3D geometry

E. Launching ANSYS Meshing

4. We are now going to double click on Mesh under Project Schematic in ANSYS Workbench to open the Mechanical window. Select Mesh in the Outline. Select Unit Systems>>Metric (mm, kg, N …) from the bottom of the graphics window. Click on Update. A coarse mesh is created.

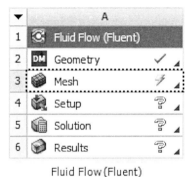

Figure 5.4a) Starting Mesh

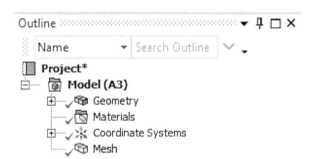

Figure 5.4b) Selection of Mesh in Outline

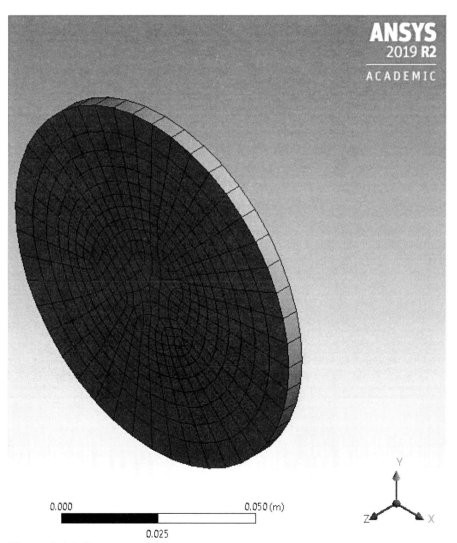

Figure 5.4c) Coarse mesh

5. Select Mesh>>Controls>>Face Meshing from the menu. Click on the cylindrical face of the mesh region in the graphics window. The face turns green. Click on the Apply button for Geometry in Details of "Face Meshing".

    Select Mesh>>Controls>>Sizing from the menu and select Edge 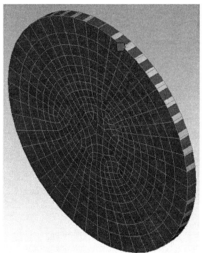. Control click on the two circumferential edges of the mesh region. Click on Apply for the Geometry in "Details of Edge Sizing". Under Definition in "Details of Edge Sizing", select Number of Divisions for Type, 500 for Number of Divisions, and Hard as Behavior.

    Repeat the selection of Mesh>>Controls>>Sizing from the menu and select Face . Control select the two plane faces and the cylindrical face of the mesh region. Enter 0.5 mm for Element Size and Hard Behavior.

    Repeat the selection of Mesh>>Controls>>Sizing from the menu and select Body . Select the body of the mesh region. Enter 5 mm for Element Size and Hard Behavior.
    Click on Update and select Mesh in the Outline. Right click in the graphics window and select Isometric View. The finished mesh is shown in the graphics window.

Figure 5.5a) Generation of Face Meshing

Figure 5.5b) Face for Face Meshing

Figure 5.5c) Mesh Control Sizing

Figure 5.5d) Round edges for sizing

Details of "Edge Sizing" - Sizing	▼ 무 □ ×
Scope	
Scoping Method	Geometry Selection
Geometry	2 Edges
Definition	
Suppressed	No
Type	Number of Divisions
Number of Divisions	500
Advanced	
Behavior	Hard
Capture Curvature	No
Capture Proximity	No
Bias Type	No Bias

Figure 5.5e) Details of edge sizing

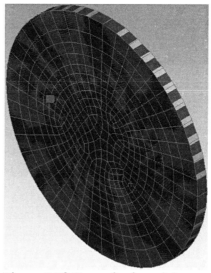

Figure 5.5f) Faces for face sizing

Details of "Face Sizing" - Sizing	▼ 무 □ ×
Scope	
Scoping Method	Geometry Selection
Geometry	3 Faces
Definition	
Suppressed	No
Type	Element Size
Element Size	0.5 mm
Advanced	
Defeature Size	Default (3.5376e-002 mm)
Influence Volume	No
Behavior	Hard
Capture Curvature	No
Capture Proximity	No

Figure 5.5g) Details of face sizing

Details of "Body Sizing" - Sizing	▼ 무 □ ×
Scope	
Scoping Method	Geometry Selection
Geometry	1 Body
Definition	
Suppressed	No
Type	Element Size
Element Size	5.0 mm
Advanced	
Defeature Size	Default (3.5376e-002 mm)
Behavior	Hard
Capture Curvature	No
Capture Proximity	No

Figure 5.5h) Details of body sizing

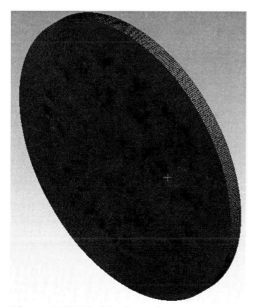

Figure 5.5i) Finished mesh

Details of "Mesh"	▼ 무 □ ×
Display	
Display Style	Use Geometry Setting
Defaults	
Physics Preference	CFD
Solver Preference	Fluent
Element Order	Linear
Element Size	Default (7.0751e-003 m)
Export Format	Standard
Export Preview Surface Mesh	No
⊞ Sizing	
⊞ Quality	
⊞ Inflation	
⊞ Assembly Meshing	
⊞ Advanced	
Statistics	
Nodes	357390
Elements	323200

Figure 5.5j) Details of mesh

6. Select Face 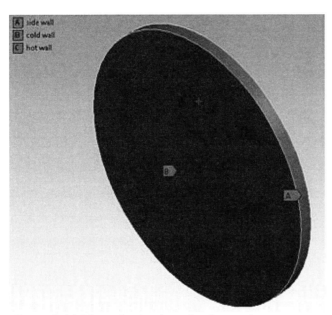 and select the cylindrical face of the mesh region, right click and select Create Named Selection. Enter *side wall* as the name and click on the OK button. Repeat this step for the upper and lower faces in the Z-direction of the mesh region and name these *cold wall* and *hot wall*, respectively.

Select File>>Export>>Mesh>>FLUENT Input File>>Export from the menu and save the mesh with the name *rayleigh-benard-3D.msh*. Select File>>Save Project from the menu and name the project "3D Rayleigh-Benard Convection". Select File>>Close Meshing to close the meshing window. Right click on Mesh in ANSYS Workbench and select Update.

Figure 5.6a) Named selections for the mesh

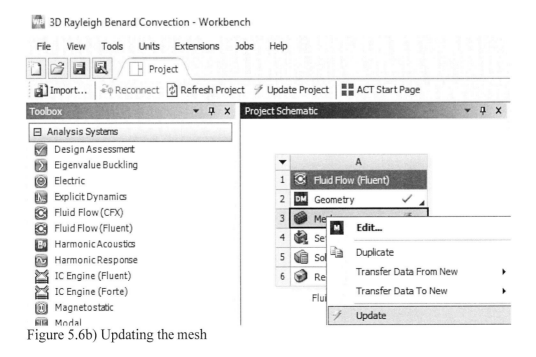

Figure 5.6b) Updating the mesh

F. Launching ANSYS Fluent

7. Double click on Setup under Project Schematic in ANSYS Workbench. Check the box for Double Precision. Select Parallel (Local Machine) as Processing Options and change the number of Processes to the number corresponding to the number of cores for your computer processor. Write down the location of the working directory that is listed under Show More Options. Click OK to launch Fluent.

Figure 5.7 ANSYS Fluent Launcher

8. Check the mesh by selecting the Check button under Mesh in General Setup. Check the scale of the mesh by selecting the Scale button. Make sure that the Domain Extent is correct and close the Scale Mesh window.

Figure 5.8a) Checking the mesh

```
Domain Extents:
   x-coordinate: min (m) = -5.000000e-02, max (m) = 5.000000e-02
   y-coordinate: min (m) = -5.000000e-02, max (m) = 5.000000e-02
   z-coordinate: min (m) = 0.000000e+00, max (m) = 4.800000e-03
Volume statistics:
   minimum volume (m3): 3.824880e-12
   maximum volume (m3): 2.648346e-10
      total volume (m3): 3.769812e-05
Face area statistics:
   minimum face area (m2): 7.968500e-09
   maximum face area (m2): 5.517387e-07
 Checking mesh...................................
Done.
```

Figure 5.8b) Console output generated by mesh check

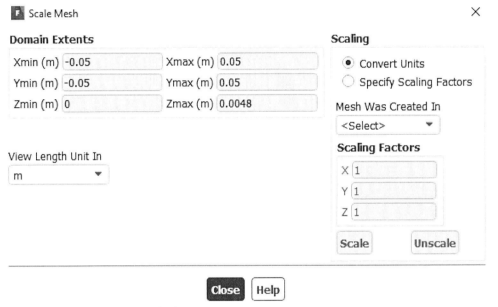

Figure 5.8c) Scale Mesh window

9. Check the Gravity box and enter -9.81 as the Gravitational Acceleration in the Z direction. Double click on Models under Setup in Outline View. Double click on the Energy model and check the box for the Energy equation. Click OK to exit the Energy Model window.

Figure 5.9a) Gravity settings   Figure 5.9b) Energy equation

10. Double click on Materials under Setup in the Outline View. Click on the Create/Edit button for Fluid on the Task Page to open the Create/Edit Materials window. Select Fluent Database…. Scroll down in the Fluent Fluid Materials window and select *water-liquid (h2o<l>)*. Click on the Copy button and Close the Fluent Database Materials window. Select *boussinesq* using the drop-down menu next to Density under Properties. Enter the value 997 (kg/m3) for the Density. Enter the value 4180 (j/kg-k) for Specific Heat, 0.607 (w/m-k) for Thermal Conductivity, and 0.000891 (kg/m-s) for Viscosity. Scroll down and enter the value 0.000247 (1/k) for the Thermal Expansion Coefficient. Click on the Change/Create button and Close the window.

Double click on Boundary Conditions under Setup in the Outline View. Click on Operating Conditions on the Task Page. Set the value for the Operating Temperature to 297.25 (k) and click on OK to close the Operating Conditions box.

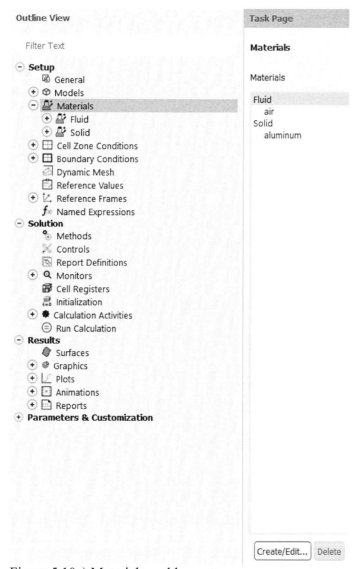

Figure 5.10a) Materials problem setup

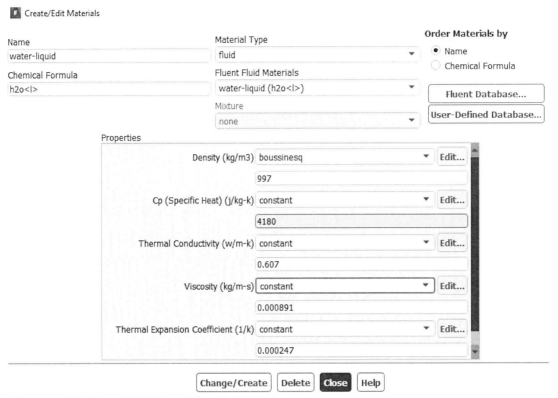

Figure 5.10b) Create/Edit Materials window

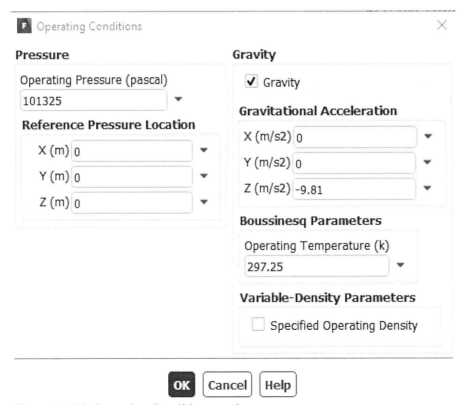

Figure 5.10c) Operating Conditions settings

11. Open Boundary Conditions under Setup in the Outline View. Double click *cold_wall* under Boundary Conditions. Select the Thermal tab and select Temperature for Thermal Conditions. Enter the value 296.5 as Temperature (k). Click OK to exit the window. Double click *hot_wall* under Boundary Conditions and set the Temperature (k) boundary condition to 298. Double click on *side_wall* under Boundary Conditions and set the Temperature (k) boundary condition to 296.5. Double click on Cell Zone Conditions under Setup in the Outline View. Double click on solid under Cell Zone Conditions. Select *water-liquid* from the Material Name drop-down menu in the Fluid window. Click OK to exit the window.

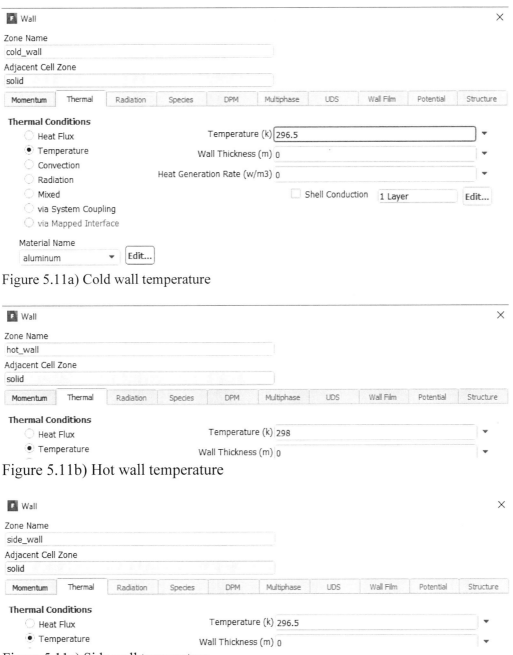

Figure 5.11a) Cold wall temperature

Figure 5.11b) Hot wall temperature

Figure 5.11c) Side wall temperature

Figure 5.11d) Fluid selection

12. Double click on Initialization under Solution in the Outline View. Select Standard Initialization under Initialization Methods. Enter 0.01 for Z Velocity (m/s), enter 297.25 as Temperature (k) and click on Initialize.

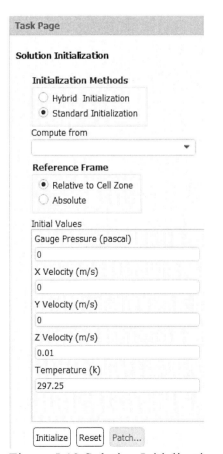

Figure 5.12 Solution Initialization settings

13. Double click on Monitors under Solution in the Outline View and double click on Residual under Monitors. Set the Absolute Criteria to 1e-6 for all equations and click OK to close the window. Double click on Methods under Solution in the Outline View and select PRESTO! from the Pressure drop down menu under Spatial Discretization. Select SIMPLE as Pressure-Velocity Coupling Scheme.

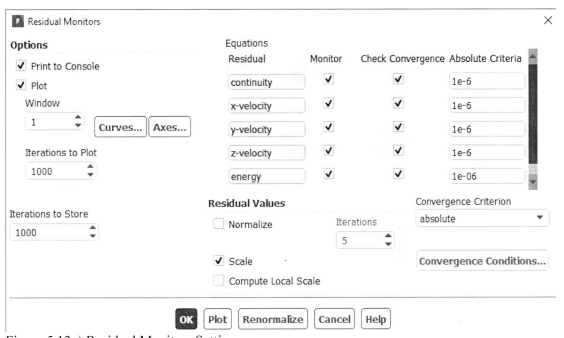

Figure 5.13a) Residual Monitors Settings

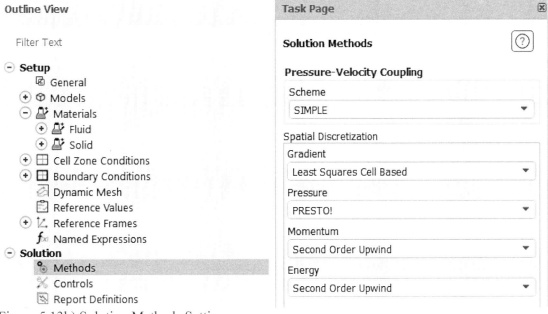

Figure 5.13b) Solution Methods Settings

14. Double click Run Calculation under Solution in the Outline View. Set the number of iterations to 3000. Click on the Calculate button. Click on the OK button in the Information window that appears when the calculations are complete.

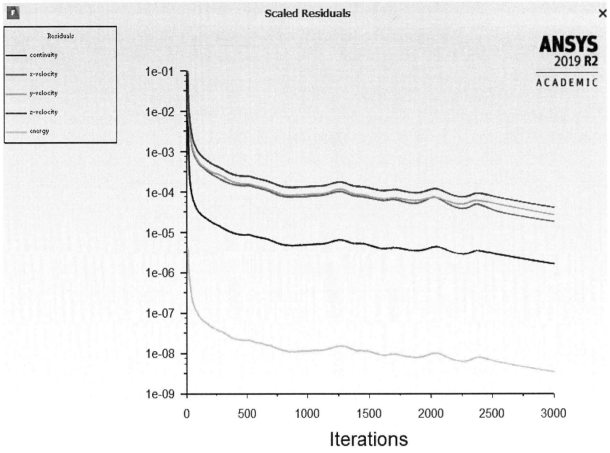

Figure 5.14 Scaled Residuals for Rayleigh-Bénard convection after 3000 iterations

G. Post-Processing

15. Double click on Graphics under Results in the Outline View. Double click on Contours in the Graphics section. Check the Filled box under Options and select Contours of Velocity and Z Velocity.

Select New Surface>>Plane from the drop-down menu in the Contours window. Check the box for Plane Tool under Options. Set (x0 (m), y0 (m), z0 (m)) to (0, -0.05, 0.0024), set (x1 (m), y1 (m), z1 (m)) to (0, 0.05, 0.0024) and (x2 (m), y2 (m), z2 (m)) to (0.05, 0, 0.0024). Enter the name *mid-plane-z=0.0024m* as the New Surface Name. Click on Create and Close the window.

Select the new plane under Surfaces in the Contours window and check the box for Contour Lines under Options. Click on the Save/Display button and Close the window. Select the x-y plane view. Repeat this step but select Contours of Temperature and Static Temperature. Click on Colormap Options. Select float as Type for Number Format and set Precision to 1. Click on Apply and Close the Colormap window. Click on the Save/Display button.

Figure 5.15a) Creation of a new x-y plane   Figure 5.15b) Contours settings

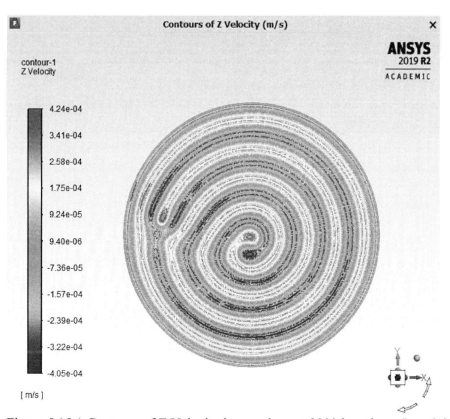

Figure 5.15c) Contours of Z Velocity in x-y plane at 3000 iterations, $Ra = 3{,}088$

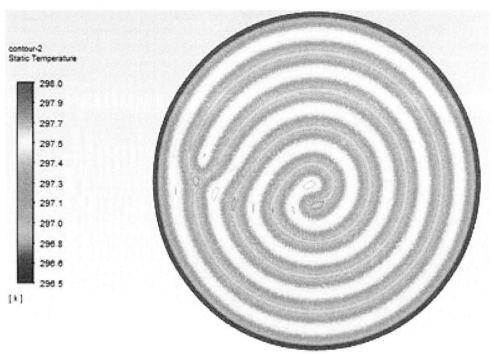

Figure 5.15d) Contours of Static Temperature in x-y plane at 3000 iterations, *Ra* = 3,088

16. Select New Surface>>Plane from the drop-down menu in the Contours window. Check the box for Plane Tool under Options. Set (x0 (m), y0 (m), z0 (m)) to (0, 0, 0), set (x1 (m), y1 (m), z1 (m)) to (0, 0, 0.0048) and (x2 (m), y2 (m), z2 (m)) to (0.05, 0, 0). Enter the name *x-z-plane-y=0* as the New Surface Name. Click on Create and Close the window.

    Select the new plane under Surfaces in the Contours window and check the box for Contour Lines under Options. Click on Colormap Options. Select float as Type for Number Format and set Precision to 1. Set Colormap Alignment to Top. Click on Apply and close the Colormap window. Click on the Save/Display button to display the Temperature field. Select the x-z plane view. Finally, display the Z Velocity field in the *x-z* plane, see Figure 5.16c). You will need to change Colormap Options. Select general as Type for Number Format and set Precision to 2.

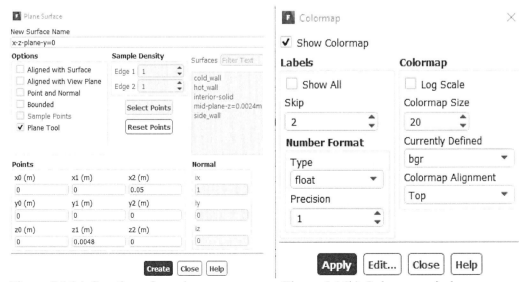

Figure 5.16a) Creation of *x-z* plane   Figure 5.16b) Colormap window

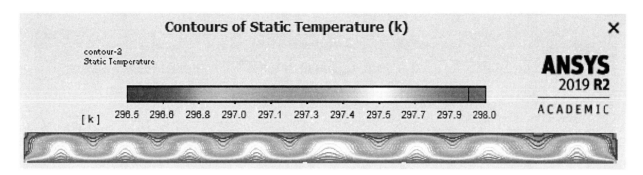

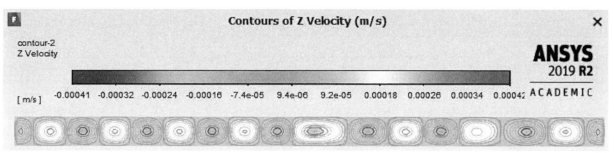

Figure 5.16c) Contours of static temp. and Z velocity in x-z plane at 3000 iterations, Ra = 3,088

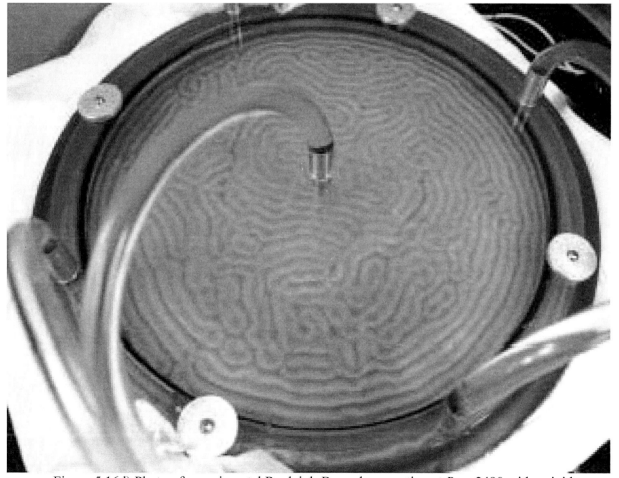

Figure 5.16d) Photo of experimental Rayleigh-Benard convection at Ra = 2490 with a rigid upper wall, Matsson[7].

H. Theory

Comparison with Neutral Stability Theory for Rayleigh-Bénard Convection

17. The instability of the flow between two parallel plates heated from below is governed by the Rayleigh number Ra.

$$Ra = \frac{g\beta\rho^2 C_p(T_1-T_2)L_c^3}{\mu k} \tag{5.1}$$

where g is acceleration due to gravity, β is the coefficient of volume expansion, ρ is density of the fluid, C_p is the specific heat, T_1 and T_2 are the temperatures of the hot and cold surfaces respectively, L_c is the distance between the surfaces (fluid layer thickness), k is thermal conductivity of the fluid, and μ is the dynamic viscosity of the fluid.

Below the critical $Ra_{crit} = 1715$ for a rigid upper surface, the flow is stable but convective currents will develop above this Rayleigh number. For the case of a free upper surface, the theory predicts a lower critical Rayleigh number at 1101. The non-dimensional wave number α of this instability is determined by

$$\alpha = \frac{2\pi L_c}{\lambda} \tag{5.2}$$

where λ is the wave length of the instability. The critical wave numbers are $\alpha_{crit} = 3.12, 2.68$ for rigid and free surface boundary conditions, respectively.

From the ANSYS Fluent simulations in this chapter, Figure 5.16c), the wave number can be determined to be

$$\alpha = \frac{2\pi \cdot 0.0048}{0.01224} = 2.46 \tag{5.3}$$

The Rayleigh number in the flow simulation is

$$Ra = \frac{9.81*0.000247*997^2*1.5*0.0048\text{^}3}{0.000891*0.607} = 3{,}088 \tag{5.4}$$

The neutral stability curve for Rayleigh-Benard convection can be given to the first approximation, see Figure 5.17.

$$Ra = \frac{(\pi^2+\alpha^2)^3}{\alpha^2\left\{1-16\alpha\pi^2\cosh^2(\frac{\alpha}{2})/[(\pi^2+\alpha^2)^2(\sinh\alpha+\alpha)]\right\}} \tag{5.5}$$

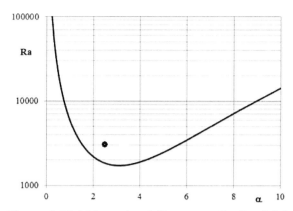

Figure 5.17a) Neutral stability curve for Rayleigh-Bénard convection. The filled circle represents result from ANSYS Fluent simulation.

I. References

1. Bénard, H. "Les tourbillons cellulaires dans une nappe liquide", *Rev. Gen. Sciences Pure Appl.* **11**, 1261-1271, 1309-1328, 1900
2. Rayleigh, L. "On convection currents in a horizontal layer of fluid when the higher temperature is on the underside.", Phil. Mag. **32**, 529-546, 1916.
3. Chandrasekhar, S. "Hydrodynamic and Hydromagnetic Stability", Dover, 1981.
4. Koschmieder, E.L. "Bénard cells and Taylor vortices", Cambridge University Press, 1993.
5. Koschmieder, E.L. and Pallas, S.G. "Heat transfer through a shallow, horizontal convecting fluid layer.", Int. J. Heat Mass Transfer **17**, 991-1002, 1974.
6. Hoard, C.Q., Robertson, C.R., and Acrivos, A. "Experiments on the cellular structure in Bénard convection", Int. J. Heat Mass Transfer **13**, 849-856, 1970.
7. Matsson J. "A Student Project on Rayleigh-Benard Convection", Annual ASEE Conference & Exposition, June 22-25, Pittsburg, Pa, 2008.

J. Exercises

5.1 Run ANSYS Fluent simulations with a rigid upper boundary condition for Rayleigh number $Ra = 2490$ and compare the results with Figure 5.16c) by plotting contours of Z velocity and contours of temperature. Determine the wave number α in the simulations and compare with the neutral stability curve as shown in Figure 5.17a).

5.2 Run ANSYS Fluent simulations with a free upper boundary condition for Rayleigh number $Ra = 2120$ and compare the results with Figure 5.17b) by plotting contours of Z velocity and contours of temperature.

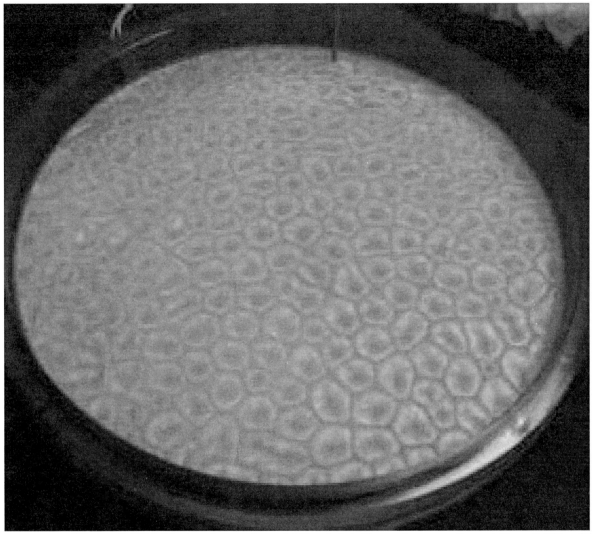

Figure 5.17b) Photo of experimental Rayleigh-Benard convection at $Ra = 2120$ with a free surface upper boundary condition (copied from Matsson[7]).

CHAPTER 6. CHANNEL FLOW

A. Objectives

- Using ANSYS Workbench to Model Geometry and Mesh
- Creating a User Defined Temperature Profile at Inlet
- Inserting Boundary Conditions
- Running Laminar Steady 2D Planar ANSYS Fluent Simulations
- Using Contour Plots for Visualizations of Pressure, Temperature and Velocity Fields
- Using XY Plots for Comparison of Inlet and Outlet Velocity and Temperature Profiles
- Comparing with Theoretical Solution Using Mathematica Code

B. Problem Description

We will study the development of the laminar flow of aqueous glycerin solution through a channel. The channel has a height of 90 mm and a length of 3,000 mm. The inlet temperature profile is linear where the bottom wall has a temperature of 0 °C and the upper wall is at 100 °C. The inlet velocity profile is laminar with a parabolic velocity profile in between the walls.

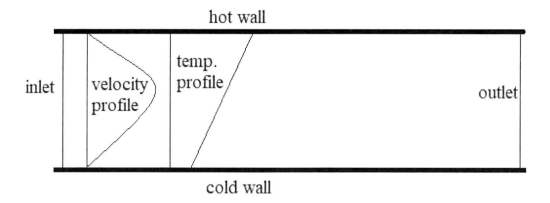

C. Launching ANSYS Workbench and Selecting Fluent

1. Start by launching the ANSYS Workbench. Double click on Fluid Flow (Fluent).

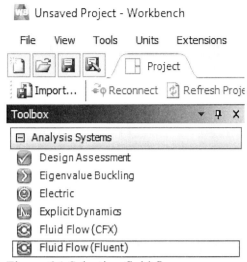

Figure 6.1 Selecting fluid flow

D. Launching ANSYS DesignModeler

2. Right click Geometry and select Properties. In Properties of Schematic A2: Geometry, select Analysis Type 2D under Advanced Geometry Options. Right-click on Geometry in the Project Schematic window and select New DesignModeler Geometry. Select meter as the desired length unit from the menu in DesignModeler.

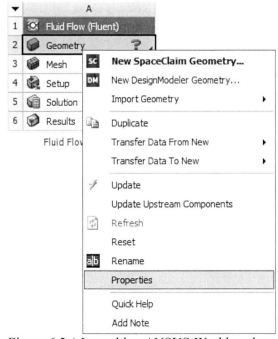

Figure 6.2a) Launching ANSYS Workbench

20	⊟ Advanced Geometry Options	
21	Analysis Type	3D ▾
22	Use Associativity	3D / 2D

Figure 6.2b) Advanced geometry options

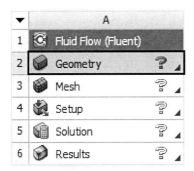

Fluid Flow (Fluent)

Figure 6.2c) Selecting the geometry

3. Select XY plane in the Tree Outline and select the Sketching tab. Select Look at Sketch 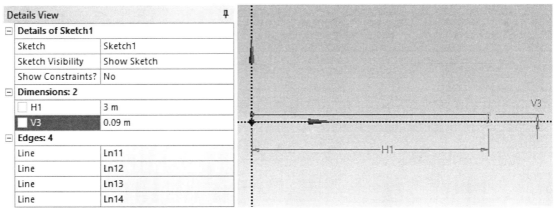.
    Draw a rectangle from the origin and set the horizontal length of the rectangle in Details View to
    3 m and the vertical height of the rectangle to 0.09 m, see Figure 6.3a). Click on the Modeling tab
    in the Tree Outline and highlight Sketch1 under XYPlane. Select Concept>>Surfaces from
    Sketches from the menu. Apply Sketch1 as the Base Object in Details View and click on
    Generate. Close DesignModeler.

Details View	📌
⊟ **Details of Sketch1**	
Sketch	Sketch1
Sketch Visibility	Show Sketch
Show Constraints?	No
⊟ **Dimensions: 2**	
☐ H1	3 m
☐ V3	0.09 m
⊟ **Edges: 4**	
Line	Ln11
Line	Ln12
Line	Ln13
Line	Ln14

Figure 6.3a) Surface from a sketch

Concept Tools Units View
- Lines From Points
- Lines From Sketches
- Lines From Edges
- 3D Curve
- Split Edges
- Surfaces From Edges
- **Surfaces From Sketches**

Figure 6.3b) Surface from a sketch

Details View	
⊟ **Details of SurfaceSk1**	
Surface From Sketches	SurfaceSk1
Base Objects	1 Sketch
Operation	Add Material
Orient With Plane Normal?	Yes
Thickness (>=0)	0 m

Figure 6.3c) Details view

E. Launching ANSYS Meshing

4. Next, we will be creating the mesh for the flow field. Double click on Mesh under Project Schematic in ANSYS Workbench. Right click on Mesh under Outline in the Meshing window and select Generate Mesh. Select Unit Systems>>Metric (mm, kg, N …) from the bottom of the graphics window.

Figure 6.4a) Coarse mesh

Select Mesh>>Controls>>Face Meshing from the menu. Select the mesh region in the graphics window and apply it as Geometry under Scope in Details of "Face Meshing".

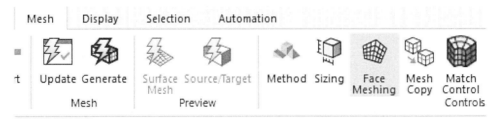

Figure 6.4b) Face meshing

Select Mesh>>Controls>>Sizing from the menu. Select Edge , control select the four edges of the rectangle and apply them as the Geometry under Scope in Details of "Edge Sizing". Set the element size to 5 mm and the Behavior to Hard. Click on Generate Mesh and select Mesh in the Outline.

Figure 6.4c) Refined mesh

Select the left vertical edge of the mesh region, right click and select Create Named Selection. Name this edge "inlet". Select the right vertical edge, right click and select Create Named Selection. Name this edge "outlet". Select the horizontal lower edge, right click and select Create Named Selection. Name this edge "cold wall". Finally, select the horizontal upper edge, right click and select Create Named Selection. Name this edge "hot wall".

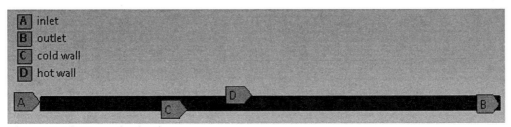

Figure 6.4d) Named selections

Select File>>Save Project from the menu and name the project "Channel Flow". Select File>>Export…>>Mesh>>FLUENT Input File>>Export from the menu in the Meshing window and name the mesh "channel-flow-mesh.msh". Close the meshing window. Right click on Mesh under the Project Schematic in ANSYS Workbench and select Update.

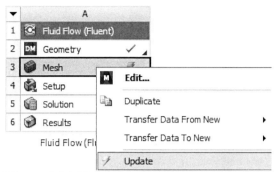

Figure 6.4e) Updating the mesh

F. Creating a UDF

5. We are now going to create a Used Defined Function for the inlet temperature profile. Start Notepad located in the Windows Accessories folder and include the following text as listed below. Save the file as a text document with the name "udf-inlet-temp-velocity-profiles.txt".

```
#include "udf.h"
DEFINE_PROFILE(inlet_t_temperature, thread, position)
{
real x[ND_ND]; /* this will hold the position vector */
real y;
face_t f;
begin_f_loop(f, thread)
{
F_CENTROID(x,f,thread);
y = x[1];
F_PROFILE(f, thread, position) =273.15+(100*y/0.09);
}
end_f_loop(f, thread)
}
DEFINE_PROFILE(inlet_u_velocity, thread, position)
{
real x[ND_ND]; /* this will hold the position vector */
real y;
face_t f;
begin_f_loop(f, thread)
{
F_CENTROID(x,f,thread);
y = x[1];
F_PROFILE(f, thread, position) =-6*0.03*(y*y-y*0.09)/(0.09*0.09*0.09);
}
end_f_loop(f, thread)
}
```

Figure 6.5 Code for UDF

G. Launching ANSYS Fluent

6. Double click Setup under Project Schematic in ANSYS Workbench. Check the Options box for Double Precision. Select Parallel Processing Options. Set the number of Processes to the number of cores for your computer processor.

   Click on the plus sign next to Show More Options, notice the location of the Working Directory and copy the file "udf-inlet-temp-velocity-profiles.txt" to this location. Click on OK to close the window.

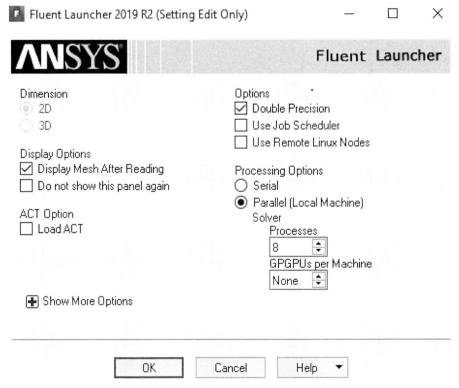

Figure 6.6a) Fluent launcher window

Select the Pressure-Based Solver under General on the Task Page and click on Units… under General, see Figure 6.6b). Scroll down the Quantities and select temperature. Set the Units to c for temperature and do the same for temperature-difference. Close the Set Units window.

Open Models under Setup in the Outline View. Double click Energy-Off under Models and check the box for Energy Equation. Click OK to close the Energy window.

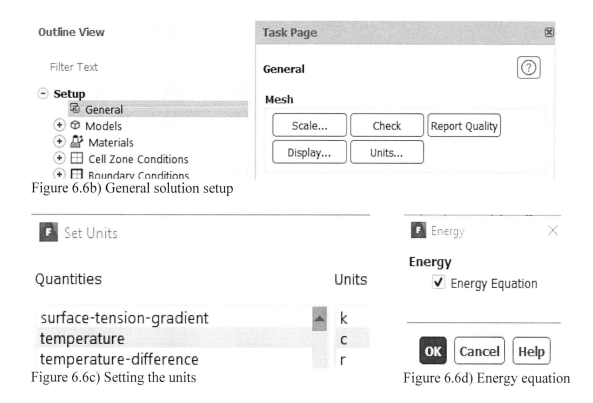

Figure 6.6b) General solution setup

Figure 6.6c) Setting the units   Figure 6.6d) Energy equation

7. Double click Materials under Setup in the Outline View. Click on Create/Edit… for Fluid on the Task Page and select Fluent Database in the new window. Scroll down in the Fluent Fluid Materials and select glycerin (c3h8o3). Click on Copy and Close the window.

Figure 6.7a) Selection of glycerin as fluid

Select piecewise-linear for Density (kg/m3) under Properties in the Create/Edit Materials window. Increase the number of points to 11 in the Piecewise-Linear Profile window. Set the Temperature (c) for Point 1 to 0 and Value (kg/m3) to 1268.4. Set the values for the remaining points as shown in Table 6.1. Click on the OK button to close the window.

Select piecewise-linear for Viscosity (kg/m-s) under Properties. Increase the number of points to 11. Set the Temperature (c) for Point 1 to 0 and Value (kg/m-s) to 7.2162. Set the values for the remaining points as shown in Table 6.1. Click on the OK button to close the piecewise-linear profile window. Click on Change/Create and Close the Create/Edit Materials window.

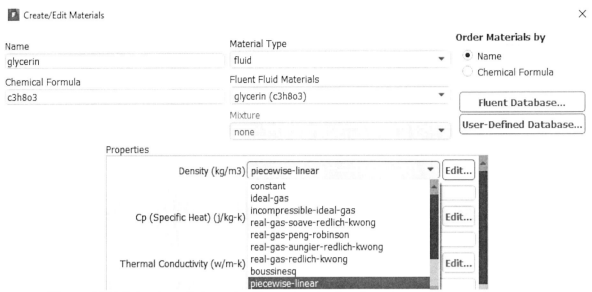

Figure 6.7b) Selection of piecewise-linear density for glycerin

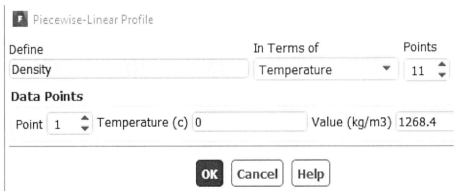

Figure 6.7c) Temperature and density for data points

Point	Temperature (c)	Density (kg/m3)	Viscosity (kg/m-s)
1	0	1268.4	7.2162
2	10	1262.2	2.3857
3	20	1256	0.92181
4	30	1249.8	0.40505
5	40	1243.7	0.19801
6	50	1237.6	0.10591
7	60	1231.5	0.06113
8	70	1225.5	0.03767
9	80	1219.5	0.024552
10	90	1213.5	0.016809
11	100	1207.6	0.012009

Table 6.1 Properties of glycerin (98 percent weight) at different temperatures

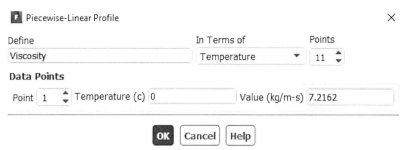

Figure 6.7d) Temperature and viscosity for data points

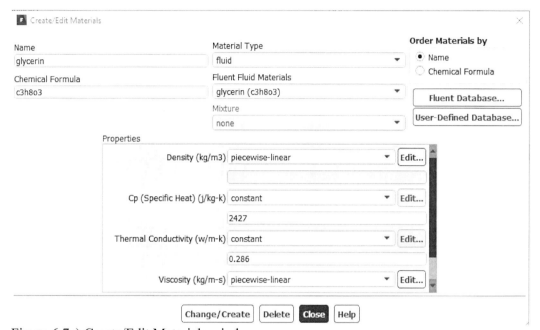

Figure 6.7e) Create/Edit Materials window

8. Open Cell Zone Conditions under Setup in the Outline View. Double click *surface_body*. Select glycerin as the Material Name and click on OK to close the window.

Figure 6.8a) Selection of glycerin as fluid

Select User-Defined>>Functions>>Interpreted… from the menu. Browse for the source file and Select Files of type: All Files (*). Find the file named "*udf-inlet-temp-velocity-profiles.txt*" in the working directory and click OK. Click on Interpret and Close the Interpreted UDFs window.

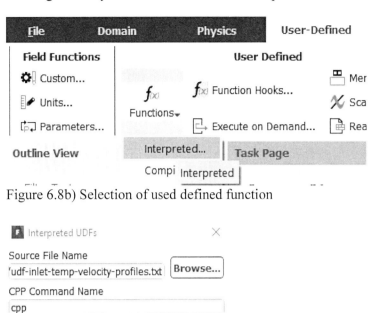

Figure 6.8b) Selection of used defined function

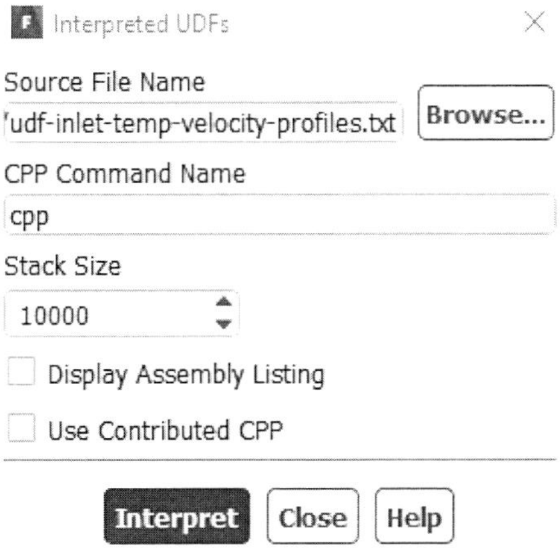

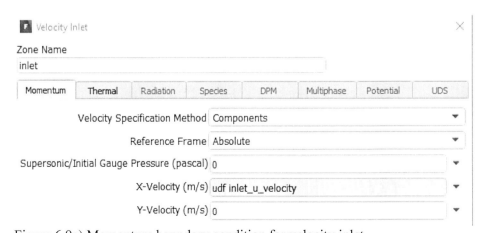

Figure 6.8c) Interpreted UDFs

9. Open Boundary Conditions under Setup in the Outline View. Double click on *inlet* under Boundary Conditions. Set the Velocity Specification Method to Components. Select *udf inlet_u_velocity* as X-Velocity (m/s). Click on the Thermal tab and select *udf inlet_t_temperature* from the Temperature drop down menu. Click OK to close the Velocity Inlet window.

Figure 6.9a) Momentum boundary condition for velocity inlet

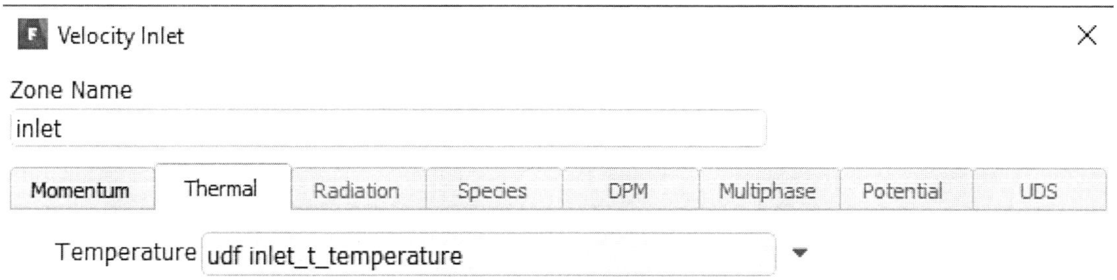

Figure 6.9b) Selection of *udf* for velocity inlet as thermal boundary condition

Double click on *cold_wall* under Boundary Conditions in the Outline View. Select the Thermal tab in the Wall window and select Temperature as Thermal Condition. Set the Temperature (c) to 0. Click OK to close the Wall window. Repeat this step for the *hot_wall* and set the temperature to 100 (c).

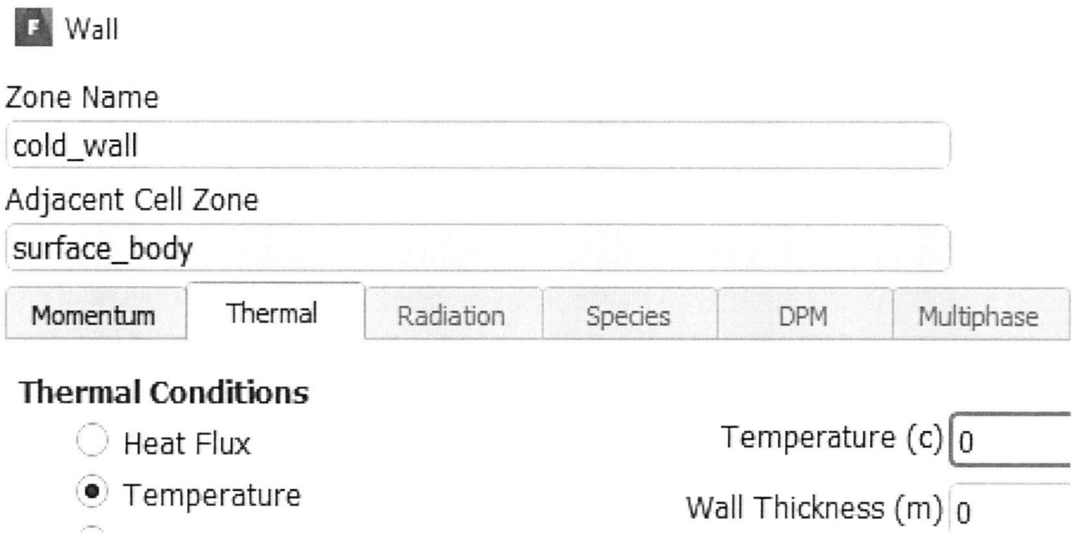

Figure 6.9c) Cold wall thermal boundary condition

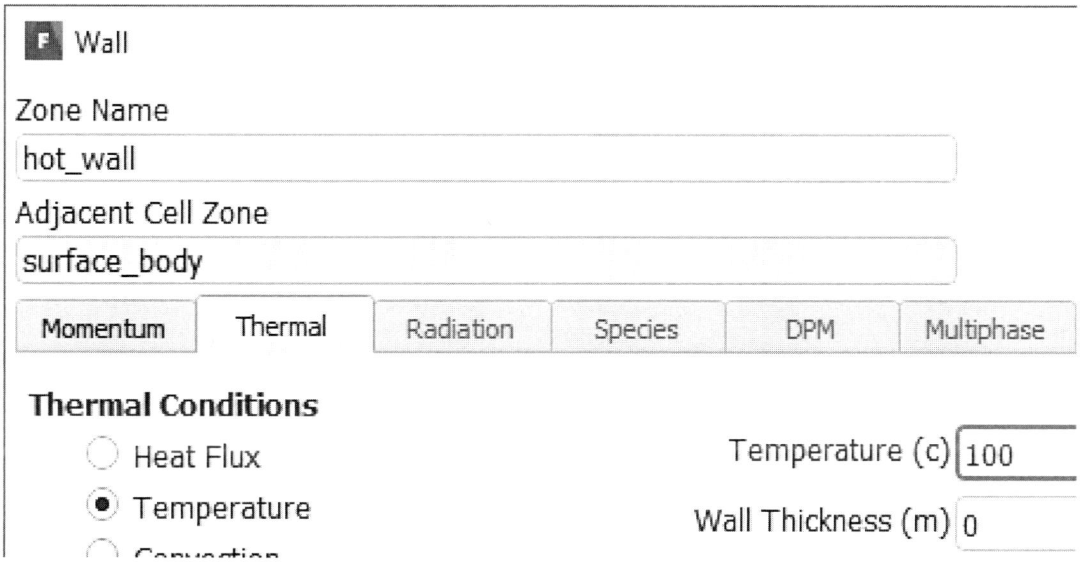

Figure 6.9d) Hot wall thermal boundary condition

10. Open Monitors under Solution in the Outline View and double click on Residual under Monitors. Set Absolute Criteria to 1e-06 for all four Residuals. Click OK to close the Residual Monitors window.

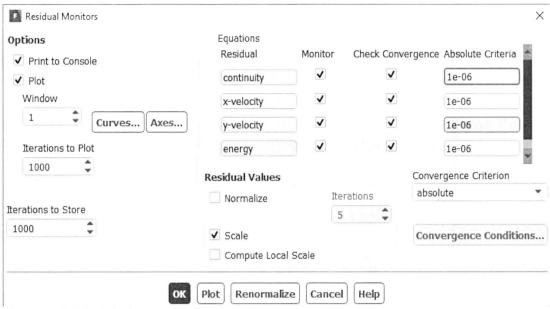

Figure 6.10a) Residual monitors window

Double click on Reference Values under Setup in the Outline View. Select *Compute from inlet* and select *surface_body* as Reference Zone. Double click on Initialization under Solution in the Outline View. Select Standard Initialization on the Task Page as Initialization Method and *Compute from inlet*. Click on *Initialize*. Double click on Run Calculation under Solution in the Outline View. Enter 10000 as *Number of Iterations*. Click on *Calculate*. Click OK when calculation is complete.

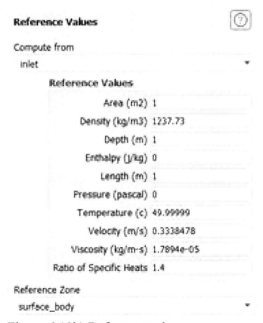

Figure 6.10b) Reference values

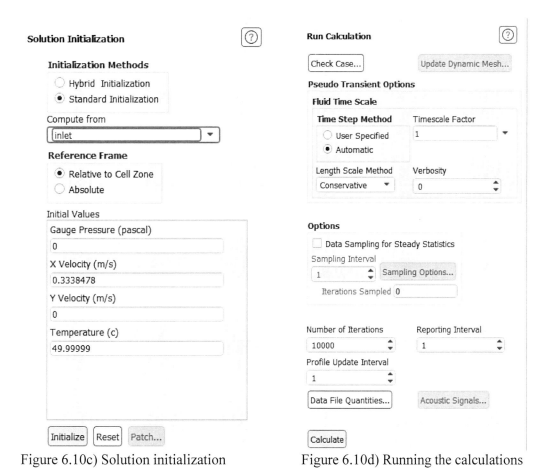

Figure 6.10c) Solution initialization   Figure 6.10d) Running the calculations

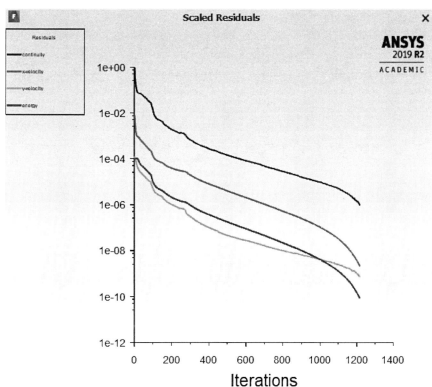

Figure 6.10e) Residuals window

H. Post-Processing

11. Open Graphics under Results in the Outline View. Double click on Contours under Graphics. Select all Surfaces and click on Colormap Options. Select float as Type and 0 for Precision. Select Top as Colormap Alignment, click on Apply and Close the Colormap window. Click on Save/Display. Display another plot of temperature contours by selecting Contours of Temperature and Static Temperature and click on Save/Display. Finally, select Contours of Velocity and X Velocity and set the Precision to 2 in the Colormap window. Click on Save/Display.

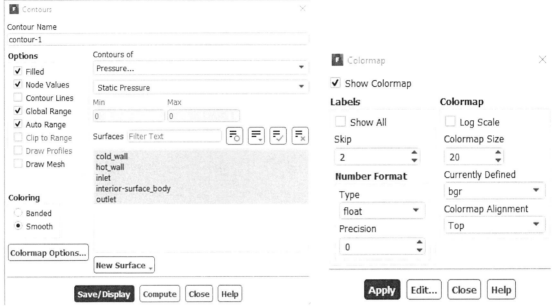

Figure 6.11a) Contours window   Figure 6.11b) Colormap window

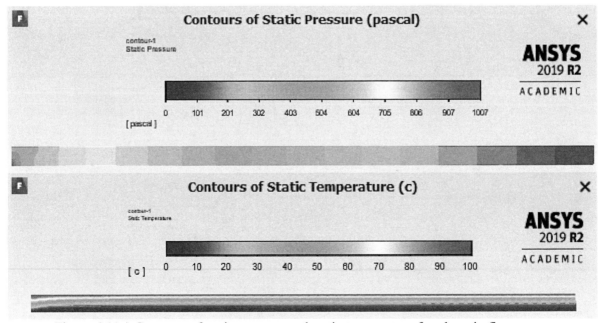

Figure 6.11c) Contours of static pressure and static temperature for glycerin flow

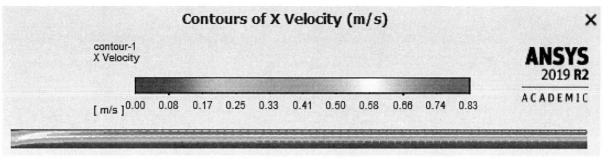

Figure 6.11d) Contours of X velocity for glycerin flow

12. Double click on XY Plot under Results and Plots in the Outline View. Uncheck Position on X Axis under Options. Select Mesh and Y-Coordinate as Y Axis Function. Select Velocity and X Velocity as X Axis Function. Click on Load File and load the file with the name *theory channel flow.dat* from the working directory. This file can be downloaded from *sdcpublications.com*. Select inlet and outlet as the Surfaces and click on Curves. Select the first Pattern for Curve # 0 and no Symbol. Click on Apply. Select the next available Pattern for Curve # 1 and no Symbol. Click on Apply. Select the next available Pattern for Curve # 2 and no Symbol. Click on Apply and Close the window.

    Click on Axes… and uncheck the box for Auto Range under Options for the X Axis. Set Minimum to 0 and Maximum to 1 under Range. Set Precision to 1 under Number Format. Click on Apply. Check the Y Axis and set the Precision to 2 under Number Format. Click on Apply. Close the window and click on Save/Plot.

    Select Temperature and Static Temperature as X Axis Function. Select inlet and outlet as the Surfaces and unselect Theory under File Data. Click on Axes…, select X Axis and check the box for Auto Range under Options. Set Precision to 0 under Number Format, click on Apply and close the window. Click on Save/Plot.

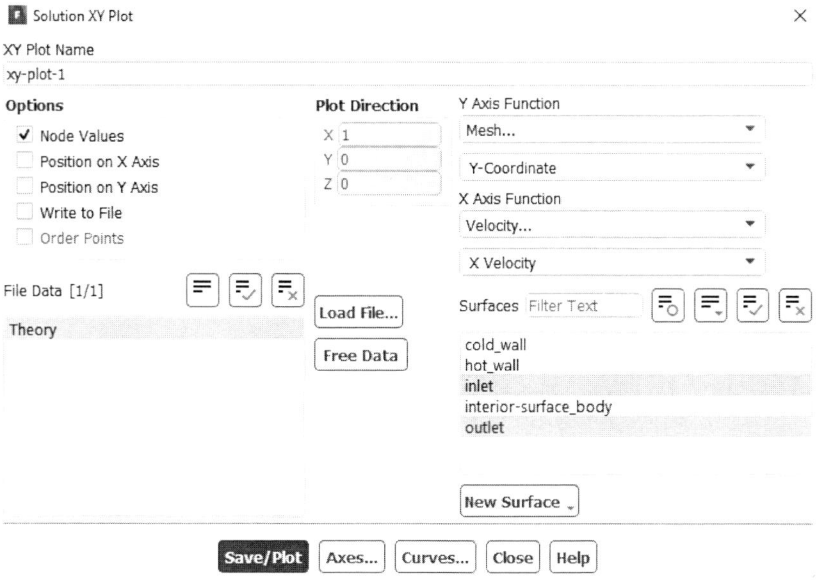

Figure 6.12a) Solution XY Plot window

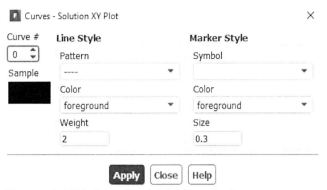

Figure 6.12b) Solution XY Plot window

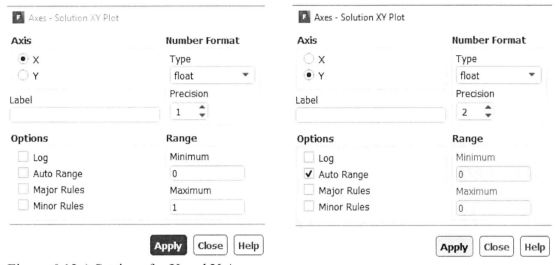

Figure 6.12c) Settings for X and Y Axes

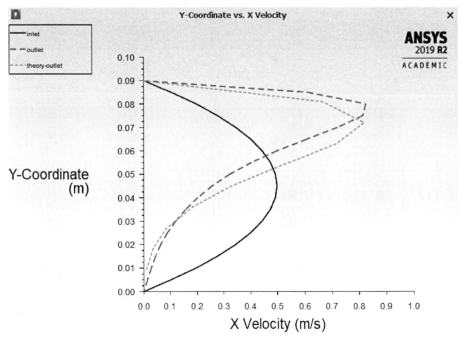

Figure 6.12d) X Velocity profiles for glycerin flow at the inlet and outlet

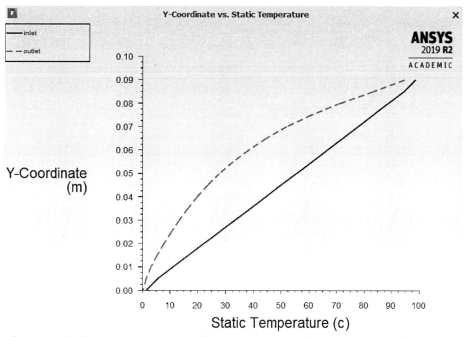

Figure 6.12e) Temperature profiles for glycerin flow at inlet and outlet

I. Theory

13. The equation of motion for the fluid for fully developed flow is given by the following equation

$$\mu \frac{d^2u}{dy^2} = \frac{dp}{dx} \qquad (6.1)$$

where u (m/s) is streamwise velocity, x (m) is streamwise coordinate, y (m) is the wall-normal coordinate, μ (kg/ms) is dynamic viscosity, and p (Pa) is the pressure. The boundary conditions are $u(0) = u\ (h) = 0$ where h is the height of the channel.

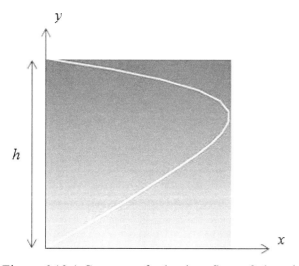

Figure 6.13a) Geometry for laminar flow of glycerin

Element i	Density (kg/m3)	Viscosity μ_i (kg/ms)	Pressure gradient $\left(\frac{dp}{dx}\right)_i$ (Pa/m)
1	1265.3	4.80095	-78.9249
2	1259.1	1.653755	-78.9249
3	1252.9	0.66343	-78.9249
4	1246.75	0.30153	-78.9249
5	1240.65	0.15196	-78.9249
6	1234.55	0.08352	-78.9249
7	1228.5	0.0494	-78.9249
8	1222.5	0.031111	-78.9249
9	1216.5	0.020681	-78.9249
10	1210.55	0.014409	-78.9249

Table 6.2 Average properties of glycerin (98 percent weight) and pressure gradient for each element

We can now compute the resistance or stiffness matrix for each element, see Moaveni[1]

$$K_i = \frac{10\mu_i}{h}\begin{pmatrix} 1 & -1 \\ -1 & 1 \end{pmatrix} \tag{6.2}$$

, and the forcing vector will be the following for each element

$$F_i = -\frac{h}{20}\left(\frac{dp}{dx}\right)_i \begin{pmatrix} 1 \\ 1 \end{pmatrix} \tag{6.3}$$

Next, we assemble the stiffness matrices into the following matrix

$$K = \frac{10}{h}\begin{pmatrix} \mu_1 & -\mu_1 & 0 & 0 & 0 & 0 & 0 & 0 & 0 & 0 & 0 \\ -\mu_1 & \mu_1+\mu_2 & -\mu_2 & 0 & 0 & 0 & 0 & 0 & 0 & 0 & 0 \\ 0 & -\mu_2 & \mu_2+\mu_3 & -\mu_3 & 0 & 0 & 0 & 0 & 0 & 0 & 0 \\ 0 & 0 & -\mu_3 & \mu_3+\mu_4 & -\mu_4 & 0 & 0 & 0 & 0 & 0 & 0 \\ 0 & 0 & 0 & -\mu_4 & \mu_4+\mu_5 & -\mu_5 & 0 & 0 & 0 & 0 & 0 \\ 0 & 0 & 0 & 0 & -\mu_5 & \mu_5+\mu_6 & -\mu_6 & 0 & 0 & 0 & 0 \\ 0 & 0 & 0 & 0 & 0 & -\mu_6 & \mu_6+\mu_7 & -\mu_7 & 0 & 0 & 0 \\ 0 & 0 & 0 & 0 & 0 & 0 & -\mu_7 & \mu_7+\mu_8 & -\mu_8 & 0 & 0 \\ 0 & 0 & 0 & 0 & 0 & 0 & 0 & -\mu_8 & \mu_8+\mu_9 & -\mu_9 & 0 \\ 0 & 0 & 0 & 0 & 0 & 0 & 0 & 0 & -\mu_9 & \mu_9+\mu_{10} & -\mu_{10} \\ 0 & 0 & 0 & 0 & 0 & 0 & 0 & 0 & 0 & -\mu_{10} & -\mu_{10} \end{pmatrix} \tag{6.4}$$

, and we assemble the forcing vector into the following

$$\boldsymbol{F} = 6h \begin{pmatrix} 1 \\ 2 \\ 2 \\ 2 \\ 2 \\ 2 \\ 2 \\ 2 \\ 2 \\ 2 \\ 1 \end{pmatrix} \tag{6.5}$$

After inclusion of boundary conditions, we get the following

$$\begin{pmatrix} 1 & 0 & 0 & 0 & 0 & 0 & 0 & 0 & 0 & 0 & 0 \\ -\mu_1 & \mu_1+\mu_2 & -\mu_2 & 0 & 0 & 0 & 0 & 0 & 0 & 0 & 0 \\ 0 & -\mu_2 & \mu_2+\mu_3 & -\mu_3 & 0 & 0 & 0 & 0 & 0 & 0 & 0 \\ 0 & 0 & -\mu_3 & \mu_3+\mu_4 & -\mu_4 & 0 & 0 & 0 & 0 & 0 & 0 \\ 0 & 0 & 0 & -\mu_4 & \mu_4+\mu_5 & -\mu_5 & 0 & 0 & 0 & 0 & 0 \\ 0 & 0 & 0 & 0 & -\mu_5 & \mu_5+\mu_6 & -\mu_6 & 0 & 0 & 0 & 0 \\ 0 & 0 & 0 & 0 & 0 & -\mu_6 & \mu_6+\mu_7 & -\mu_7 & 0 & 0 & 0 \\ 0 & 0 & 0 & 0 & 0 & 0 & -\mu_7 & \mu_7+\mu_8 & -\mu_8 & 0 & 0 \\ 0 & 0 & 0 & 0 & 0 & 0 & 0 & -\mu_8 & \mu_8+\mu_9 & -\mu_9 & 0 \\ 0 & 0 & 0 & 0 & 0 & 0 & 0 & 0 & -\mu_9 & \mu_9+\mu_{10} & -\mu_{10} \\ 0 & 0 & 0 & 0 & 0 & 0 & 0 & 0 & 0 & 0 & 1 \end{pmatrix} \begin{pmatrix} u_1 \\ u_2 \\ u_3 \\ u_4 \\ u_5 \\ u_6 \\ u_7 \\ u_8 \\ u_9 \\ u_{10} \\ u_{11} \end{pmatrix} = \frac{6h^2}{10} \begin{pmatrix} 0 \\ 2 \\ 2 \\ 2 \\ 2 \\ 2 \\ 2 \\ 2 \\ 2 \\ 2 \\ 0 \end{pmatrix} \tag{6.6}$$

with the following solution

$$\boldsymbol{u} = \begin{pmatrix} 0 \\ 0.0051 \\ 0.0178 \\ 0.0447 \\ 0.0930 \\ 0.1677 \\ 0.2647 \\ 0.3631 \\ 0.4153 \\ 0.3371 \\ 0 \end{pmatrix} \tag{6.7}$$

```
h = 0.09; n = 10; w = 1; dpdx = -78.9249; a = -dpdx * h / n;
μ = {4.80095, 1.653755, 0.66343, 0.30153, 0.15196, 0.08352, 0.0494, 0.031111, 0.020681, 0.014409};
ρ = {1265.3, 1259.1, 1252.9, 1246.75, 1240.65, 1234.55, 1228.5, 1222.5, 1216.5, 1210.55};

{a1, b1, c1} = {Array[-μ[[#]] &, n - 1], Array[μ[[# - 2]] + μ[[# - 1]] &, n, {2, 11}], Array[-μ[[# - 1]] &, n, {2, 11}]};
K = (n / h) * SparseArray[{Band[{1, 2}] → c1, Band[{1, 1}] → b1, Band[{2, 1}] → a1}, 11];
K[[1, 1]] = h / n;
K[[1, 2]] = 0;
K[[n + 1, n + 1]] = h / n;
MatrixForm[Normal[K]];

s = LinearSolve[K, {0, a, a, a, a, a, a, a, a, a, 0}];

ṁ = Σ_{i-1}^{n} ρ[[i]] * w * (h / n) * (s[[i]] + s[[i + 1]]) / 2;

ListLinePlot[Array[{s[[#]], (# - 1) * h / n} &, n + 1, {1, n + 1}], AxesLabel → {"u (m/s)", "y (m)"}, PlotLabels → {"Theory"}]

mylist = Array[{s[[#]], (# - 1) * h / n} &, n + 1, {1, n + 1}];
TableOfValues1 = Prepend[mylist, {"((xy/key/label \"theory-outlet\")"}];
TableOfValues1 = Prepend[TableOfValues1, {""}];
TableOfValues1 = Prepend[TableOfValues1, {"(labels \"X Velocity\" \"Y-Coordinate\")"}];
TableOfValues1 = Prepend[TableOfValues1, {"(title \"Theory\")"}];
TableOfValues1 = Append[TableOfValues1, {")"}];
Grid[TableOfValues1]
Export["theory.dat", TableOfValues1]
```

Figure 6.13b) Mathematica code for theoretical solution

J. References

1. S. Moaveni, Finite Element Analysis: Theory and Applications with ANSYS, 3rd Ed., Prentice Hall, 2007.

K. Exercises

6.1 Replace the fluid with engine oil from the Fluent Database and enter the piecewise-linear values for the four points as listed in the table below. Increase the Gage Total Pressure at the inlet to 500 Pa. Include residuals window, contour plots of Static Pressure, Static Temperature, X Velocity, and the X Velocity profile.

Point	Temperature (c)	Density (kg/m3)	Viscosity (kg/m-s)
1	20	881.5	0.23939
2	30	875.4	0.12842
3	40	869.3	0.07455
4	50	863	0.04643

Table 6.3 Properties for engine oil (SAE 30)

6.2 Change the size of the computational domain to 6 m in length and 0.2 m in height and change the mesh size to 0.015 m in horizontal direction and 0.01 m in the vertical direction. Modify the temperature of the cold lower wall to 0 (c) and 100 (c) for the upper hot wall. Rewrite and reinterpret the *udf* file for the new temperatures of the cold and hot wall and modify the *udf* file for the change in height of the computational domain. Replace the fluid with engine oil from the Fluent Database and enter the piecewise-linear values for the 11 points as listed in the table below. Increase the Gage Total Pressure at the inlet to 1000 pascal. Include *udf* code, zoomed in mesh that shows details, residuals window, contour plots of Static Pressure, Static Temperature, X Velocity, and the X Velocity profile.

Point	Temperature (c)	Density (kg/m3)	Viscosity (kg/m-s)
1	0	867.4	0.75352
2	10	860.9	0.37865
3	20	854.5	0.20689
4	30	848.3	0.12190
5	40	842.1	0.076551
6	50	835.8	0.050861
7	60	829.5	0.035409
8	70	823.2	0.025631
9	80	817	0.019181
10	90	810.6	0.014742
11	100	804.5	0.011619

Table 6.4 Properties for engine oil (SAE 5W-40)

Notes:

CHAPTER 7. ROTATING FLOW IN A CAVITY

A. Objectives

- Using ANSYS Fluent to Study Rotating Flow in a Cavity
- Inserting Boundary Conditions and Rotation
- Running Laminar 2D Axi-Symmetric ANSYS Fluent Simulations with Swirl
- Using XY Plots for Profiles of Velocity Components
- Comparing with Results Using Mathematica Code
- Using Contour Plots for Visualizations of Streamlines and Velocity Components
- Using Pathlines to Visualize the Flow Patterns and Compare with Experiments

B. Problem Description

We will study the rotating flow in a cavity and we will analyze the problem using ANSYS Fluent. The rotating cavity filled with water has a cylindrical geometry with a diameter of 95 mm and a height with the same dimension. The top lid is rotating with a rotational speed of 0.445 rad/s while the remaining walls of the cavity are stationary.

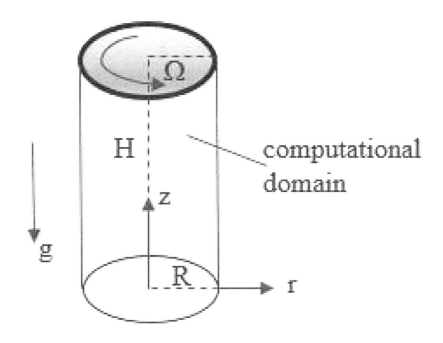

C. Launching ANSYS Workbench and Selecting Fluent

1. Start by launching ANSYS Workbench. Double click on Fluid Flow (Fluent) under Analysis Systems in Toolbox. Right click on Geometry in the Project Schematic and select Properties. Select 2D Analysis Type in Advanced Geometry Options under Properties of Schematic A2: Geometry.

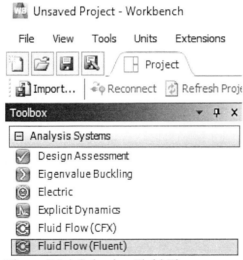

Figure 7.1a) Selecting Fluid Flow

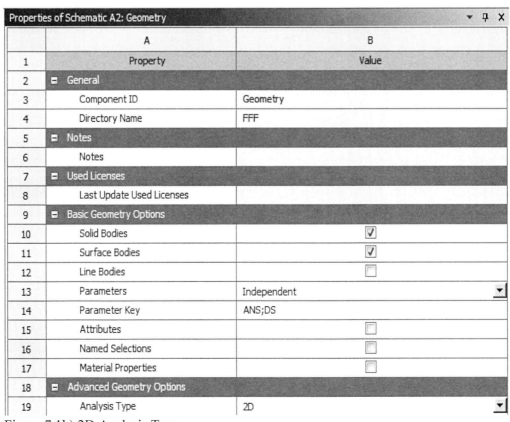

Figure 7.1b) 2D Analysis Type

D. Launching ANSYS DesignModeler

2. Right click on Geometry under Project Schematic in ANSYS Workbench and select New DesignModeler Geometry. Select **Units Millimeter** from the menu in DesignModeler.

   Select the XYPlane in Tree Outline. Look At Face/Plane/Sketch . Select the Sketching tab and Rectangle under the Draw tab. Draw a rectangle from the origin in the first quadrant. Select the Dimensions tab. Click on the left vertical edge of the rectangle and the lower horizontal edge. Enter 47.5 mm as the vertical dimension and 95 mm as the horizontal dimension. Select Concept>>Surfaces from Sketches from the menu. Select Sketch 1 under XY Plane in the Tree Outline. Apply the Sketch as Base Object in the Details View. Click on Generate and close DesignModeler.

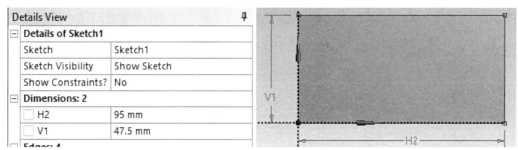

Figure 7.2 Surface sketch of the rectangle

E. Launching ANSYS Meshing

3. Double click on Mesh under Project Schematic in ANSYS Workbench. In the Meshing window, right-click on Mesh under Project and select Update. Select Mesh>>Controls>>Face Meshing from the menu. Select the rectangle in the graphics window and Apply it as Geometry in Details of Face Meshing.

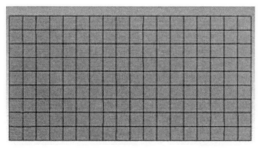

Figure 7.3a) Coarse mesh   Figure 7.3b) Face meshing

Select Mesh>>Controls>>Sizing from the menu. Select the Edge tool ⌗ , control click on the two vertical edges of the rectangle and Apply them as Geometry in Details of Sizing. Select Number of Divisions as Type and enter 20. Select Hard as Behavior. Select the third Bias type from the drop-down menu and enter 5.0 as Bias Factor. Repeat this step but select the two horizontal edges and 40 as the Number of Divisions. Use the same Bias type and a Bias Factor of 5.0. Right-click on Mesh and select Update.

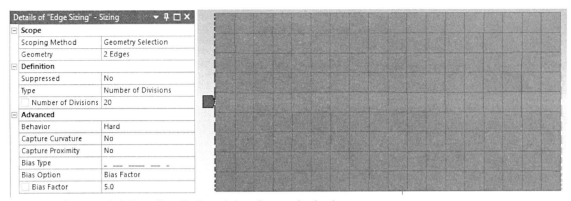

Figure 7.3c) Details of edge sizing for vertical edges

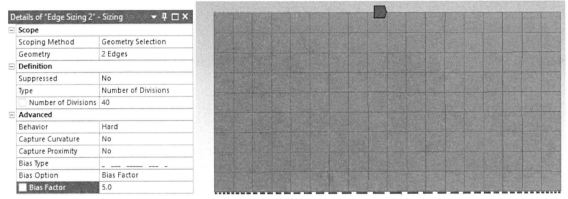

Figure 7.3d) Details of edge sizing for horizontal edges

4. Control-select the upper horizontal edge and left vertical edge, right-click and select Create Named Selection. Enter the name *wall* and click OK to close the window. Select the right vertical edge, right click and select Create Named Selection. Enter the name *lid*. Finally, name the lower horizontal edge as *symmetry*. Select File>>Save Project from the menu and enter the name "Rotating Lid Flow in Cylinder". Select File>>Export...>>Mesh>>FLUENT Input File>>Export from the menu in ANSYS Mechanical and save the mesh with the name "rotating-lid-cylinder-flow-mesh.msh". Close the Meshing window. Right-click on Mesh in the Project Schematic of ANSYS Workbench and select Update.

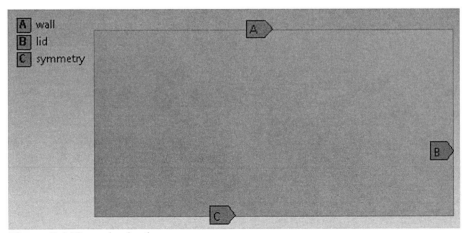

Figure 7.4 Named selections

F. Launching ANSYS Fluent

5. Double-click on Setup under Project Schematic in ANSYS Workbench. Select Double Precision and select Parallel Processing Options. Set the number of Processes equal to the number of processor cores on your computer. Click on the OK button in the Fluent Launcher window.

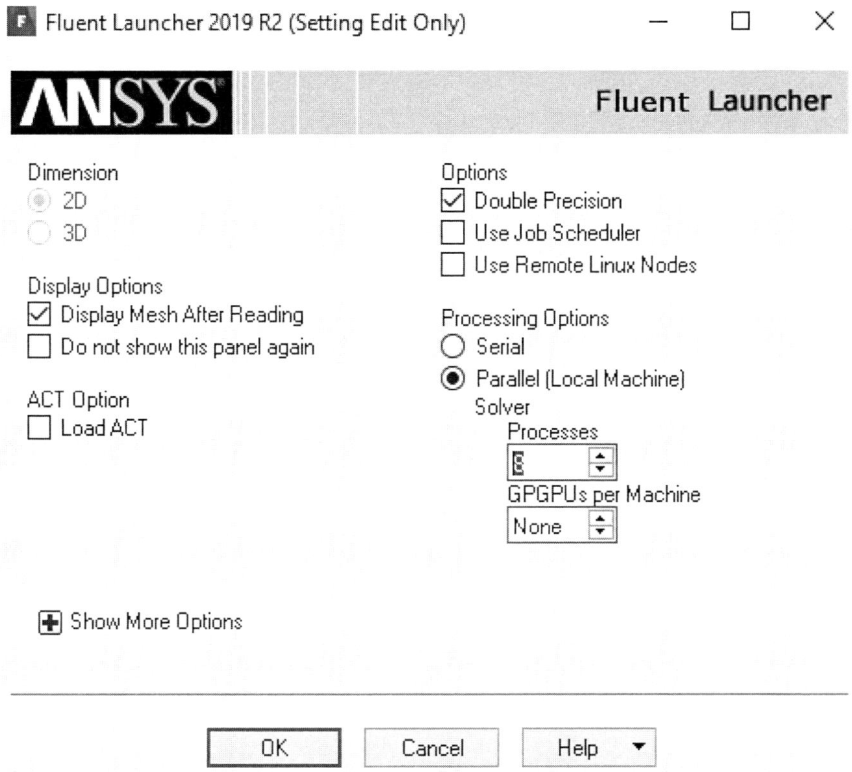

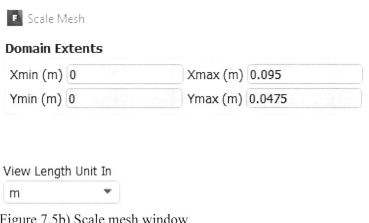

Figure 7.5a) Fluent launcher window

Click on Check and Scale… under Mesh in General on the Task Page to verify the Domain Extents. Close the Scale Mesh window. Select Axisymmetric Swirl as 2D Space Solver. Select Relative Velocity Formulation. Check the box for Gravity. Enter -9.81 as Gravitational Acceleration in the X direction.

Scale Mesh

Domain Extents

Xmin (m) 0   Xmax (m) 0.095

Ymin (m) 0   Ymax (m) 0.0475

View Length Unit In

m

Figure 7.5b) Scale mesh window

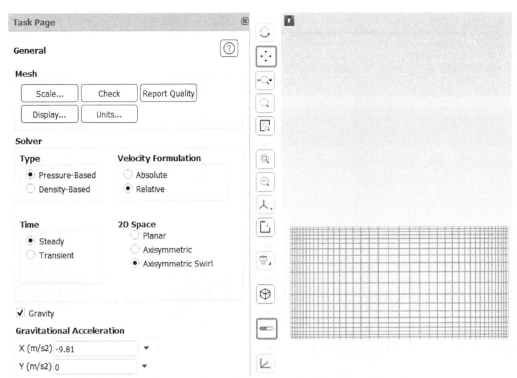

Figure 7.5c) Selecting axisymmetric swirl and gravitational acceleration

6.   Next, we double click on Materials under Setup in the Outline View. Select Fluid under Materials on the Task Page and click on Create/Edit…. Click on Fluent Database… in the Create/Edit Materials window. Scroll down in the Fluent Fluid Material section and select water-liquid (h2o<l>). Click on Copy at the bottom of the Fluent Database Materials window. Close the two windows.

Figure 7.6a) Selecting the Fluent database

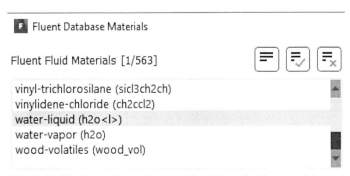

Figure 7.6b) Selection of water-liquid as fluid material

7. Open Cell Zone Conditions under Setup in the Outline View. Double click on
    surface_body under Cell Zone Conditions. Select water-liquid as Material Name. Check
    the box for Frame Motion and enter Speed (rad/s) -0.4449 as Rotational Velocity. Click
    OK to close the Fluid window.

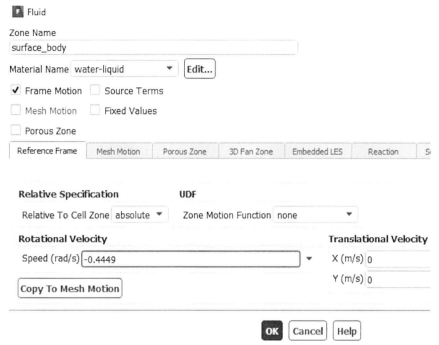

Figure 7.7 Selection of water-liquid and frame motion for the surface body

8. Double click on Boundary Conditions under Setup in the Outline View. Select symmetry
    under Zone in Boundary Conditions on the Task Page. Choose axis from the Type drop-
    down menu, rename the Zone Name to *axis* and click OK in the Axis window.

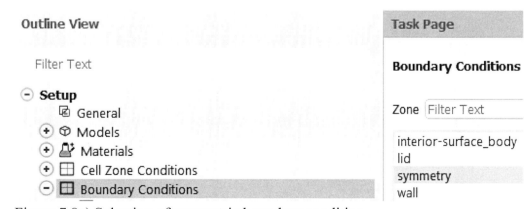

Figure 7.8a) Selection of symmetric boundary condition

Figure 7.8b) Selection of axis boundary condition

Select *lid* under Zone in Boundary Conditions on the Task Page. Click on the Edit… button for wall Type. Select *Moving Wall* under Wall Motion. Check Absolute and Rotational under Motion and enter 0.4449 as Speed (rad/s). Click OK to close the window. Repeat this step for the *wall* Zone, use Absolute and Rotational Motion and enter 0 as Speed (rad/s), see Figure 7.8d).

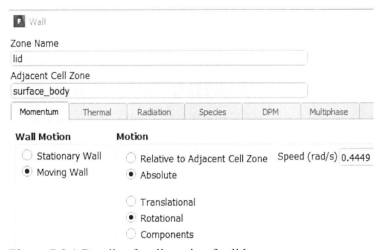

Figure 7.8c) Details of wall motion for lid

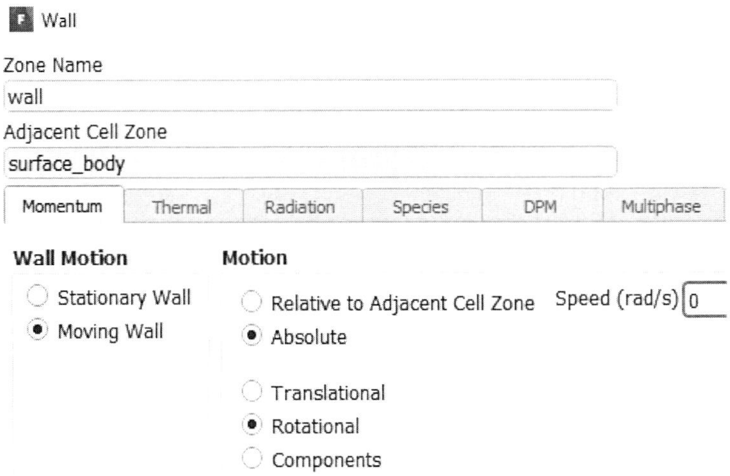

Figure 7.8d) Details of wall motion for wall

9. Double click on Methods under Solution in the Tree and choose PRESTO! for Pressure Spatial Discretization on the Task Page. Select SIMPLEC as the Pressure-Velocity Coupling Scheme. Select Green-Gauss Node Based Gradient under Spatial Discretization. Select QUICK for both Momentum and Swirl Velocity under Spatial Discretization.

    Double click on Controls under Solution in the Tree. Set all Under-Relaxation Factors to 1 except Momentum that is set to 0.7.

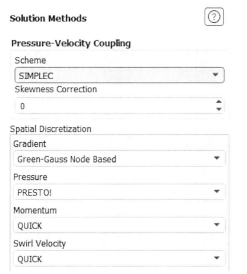

Figure 7.9a) Solution methods   Figure 7.9b) Under-relaxation factors

10. Double click on Monitors and Residual under Solution in the Outline View. Make sure that the box for Plot under Options is checked. Set the Absolute Criteria to 1e-12 for all four residuals and click OK to close the window.

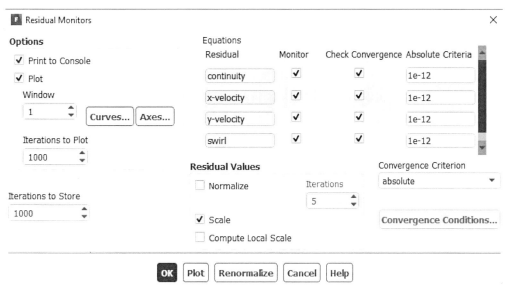

Figure 7.10 Residual monitors window

11. Double click on Initialization under Solution in the Outline View and select Standard Initialization as Initialization Method. Set Swirl Velocity (m/s) to 0.02. This value is approximately the speed of rotation 0.4449 rad/s times the radius 0.0475m. Click on Initialize. Double click on Run Calculation under Solution in the Outline View and set the Number of Iterations to 2000. Click on the *Calculate* button on the Task Page. Click OK in the Information window when the calculation is complete.

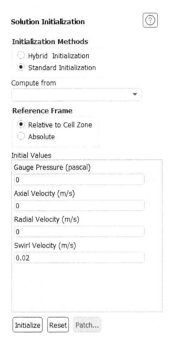

Figure 7.11a) Solution initialization

Double click on Run Calculation under Solution in the Tree and set the Number of Iterations to 2000. Click on the *Calculate* button on the Task Page. Click OK in the Information window when the calculation is complete.

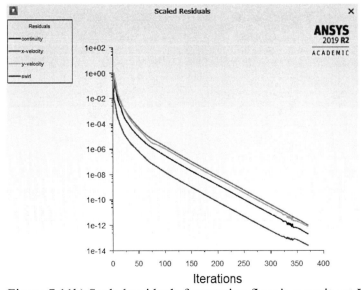

Figure 7.11b) Scaled residuals for rotating flow in a cavity at Re = 1000

G. Post-Processing

12. Open Graphics under Results in Outline View and double click on Contours under Graphics. Select Contours of Velocity and Stream Function. Select all surfaces including *interior-surface_body*. Click on Save/Display.

Figure 7.12a) Contours window

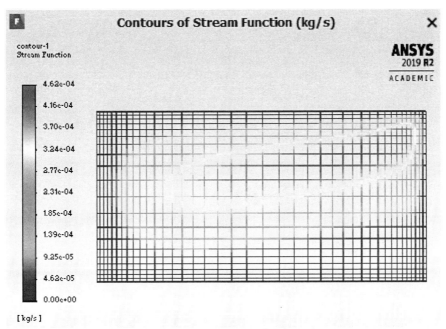

Figure 7.12b) Streamlines for Re = 1,000 and H/R = 2

13. Open Plots and double click on XY Plot under Results in the Outline View. Uncheck Position on X Axis and Position on Y Axis under Options. Select Velocity… and Swirl Velocity as Y Axis Function. Select Mesh… and X-Coordinate as X Axis Function. Select New Surface>>Line/Rake…. Enter x0 (m) 0 and x1 (m) 0.095. Enter y0 (m) 0.0285 and y1 (m) 0.0285. Enter *y=0.0285m* as the New Surface Name and click on Create. Close the Line/Rake Surface window.

Select *y=0.0285m* under Surfaces in the Solution XY Plot window and click on Axes…. Set Precision to 2 under Number Format for X Axis. Click on Apply. Set Precision to 3 under Number Format for Y Axis. Click on Apply. Close the Axes window.

Put the file $swirl - velocity - y = 0.0285m.dat$ in the working directory. This and other files can be downloaded from *sdcpublications.com*. Click on Load File… and read the file $swirl - velocity - y = 0.0285m.dat$ from the working directory. Click on Save/Plot. Repeat this step but instead load $radial - velocity - y = 0.0285m.dat$ and $axial - velocity - y = 0.0285m.dat$ and plot the Radial Velocity and the Axial Velocity components, respectively.

Create another Line/Rake… with x0 (m) 0.0475 and x1 (m) 0.0475. Enter y0 (m) 0 and y1 (m) 0.0475. Enter *x=0.0475m* as the New Surface Name. Plot the three velocity components versus Y-Coordinate and compare with loaded files. Close the Solution XY Plot window.

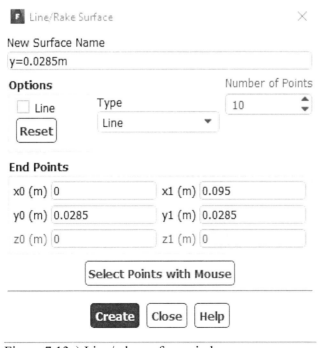

Figure 7.13a) Line/rake surface window

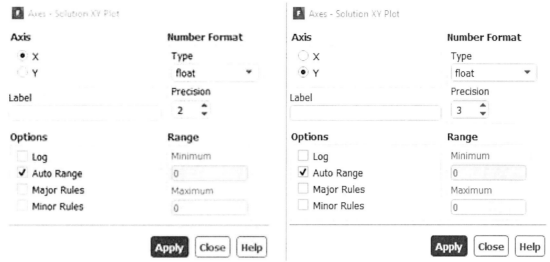

Figure 7.13b) X Axes settings   Figure 7.13c) Y Axes settings

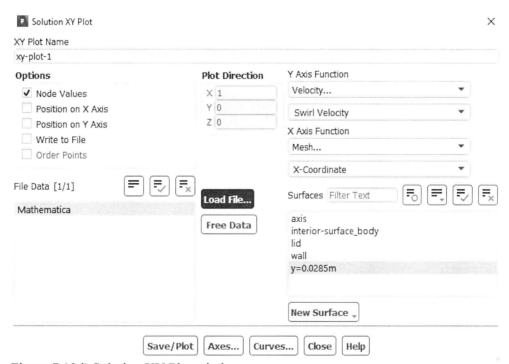

Figure 7.13d) Solution XY Plot window

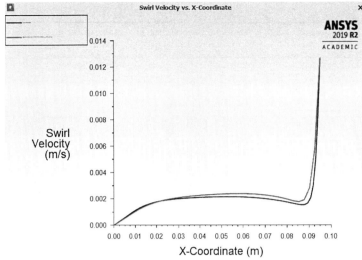

Figure 7.13e) Swirl velocity versus x (Re = 1,000 and H/R = 2) at y = 0.0285 m

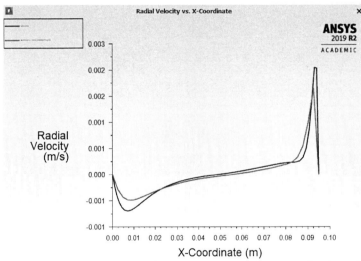

Figure 7.13f) Radial velocity versus x (Re = 1,000 and H/R = 2) at y = 0.0285 m

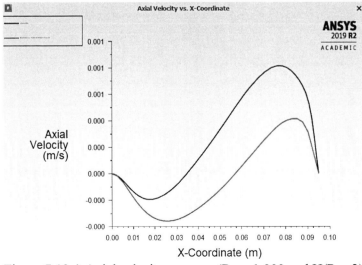

Figure 7.13g) Axial velocity versus x (Re = 1,000 and H/R = 2) at y = 0.0285m

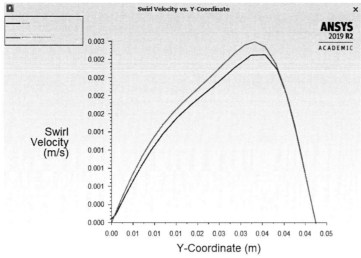

Figure 7.13h) Swirl velocity versus *y* (Re = 1,000 and H/R = 2) at *x* = 0.0475m

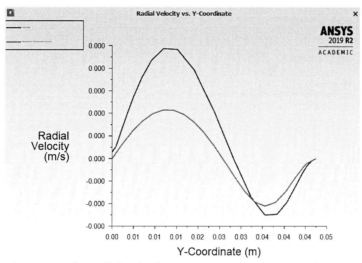

Figure 7.13i) Radial velocity versus *y* (Re = 1,000 and H/R = 2) at *x* = 0.0475m

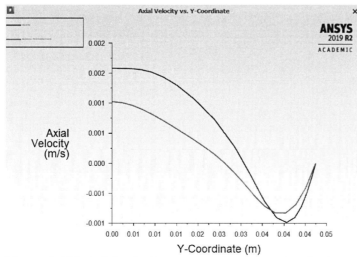

Figure 7.13j) Axial velocity versus *y* (Re = 1,000 and H/R = 2) at *x* = 0.0475m

151

14. Double click on Graphics and Contours under Results in the Outline View. Select Contours of Velocity and Stream Function. Select axis, interior-surface_body, lid and wall under Surfaces. Click on Save/Display.

Select the View tab in the menu and click on Views…. Select *axis* as Mirror Plane and click on Apply. Click on the Camera… button in the Views window. Use your left mouse button to rotate the dial counter-clockwise until the cavity appears upright. Close the Camera Parameters window. Click on the Save button under Actions in the Views window and close the windows.

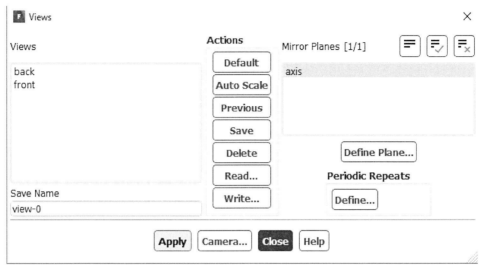

Figure 7.14a) Views window

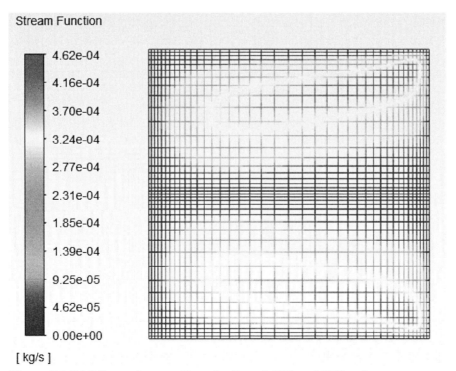

Figure 7.14b) Mirrored streamlines for Re = 1,000 and H/R = 2

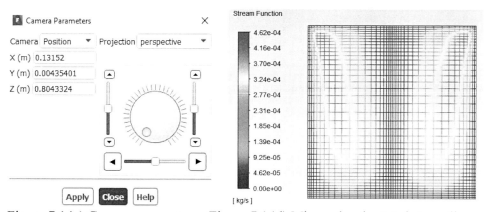

Figure 7.14c) Camera parameters   Figure 7.14d) Mirrored and rotated streamlines

Double click on Graphics and Contours under Results in the Outline View. Select Contours of Velocity… and Stream Function. Do not select any surfaces. Click on Save/Display. Select the Viewing tab in the menu and click on Views…. Select *view-0* under Views and axis under Mirror Planes and click on Apply. Close the Views window. Select Contours of Velocity… and Swirl Velocity in the Contours window. Click on Save/Display. Repeat this for Radial Velocity and Axial Velocity. Close the Contours window.

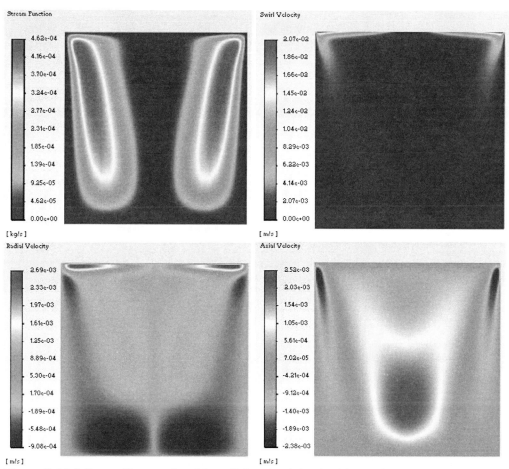

Figure 7.14e) Streamlines and swirl, radial and axial velocities and Re=1000

153

15. Start another separate session of ANSYS Workbench and ANSYS Fluent 2019 R2. Select 2D Dimension, Double Precision and select Parallel Processing Options. Set the number of Processes equal to the number of processor cores on your computer. Click on the OK button in the Fluent Launcher window. Copy the file *rotating-flow-mesh-lambda=2.5.msh* into the working directory.

Select File>>Import>>Mesh from the Fluent menu. Answer Yes to the question that you get on the screen. Select the file *rotating-flow-mesh-lambda=2.5.msh.* Double click on General under Setup in Outline View. Click on Display... under Mesh and General on the Task Page. Select all Surfaces and click on Display in the Mesh Display window. Close the window. Select Axisymmetric Swirl as 2D Space Solver. Select Relative Velocity Formulation. Check the box for Gravity. Enter -9.81 as Gravitational Acceleration in the X direction. Repeat steps *6* to *11* in this chapter. Enter -1 rad/s as Rotational Velocity in step *7*. Set the Speed of the Lid in step *8* to 1 rad/s corresponding to *Re* = 2,245 and set the Swirl Velocity (m/s) to 0.0475 in step *11*.

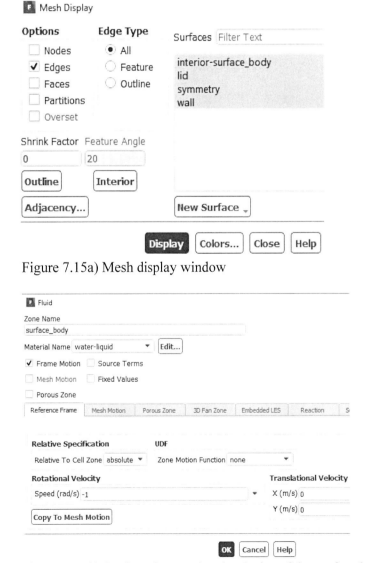

Figure 7.15a) Mesh display window

Figure 7.15b) Settings for rotational velocity of the surface body

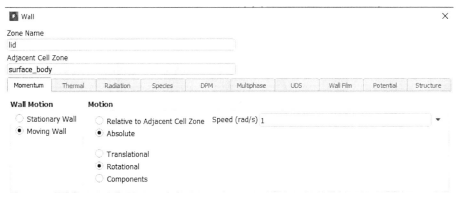

Figure 7.15c) Settings for speed of the lid corresponding to $Re = 2,245$

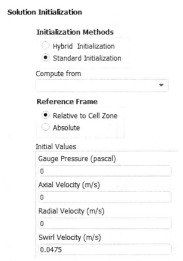

Figure 7.15d) Settings for solution initialization

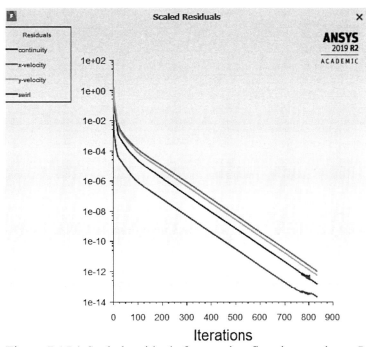

Figure 7.15e) Scaled residuals for rotating flow in a cavity at $Re = 2245$

16. Double click on Graphics and Contours under Results in the Outline View. Select Contours of Velocity and Stream Function. Click on Save/Display. Select the View tab in the menu and click on Views.... Select *axis* as Mirror Plane and click on Apply. Click on the Camera... button in the Views window. Use your left mouse button to rotate the dial counter-clockwise until the cavity appears upright. Close the Camera Parameters window. Click on the Save button under Actions in the Views window and close the windows.

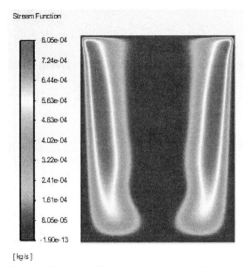

Figure 7.16a) Mirrored and rotated streamlines for Re = 2245 and H/R = 2.5

Double click on Graphics and Pathlines under Results in the Outline View. Select Color by Velocity and Velocity Magnitude. Select *interior-surface_body* under Release from Surfaces. Set the Step Size (m) to 0.02, the Number of Steps to 500 and Path Skip to 20. Click on Save/Display.

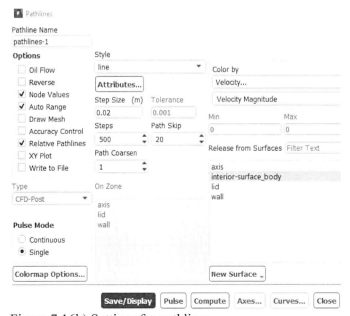

Figure 7.16b) Settings for pathlines

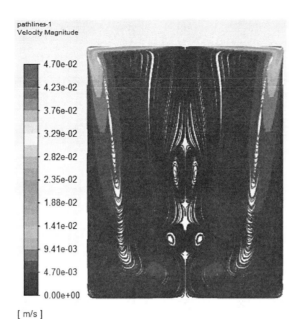

Figure 7.16c) Pathlines at Re = 2245 and H/R = 2.5

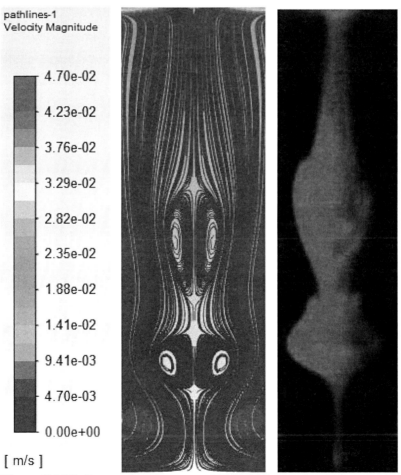

Figure 7.16d) Comparison between ANSYS Fluent simulations and experimental visualizations at Re = 2245, H/R = 2.5

H. Theory

17. We define the Reynolds number as

$$Re = \Omega R^2 / \nu \qquad (7.1)$$

where Ω (rad/s) is the angular velocity of the lid, R (m) is the radius of the cylindrical container and ν (m²/s) is kinematic viscosity. The aspect ratio of the cylindrical container is defined as

$$\lambda = H/R \qquad (7.2)$$

where H (m) is the height of the cylindrical container.

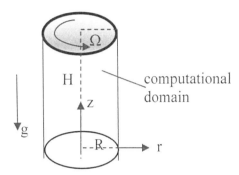

Figure 7.17a) Geometry for cylinder with rotating lid

The incompressible Navier-Stokes equations in cylindrical coordinates (r, θ, z) with velocity components $\big(u_r(r, \theta, z, t), u_\theta(r, \theta, z, t), u_z(r, \theta, z, t)\big)$ are given by the following equations:

Continuity equation: $\quad \dfrac{1}{r}\dfrac{\partial(r u_r)}{\partial r} + \dfrac{1}{r}\dfrac{\partial u_\theta}{\partial \theta} + \dfrac{\partial u_z}{\partial z} = 0 \qquad (7.3)$

r-component: $\quad \rho\left(\dfrac{\partial u_r}{\partial t} + u_r\dfrac{\partial u_r}{\partial r} + \dfrac{u_\theta}{r}\dfrac{\partial u_r}{\partial \theta} - \dfrac{u_\theta^2}{r} + u_z\dfrac{\partial u_r}{\partial z}\right) =$

$\quad -\dfrac{\partial p}{\partial r} + \mu\left[\dfrac{1}{r}\dfrac{\partial}{\partial r}\left(r\dfrac{\partial u_r}{\partial r}\right) - \dfrac{u_r}{r^2} + \dfrac{1}{r^2}\dfrac{\partial^2 u_r}{\partial \theta^2} - \dfrac{2}{r^2}\dfrac{\partial u_\theta}{\partial \theta} + \dfrac{\partial^2 u_r}{\partial z^2}\right] \qquad (7.4)$

θ-component: $\quad \rho\left(\dfrac{\partial u_\theta}{\partial t} + u_r\dfrac{\partial u_\theta}{\partial r} + \dfrac{u_\theta}{r}\dfrac{\partial u_\theta}{\partial \theta} + \dfrac{u_r u_\theta}{r} + u_z\dfrac{\partial u_\theta}{\partial z}\right) =$

$\quad -\dfrac{1}{r}\dfrac{\partial p}{\partial \theta} + \mu\left[\dfrac{1}{r}\dfrac{\partial}{\partial r}\left(r\dfrac{\partial u_\theta}{\partial r}\right) - \dfrac{u_\theta}{r^2} + \dfrac{1}{r^2}\dfrac{\partial^2 u_\theta}{\partial \theta^2} + \dfrac{2}{r^2}\dfrac{\partial u_r}{\partial \theta} + \dfrac{\partial^2 u_\theta}{\partial z^2}\right] \qquad (7.5)$

z-component: $\quad \rho\left(\dfrac{\partial u_z}{\partial t} + u_r\dfrac{\partial u_z}{\partial r} + \dfrac{u_\theta}{r}\dfrac{\partial u_z}{\partial \theta} + u_z\dfrac{\partial u_z}{\partial z}\right) =$

$\quad -\dfrac{\partial p}{\partial z} + \mu\left[\dfrac{1}{r}\dfrac{\partial}{\partial r}\left(r\dfrac{\partial u_z}{\partial r}\right) + \dfrac{1}{r^2}\dfrac{\partial^2 u_z}{\partial \theta^2} + \dfrac{\partial^2 u_z}{\partial z^2}\right] \qquad (7.6)$

where ρ (kg/m³) is density, g (m/s²) is acceleration due to gravity and μ (kg/m-s) is dynamic viscosity. For axisymmetric flow there is no θ dependence for the velocity components so they can be expressed as $\left(u_r(r,z), u_\theta(r,z), u_z(r,z)\right)$. This together with a steady flow will reduce the equations above to the following equations:

Continuity equation:
$$\frac{1}{r}\frac{\partial(r u_r)}{\partial r} + \frac{\partial u_z}{\partial z} = 0 \tag{7.7}$$

r-component:
$$\rho\left(u_r\frac{\partial u_r}{\partial r} - \frac{u_\theta^2}{r} + u_z\frac{\partial u_r}{\partial z}\right) = -\frac{\partial p}{\partial r} + \mu\left[\frac{1}{r}\frac{\partial}{\partial r}\left(r\frac{\partial u_r}{\partial r}\right) - \frac{u_r}{r^2} + \frac{\partial^2 u_r}{\partial z^2}\right] \tag{7.8}$$

θ-component:
$$\rho\left(u_r\frac{\partial u_\theta}{\partial r} + \frac{u_r u_\theta}{r} + u_z\frac{\partial u_\theta}{\partial z}\right) = \mu\left[\frac{1}{r}\frac{\partial}{\partial r}\left(r\frac{\partial u_\theta}{\partial r}\right) - \frac{u_\theta}{r^2} + \frac{\partial^2 u_\theta}{\partial z^2}\right] \tag{7.9}$$

z-component:
$$\rho\left(u_r\frac{\partial u_z}{\partial r} + u_z\frac{\partial u_z}{\partial z}\right) = -\frac{\partial p}{\partial z} + \mu\left[\frac{1}{r}\frac{\partial}{\partial r}\left(r\frac{\partial u_z}{\partial r}\right) + \frac{\partial^2 u_z}{\partial z^2}\right] \tag{7.10}$$

We make the velocity components and pressure non-dimensional using the following relations:

$$u_r^* = u_r/(\Omega R), u_\theta^* = u_\theta/(\Omega R), u_z^* = u_z/\Omega R, p^* = p/(\rho\Omega^2 R^2) \tag{7.11}$$

and we make the coordinates non-dimensional using the following relations:

$$r^* = r/R, \theta^* = \theta, z^* = z/R \tag{7.12}$$

The continuity equation and the different component equations in non-dimensional form after skipping the $*$ superscript symbol:

$$\frac{\partial u_r}{\partial r} + \frac{u_r}{r} + \frac{\partial u_z}{\partial z} = 0 \tag{7.13}$$

$$u_r\frac{\partial u_r}{\partial r} - \frac{u_\theta^2}{r} + u_z\frac{\partial u_r}{\partial z} = -\frac{\partial p}{\partial r} + \frac{1}{Re}\left[\frac{\partial^2 u_r}{\partial r^2} + \frac{1}{r}\frac{\partial u_r}{\partial r} - \frac{u_r}{r^2} + \frac{\partial^2 u_r}{\partial z^2}\right] \tag{7.14}$$

$$u_r\frac{\partial u_\theta}{\partial r} + \frac{u_r u_\theta}{r} + u_z\frac{\partial u_\theta}{\partial z} = \frac{1}{Re}\left[\frac{\partial^2 u_\theta}{\partial r^2} + \frac{1}{r}\frac{\partial u_\theta}{\partial r} - \frac{u_\theta}{r^2} + \frac{\partial^2 u_\theta}{\partial z^2}\right] \tag{7.15}$$

$$u_r\frac{\partial u_z}{\partial r} + u_z\frac{\partial u_z}{\partial z} = -\frac{\partial p}{\partial z} + \frac{1}{Re}\left[\frac{\partial^2 u_z}{\partial r^2} + \frac{1}{r}\frac{\partial u_z}{\partial r} + \frac{\partial^2 u_z}{\partial z^2}\right] \tag{7.16}$$

The boundary conditions are the following:

$$u_r(0,z) = u_r(1,z) = u_r(r,0) = u_r(r,2) = 0 \tag{7.17}$$

$$u_\theta(0,z) = u_\theta(1,z) = u_\theta(r,0) = 0, \; u_\theta(r,2) = \Omega r \tag{7.18}$$

$$\frac{\partial u_z(0,z)}{\partial r} = u_z(1,z) = u_z(r,0) = u_z(r,2) = 0 \tag{7.19}$$

```
Remove[XandYGrid,MakeVariables,FDMatrices];
XandYGrid[domain_List,pts_List]:=MapThread[N@Range[Sequence@@#1,Abs[Subtract@@#1]/#2]&,{domain,pts-1}];
BoundaryIndex[rgridlen_,zgridlen_]:=Module[{tmp,left,right,bot,top},tmp=Table[(n-1)zgridlen+Range[1,zgridlen],{n,1,rgridlen}];
  {left,right}=tmp[[{1,-1}]];{bot,top}=Transpose[{First[#],Last[#]}&/@tmp];{top,right[[2;;-2]],bot,left[[2;;-2]]}];
Attributes[MakeVariables]={Listable};MakeVariables[var_,n_]:=Table[Unique[var],{n}];
FDMatrices[deriv_,rzgrid_,difforder_]:=Map[NDSolve`FiniteDifferenceDerivative[#,rzgrid,"DifferenceOrder"→difforder]["Differen
tiationMatrix"]&,deriv];

Options[DrivenCylinderCavitySolver]={"InitialGuess"→1};
DrivenCylinderCavitySolver[Rey_,domain_List,pts_List,difforder_,OptionsPattern[]]:=Module[{rzgrid,rrgrid,rgrid,r2grid,nr,nz,top,r
ight,bot,left,ur,uz,uθ,p,urvar,uzvar,uθvar,pvar,dr,dz,dr2,dz2,eqnur,eqnuz,eqnuθ,eqncont,bcindx,sol,boundaries,deqns,dvars,grid}
,(*Get the grid and differentiation matrices*)rzgrid=XandYGrid[domain,pts];rrgrid=rzgrid[[1]];
  grid=Flatten[Outer[List,Sequence@@rzgrid],1];rgrid=grid[[All,1]];r2grid=rgrid*rgrid;
  {nr,nz}=Map[Length,rzgrid];{top,right,bot,left}=BoundaryIndex[nr,nz];
  {dr,dz,dr2,dz2}=FDMatrices[{{1,0},{0,1},{2,0},{0,2}},rzgrid,difforder];
  (*Get the discretized axisymmetric Navier Stokes equations*){urvar,uzvar,uθvar,pvar}=MakeVariables[{ur,uz,uθ,p},nr*nz];
  eqnur=r2grid urvar (dr.urvar)-rgrid uθvar uθvar+r2grid uzvar (dz.urvar)+r2grid(dr.pvar)-r2grid (1/Rey) (dr2+dz2).urvar-
rgrid(1/Rey) (dr.urvar)+(1/Rey) urvar;
  eqnuz=rgrid urvar(dr.uzvar)+rgrid uzvar (dz.uzvar)+rgrid(dz.pvar)-rgrid (1/Rey) (dr2+dz2).uzvar-(1/Rey) (dr.uzvar);
  eqnuθ=r2grid urvar (dr.uθvar)+rgrid urvar uθvar+r2grid uzvar (dz.uθvar)-r2grid (1/Rey) (dr2+dz2).uθvar-rgrid(1/Rey)
(dr.uθvar)+(1/Rey) uθvar;
  eqncont=rgrid (dr.urvar)+urvar+rgrid(dz.uzvar);
  (*Apply the boundary conditions and solve the
system*)boundaries=Join[top,right,bot,left];eqnur[[boundaries]]=urvar[[boundaries]];
  eqnuz[[boundaries]]=uzvar[[boundaries]];eqnuz[[left]]=(dr[[left]].uzvar);
  eqnuθ[[boundaries]]=uθvar[[boundaries]];eqnuθ[[top]]=uθvar[[top]]-(rrgrid-1);
  eqncont[[top[[1]]]]=pvar[[top[[1]]]];
  {deqns,dvars}={Join[eqnur,eqnuz,eqnuθ,eqncont],Join[urvar,uzvar,uθvar,pvar]};
  sol=dvars/.Quiet@FindRoot[deqns,Thread[{dvars,OptionValue["InitialGuess"]}]];
  (*Get Interpolating
functions*)grid=Flatten[Outer[List,Sequence@@rzgrid],1];Map[Interpolation@Join[grid,Transpose@List@#,2]&,Partition[sol,Len
gth[grid]]]];

(* Calculate Solution *)
Timing[res={ur,uz,uθ,p}=DrivenCylinderCavitySolver[1000,{{1,2},{0,2}},{30,60},4]]
StreamDensityPlot[{ur[r,z],uz[r,z]},{r,1,2},{z,0,2},AspectRatio→2,PlotLabel→Style[Text["Streamfunction at Re = 1000"]]]

(* Plot Results and Save Velocity Profiles for uθ *)
SetDirectory["C:\\Users\\johne"];r1=1;omega=0.4449;radius=0.0475;
Plot[uθ[0.6+r1,z]*omega*radius,{z,0,2},PlotRange→{{0,2},{0,0.014}},AxesLabel→{z,Uθ[m/s]},PlotLabel→Style[Text["r=1.6,
Re=1000"]]]
mylist=Table[{uθ[0.6+r1,z]*omega*radius,z*radius},{z,0,2,0.05}];
Plotex[mylist];Export["swirl-velocity-y=0.0285m.dat",TableOfValues1];

Plot[uθ[r,1]*omega*radius,{r,0+r1,1+r1},AxesLabel→{r+1,Uθ[m/s]},PlotLabel→Style[Text["z=1, Re=1000"]]]
mylist=Table[{uθ[r,1]*omega*radius,(r-r1)*radius},{r,0+r1,1+r1,0.05}];Plotex[mylist];Export["swirl-velocity-
x=0.0475m.dat",TableOfValues1];

Plotex[n_]:=(mylist[[All,{1,2}]]]=n[[All,{2,1}]];TableOfValues1=Prepend[mylist,{""}];
  TableOfValues1=Prepend[TableOfValues1,{"((xy/key/label \"Mathematica - Finite Difference Solution\")"}];
  TableOfValues1=Prepend[TableOfValues1,{""}];
  TableOfValues1=Prepend[TableOfValues1,{"(labels \"Swirl Velocity (m/s)\" \"Position (m)\")"}];
  TableOfValues1=Prepend[TableOfValues1,{"(title
\"Mathematica\")"}];TableOfValues1=Append[TableOfValues1,{")"}];Grid[TableOfValues1];)

(* Plot Results and Save Velocity Profiles for ur *)
SetDirectory["C:\\Users\\johne"];r1=1;omega=0.4449;radius=0.0475;
Plot[ur[0.6+r1,z]*omega*radius,{z,0,2},PlotRange→{{0,2},{-0.001,0.0025}},AxesLabel→{z,Ur[m/s]},PlotLabel→Style[Text["r=1.6,
Re=1000"]]]
mylist=Table[{ur[0.6+r1,z]*omega*radius,z*radius},{z,0,2,0.05}];
Plotex[mylist];Export["radial-velocity-y=0.0285m.dat",TableOfValues1];

Plot[ur[r,1]*omega*radius,{r,0+r1,1+r1},AxesLabel→{r+1,Ur[m/s]},PlotLabel→Style[Text["z=1, Re=1000"]]]
mylist=Table[{ur[r,1]*omega*radius,(r-r1)*radius},{r,0+r1,1+r1,0.05}];Plotex[mylist];Export["radial-velocity-
x=0.0475m.dat",TableOfValues1];
```

```
Plotex[n_]:=(mylist[[All,{1,2}]]=n[[All,{2,1}]];TableOfValues1=Prepend[mylist,{""}];
 TableOfValues1=Prepend[TableOfValues1,{"((xy/key/label \"Mathematica - Finite Difference Solution\")"}];
 TableOfValues1=Prepend[TableOfValues1,{""}];
 TableOfValues1=Prepend[TableOfValues1,{"(labels \"Radial Velocity (m/s)\" \"Position (m)\")"}];
 TableOfValues1=Prepend[TableOfValues1,{"(title
\"Mathematica\")"}];TableOfValues1=Append[TableOfValues1,{")"}];Grid[TableOfValues1];)

(* Plot Results and Save Velocity Profiles for uz *)
SetDirectory["C:\\Users\\johne"];r1=1;omega=0.4449;radius=0.0475;
Plot[uz[0.6+r1,z]*omega*radius,{z,0,2},PlotRange→{{0,2},{-0.0004,0.0010}},AxesLabel→{z,Uz[m/s]},PlotLabel→Style[Text["r=1.6,
Re=1000"]]]
mylist=Table[{uz[0.6+r1,z]*omega*radius,z*radius},{z,0,2,0.05}];
Plotex[mylist];Export["axial-velocity-y=0.0285m.dat",TableOfValues1];

Plot[uz[r,1]*omega*radius,{r,0+r1,1+r1},AxesLabel→{r+1,Uz[m/s]},PlotLabel→Style[Text["z=1, Re=1000"]]]
mylist=Table[{uz[r,1]*omega*radius,(r-r1)*radius},{r,0+r1,1+r1,0.05}];Plotex[mylist];Export["axial-velocity-
x=0.0475m.dat",TableOfValues1];

Plotex[n_]:=(mylist[[All,{1,2}]]=n[[All,{2,1}]];TableOfValues1=Prepend[mylist,{""}];
 TableOfValues1=Prepend[TableOfValues1,{"((xy/key/label \"Mathematica - Finite Difference Solution\")"}];
 TableOfValues1=Prepend[TableOfValues1,{""}];
 TableOfValues1=Prepend[TableOfValues1,{"(labels \"Axial Velocity (m/s)\" \"Position (m)\")"}];
 TableOfValues1=Prepend[TableOfValues1,{"(title
\"Mathematica\")"}];TableOfValues1=Append[TableOfValues1,{")"}];Grid[TableOfValues1];)
```

Figure 7.17b) Mathematica 8.0 code for cylinder with rotating lid

I. References

1. ANSYS Fluid Dynamics Verification Manual, Release 15.0, November 2013.
2. Granger, R.A., Experiments in Fluid Mechanics, Dryden Press, 1988.
3. Michelsen, J.A., Modeling of Laminar Incompressible Rotating Fluid Flow, AFM 86-05, Ph.D. thesis, Department of Fluid Mechanics, Technical University of Denmark, 1986.
4. Mokhasi, Paritosh, Using Mathematica to Simulate and Visualize Fluid Flow in a Box, 2013.
5. Sorensen, J.N. and Loc,T.P., Higher-Order Axisymmetric Navier-Stokes Code: Description and Evolution of Boundary Conditions, *International Journal For Numerical Methods in Fluids*, 9:1517-1537, 1989.
6. Sorensen, J.N. and Christensen, E.A., Direct Numerical Simulation of Rotating Fluid Flow in a Closed Cylinder, *Physics of Fluids* 7:764, 1995.

J. Exercises

7.1 Use ANSYS Fluent to study the rotating cavity filled with water that has a cylindrical geometry with a radius of 100 mm and a height 300 mm. The top lid is rotating with a Reynolds number $Re = \frac{\Omega R^2}{v} = 2,800$ while the remaining walls of the cavity are stationary. Visualize pathlines, streamlines, swirl velocity, radial velocity and axial velocity for this flow case.

7.2 Use ANSYS Fluent to study the rotating cavity filled with water that has a cylindrical geometry with a radius of 100 mm and a height 150 mm. The top lid is rotating with a Reynolds number $Re = \frac{\Omega R^2}{v} = 1{,}400$ while the remaining walls of the cavity are stationary. Visualize pathlines, streamlines, swirl velocity, radial velocity and axial velocity for this flow case.

7.3 Use ANSYS Fluent to study a rotating cavity filled with water that has a frustum geometry with a bottom radius of 50 mm, top radius of 100 mm and a height 150 mm. The top lid is rotating with a Reynolds number $Re = \frac{\Omega Rt^2}{v} = 2{,}000$ while the remaining walls of the cavity are stationary. Visualize pathlines, streamlines, swirl velocity, radial velocity and axial velocity for this flow case.

7.4 Use ANSYS Fluent to study a rotating cavity filled with water that has a frustum geometry with a bottom radius of 50 mm, top radius of 100 mm and a height 150 mm. The top lid is rotating with a Reynolds number $Ret = \frac{\Omega t Rt^2}{v} = 2{,}000$ and the bottom is rotating with the same Reynolds number $Reb = \frac{\Omega b Rb^2}{v} = 2{,}000$ while the remaining walls of the cavity are stationary. Visualize pathlines, streamlines, swirl velocity, radial velocity and axial velocity for this flow case.

CHAPTER 8. SPINNING CYLINDER

A. Objectives

- Using ANSYS Fluent to Study the Fluid in an Open Cylinder with a Free Surface and Solid Body Rotation
- Inserting Boundary Conditions and System Rotation
- Using Volume of Fluid Model for Multiphase Flow with Surface Tension
- Running Laminar 2D Axisymmetric ANSYS Fluent Simulations with Swirl
- Using Contour Plots for Visualizations of Volume Fraction and Swirl Velocity
- Using Excel for Free Surface Plots

B. Problem Description

We will study the startup flow in a partially filled spinning open cylindrical container where the fluid has a free surface. We will analyze the problem using ANSYS Fluent. The cylindrical container has a diameter of 304.8 mm and the same height. The rotational speed of the cylinder is 12 rad/s.

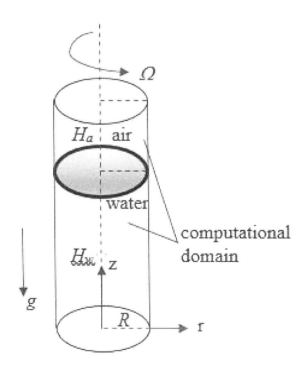

C. Launching ANSYS Workbench and Selecting Fluent

1. Start by launching ANSYS Workbench. Launch Fluid Flow (Fluent) that is available under Analysis Systems in ANSYS Workbench. Select Geometry under Project Schematic, right click and select Properties. Select 2D Analysis Type under Advanced Geometry Options. Right click on Geometry in Project Schematic and select New DesignModeler Geometry to start DesignModeler.

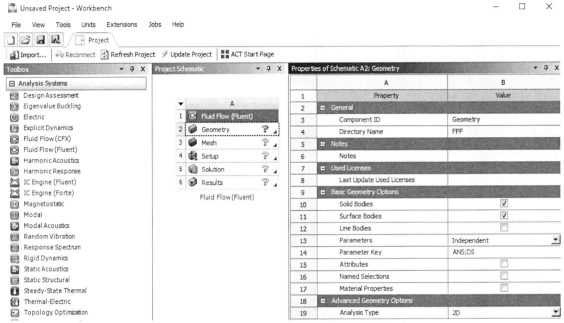

Figure 8.1 Launching ANSYS Fluent and selecting 2D analysis type

D. Launching ANSYS DesignModeler

2. Select Units>>Millimeter from the menu in DesignModeler. Select the XYPlane in the Tree Outline. Select Look At Face/Plane/Sketch 🔍. Select the Sketching tab and Rectangle. Draw a rectangle from the origin in the first quadrant of the graphics window.

Select Dimensions and click on the left vertical edge of the rectangle and the lower horizontal edge. Enter 304.8 mm as the horizontal dimension and 152.4 mm as the vertical dimension. Right click in the graphics window and select Zoom to Fit.

Select Concept>>Surfaces from Sketches from the menu. Select Sketch 1 under XY Plane in the Tree Outline. Apply the sketch as a Base Object in Details View. Click on Generate and close DesignModeler.

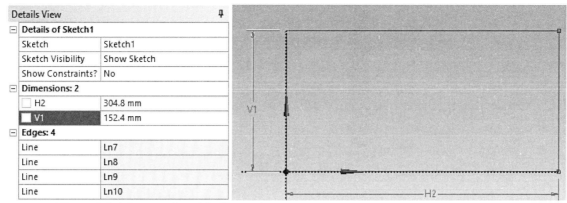

Figure 8.2a) Rectangle with dimensions

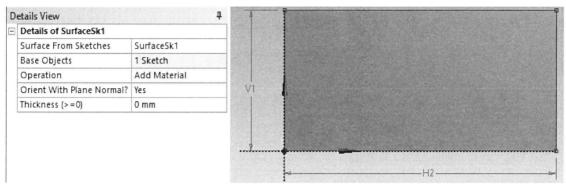

Figure 8.2b) Surface sketch for the rectangle

E. Launching ANSYS Meshing

3. Double click on Mesh under Project Schematic in ANSYS Workbench. Right-click on Mesh under Project and Model (A3) in the Meshing window and select Update. Select Mesh>>Controls>Face Meshing from the menu. Click on the rectangle and Apply it as Geometry in Details of Face Meshing.

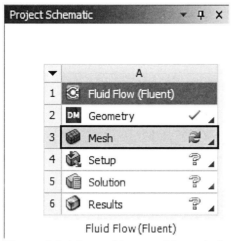

Figure 8.3a) Launching meshing window

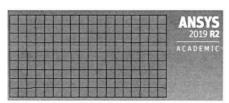

Figure 8.3b) Coarse mesh

165

Figure 8.3c) Selecting face meshing

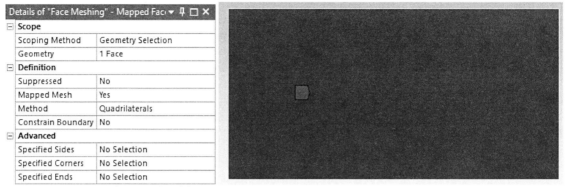

Figure 8.3d) Details of face meshing

Select Mesh>>Controls>>Sizing from the menu. Select the Edge tool 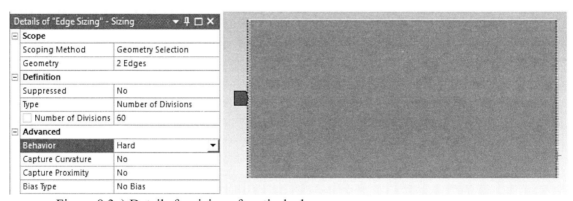, control click on the two vertical edges and Apply them as Geometry in Details of Sizing. Select Number of Divisions as Type and enter 60. Select Hard as Behavior. Repeat this step but select the two horizontal edges and 120 as the Number of Divisions and Hard as Behavior. Right click on Mesh and select Update.

Figure 8.3e) Details for sizing of vertical edges

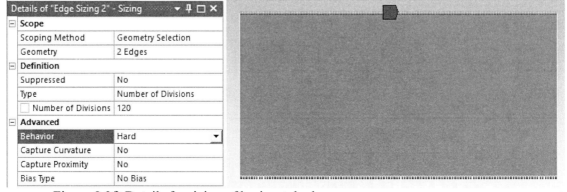

Figure 8.3f) Details for sizing of horizontal edges

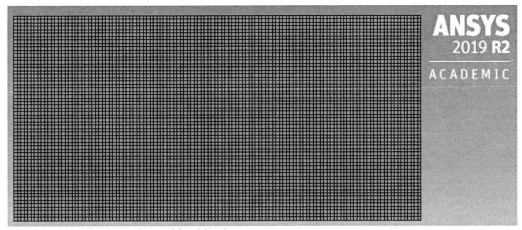

Figure 8.3g) Final mesh used in this chapter

Select the lower horizontal edge, right click and select Create Named Selection. Enter the name *symmetry-2* and click OK to close the window. Control-select the right vertical edge and the upper horizontal edge, right click and select Create Named Selection. Enter the name *wall-1*. Name the left vertical edge as *pressure-inlet-4*. Finally, select the face tool 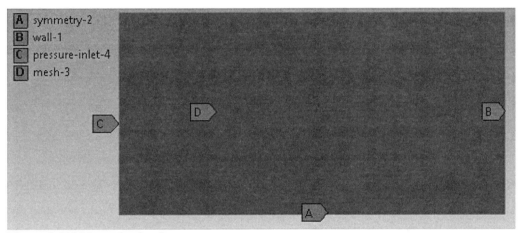, select the interior of the mesh, right click and name it *mesh-3*.

Figure 8.3h) Named selections

Select File>>Export...>>Mesh>>FLUENT Input File>>Export from the menu. Save the mesh with the name *spinning-cylinder.msh*. Select File>>Save Project from the menu and save the project with the name *Spinning Cylinder.wbpj*. Close the meshing window. Right click on Mesh in the Project Schematic and select Update.

F. Launching ANSYS Fluent

4. Double click on Setup under Project Schematic in ANSYS Workbench. Check the box for Double Precision and uncheck the box for Display Mesh After Reading. Click on plus sign next to Show More Options and write down the location of your *working directory*. You will need this information later. Select Parallel Processing Options and set the number of processes equal to the number of processor cores for your computer. Click on the OK button.

   Click on Display under General in Mesh on the Task Page in ANSYS Fluent. Select all Surfaces and click on Display in the Mesh Display window and close the same window.

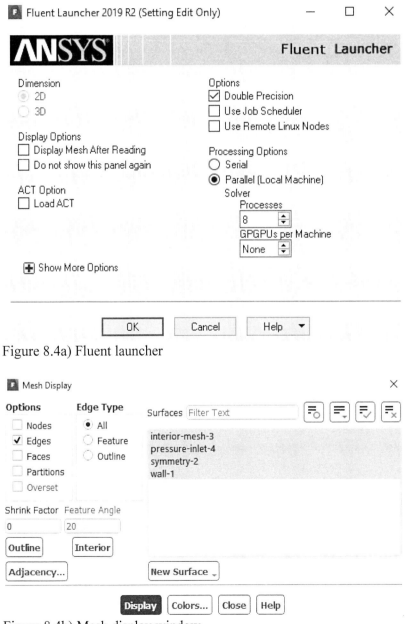

Figure 8.4a) Fluent launcher

Figure 8.4b) Mesh display window

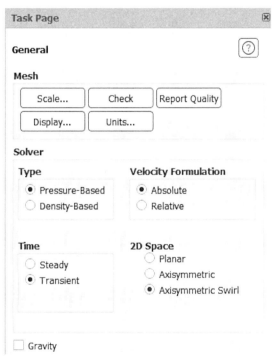

Figure 8.4c) Cylinder with mesh in ANSYS Fluent

5. Select Axisymmetric Swirl for 2D Space in the General Solver settings on the Task Page in ANSYS Fluent. Select Transient for Time in the General Solver settings. Open Models and double click on Multiphase under Setup in the Outline View. Select the Volume of Fluid Model and check the box for Implicit Body Force under Body Force Formulation. Click OK to close the Multiphase Model window.

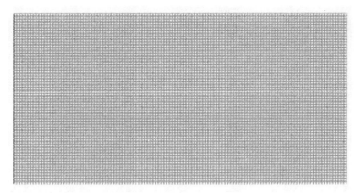

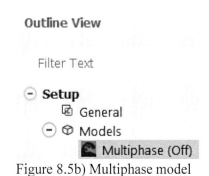

Figure 8.5a) General settings   Figure 8.5b) Multiphase model

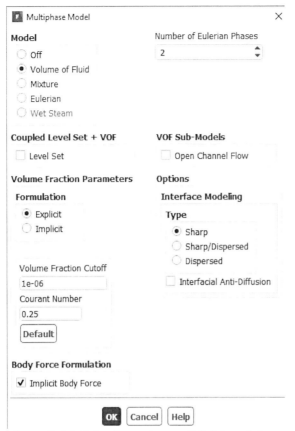

Figure 8.5c) Selecting volume of fluid model

6. Next, we double click on Materials under Setup in the Outline View. Select Fluid under Materials on the Task Page and click on Create/Edit…. Click on Fluent Database… in the Create/Edit Materials window. Scroll down in the Fluent Fluid Material section and select *water-liquid (h2o<l>)*. Click Copy at the bottom of the Fluent Database Materials window. Close the two windows.

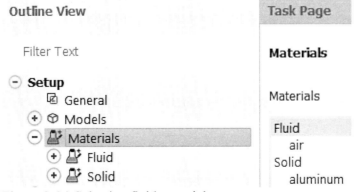

Figure 8.6a) Selecting fluid materials

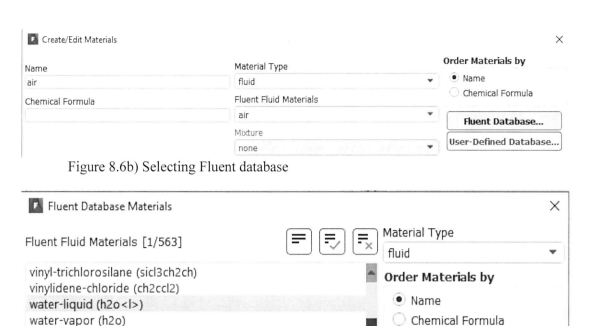

Figure 8.6b) Selecting Fluent database

Figure 8.6c) Selection of water-liquid as fluid material

7. Select the Physics tab in the menu and select Phases>>List/Show All…. Select phase-1-Primary Phase and click on the Edit… button. Enter *air* as name for the Primary Phase. Click on OK to close the window. Select phase-2-Secondary Phase and click on the Edit… button. Select *water-liquid* as the Phase Material and enter *water* as the Name for the Secondary Phase. Click on OK to close the window. Click on Interaction… and select the Surface Tension tab in the Phase Interaction window. Check the box for Surface Tension Force Modeling and select constant for Surface Tension Coefficients (n/m). Enter 0.07286 as the value. Select OK to close the Phase Interaction window and Close the Phases window.

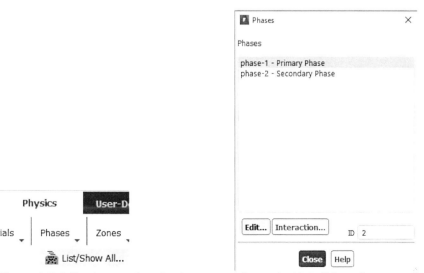

Figure 8.7a) Setting up the physics   Figure 8.7b) Editing phase-1-Primary Phase

Figure 8.7c) Name for phase-1   Figure 8.7d) Editing phase-2

Figure 8.7e) Name for phase-2

Figure 8.7f) Entering value for surface tension between water and air

8. Select the Physics tab in the menu and select Operating Conditions… under Solver. Check the box for Gravity and enter 9.81 m/s2 for Gravitational Acceleration in the X direction. Check the box for Specified Operating Density. Click on the OK button to close the window.

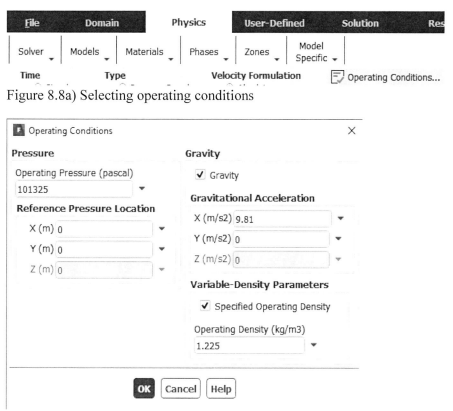

Figure 8.8a) Selecting operating conditions

Figure 8.8b) Including gravity and specified operating density

9. Double click on Boundary Conditions under Setup in the Outline View. Select *symmetry-2* under Zone in Boundary Conditions on the Task Page. Choose *axis* from the Type drop-down menu, change the zone name to *axis-2* and click OK in the Axis window. Select *pressure-inlet-4* under Zone in Boundary Conditions on the Task Page. Click on the Edit… button. Leave the Gauge Total Pressure at 0 and click OK to close the window.

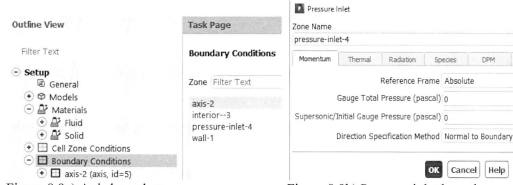

Figure 8.9a) Axis boundary   Figure 8.9b) Pressure-inlet boundary

10. For *pressure-inlet-4*, select water from the Phase drop-down menu under Boundary Conditions on the Task Page. Click on the Edit… button and make sure that the value for the Volume Fraction is 0 and click OK to close the window.

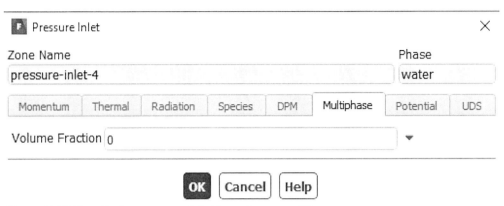

Figure 8.10 Details for pressure-inlet boundary condition

11. For *wall-1*, select mixture from the Phase drop-down menu under Boundary Conditions on the Task Page. Click on the Edit… button and select Moving Wall for Wall Motion. Choose Rotational Motion and set the Speed (rad/s) to 12. Click OK to exit the Wall window.

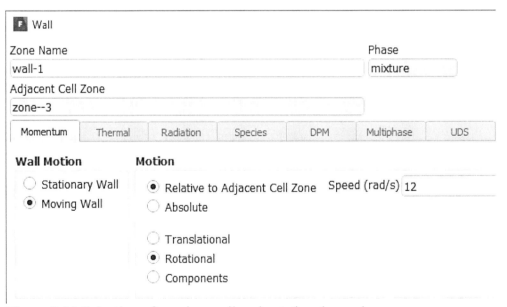

Figure 8.11 Selection of moving wall and rotational speed

12. Double click on Methods under Solution in the Outline View and choose Body Force Weighted for Pressure and First Order Upwind for Momentum under Spatial Discretization. Select SIMPLE as the Pressure-Velocity Coupling Scheme.

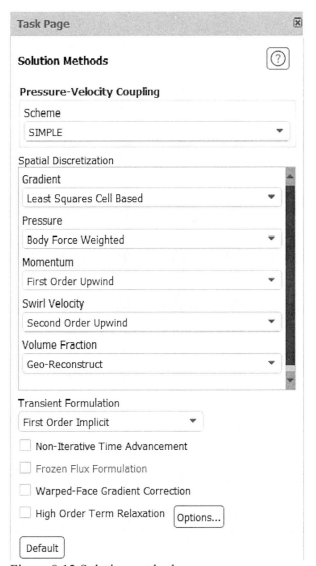

Figure 8.12 Solution methods

13. We are going to define a point close to the outer edge of the cylinder to enable the plotting of the swirl velocity over time. Select the Results tab from the menu and Create Point. Set the x0 (m) and y0 (m) coordinates to 0.2339 and 0.1372, respectively. Click Create and Close the window.

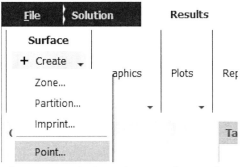

Figure 8.13a) Creating a point surface

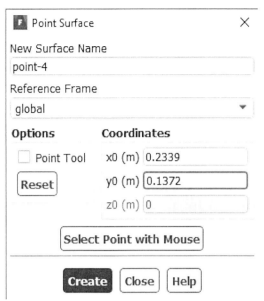

Figure 8.13b) Point surface window

14. Open Monitors and double click on Report Plots under Solution in the Outline View. Click on New… in the Report Plot Definitions window. Select New>>Surface Report>>Vertex Average… in the New Report Plot window. Check the Report File, Report Plot and Print to Console boxes under Create in the Surface Report Definition window. Select Vertex Average as Report Type. Select Velocity and Swirl Velocity as Field Variable. Select *point-4* in the Surfaces list. Enter *swirl-velocity.out* as Name. Click OK to exit the Surface Report Definition window. Click OK to close the New Report Plot window. Close the Report Plot Definitions window. Double click on Initialization under Solution in the Tree and select Compute from *pressure-inlet-4* on the Task Page. Click on Initialize.

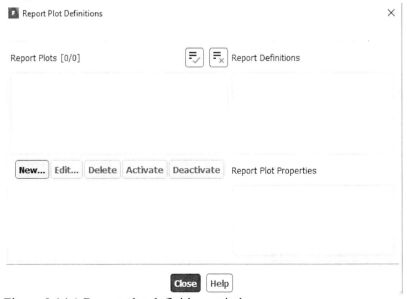

Figure 8.14a) Report plot definitions window

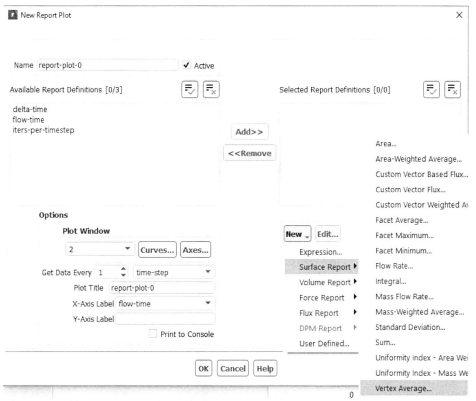

Figure 8.14b) New report plot window

Figure 8.14c) Surface report definition

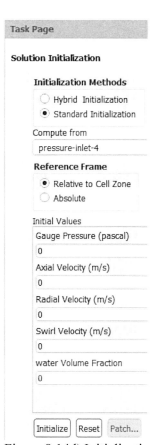

Figure 8.14d) Initialization

177

15. Select the *Domain* tab in the menu and select Adapt>>Refine/Coarsen…. Select Cell Registers>>New>>Region from the Adaption Controls window. Set X Min (m) to 0.2058, X Max (m) to 0.3048, and Y Max (m) to 0.1524. Click on Display Options…. Select red as Color and no Symbol. Check the box for Filled and uncheck the boxes for Wireframe and Marker under Options. Click on OK. Click on Save/Display in the Region Register window. Close the windows.

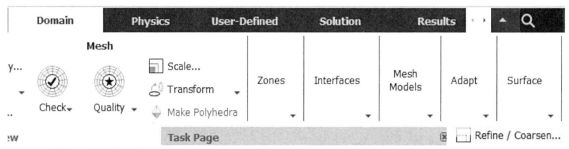

Figure 8.15a) Domain adaption

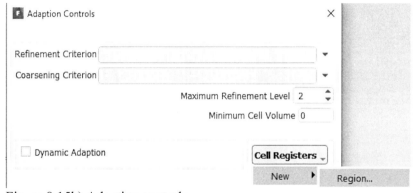

Figure 8.15b) Adaption controls

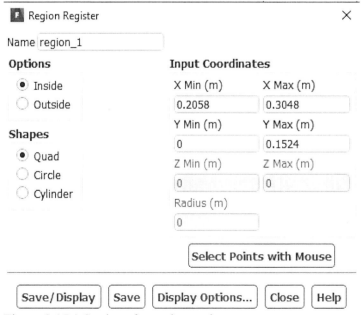

Figure 8.15c) Settings for region register

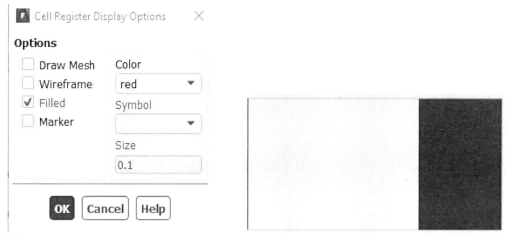

Figure 8.15d) Cell register display   Figure 8.15e) Bottom 33% of cylinder

16. Click on the Patch button on the Solution Initialization Task Page.
Select *water* as Phase in the Patch window and select Volume Fraction as Variable.
Select region_0 as Registers to Patch and set the Value to 1. Click on the Patch button.
You have now defined the lower third of the cylinder to be filled with water. Select
Mixture as Phase and choose Swirl Velocity as Variable. Set the Value (m/s) to 0 and
click on the Patch button. Close the Patch window.

Figure 8.16a) Patching settings for water

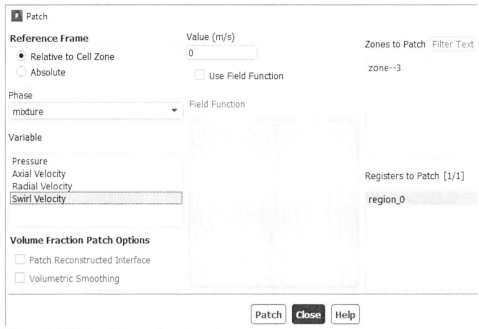

Figure 8.16b) Patching settings for mixture

17. Double click on Graphics and Contours under Results in the Outline View. Select Contours of Velocity and Swirl Velocity. Select Colormap Options… and set the Colormap Size to 30. Click on Apply and Close the Colormap window. Unselect all Surfaces and click on Save/Display. Close the Contours window.

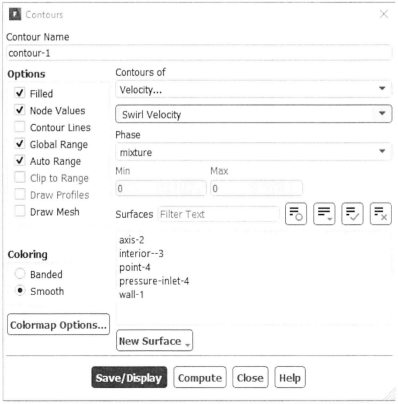

Figure 8.17a) Contours window

Select the View tab in the menu and click on Views…. Select *axis-2* as Mirror Plane and click on Apply. Zoom out and translate the view if needed so that the entire cylinder is visible in the graphics window. Click on the Camera… button in the Views window. Use your left mouse button to rotate the dial clockwise until the bowl rotates 90 degrees clockwise and appears upright. Close the Camera Parameters window. Click on the Save button under Actions in the Views window and Close the Views window.

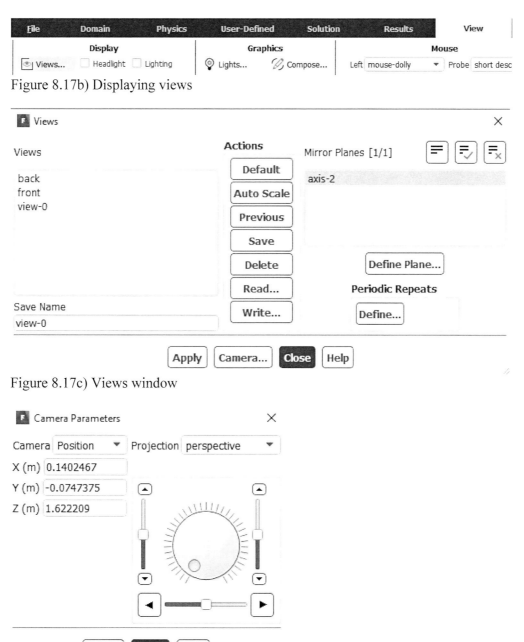

Figure 8.17b) Displaying views

Figure 8.17c) Views window

Figure 8.17d) Camera parameters window

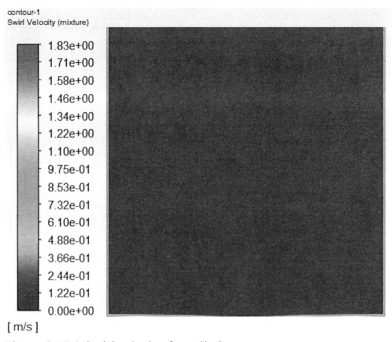

Figure 8.17e) Swirl velocity for cylinder

18. Double click on Contours under Results and Graphics in the Outline View. Select Contours of Phases… and Volume Fraction. Select *water* as the Phase. Unselect all Surfaces. Click on Save/Display and Close the Contours window. Double click on Run Calculation under Solution in the Outline View and set the Time Step Size to 0.01 s. Set the Number of Time Steps to 10000. Click on the Calculate button on the Task Page. Click OK in the Information window when the calculation is complete.

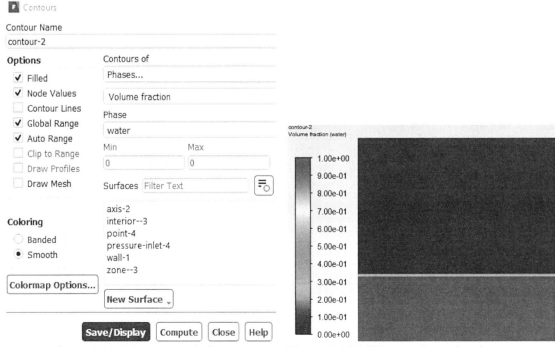

Figure 8.18a) Contours window   Figure 8.18b) Water volume fraction

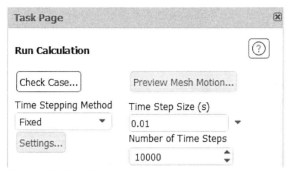

Figure 8.18c) Calculation settings

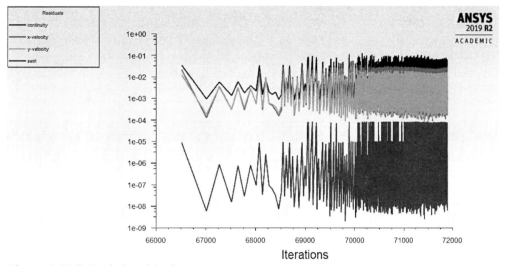

Figure 8.18d) Scaled residuals

G. Post-Processing

19. Select File>>Export>>Data… from the menu. Save the data file in the *working directory* folder with the name *t=100s.dat.* Select the View tab in the menu and click on Views. Select *view-0*, click on Apply and Close the window.

    Select the Results tab from the menu and select Surface>>Create>>Iso-Surface…. Select Surface of Constant Phases… and Volume Fraction. Select *air* as the Phase and set Iso-Values to 0.5. Select mesh-3 under From Zones and mesh-3 under From Surface. Click on Create.

    Select *water* as the Phase and set Iso-Values to 0.5. Select mesh-3 under From Zones and mesh-3 under From Surface. Enter *free-surface* as New Surface Name and click on Create. Close the window.

    Select File>>Export>>Solution Data… from the menu. Select ASCII as File Type, Node under Location and Space as Delimeter. Select mesh-3 under Cell Zones and free-surface under Surfaces. Select Volume fraction (water) under Quantities. Click on Write and save the ASCII File in the working directory with the name "free-surface-coordinates-t100s". Close the Export window.

Open the saved file in Excel and answer Yes to the question that you get. Click on Next in the Text Import Wizard – Step 1 of 3. Click on Next in Text Import Wizard – Step 2 of 3. Click on Finish in Text Import Wizard – Step 3 of 3. Plot the free surface in comparison with the final parabolic shape for the free surface, see Figures 8.19d), 8.19e) and the theory section for the definition of the two coordinate systems (x, y) and (r, z):

$$z = H_w + H_a - x = 0.3048 - x, \ r = y \tag{8.1}$$

$$H(r,\text{t}) = Z(r,t) - H_w = z - H_w \tag{8.2}$$

Double click on contour-2 under Contours that is located under Results and Graphics in the Outline View. Click on Save/Display in the Contours window to display the volume fraction (water) at $t = 100$ s, see Figure 8.19f). Close the Contours window. Select the View tab in the menu and click on Views. Select *view-0*, click on Apply and Close the window. Repeat this step but instead double click on contour-1 to display swirl velocity, see Figure 8.19g). Continue to run the calculations to $t = 200$ s and $t = 300$ s and plot the free surface evaluations, volume fraction of water and swirl velocity.

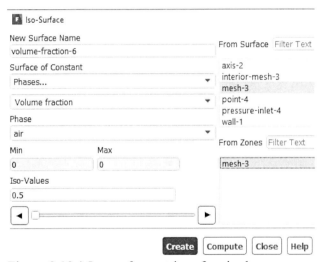

Figure 8.19a) Iso-surface settings for air phase

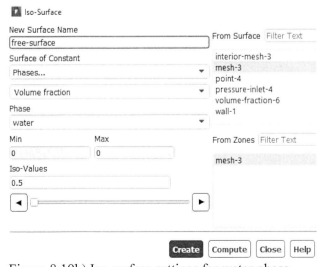

Figure 8.19b) Iso-surface settings for water phase

184

Figure 8.19c) Export settings

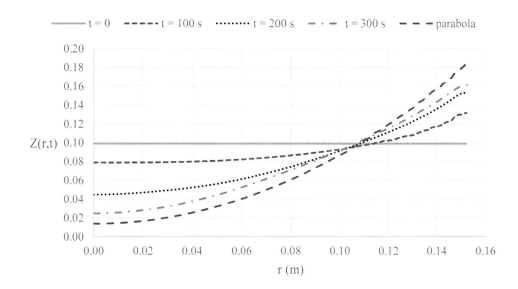

Figure 8.19d) Fluent dimensional free surface elevation at different times.

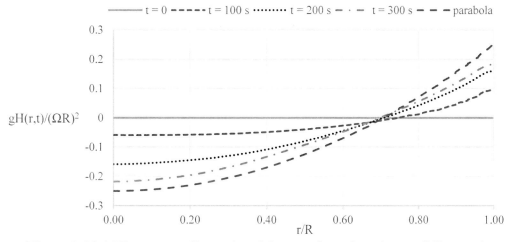

Figure 8.19e) Fluent non-dimensional free surface elevation at different times.

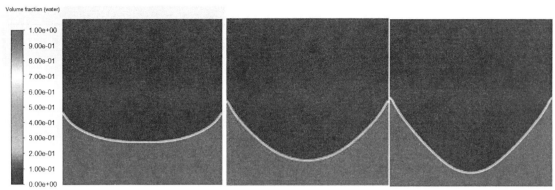

Figure 8.19f) Contours of water volume fraction at $t = 100$, 200, and 300 s

Figure 8.19g) Contours of swirl velocity at $t = 100$, 200, and 300 s

H. Theory

20. We start by defining the Reynolds number for this flow case as

$$Re = \frac{\Omega R^2}{v} = \frac{12*0.1524^2}{1.0038*10^{-6}} = 277,650 \tag{8.3}$$

where Ω (rad/s) is the angular velocity of the cylinder, R (m) is the inside radius of the cylindrical container and v (m²/s) is kinematic viscosity. Another non-dimensional number that is commonly used in the Ekman number that is the inverse of the Reynolds number. The initial height of water is $H_w = 0.099$ m and the initial height of air in the cylinder is $H_a = 0.2058$ m. The initial condition for the location of the free surface without rotation can be described as $Z(r,0) = H_w$. Next, we assume that the cylinder has been rotating long enough with constant angular velocity so that the fluid has attained solid-body rotation. We can then describe the shape of the surface as a parabola with the following function for the elevation of the free surface

$$Z(r, \infty) = H_w + \frac{\Omega^2}{2g}\left(r^2 - \frac{R^2}{2}\right) \tag{8.4}$$

We can now define the deviation for the height of the free surface from the initial height H_w as

$$H(r, \infty) = Z(r, \infty) - H_w = \frac{\Omega^2}{2g}\left(r^2 - \frac{R^2}{2}\right) \tag{8.5}$$

Then, we can modify equation (8.3) and define a non-dimensional variable related to the deviation of the free surface from the initial height, see Figure 8.19f).

$$\frac{gH(r,\infty)}{\Omega^2 R^2} = \frac{1}{2}\left[\left(\frac{r}{R}\right)^2 - \frac{1}{2}\right]$$

(8.6)

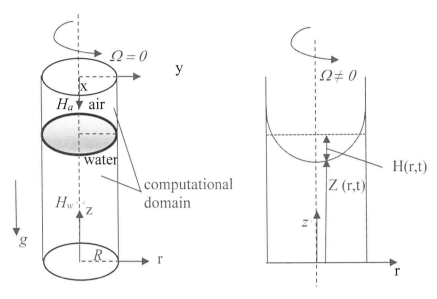

Figure 8.20 Geometry and shape of free surface for cylinder without and with solid body rotation

Generally, the incompressible Navier-Stokes equations in cylindrical coordinates (r, θ, z) with velocity components $\big(u_r(r, \theta, z, t), u_\theta(r, \theta, z, t), u_z(r, \theta, z, t)\big)$ are given by the following equations:

Continuity equation: $\quad \frac{1}{r}\frac{\partial(ru_r)}{\partial r} + \frac{1}{r}\frac{\partial u_\theta}{\partial \theta} + \frac{\partial u_z}{\partial z} = 0$

(8.7)

r-component: $\quad \rho\left(\frac{\partial u_r}{\partial t} + u_r\frac{\partial u_r}{\partial r} + \frac{u_\theta}{r}\frac{\partial u_r}{\partial \theta} - \frac{u_\theta^2}{r} + u_z\frac{\partial u_r}{\partial z}\right) =$

$-\frac{\partial p}{\partial r} + \mu\left[\frac{1}{r}\frac{\partial}{\partial r}\left(r\frac{\partial u_r}{\partial r}\right) - \frac{u_r}{r^2} + \frac{1}{r^2}\frac{\partial^2 u_r}{\partial \theta^2} - \frac{2}{r^2}\frac{\partial u_\theta}{\partial \theta} + \frac{\partial^2 u_r}{\partial z^2}\right]$

(8.8)

θ-component: $\quad \rho\left(\frac{\partial u_\theta}{\partial t} + u_r\frac{\partial u_\theta}{\partial r} + \frac{u_\theta}{r}\frac{\partial u_\theta}{\partial \theta} + \frac{u_r u_\theta}{r} + u_z\frac{\partial u_\theta}{\partial z}\right) =$

$-\frac{1}{r}\frac{\partial p}{\partial \theta} + \mu\left[\frac{1}{r}\frac{\partial}{\partial r}\left(r\frac{\partial u_\theta}{\partial r}\right) - \frac{u_\theta}{r^2} + \frac{1}{r^2}\frac{\partial^2 u_\theta}{\partial \theta^2} + \frac{2}{r^2}\frac{\partial u_r}{\partial \theta} + \frac{\partial^2 u_\theta}{\partial z^2}\right]$

(8.9)

z-component: $\quad \rho\left(\frac{\partial u_z}{\partial t} + u_r\frac{\partial u_z}{\partial r} + \frac{u_\theta}{r}\frac{\partial u_z}{\partial \theta} + u_z\frac{\partial u_z}{\partial z}\right) =$

$-\frac{\partial p}{\partial z} + \mu\left[\frac{1}{r}\frac{\partial}{\partial r}\left(r\frac{\partial u_z}{\partial r}\right) + \frac{1}{r^2}\frac{\partial^2 u_z}{\partial \theta^2} + \frac{\partial^2 u_z}{\partial z^2}\right]$

(8.10)

where ρ (kg/m³) is density, g (m/s²) is acceleration due to gravity and μ (kg/m-s) is dynamic viscosity. For axisymmetric flow there is no θ dependence for the velocity components so they can be expressed as $\big(u_r(r, z, t), u_\theta(r, z, t), u_z(r, z, t)\big)$. This will reduce the equations above to the following equations:

Continuity equation: $\quad \frac{1}{r}\frac{\partial(ru_r)}{\partial r} + \frac{\partial u_z}{\partial z} = 0$ (8.11)

r-component: $\quad \rho\left(\frac{\partial u_r}{\partial t} + u_r\frac{\partial u_r}{\partial r} - \frac{u_\theta^2}{r} + u_z\frac{\partial u_r}{\partial z}\right) =$
$$-\frac{\partial p}{\partial r} + \mu\left[\frac{1}{r}\frac{\partial}{\partial r}\left(r\frac{\partial u_r}{\partial r}\right) - \frac{u_r}{r^2} + \frac{\partial^2 u_r}{\partial z^2}\right]$$ (8.12)

θ-component: $\quad \rho\left(\frac{\partial u_\theta}{\partial t} + u_r\frac{\partial u_\theta}{\partial r} + \frac{u_r u_\theta}{r} + u_z\frac{\partial u_\theta}{\partial z}\right) =$
$$\mu\left[\frac{1}{r}\frac{\partial}{\partial r}\left(r\frac{\partial u_\theta}{\partial r}\right) - \frac{u_\theta}{r^2} + \frac{\partial^2 u_\theta}{\partial z^2}\right]$$ (8.13)

z-component: $\quad \rho\left(\frac{\partial u_z}{\partial t} + u_r\frac{\partial u_z}{\partial r} + u_z\frac{\partial u_z}{\partial z}\right) = -\frac{\partial p}{\partial z} + \mu\left[\frac{1}{r}\frac{\partial}{\partial r}\left(r\frac{\partial u_z}{\partial r}\right) + \frac{\partial^2 u_z}{\partial z^2}\right]$ (8.14)

We make the velocity components and pressure non-dimensional using the following relations:

$$u_r^* = u_r/\Omega R, u_\theta^* = u_\theta/\Omega R, u_z^* = u_z/\Omega R, p^* = p/\rho\Omega^2 R^2$$ (8.15)

and we make the coordinates non-dimensional using the following relations:

$$r^* = \frac{r}{R}, \theta^* = \theta, \; z^* = \frac{z}{R}, \; t^* = t\,\Omega$$ (8.16)

The continuity equation and the different component equations in non-dimensional form after skipping the $*$ superscript symbol:

$$\frac{\partial u_r}{\partial r} + \frac{u_r}{r} + \frac{\partial u_z}{\partial z} = 0$$ (8.17)

$$\frac{\partial u_r}{\partial t} + u_r\frac{\partial u_r}{\partial r} - \frac{u_\theta^2}{r} + u_z\frac{\partial u_r}{\partial z} = -\frac{\partial p}{\partial r} + \frac{1}{Re}\left[\frac{\partial^2 u_r}{\partial r^2} + \frac{1}{r}\frac{\partial u_r}{\partial r} - \frac{u_r}{r^2} + \frac{\partial^2 u_r}{\partial z^2}\right]$$ (8.18)

$$\frac{\partial u_\theta}{\partial t} + u_r\frac{\partial u_\theta}{\partial r} + \frac{u_r u_\theta}{r} + u_z\frac{\partial u_\theta}{\partial z} = \frac{1}{Re}\left[\frac{\partial^2 u_\theta}{\partial r^2} + \frac{1}{r}\frac{\partial u_\theta}{\partial r} - \frac{u_\theta}{r^2} + \frac{\partial^2 u_\theta}{\partial z^2}\right]$$ (8.19)

$$\frac{\partial u_z}{\partial t} + u_r\frac{\partial u_z}{\partial r} + u_z\frac{\partial u_z}{\partial z} = -\frac{\partial p}{\partial z} + \frac{1}{Re}\left[\frac{\partial^2 u_z}{\partial r^2} + \frac{1}{r}\frac{\partial u_z}{\partial r} + \frac{\partial^2 u_z}{\partial z^2}\right]$$ (8.20)

The boundary conditions excluding surface tension are the following:

$$u_r(0,z,t) = u_\theta(0,z,t) = \frac{\partial u_z(0,z,t)}{\partial r} = 0, \; , \; 0 \leq z \leq h(0,t)$$ (8.21)

$$u_r(1,z,t) = u_z(1,z,t) = 0, \; u_\theta(1,z,t) = 1, \; 0 \leq z \leq h(1,t)$$ (8.22)

$$p = \frac{\partial h}{\partial t} + u_r\frac{\partial h}{\partial r} - u_z = 0, \; z = h(r,t)$$ (8.23)

and the initial conditions are
$$u_r(r,z,0) = u_\theta(r,z,0) = u_z(r,z,0) = 0, \; 0 \leq r \leq 1, 0 \leq z \leq H_w/R$$ (8.24)

I. References

1. Greenspan, H.P. and Howard, L.N., "On a Time-Dependent Motion of a Rotating Fluid", *Journal of Fluid Mechanics,* **17**, 3, 385-404, (1963).
2. Kim, K.Y. and Hyun, J.M., "Solution for Spin-Up from Rest of Liquid with a Free Surface", *AIAA Journal,* **34**, 7, 1441-1446, (1996).
3. Van de Konijnenberg, J.A, van Heijst, G.J.F., "Nonlinear spin-up in a circular cylinder", *Phys. Fluids,* **7** (12), (1995).

J. Exercises

8.1 Use ANSYS Fluent to continue running the simulations in this chapter and include free surface elevation plots at $t = 150$ s and $t = 200$ s as shown in Figures 8.19f) and 8.19g). Include contours of water volume fraction and swirl velocity at $t = 150$ and 200 s.

8.2 Use ANSYS Fluent to rerun the calculations shown in this chapter but change the rotational speed to 8 rad/s. Include free surface elevation plots at $t = 100$, 150 and 200 s as shown in Figures 8.19f) and 8.19g). Include contours of water volume fraction and swirl velocity at $t = 100$, 150 and 200 s. Determine the Reynolds number.

8.3 Use ANSYS Fluent to rerun the calculations shown in this chapter but change the rotational speed to 16 rad/s. Include free surface elevation plots at $t = 100$, 150 and 200 s as shown in Figures 8.19f) and 8.19g). Include contours of water volume fraction and swirl velocity at $t = 100$, 150 and 200 s. Determine the Reynolds number.

8.4 Use ANSYS Fluent to rerun the calculations shown in this chapter but change the rotational speed to 10 rad/s. Also, change the radius of the cylinder to R = 0.2 m with everything else being the same. Include free surface elevation plots at $t = 100$, 150 and 200 s as shown in Figures 8.19f) and 8.19g). Include contours of water volume fraction and swirl velocity at $t = 100$, 150 and 200 s. Determine the Reynolds number.

8.5 Use ANSYS Fluent to rerun the calculations shown in this chapter but change the rotational speed to 10 rad/s. Also, change the geometry to a frustum shape with bottom radius of the cylinder $R_{bottom} = 0.1$ m and top radius $R_{top} = 0.2$ m with everything else being the same. Include free surface elevation plots at $t = 100$, 150 and 200 s as shown in Figures 8.19f) and 8.19g). Include contours of water volume fraction and swirl velocity at $t = 100$, 150 and 200 s. Determine the Reynolds number based on the average radius.

Notes:

CHAPTER 9. KELVIN-HELMHOLTZ INSTABILITY

A. Objectives

- Using ANSYS Workbench to Create Geometry and Mesh for Kelvin-Helmholtz Instability
- Inserting Wall Boundary Conditions and an Acceleration Due to Gravity Vector Corresponding to a Tilt Angle of 4 degrees for the Tube.
- Using Volume of Fluid Model for Multiphase Flow with Surface Tension
- Running Laminar Transient 2D Planar ANSYS Fluent Simulations
- Using Contour Plots of Volume Fraction and a Movie for Visualizations

B. Problem Description

The Kelvin-Helmholtz instability is a classical problem originally studied by Helmholtz[1] and Kelvin[2]. The mechanism causing the instability has been studied in detail by Lamb[3], Bachelor[4], Drazin and Reid[5], Chandrasekahr[6], Craik[7], and many others. The Kelvin-Helmholtz instability can appear at the interface of two fluid layers flowing with different velocities and with different densities. For a complete review of this instability, please see Thorpe[8]. Thorpe[9-12] found that the Kelvin-Helmholtz instability can be generated and visualized by tilting a tube that contains two fluids at different densities.

We will study the Kelvin-Helmholtz instability and analyze the problem using ANSYS Fluent. The length of the tube is 2,400 mm and the diameter 200 mm.

(fresh water) $\rho_1 = 998.2$ kg/m^3, $\mu_1 = 0.001002$ kg/ms, $\gamma_1 = 0.07274$ N/m

(salt water) $\rho_2 = 1074.9$ kg/m^3, $\mu_2 = 0.001259$ kg/ms, $\gamma_2 = 0.07422$ N/m

C. Launching ANSYS Workbench and Selecting Fluent

1. Start by launching the ANSYS Workbench. Double click on Fluid Flow (Fluent) under Analysis Systems in the Toolbox.

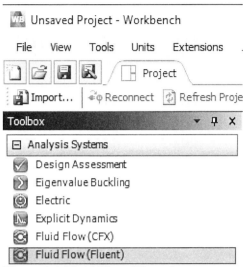

Figure 9.1 Fluid Flow (Fluent)

D. Launching ANSYS DesignModeler

2. Right click on Geometry in the Project Schematic and select Properties. Select 2D Analysis Type under Advanced Geometry Options in Properties of Schematic A2: Geometry. Right click on Geometry and select New DesignModeler Geometry. Select Units>>Millimeter from the menu as the length unit in DesignModeler.

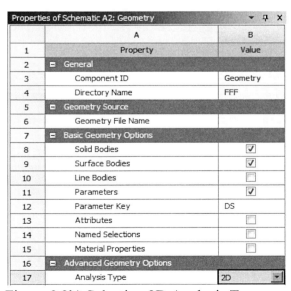

Figure 9.2a) Selecting Geometry   Figure 9.2b) Selecting 2D Analysis Type

3. Next, we will be creating the mesh for the simulation. Select XYPlane from the Tree Outline. Select Look at Sketch 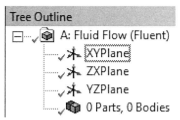. Click on the Sketching tab on the left-hand side. Select Draw and sketch a Rectangle from the origin. Select the Dimensions tab in the Sketching Toolboxes. Select one of the vertical edges of the rectangle and enter a length of 200 mm. Select one of the horizontal edges of the rectangle and enter a length of 2400 mm.

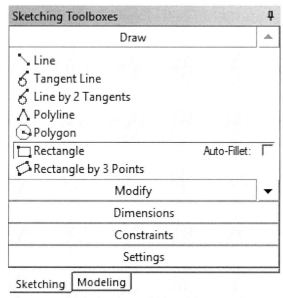

Figure 9.3a) Selection of XYPlane

Figure 9.3b) Selection of Sketching Toolboxes and Rectangle

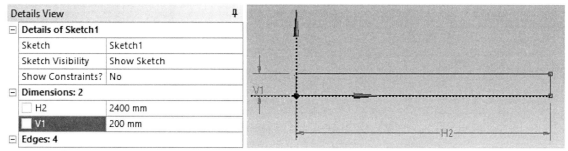

Figure 9.3c) Dimensions for rectangle in Details View

193

4. Click on the Modeling tab. Select Concept>>Surfaces from Sketches from the menu. Select Sketch1 under XYPlane in the Tree Outline on the left and select Apply as Base Objects in Details View. Click on Generate in the toolbar. The rectangle turns gray. Right click in the graphics window and select Zoom to Fit. Close the DesignModeler window.

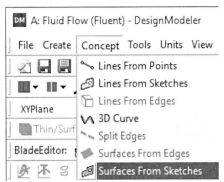

Figure 9.4a) Selecting Surfaces from Sketches

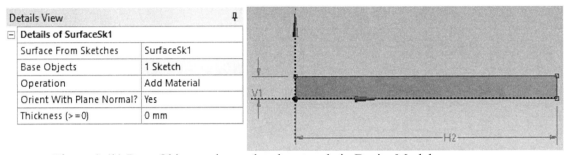

Figure 9.4b) Base Object and completed rectangle in DesignModeler

E. Launching ANSYS Meshing

5. We are now going to double click on Mesh in ANSYS Workbench to open the Meshing window. Select Mesh in the Outline. Click on Update under Mesh in the menu. A coarse mesh is created.

Select Mesh>>Controls>>Face Meshing from the menu. Click on the rectangle in the graphics window that turns green. Select the yellow region next to Geometry that is labeled No Selection and click on the Apply button for Geometry in Details of "Face Meshing".

Select Mesh>>Controls>>Sizing from the menu and select the Edge ⬚ selection filter. Click on the upper horizontal edge of the rectangle and control select the lower horizontal edge. Click on Apply for the Geometry in "Details of Edge Sizing". Under Definition in "Details of Edge Sizing", select Number of Divisions as Type, 480 as Number of Divisions, and Hard as Behavior.

Repeat the selection of Mesh>>Controls>>Sizing from the menu and control-select the two vertical edges of the rectangle. Enter 40 for Number of Divisions and Hard Behavior. Choose the Bias Type ----- --- - --- ----- and enter 3.0 as Bias Factor. Select Mesh>>Update in the menu and select Mesh in the Outline. The finished mesh is shown in the graphics window.

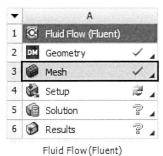

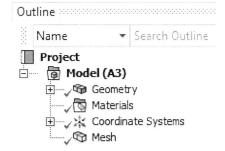

Figure 9.5a) Starting Mesh   Figure 9.5b) Selection of Mesh in Outline

Figure 9.5c) Coarse mesh

Figure 9.5d) Face Meshing

Figure 9.5e) Applied Geometry in Details

Figure 9.5f) Mesh Control Sizing

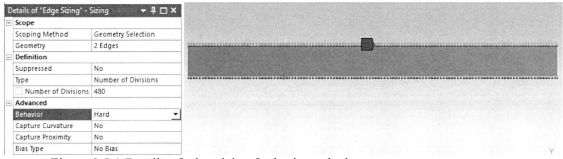

Figure 9.5g) Details of edge sizing for horizontal edges

195

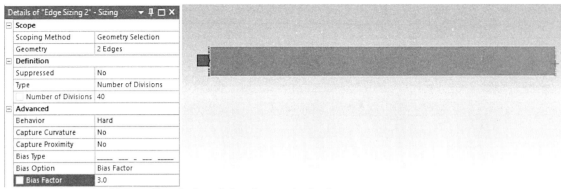

Figure 9.5h) Details of edge sizing for vertical edges

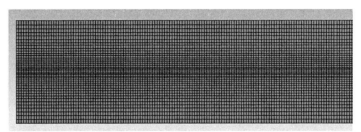

Figure 9.5i) Details of finished mesh

6. We are now going to rename the edges for the rectangle. Select the Edge filter ⬚ and control-select the four edges of the rectangle, right click and select Create Named Selection. Enter *wall* as the name for the selection group and click on the OK button.

Select File>>Export...>>Mesh>>FLUENT Input File>>Export from the menu and save the mesh with the name "*khi-mesh.msh*" in the working directory. Select File>>Save Project from the menu and save the project with the name "Kelvin-Helmholtz Instability". Close the Meshing window. Right click on Mesh in ANSYS Workbench in the Project Schematic and select Update.

Figure 9.6a) Selection of a name for the four edges of the rectangle

Figure 9.6b) Named selections

F. Launching ANSYS Fluent

7. Double-click on Setup under Project Schematic in ANSYS Workbench. Select Double Precision and select Parallel Processing Options. Set the number of Processes equal to the number of processor cores for your computer. Click on the plus sign next to Show More Options and take a note of the location of the Working Directory. Click on the OK button in the Fluent Launcher window.

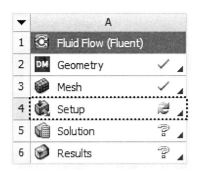

Figure 9.7a) Starting Setup

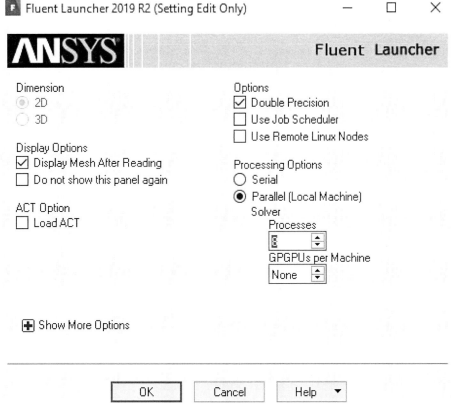

Figure 9.7b) Fluent launcher window

8. Check the mesh by selecting the Check button under Mesh in General on Task Page. Check the scale of the mesh by selecting the Scale button. Make sure that the Domain Extent is correct and close the Scale Mesh window.

Figure 9.8a) Mesh Check

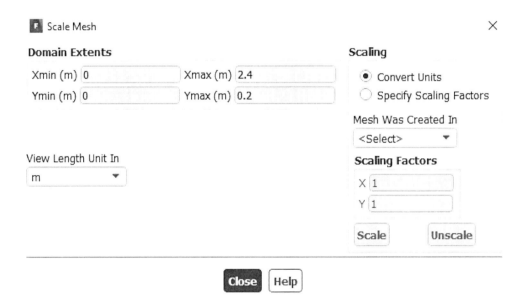

Figure 9.8b) Scale Mesh window

9. Select Transient Time for the Solver in General on the Task Page. Check the Gravity box and enter -9.71453 m/s2 as the Gravitational Acceleration in the Y direction. Enter -1.365288 m/s2 as the Gravitational Acceleration in the X direction. These components correspond to a tilt angle of 8 degrees for the tube.

Open Models and double click on Multiphase (Off) under Setup in the Outline View. Select the Volume of Fluid Model. Click OK to exit the Multiphase Model window.

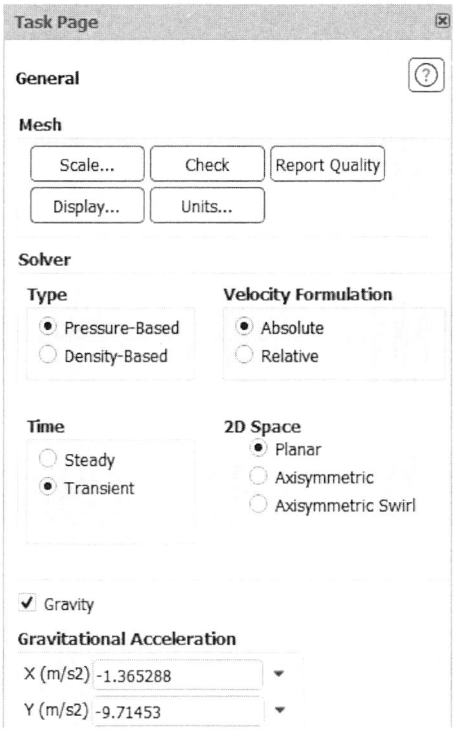

Task Page

General

Mesh

| Scale... | Check | Report Quality |
| Display... | Units... |

Solver

Type
- ● Pressure-Based
- ○ Density-Based

Velocity Formulation
- ● Absolute
- ○ Relative

Time
- ○ Steady
- ● Transient

2D Space
- ● Planar
- ○ Axisymmetric
- ○ Axisymmetric Swirl

☑ Gravity

Gravitational Acceleration

X (m/s2) -1.365288

Y (m/s2) -9.71453

Outline View

Filter Text

⊖ **Setup**
- General
- ⊖ Models
  - **Multiphase (Off)**
  - Energy (Off)
  - Viscous (Laminar)
  - Radiation (Off)
  - Heat Exchanger (Off)
  - Species (Off)
  - ⊕ Discrete Phase (Off)
  - Solidification & Melting (Off)
  - Acoustics (Off)
  - Structure (Off)
  - Electric Potential (Off)

Figure 9.9a) General Setup

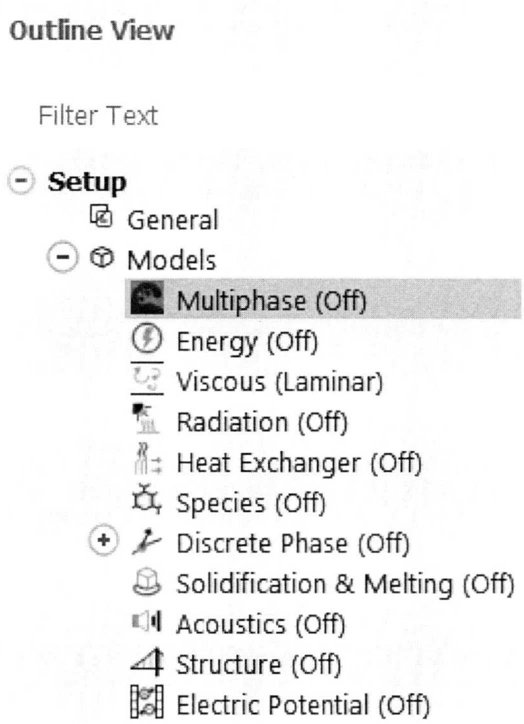

Figure 9.9b) Models Problem Setup

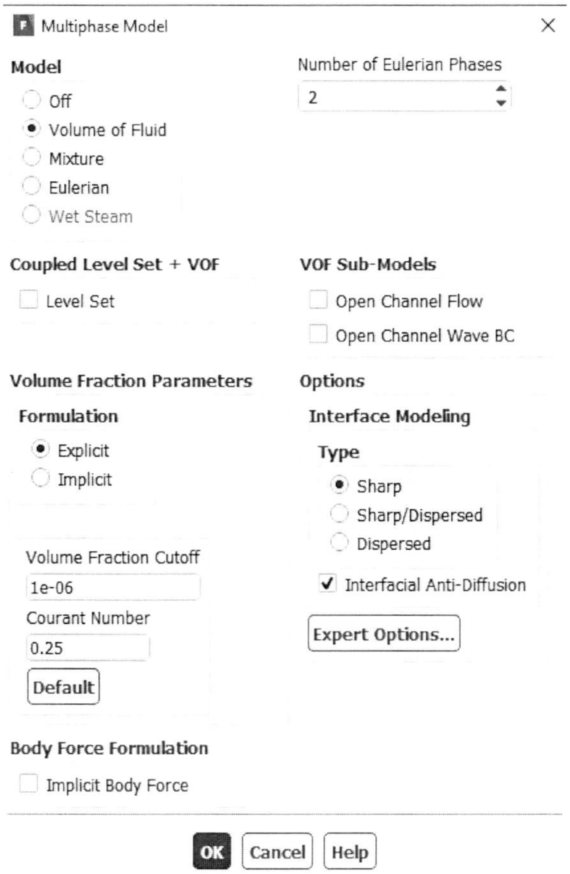

Multiphase Model ✕

Model
- ○ Off
- ● Volume of Fluid
- ○ Mixture
- ○ Eulerian
- ○ Wet Steam

Number of Eulerian Phases

2

Coupled Level Set + VOF
- ☐ Level Set

VOF Sub-Models
- ☐ Open Channel Flow
- ☐ Open Channel Wave BC

Volume Fraction Parameters

Formulation
- ● Explicit
- ○ Implicit

Volume Fraction Cutoff

1e-06

Courant Number

0.25

Default

Options

Interface Modeling

Type
- ● Sharp
- ○ Sharp/Dispersed
- ○ Dispersed

☑ Interfacial Anti-Diffusion

Expert Options...

Body Force Formulation
- ☐ Implicit Body Force

OK | Cancel | Help

Figure 9.9c) Multiphase model

10. Double click on Materials under Setup in the Outline View. Click on the Create/Edit button for Fluid on the Task Page to open the Create/Edit Materials window. Click on Fluent Database. Scroll down in the Fluent Fluid Materials window and select *water-liquid (h2o<l>)*. Click on the Copy button and Close the Fluent Database Materials window. Click on the Change/Create button and the Close button in the Create/Edit Materials window.

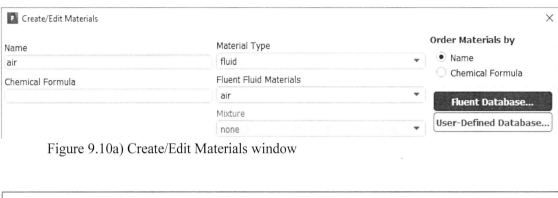

Figure 9.10a) Create/Edit Materials window

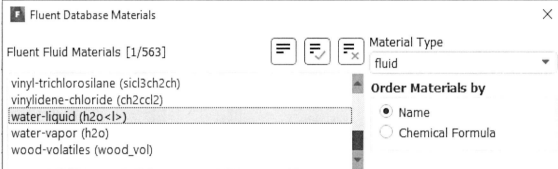

Figure 9.10b) Selecting water-liquid as FLUENT Fluid Material

Repeat these steps above and select *water-liquid*. You will get a New Material Name window when you click on the Copy button in the Fluent Database Materials window. Enter *salt-water-liquid* as the New Name and click OK. Close the Fluent Database Materials window. Click on the Change/Create button and the Close button in the Create/Edit Materials window.

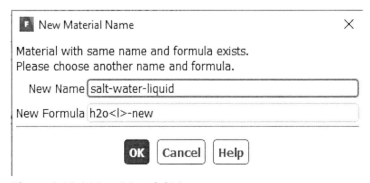

Figure 9.10c) New Material Name

11. Open Models, Multiphase (Volume of Fluid) and Phases under Setup in the Outline View. Double click on phase-1-Primary Phase. Select *water-liquid* from Phase Materials and enter *fresh-water* as the name of the Primary Phase. Click on the OK button to exit.

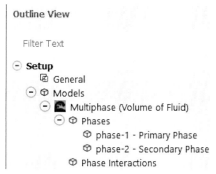

Figure 9.11a) Phases Problem Setup

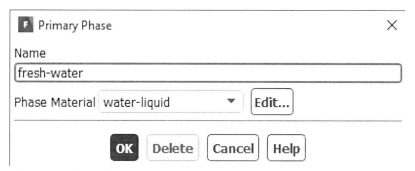

Figure 9.11b) Primary Phase Setup

Repeat these steps for the Secondary Phase to select *salt-water-liquid* and enter the name *salt-water*.

Double click on Phase Interactions under Models and Multiphase in Setup. Click on the Surface Tension tab, check the Surface Tension Force Modeling box, select constant from the Surface Tension Coefficients drop down menu, enter the value 0.00148 n/m and click on the OK button.

Select salt-water-liquid under Materials and Fluid on the Task Page and click on Create/Edit. Enter 1074.9 as Density (kg/m3) and 0.001259 as Viscosity (kg/m-s). Click on Change/Create and Close the window. For a reference of the dynamic viscosity value used for the salt-water, see Sharqawy, Lienhard, and Zubair[13].

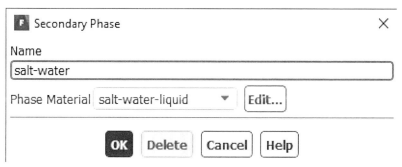

Figure 9.11c) Secondary Phase Setup

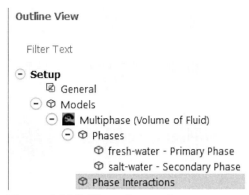

Figure 9.11d) Phase Interactions

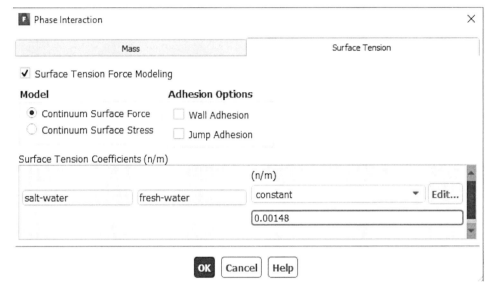

Figure 9.11e) Phase interaction window

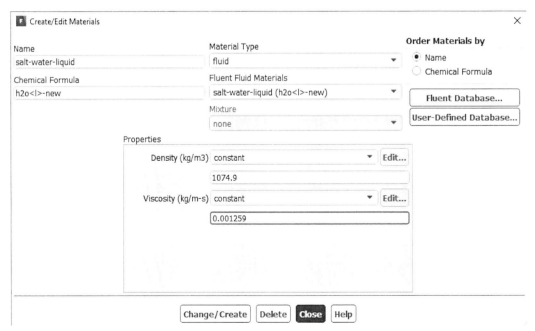

Figure 9.11f) Values of density and viscosity for salt-water

12. Double click on Methods under Solution in the Tree. Select Default settings except for First Order Upwind for Momentum. Double click on Initialization under Solution in the Outline View, select Standard Initialization and click on Initialize.

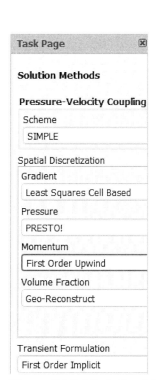

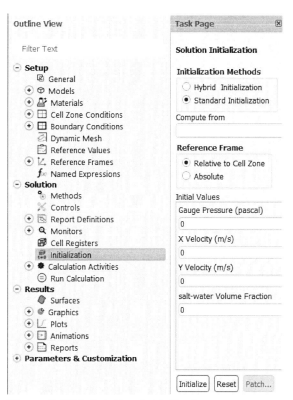

Figure 9.12a) Solution Methods   Figure 9.12b) Solution Initialization

13. Select the Domain tab in the menu and select Adapt>>Refine/Coarsen…. Select Cell Registers>>New>>Region in the Adaption Controls window. Enter 2.4 for X Max, and 0.1 for Y Max. Click on the Save button to close the window. Click OK to close the Adaption Controls window.

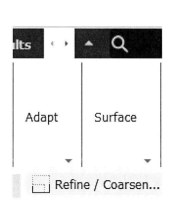

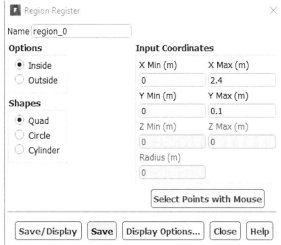

Figure 9.13a) Adapting a Region   Figure 9.13b) Region Adaption Settings

Click on the Patch… button on the Task Page for Solution Initialization and select *salt-water* as the phase. Select Volume Fraction as the Variable and region_0 as Registers to Patch. Set the value to 1 and click on the Patch button.

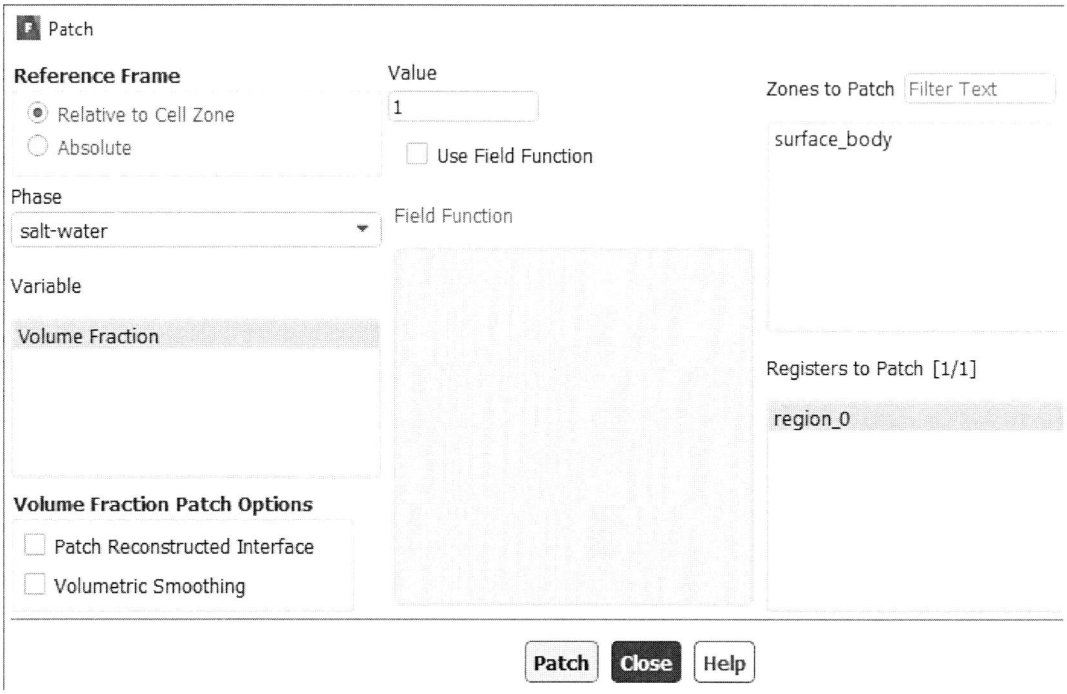

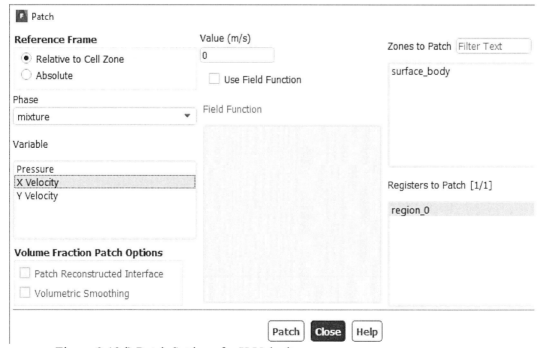

Figure 9.13c) Patch Settings for Volume Fraction

Select mixture for the phase. Select X Velocity as the Variable and region_0 as Registers to Patch. Set the value to 0 and click on the Patch button and close the window.

Figure 9.13d) Patch Settings for X Velocity

14. Open Graphics and double click on Contours under Results in the Outline View. Select Phases and Volume fraction under Contours of and select *fresh-water* as the Phase. Click on Colormap Options and select Top as Colormap Alignment. Set Type to float and Precision to 1 as Number Format. Click on Apply and Close the Colormap window. Click on the Save/Display button and Close the window.

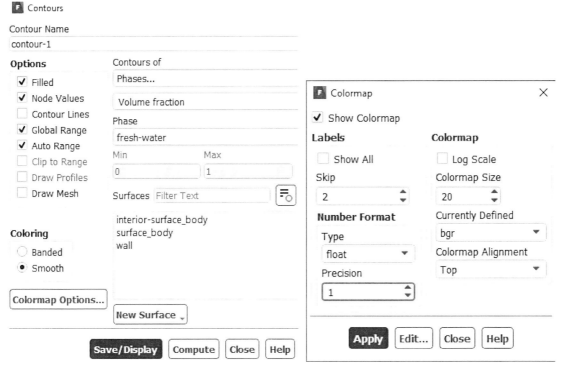

Figure 9.14a) Contours and colormap settings

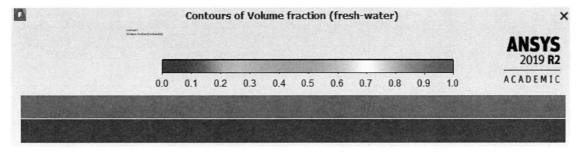

Figure 9.14b) Contours of Volume Fraction (fresh-water)

15. Open Calculation Activities and double click on Solution Animations under Solution in the Outline View. Enter *khi-animation* as the name and select *contour-1* as Animation Object. Set Record after every to 10 time-step. Click on the OK button to close the Animation Definition window.

    Double click on Run Calculation under Solution, enter 0.01 as Time Step Size, and 200 for Number of Time Steps. Click on the Calculate button. Click OK when the calculation is complete.

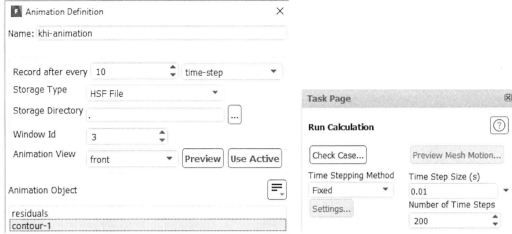

Figure 9.15a) Animation definition window   Figure 9.15b) Running calculations

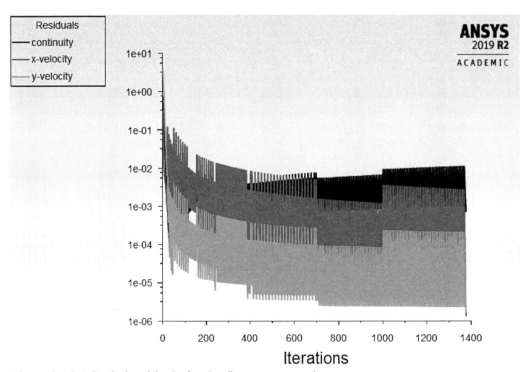

Figure 9.15c) Scaled residuals for the first two seconds.

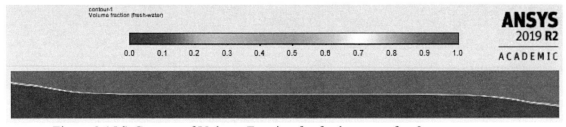

Figure 9.15d) Contour of Volume Fraction for fresh-water after 2 s

G. Post-Processing

16. Enter 100 for Number of Time Steps and continue running the calculations twice followed by entering 50 for the Number of Time Steps. Next, continue running the calculations six more times for a total of 7 seconds. These ANSYS Fluent simulations can be compared with experiments of this instability, see Matsson and Boiselle[14].

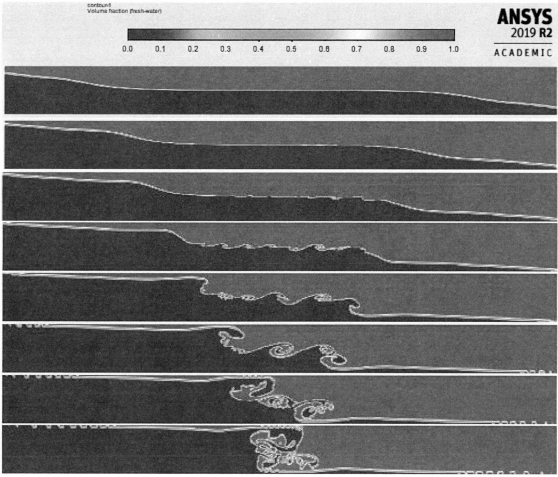

Figure 9.16a) Contour of Volume Fraction for fresh-water after 3, 4, 4.5, 5, 5.5, 6, 6.5, 7 s

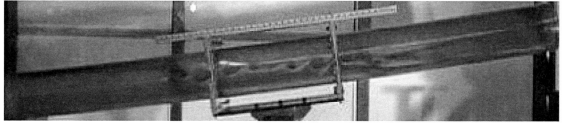

Figure 9.16b) Experiments of Kelvin-Helmholtz instability at t = 5.0 s (8° tilt angle), from Matsson and Boisselle[1]

Select File>>Write>Case & Data… from the menu. Save the file with the name *khi-computation.cas*.

Double click on Animations and Solution Animation Playback under Results in the Outline View. Set the Replay Speed to low and select Play Once as Playback Mode. Select MPEG as Write/Record Format. Click on the Write button. This will create the mpeg movie in your working directory. Close the Playback window. The movie can be viewed using, for example, VLC Media Player.

In VLC Media Player select Media>>Open File… from the menu. Open the movie from the working directory. Select Playback>>Speed>>Slower several times from the menu in the VLC Media Player until you have a suitable speed for the movie.

H. Theory

17. We will look at the inviscid theory for the Kelvin-Helmholtz instability in terms of a sinusoidal disturbance between two fluids with velocities U_1, U_2 and densities ρ_1, ρ_2.

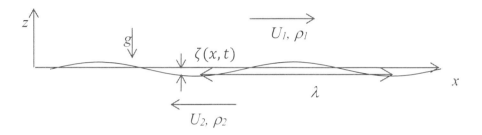

Figure 9.17 Development of Kelvin Helmholtz instability from a perturbation

The velocity vector in a Cartesian coordinate system can be described as

$$\bar{U} = u_x \bar{e}_x + u_y \bar{e}_y + u_z \bar{e}_z \tag{9.1}$$

where u_x, $u_y = 0$ and u_z are the velocity components in the streamwise, spanwise and normal directions, respectively. Euler equations of motion can be written as

$$\frac{\partial u_x}{\partial t} + u_x \frac{\partial u_x}{\partial x} + u_z \frac{\partial u_x}{\partial z} = -\frac{1}{\rho} \frac{\partial P}{\partial x} \tag{9.2}$$

$$\frac{\partial u_z}{\partial t} + u_x \frac{\partial u_z}{\partial x} + u_z \frac{\partial u_z}{\partial z} = -\frac{1}{\rho} \frac{\partial P}{\partial z} - g \tag{9.3}$$

$$\frac{\partial u_x}{\partial x} + \frac{\partial u_z}{\partial z} = 0 \tag{9.4}$$

The velocity components can be divided into mean flow components in the main streamwise direction plus a perturbation

$$\bar{U} = (U(z) + u)\bar{e}_x + w\bar{e}_z \tag{9.5}$$

and the pressure is $\qquad P = P_0 - \rho g z + p \tag{9.6}$

A perturbation is introduced in the form

$$u, w, p = [u_n(z), w_n(z), p_n(z)]e^{i(kx-\omega t)} \tag{9.7}$$

where k is the streamwise wave number, ω is the frequency and $u_n(z), w_n(z), p_n(z)$ are eigenfunctions. The linearized Euler equations can be written as

$$i(kU - \omega)u_n + \frac{ik}{\rho}p_n = 0 \tag{9.8}$$

$$i(kU - \omega)w_n + \frac{1}{\rho}p_n' = 0 \tag{9.9}$$

$$iku_n + w_n' = 0 \tag{9.10}$$

From equations (9.8) – (9.10) we can find the equation for w_n

$$w_n'' - k^2 w_n = 0 \tag{9.11}$$

with the general solution

$$w_n = c_1 e^{-kz} + c_2 e^{kz} \tag{9.12}$$

To get exponentially decaying solutions far from the interface, we set c_1 and c_2 equal to zero in the lower and upper layers, respectively. The interface location is defined by

$$z = \zeta(x, t) = ae^{i(kx-\omega t)} \tag{9.13}$$

The normal velocity w at the interface is given by the material derivative of $\zeta(x, t)$

$$w = w_n(z)e^{i(kx-\omega t)} = \frac{D\zeta}{Dt} = \frac{\partial \zeta}{\partial t} + U\frac{\partial \zeta}{\partial x} =$$
$$i(kU - \omega)\,\zeta = i(kU - \omega)ae^{i(kx-\omega t)} \tag{9.14}$$

, we find that $c_1 = i(kU_1 - \omega)a$, $c_2 = -i(kU_2 + \omega)a$

$$w_{n,1} = i(kU_1 - \omega)ae^{-kz}$$
$$w_{n,2} = -i(kU_2 + \omega)ae^{kz} \tag{9.15}$$

We can now find the pressure eigenfunctions in the upper and lower layers from equation (9.9).

$$p_{n,1} = -\rho_1(kU_1 - \omega)^2 ae^{-kz}/k$$
$$p_{n,2} = \rho_2(kU_2 + \omega)^2 ae^{kz}/k \tag{9.16}$$

Next, we use equation (9.6) and set the pressures identical at the interface to get the dispersion relation

$$P_0 - \rho_1 g\zeta + p_{n,1}e^{i(kx-\omega t)} = P_0 - \rho_2 g\zeta + p_{n,2}e^{i(kx-\omega t)} \tag{9.17}$$

$$(\rho_2 - \rho_1)gk = \rho_2(kU_2 + \omega)^2 + \rho_1(kU_1 - \omega)^2 \tag{9.18}$$

and we find the following equation for the frequency

$$\omega = \frac{k}{\rho_1 + \rho_2}[(\rho_1 U_1 - \rho_2 U_2) \pm \sqrt{\frac{2(\rho_2^2 - \rho_1^2)g}{k} - \rho_1 \rho_2 (U_1 + U_2)^2}] \qquad (9.19)$$

The frequency is complex with the associated growth of Kelvin-Helmholtz instability waves when the expression under the square root is negative

$$\frac{2(\rho_2^2 - \rho_1^2)g}{k} < \rho_1 \rho_2 (U_1 + U_2)^2 \qquad (9.20)$$

Using the definition of wave number as inversely proportional to the wave-length

$$k = \frac{2\pi}{\lambda} \qquad (9.21)$$

We find that waves are amplified and develop when their wave-length fulfills the following condition as shown in equation (9.22). A boundary below or above the interface can destabilize the flow as shown by Hazel[15].

$$\lambda < \frac{\pi \rho_1 \rho_2 (U_1 + U_2)^2}{g(\rho_2^2 - \rho_1^2)} \qquad (9.22)$$

I. References

1. Helmholtz H. "On discontinuous movement of fluids", *Phil. Mag.* (4) **36**, 337, (1868).
2. Kelvin L. "Hydrokinetic solutions and observations", *Phil. Mag.* (4) **42**, 362, (1871).
3. Lamb H. "Hydrodynamics", *Cambridge University Press*, (1932).
4. Batchelor G.K. "An introduction to fluid dynamics", *Cambridge University Press*, (1967).
5. Drazin P.G. and Reid W.H. "Introduction to hydrodynamic instability", *Cambridge University Press*, (1981).
6. Chandrasekhar S. "Hydrodynamic and Hydromagnetic Stability", *Dover Publications, Inc.*, New York (1961).
7. Craik A.D.D. "Wave interactions and fluid flows", *Cambridge University Press*, (1985).
8. Thorpe S.A. "Transitional phenomena and the development of turbulence in stratified fluids: a review", *J. Geophys. Res.*, **92**, 5231 (1987).
9. Thorpe S.A. "A method of producing a shear flow in a stratified fluid", *J. Fluid Mech.*, **32**, 693 (1968).
10. Thorpe S.A. "Experiments on the instability of stratified shear flows: miscible fluids", *J. Fluid Mech.*, **46**, 299 (1971).
11. Thorpe S.A. "Turbulence in stably stratified fluids: a review of laboratory experiments", *Boundary-Layer Meteorol.*, **5**, 95 (1973).
12. Thorpe S.A. "Experiments on the instability and turbulence in a stratified shear flow", *J. Fluid Mech.*, **61**, 731 (1973).
13. Sharqawy M.H, Lienhard J.H., and Zubair S.M. "Thermophysical Properties of Sea Water: A Review of existing Correlations and Data, Desalination, and Water Treatment", *Desalination and Water Treatment*, **16**, 354 (2010).
14. Matsson J. and Boisselle J. "A Senior Design Project on the Kelvin-Helmholtz Instability", 122nd ASEE Annual Conference and Exposition, June 14-17, 2015, Seattle, WA.
15. Hazel P. "Numerical Studies of the stability of inviscid stratified shear flows", *J. Fluid Mech.*, **51**, 39 (1972).

J. Exercises

9.1 Run the ANSYS Fluent simulations for a tube tilt angle of 4 degrees and show the development of the instability using contours of volume fraction for fresh water for the same fluids as used in this chapter.

9.2. Run the ANSYS Fluent simulations for a tube tilt angle of 12 degrees and show the development of the instability using contours of volume fraction for fresh water for the same fluids as used in this chapter.

9.3 Run the ANSYS Fluent simulations shown in this chapter but instead use a transient 3D geometry and mesh for the model. Use a tube tilt angle of 4 degrees and use contours of volume fraction for fresh water to visualize the flow for the same fluids as used in this chapter.

9.4 Run the ANSYS Fluent simulations shown in this chapter but instead use a transient 3D geometry and mesh for the model. Use a tube tilt angle of 8 degrees and use contours of volume fraction for fresh water to visualize the flow for the same fluids as used in this chapter.

9.5 Run the ANSYS Fluent simulations shown in this chapter but instead use a transient 3D geometry and mesh for the model. Use a tube tilt angle of 12 degrees and use contours of volume fraction for fresh water to visualize the flow for the same fluids as used in this chapter.

Notes:

CHAPTER 10. RAYLEIGH-TAYLOR INSTABILITY

A. Objectives

- Using ANSYS Workbench to Create Geometry and Mesh for Rayleigh-Taylor Instability
- Inserting Symmetry and Wall Boundary Conditions
- Using Volume of Fluid Model for Multiphase Flow
- Using a User Defined Function to Trigger the Rayleigh-Taylor Instability
- Running Laminar Transient 2D Planar ANSYS Fluent Simulations
- Using Contour Plots of Volume Fractions and a Movie for Visualizations

B. Problem Description

We will study the Rayleigh-Taylor instability and will analyze the problem using ANSYS. The Geometry for Rayleigh-Taylor instability (total height 1 m, width 0.25 m) is shown below. The heavier fluid is initially on top of the lighter fluid.

Salt-water
$\rho_1 = 1075$ kg/m^3
$\mu_1 = 0.00126$ kg/m-s

$H = 1$ m

Fresh-water
$\rho_2 = 998.2$ kg/m^3
$\mu_2 = 0.001$ kg/m-s

$D = 0.25$ m

C. Launching ANSYS Workbench and Selecting Fluent

1. Start by launching ANSYS Workbench. Double click on Fluid Flow (Fluent).

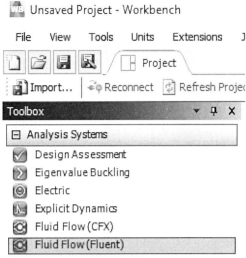

Figure 10.1 Selecting Fluent

D. Launching ANSYS DesignModeler

2. Right click on Geometry under Project Schematic in ANSYS Workbench and select Properties. Select 2D Analysis Type under Advanced Geometry Options in Properties of Schematic A2: Geometry. Right click on Geometry and select New DesignModeler Geometry to open ANSYS DesignModeler. **Select Units>>Millimeter from the menu as the length unit in DesignModeler.**

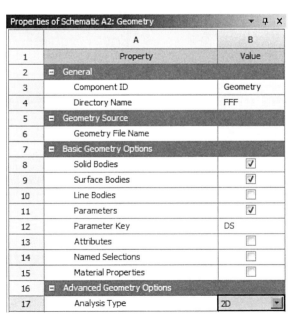

Figure 10.2a) Selecting Geometry   Figure 10.2b) Selecting 2D Analysis Type

3.   Next, we will be creating the mesh for the simulation. Select XYPlane in the Tree Outline. Select Look at Sketch 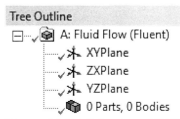 . Click on the Sketching tab and Draw a Rectangle from the origin. Select the Dimensions tab in the Sketching Toolboxes. Click on one of the vertical edges of the rectangle and enter a vertical length of 1,000 mm. Click on one of the horizontal edges and a horizontal length of 250 mm.

Figure 10.3a) Selection of XYPlane in the Tree Outline

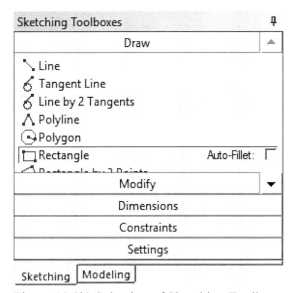

Figure 10.3b) Selection of Sketching Toolboxes and Rectangle

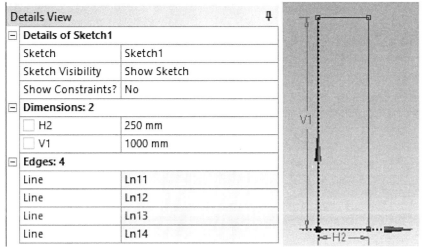

Figure 10.3c) Dimensions in Details View

4. Click on the Modeling tab and select Concept>>Surfaces from Sketches in the menu. Open XYPlane in the Tree Outline, select Sketch1 as Base Objects and select Apply in Details View. Click on ⚡Generate in the toolbar. The rectangle turns gray. Right click in the graphics window, select Zoom to Fit and close DesignModeler.

Figure 10.4 Completed rectangle in DesignModeler

E. Launching ANSYS Meshing

5. We are now going to double click on Mesh in ANSYS Workbench to open the Meshing window. Select Mesh in the Outline. Click on Update. A coarse mesh is created. Select Mesh>>Controls>>Face Meshing from the menu. Click on the rectangle in the graphics window. Apply the Geometry in Details of "Face Meshing".

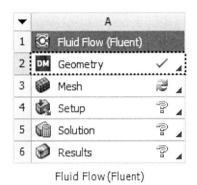

Figure 10.5a) Starting Mesh

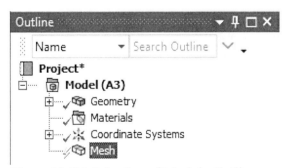

Figure 10.5b) Selection of Mesh in Outline

Figure 10.5c) Generation of Face Meshing

Details of "Face Meshing" - Mapped Fa ▼ 廿 □ ✕	
Scope	
Scoping Method	Geometry Selection
Geometry	1 Face
Definition	
Suppressed	No
Mapped Mesh	Yes
Method	Quadrilaterals
Constrain Boundary	No
Advanced	
Specified Sides	No Selection
Specified Corners	No Selection
Specified Ends	No Selection

Figure 10.5d) Applying Geometry in Details of "Face Meshing"

6. Select Mesh>>Controls>>Sizing from the menu and select Edge . Control-select the four edges of the rectangle. Click on Apply for the Geometry in "Details of Edge Sizing". Under Definition in "Details of Edge Sizing", select Element Size as Type, 2.0 mm as Element Size, and Hard as Behavior. Click on Update and select Mesh in the Outline. The finished mesh is shown below.

Figure 10.6a) Mesh Control Sizing

Details of "Edge Sizing" - Sizing ▼ 廿 □ ✕	
Scope	
Scoping Method	Geometry Selection
Geometry	4 Edges
Definition	
Suppressed	No
Type	Element Size
Element Size	2.0 mm
Advanced	
Behavior	Hard
Capture Curvature	No
Capture Proximity	No
Bias Type	No Bias

Figure 10.6b) Details of "Edge Sizing"

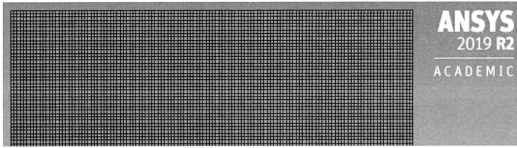

Figure 10.6c) Details of finished mesh

7. We are now going to rename the edges for the rectangle. Use the Edge tool , control-select the left and right edges of the rectangle, right click and select Create Named Selection. Enter *symmetry* as the name and click on the OK button.

Repeat this step for the upper and lower horizontal edges (control select both edges) of the rectangle and name them *wall*. Select File>>Export...>>Mesh>>FLUENT Input File>>Export from the menu and save the mesh with the name "*rt-mesh.msh*". Select File>>Save Project from the menu. Save the project with the name "Rayleigh-Taylor-Instability". Select File>>Close Meshing. Right click on Mesh under Project Schematic in ANSYS Workbench and select Update.

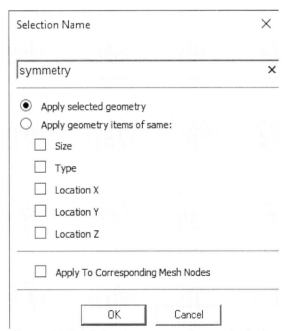

Figure 10.7a) Selecting a name for vertical edges

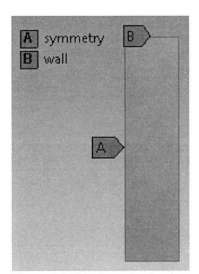

Figure 10.7b) Named selections

F. Preparation for Compiling UDFs in Windows 7 or Windows 10

8. If you are using Windows 10, please proceed with step 9.

   Using Windows 7, select Windows ![] in the lower left corner on your computer monitor and click on ![Control Panel]. Double click on ![] Programs and Features and uninstall all programs with "Microsoft Visual C++ 2010…".

   Download Microsoft Windows SDK from the following link
   https://www.microsoft.com/en-us/download/details.aspx?id=8279
   and run the installer. For the installation options, only install "Windows Headers and Libraries" and "Tools" under *Windows Native Code Development* and uncheck all the other installation options.

   Download Microsoft Visual C++ 2010 Compilers Update for Windows SDK from the following link and run the installer.
   http://www.microsoft.com/en-us/download/details.aspx?display?displaylang=en&id=4422

   Download Microsoft Visual C++ 2010 from the following links and run installers.
   http://www.microsoft.com/en-us/download/details.aspx?id=14632
   http://www.microsoft.com/en-us/download/details.aspx?id=5555

   Select Windows ![] in the lower left corner on your computer screen and select

   Run the following command at the command prompt.
   "C:\Program Files\Microsoft SDKs\Windows\v7.1\Bin\SetEnv.Cmd"

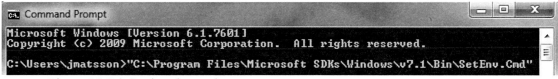

Figure 10.8a) Setting the environment

   Next, run this command to launch ANSYS Fluent (you can copy and paste the command):
   "C:\Program Files\ANSYS Inc\ANSYS Student\v192\fluent\ntbin\win64\fluent.exe"

   This command will be slightly modified if you are not running ANSYS Student… or if you are running a different version of ANSYS.

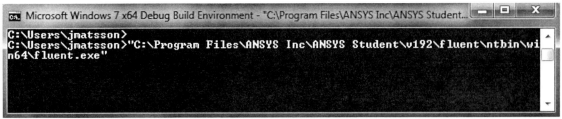

Figure 10.8b) Launching ANSYS Fluent

If you need more information on installations for Compiling UDFs on Windows 7, please see the following link:
https://inside.mines.edu/~rgilmore/mio/using_UDF_in_Fluent.html

9. Using Windows 10, select Windows ⊞ in the lower left corner on your computer monitor and click on ▣ Windows System and ▣ Control Panel. Double click on Programs and Features. Uninstall Microsoft Visual C++ 2019 if you have it installed and go to *www.visualstudio.com*. Choose Visual Studio IDE, Downloads for Windows, Community 2019. Run Visual Studio Installer and install the software.

    Make sure that you have the selections checked as shown in Figures 10.9a) and 10.9b). Restart your computer after installation.

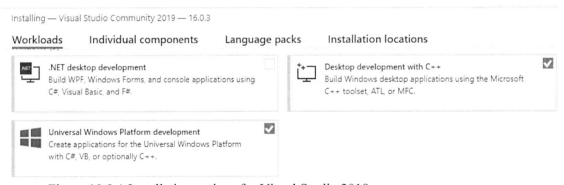

Figure 10.9a) Installation options for Visual Studio 2019

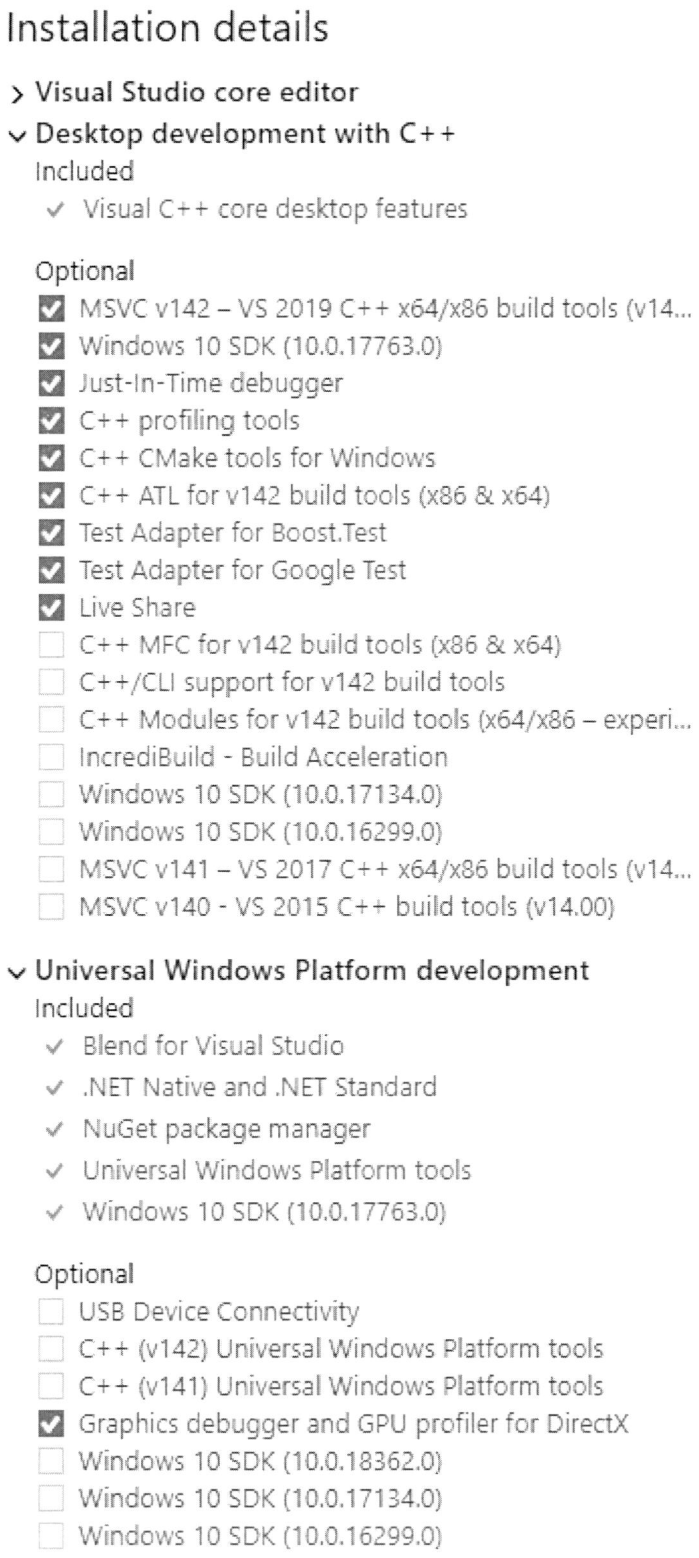

Installation details

> Visual Studio core editor

∨ Desktop development with C++
Included
  ✓ Visual C++ core desktop features

Optional
  ☑ MSVC v142 – VS 2019 C++ x64/x86 build tools (v14...
  ☑ Windows 10 SDK (10.0.17763.0)
  ☑ Just-In-Time debugger
  ☑ C++ profiling tools
  ☑ C++ CMake tools for Windows
  ☑ C++ ATL for v142 build tools (x86 & x64)
  ☑ Test Adapter for Boost.Test
  ☑ Test Adapter for Google Test
  ☑ Live Share
  ☐ C++ MFC for v142 build tools (x86 & x64)
  ☐ C++/CLI support for v142 build tools
  ☐ C++ Modules for v142 build tools (x64/x86 – experi...
  ☐ IncrediBuild - Build Acceleration
  ☐ Windows 10 SDK (10.0.17134.0)
  ☐ Windows 10 SDK (10.0.16299.0)
  ☐ MSVC v141 – VS 2017 C++ x64/x86 build tools (v14...
  ☐ MSVC v140 - VS 2015 C++ build tools (v14.00)

∨ Universal Windows Platform development
Included
  ✓ Blend for Visual Studio
  ✓ .NET Native and .NET Standard
  ✓ NuGet package manager
  ✓ Universal Windows Platform tools
  ✓ Windows 10 SDK (10.0.17763.0)

Optional
  ☐ USB Device Connectivity
  ☐ C++ (v142) Universal Windows Platform tools
  ☐ C++ (v141) Universal Windows Platform tools
  ☑ Graphics debugger and GPU profiler for DirectX
  ☐ Windows 10 SDK (10.0.18362.0)
  ☐ Windows 10 SDK (10.0.17134.0)
  ☐ Windows 10 SDK (10.0.16299.0)

Figure 10.9b) Installation details for Visual Studio 2019

Select Windows  in the lower left corner on your computer screen and select

Visual Studio 2019 New and **x64 Native Tools Command Promp...**.

x64 Native Tools Command Prompt for VS 2019

```
********************************************************************************
** Visual Studio 2019 Developer Command Prompt v16.0.3
** Copyright (c) 2019 Microsoft Corporation
********************************************************************************
[vcvarsall.bat] Environment initialized for: 'x64'

C:\Program Files (x86)\Microsoft Visual Studio\2019\Community>
```
Figure 10.9c) Command Prompt for Visual Studio 2019 x64

Next, run this command including " at the beginning and end to launch ANSYS Fluent (you can copy and paste the command):
"C:\Program Files\ANSYS Inc\ANSYS Student\v194\fluent\ntbin\win64\fluent.exe"
This command will be slightly modified if you are not running ANSYS Student… or if you are running a different version of ANSYS.

```
C:\Program Files (x86)\Microsoft Visual Studio\2019\Community>
"C:\Program Files\ANSYS Inc\ANSYS Student\v194\fluent\ntbin\wi
n64\fluent.exe"
```
Figure 10.9d) Launching ANSYS Fluent from VS 2019 command prompt

G. Launching ANSYS Fluent

10. Select the 2D and Double Precision solver for ANSYS Fluent. Click on the plus sign next to Show More Options and note the location for your *working directory*. In this case the location of the *working directory* is *C:\Users\John Matsson*.
Select Parallel under Processing Options. Set the number of Processes equal to the number of processor cores for your computer. Click OK to start ANSYS Fluent. Select File>>Read>>Mesh… from the menu. Copy the file *rt-mesh.msh* to the working directory. Read the file *rt-mesh.msh* from the working directory. The mesh file can also be downloaded from *sdcpublications.com*. Click on Display… under Mesh in General on the Task Page. Click on Display in the Mesh Display window and Close the window.

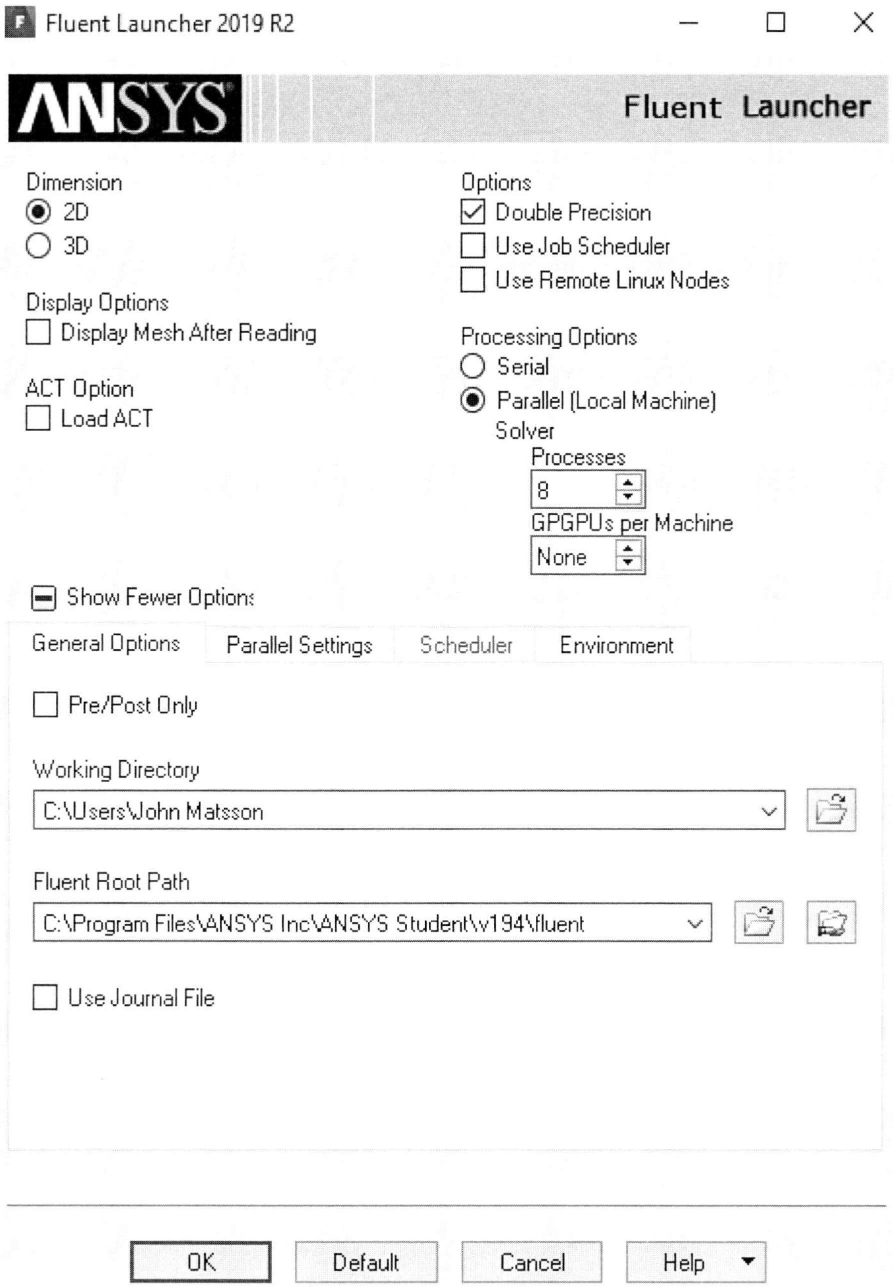

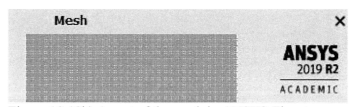

Figure 10.10a) ANSYS Fluent Launcher

Figure 10.10b) A part of the mesh in ANSYS Fluent

11. Check the mesh in ANSYS Fluent by selecting the Check button under Mesh in General Problem Setup. Check the scale of the mesh by selecting the Scale button. Make sure that the Domain Extent is correct and close the Scale Mesh window.

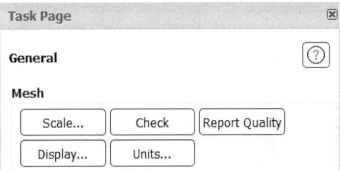

Figure 10.11a) Mesh check

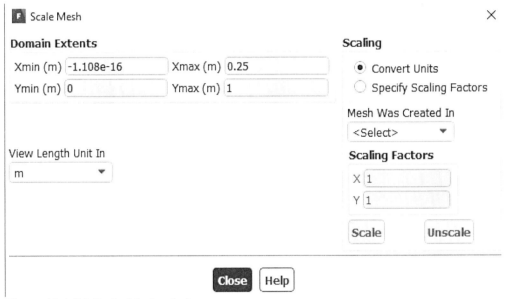

Figure 10.11b) Scale Mesh window

12. Select Transient Time for the Solver in General Problem Setup. Check the Gravity box and enter -9.81 as the Gravitational Acceleration in the Y direction.

Open Models and double click on Multiphase (Off) under Setup in the Outline View. Select the Volume of Fluid Model. Check the box for Implicit Body Force. Click OK to exit the Multiphase Model window.

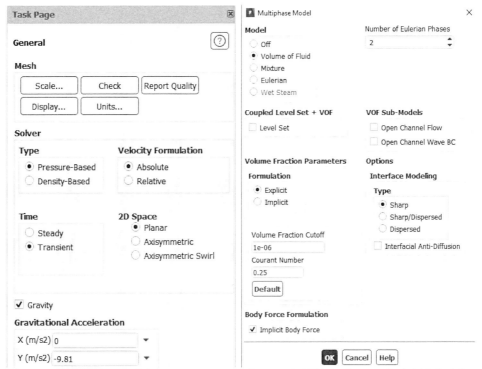

Figure 10.12a) General Setup   Figure 10.12b) Volume of Fluid Model

13. Double click on Materials, Fluid and air under Setup in the Outline View. Change the Name from *air* to *light-fluid*. Change the Density (kg/m3) to 998.2 and the Viscosity (kg/m-s) to 0.001002. Click on the Change/Create button and answer *Yes* to the question that appears and Close the window.

Click on Create/Edit for Fluid under Materials on the Task Page. Click on Fluent Database. Scroll down in the Fluent Fluid Materials window and select *water-liquid (h2o<l>)*. Click on the Copy button and Close the Fluent Database Materials window. Change the Name from *water-liquid* to *heavy-fluid*. Change the Density (kg/m3) to 1074.9 and the Viscosity (kg/m-s) to 0.001259. Erase the Chemical Formula. Click on the Change/Create button, answer *Yes* to the question that appears and Close the window.

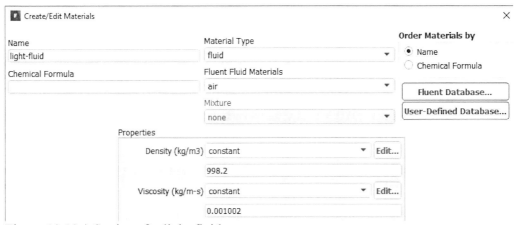

Figure 10.13a) Settings for light-fluid

225

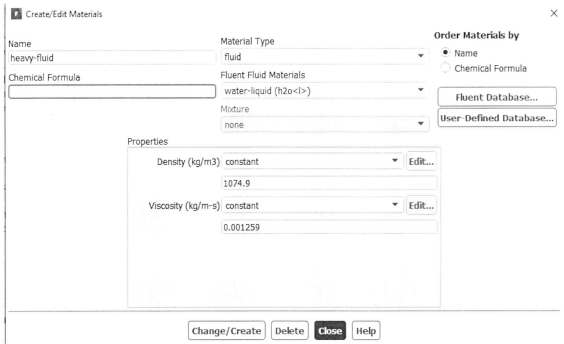

Figure 10.13b) Settings for heavy-fluid

14. Open Models, Multiphase and Phases under Setup in the Outline View. Double click on phase-1-Primary Phase. Select *light-fluid* as Phase Materials and enter *light-fluid* as the name of the Primary Phase. Click on the OK button to exit. Repeat this step to select and name *heavy-fluid* as the Secondary Phase.

Double click on Phase Interaction under Models and Multiphase under Setup in the Outline View, click on the Surface Tension tab, check the Surface Tension Force Modeling box, select constant from the Surface Tension Coefficients drop down menu, enter the value 0.00148 and click on the OK button.

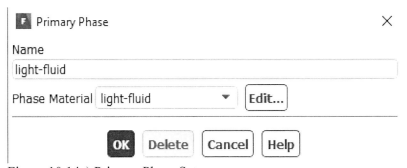

Figure 10.14a) Primary Phase Setup

Figure 10.14b) Secondary Phase Setup

Figure 10.14c) Phase interaction toolbox

15. Copy the files *rayleigh-taylor.c* and *udfconfig.h* to your *working directory*. These files are available for download at *sdcpublications.com*. Select User-Defined>>Functions>>Interpreted… from the menu. Browse for the file *rayleigh-taylor.c,* select the file and click OK. Click on the Interpret button. Close the window.

```
#include "udf.h"
DEFINE_INIT(init_cos, domain)
{
cell_t c;
Thread*thread;
real xc[ND_ND];
thread_loop_c(thread,domain)
{
begin_c_loop_all(c,thread)
{
C_CENTROID(xc,c,thread);
if(xc[1] <= 0.5+0.05*cos(2*3.141592654/0.25*xc[0]))
{
C_V(c,thread)=0;
}
else
{
C_V(c,thread)=-0.1;
}
}
end_c_loop_all (c,thread)
}
}
```

Figure 10.15a) Code for the *rayleigh-taylor.c* file

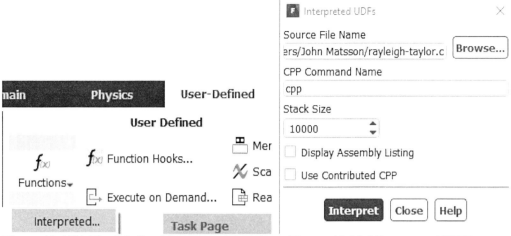

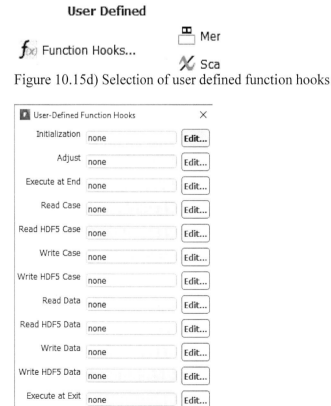

Figure 10.15b) Used defined interpreted function   Figure 10.15c) Interpreted UDFs

Select User-Defined>>Functions Hook from the menu. Click on the Edit button next to Initialization. Select *init_cos* from Available Initialization Functions and click on the Add button to move it over to the Selected Initialization Functions. Click on OK buttons to close windows.

Figure 10.15d) Selection of user defined function hooks

Figure 10.15e) User defined function hooks window

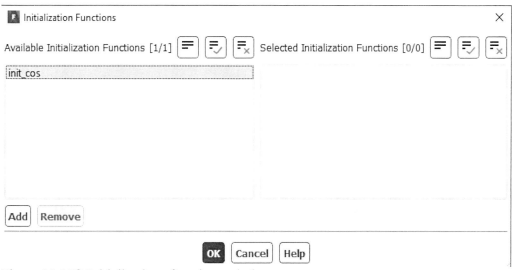

Figure 10.15f) Initializations functions window

16. Double click on Boundary Conditions under Setup in the Outline View. Click on the Operating Conditions on the Task Page in the Boundary Conditions section. Check the box for Specified Operating Density and enter the value 998.2 for Operating Density (this is the value for the less dense fluid). Click OK to close the window.

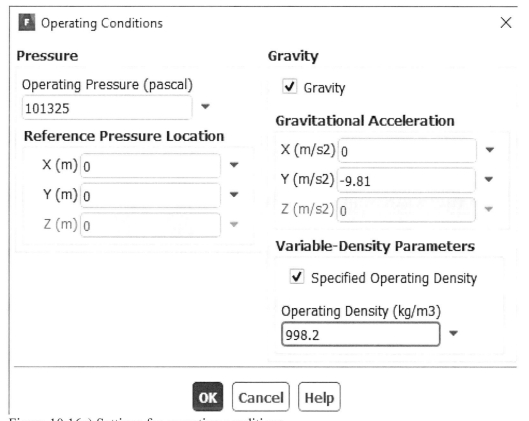

Figure 10.16a) Settings for operating conditions

Double click on Methods under Solution in the Outline View. Select Default settings except for First Order Upwind for Momentum and Body Force Weighted for Pressure.

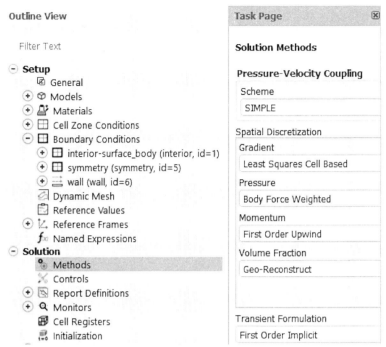

Figure 10.16b) Solution Methods Problem Setup

17. Double click on Initialization under Solution in the Tree, set the Y Velocity to -0.1 and click on the Initialize button.

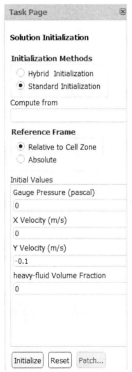

Figure 10.17 Solution initialization settings

18. Select the *Domain* tab in the menu and choose Adapt>>Refine/Coarsen. Select Cell Registers>>New>>Region… in the Adaption Controls window. Enter 0.25 for X Max, 0.5 for Y Min, and 1 for Y Max. Click on the Save button and click OK to close the window.

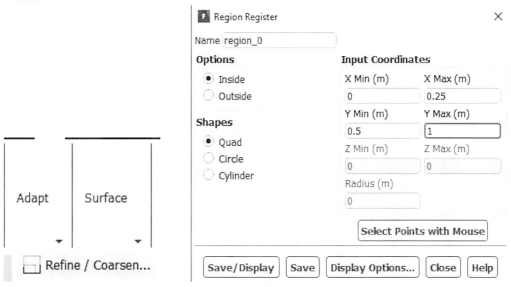

Figure 10.18a) Adaption   Figure 10.18b) Region Adaption Settings

19. Click on the Patch button on the Task Page and select *heavy-fluid* as the phase. Select Volume Fraction as the Variable and region_0 as Registers to Patch. Set the value to 1, click on the Patch button and close the window.

Click on the Patch button on the Task Page and select *mixture* for the phase. Select Y Velocity as the Variable and region_0 as Registers to Patch. Set the value to -0.1 and click on the Patch button and close the window.

Figure 10.19a) Patch Settings for Volume Fraction

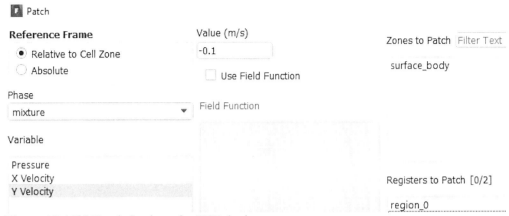

Figure 10.19b) Patch Settings for Y Velocity

20. Double click on Graphics and Contours under Results in the Outline View. Select Phases… and Volume fraction under Contours of and select *heavy-fluid* as the Phase. Click on Colormap Options…, set Type to float and Precision to 1 under Number Format, click on Apply and Close the Colormap window. Click on the Save/Display button and Close the Contours window.

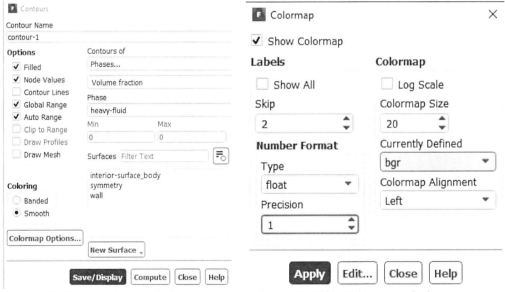

Figure 10.20a) Contours window   Figure 10.20b) Colormap window

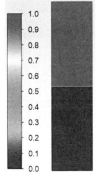

Figure 10.20c) Contours of Volume Fraction (heavy-fluid)

21. Double click on Calculation Activities and Solution Animations under Solution in the Outline View. Enter *rayleigh-taylor-instability* as the Name, enter Record after every 10 and select time-step. Set the Window ID to 2 and select contour-1 under Animation Object. Click OK to close the Animation Definition window.

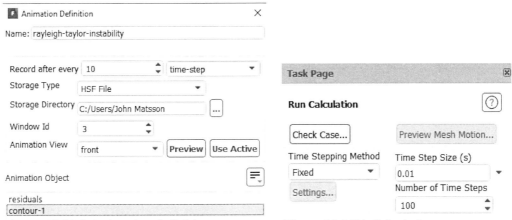

Figure 10.21a) Animation definition   Figure 10.21b) Calculations

Double click on Run Calculation under Solution, enter 0.01 as Time Step Size, and 100 for Number of Time Steps. Click on the Calculate button. Continue running the calculations with 20 as Number of Time Steps 14 more times for a total of 3.8 seconds. Select File>>Write>Case & Data… from the menu. Save the file with the name *rt-computation.cas*.

H. Post-Processing

22. Double click on Animations and Solution Animation Playback under Results in the Outline View. Set the Replay Speed to low and select Play Once as Playback Mode. Select MPEG as Write/Record Format. Click on the Write button. This will create the mpeg movie in your working directory. Close the Playback window. The movie can be viewed using, for example, VLC Media Player.
In VLC Media Player select Media>>Open File… from the menu. Open the movie from the working directory. Select Playback>>Speed>>Slower several times from the menu in the VLC Media Player until you have a suitable speed for the movie.

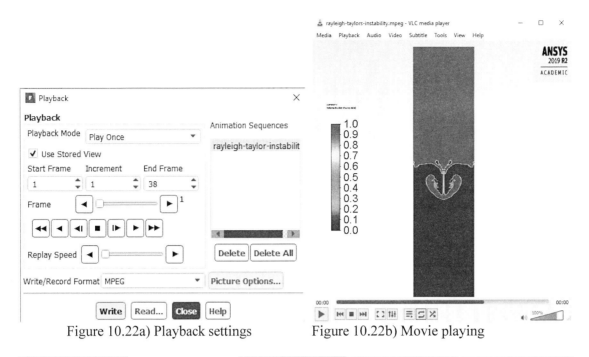

Figure 10.22a) Playback settings   Figure 10.22b) Movie playing

Figure 10.22c) Volume Fraction Contours after 1, 1.2, 1.4, 1.6 and 1.8 s

Figure 10.22d) Volume Fraction Contours after 2, 2.2, 2.4, 2.6, 2.8, 3, 3.2, 3.4, 3.6 and 3.8 s

I. Theory

23. We will look at the inviscid theory for the Rayleigh-Taylor instability in the same way as we did for the Kelvin-Helmholz instability in terms of a sinusoidal disturbance between two fluids with densities ρ_1, ρ_2.

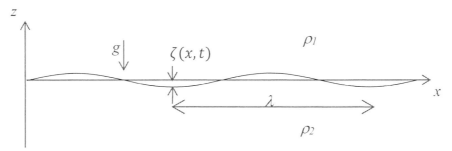

Figure 10.23 Development of Rayleigh-Taylor instability from a perturbation

The velocity vector in a Cartesian coordinate system can be described as

$$\overline{U} = u_x \overline{e}_x + u_y \overline{e}_y + u_z \overline{e}_z \tag{10.1}$$

where u_x, $u_y = 0$, u_z are the velocity components in the streamwise, spanwise and normal directions, respectively. Euler equations of motion can be written as

$$\frac{\partial u_x}{\partial t} + u_x \frac{\partial u_x}{\partial x} + u_z \frac{\partial u_x}{\partial z} = -\frac{1}{\rho} \frac{\partial P}{\partial x} \tag{10.2}$$

$$\frac{\partial u_z}{\partial t} + u_x \frac{\partial u_z}{\partial x} + u_z \frac{\partial u_z}{\partial z} = -\frac{1}{\rho} \frac{\partial P}{\partial z} - g \tag{10.3}$$

$$\frac{\partial u_x}{\partial x} + \frac{\partial u_z}{\partial z} = 0 \tag{10.4}$$

The velocity components can be divided into mean flow components in the main streamwise direction plus a perturbation (no mean flow components in this case)

$$\overline{U} = u \overline{e}_x + w \overline{e}_z \tag{10.5}$$

and the pressure is $\quad P = P_0 - \rho g z + p \tag{10.6}$

A perturbation is introduced in the form

$$u, w, p = [u_n(z), w_n(z), p_n(z)] e^{i(kx - \omega t)} \tag{10.7}$$

where $k = 2\pi / \lambda$ is the wave number, λ is the wave length, ω is the frequency and $u_n(z), w_n(z), p_n(z)$ are eigenfunctions. The linearized Euler equations can be written as

$$-i\omega u_n + \frac{ik}{\rho} p_n = 0 \tag{10.8}$$

$$-i\omega w_n + \frac{1}{\rho} p_n' = 0 \tag{10.9}$$

$$ik u_n + w_n' = 0 \tag{10.10}$$

From equations (10.8) – (10.10) we can find the equation for w_n

$$w_n'' - k^2 w_n = 0 \tag{10.11}$$

with the general solution

$$w_n = c_1 e^{-kz} + c_2 e^{kz} \tag{10.12}$$

To get exponentially decaying solutions far from the interface, we set c_1 and c_2 equal to zero in the lower and upper layers, respectively. The interface location is defined by

$$z = \zeta(x,t) = \mathcal{R}\{a e^{i(kx-\omega t)}\} \tag{10.13}$$

where $\mathcal{R}$ stands for the real part and a is the amplitude of the initial disturbance. The normal velocity w at the interface is given by the material derivative of $\zeta(x,t)$

$$w = w_n(z)e^{i(kx-\omega t)} = \frac{D\zeta}{Dt} = \frac{\partial \zeta}{\partial t} = -i\omega \, \zeta = -i\omega a e^{i(kx-\omega t)} \tag{10.14}$$

We find the following results: $c_1 = -i\omega a$, $c_2 = -i\omega a$

$$w_{n,1} = -i\omega a e^{-kz}, \; w_{n,2} = -i\omega a e^{kz} \tag{10.15}$$

We can now find the pressure eigenfunctions in the upper and lower layers from equation (10.9)

$$p_{n,1} = -\rho_1 \omega^2 a e^{-kz}/k \tag{10.16}$$
$$p_{n,2} = \rho_2 \omega^2 a e^{kz}/k \tag{10.17}$$

Next, we use equation (10.6) and set the pressures identical at the interface to get the dispersion relation

$$P_0 - \rho_1 g\zeta + p_{n,1}e^{i(kx-\omega t)} = P_0 - \rho_2 g\zeta + p_{n,2}e^{i(kx-\omega t)} - \sigma k^2 \zeta \tag{10.18}$$

$$(\rho_2 - \rho_1)gk = (\rho_2 + \rho_1)\omega^2 - \sigma k^3 \tag{10.19}$$

where σ is surface tension. We find the following equation for the frequency without surface tension

$$\omega = \sqrt{\frac{(\rho_2-\rho_1)gk}{\rho_1+\rho_2}} = i\sqrt{\frac{(\rho_1-\rho_2)gk}{\rho_1+\rho_2}} = i\sqrt{gkAt} \tag{10.20}$$

and including surface tension

$$\omega = \sqrt{\frac{(\rho_2-\rho_1)gk+\sigma k^3}{\rho_1+\rho_2}} = i\sqrt{\frac{(\rho_1-\rho_2)gk-\sigma k^3}{\rho_1+\rho_2}} = i\sqrt{gkAt(1-\frac{4\pi^2}{Bo})} \tag{10.21}$$

where $At = (\rho_1 - \rho_2)/\rho_1+\rho_2$ is non-dimensional Atwood number and $Bo = (\rho_1 - \rho_2)gD^2/\sigma$ is non-dimensional Bond number. The frequency is complex with the associated growth of waves when the expression under the square root without surface tension is negative for

$$\rho_2 - \rho_1 < 0 \qquad \text{or} \qquad \rho_2 < \rho_1 \tag{10.22}$$

and including surface tension we get

$$(\rho_2 - \rho_1)gk + \sigma k^3 < 0 \qquad \text{or} \qquad \lambda > 2\pi\sqrt{\frac{\sigma}{(\rho_1 - \rho_2)g}} \tag{10.23}$$

The Bond number $Bo > 4\pi^2$ will give growth of waves when $\lambda = D$. The interface location can now be written as

$$z = \zeta(x,t) = \mathcal{R}\left\{ae^{\sqrt{gkAt(1-\frac{4\pi^2}{Bo})}\,t}e^{ikx}\right\} = ae^{\sqrt{gkAt(1-\frac{4\pi^2}{Bo})}\,t}\cos(kx) \tag{10.24}$$

and we see that surface tension has a very small but stabilizing effect. In ANSYS Fluent simulations we used $a = 0.05$ m, $k = 8\pi$ m^{-1}, $g = 9.81$ m/s^2, $\lambda = D = 0.25$ m, $\sigma = 0.00148$ N/m, $\rho_1 = 1074.9\,\frac{kg}{m^3}$, $\rho_2 = 998.2\,\frac{kg}{m^3}$. The Atwood and Bond numbers used in ANSYS Fluent are

$$At = \frac{1074.9 - 998.2}{1074.9 + 998.2} = 0.037 \tag{10.25}$$

$$Bo = \frac{(1074.9 - 998.2)*9.81*0.25^2}{0.00148} = 31,775 \tag{10.26}$$

There are a few more non-dimensional parameters in this problem that we can define such as the aspect ratio for the rectangular computational domain $H/D = 4$, the density ratio $\rho_1/\rho_2 = 1.077$, the dynamic viscosity ratio $\mu_1/\mu_2 = 1.256$ and non-dimensional time $\tau = t\sqrt{gkAt(1 - \frac{4\pi^2}{Bo})}$. The interface location is

$$z = \zeta(x,t) \approx \frac{e^{3t}}{20}\cos(8\pi x) \tag{10.27}$$

Using the inviscid theory, we find that the wave-length with surface tension included according to equation (10.23) must be $\lambda > 0.0088\,m$ to get growth of waves.

J. References

1. Andrews, M.J. and Dalziel, S.B. "Small Atwood number Rayleigh-Taylor Experiments", *Phil. Trans. R. Soc. A*, **368**, 1663-1679, (2010).
2. Chandrasekhar S. "Hydrodynamic and Hydromagnetic Stability", *Dover Publications, Inc.*, New York (1961).
3. Drazin P.G. and Reid W.H. "Introduction to hydrodynamic instability", *Cambridge University Press*, (1981).
4. Sharqawy M.H, Lienhard J.H., and Zubair S.M. "Thermophysical Properties of Sea Water: A Review of existing Correlations and Data, Desalination, and Water Treatment", *Desalination and Water Treatment*, **16**, 354 (2010).

5. Strubelj, L., and Tiselj, I., "Numerical Simulations of Basic Interfacial Instabilities with Improved Two-Fluid Model", *International Conference Nuclear Energy for New Europe*, September 14–17, Bled, Slovenia, (2009).
6. Strubelj, L., and Tiselj, I., "Numerical Simulations of Rayleigh-Taylor Instability with Two-Fluid Model and Interface Sharpening", *Proceedings of ASME Fluids Engineering Division Summer Conference*, August 10-14, Jacksonville, FL, (2008).
7. Tryggvason, G., "Numerical Simulations of the Rayleigh-Taylor Instability", *Journal of Computational Physics*, **75**, 253-282, (1988).

K. Exercises

10.1 Use ANSYS Fluent to study the same problem as we completed in this chapter but instead complete transient 2D axisymmetric simulations. Visualize the instability using contours of volume fraction for the heavy fluid.

10.2 Use ANSYS Fluent to study the same problem as we completed in this chapter but instead use the following dimensions $H = 2$ m, $D = 0.25$ m. Visualize the instability using contours of volume fraction for the heavy fluid.

10.3 Use ANSYS Fluent to study the same problem as we completed in this chapter but instead use a frustum shaped geometry with the following dimensions $H = 1$ m, $D_{bottom} = 0.25$ m and $D_{top} = 0.5$ m. Visualize the instability using contours of volume fraction for the heavy fluid.

Notes:

CHAPTER 11. FLOW UNDER A DAM

A. Objectives

- Using ANSYS Workbench to Model Seepage Flow of Water under a Concrete Dam
- Inserting Boundary Conditions and a Porous Medium Zone with Viscous and Inertial Resistance
- Running Laminar Steady 2D Planar ANSYS Fluent Simulations
- Using Contour Plots for Static Pressure and Velocity Magnitude
- Using XY Plots for Visualizations of Velocity and Pressure
- Comparing ANSYS Fluent Results with Results Using Mathematica

B. <u>Problem Description</u>

We will study the seepage flow of water under a concrete dam using ANSYS Fluent. The dimensions and water levels are shown below.

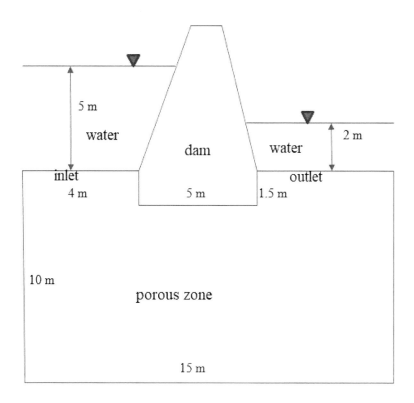

C. Launching ANSYS Workbench and Selecting Fluent

1. Start by launching ANSYS Workbench. Double click on Fluid Flow (Fluent) under Analysis Systems in the Toolbox.

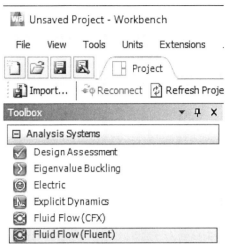

Figure 11.1 Selecting Fluid Flow (Fluent)

D. Launching ANSYS DesignModeler

2. Right click Geometry under Project Schematic in ANSYS Workbench and select Properties. In Properties of Schematic A2: Geometry, select Analysis Type 2D under Advanced Geometry Options. Right click on Geometry in the Project Schematic window and select New DesignModeler Geometry.

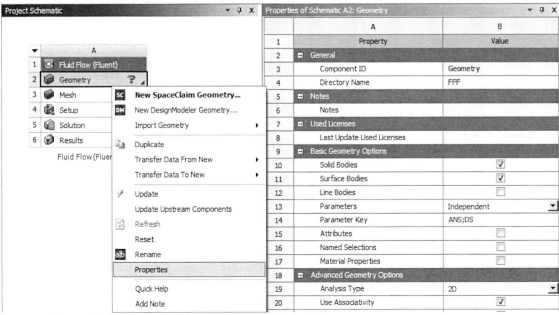

Figure 11.2a) Selecting properties and 2D analysis type

242

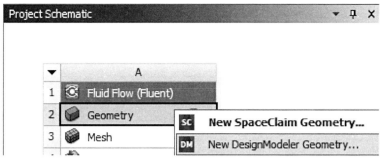

Figure 11.2b) Selecting new DesignModeler geometry

3. Select the Sketching tab in the Tree Outline and select Line under Draw. Click on Look at Face/Plane/Sketch 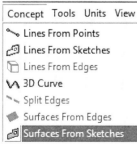. Draw a horizontal line to the right from the origin of the coordinate system in the graphics window. Make sure you have the letters *P* at the origin, *H* along the line and *C* when you end the line.

   Click on the Dimensions tab under Sketching Toolboxes and click on the new line. Enter 15 m for the length of the line. Continue adding lines with lengths as shown in Fig. 11.3a).

   Select Concepts>>Surfaces from Sketches from the menu. Click on Sketch 1 under XYPlane in the Tree Outline and select Apply for Base Objects in Details View. Click on Generate. Close DesignModeler.

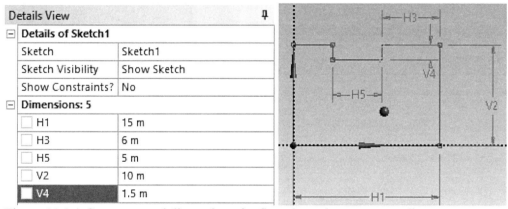

Figure 11.3a) Geometry and dimensions for flow through a porous medium

Figure 11.3b) Creating surfaces from Sketches

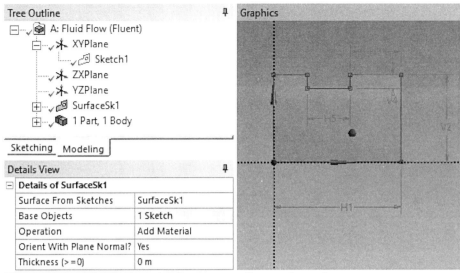

Figure 11.3c) Finished model for seepage flow under a dam

E. Launching ANSYS Meshing

4. Double click on Mesh under the Project Schematic in ANSYS Workbench. Select Mesh under Model (A3) and Project in the Outline. Right click on Mesh and select Update.

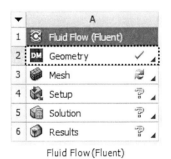

Figure 11.4a) Mesh in ANSYS

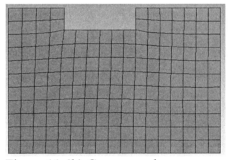

Figure 11.4b) Coarse mesh

Select Mesh>>Controls>>Face Meshing from the menu. Select the face of the mesh region. Apply the Geometry under Details of "Face Meshing".

Figure 11.4c) Face meshing

Select Mesh>>Controls>>Sizing from the menu and select the face of the mesh region. Apply the Geometry under Details of "Face Sizing". Set the Element Size to 50 mm and set the Behavior to Hard. Right click on Mesh in the tree outline and select Generate Mesh.

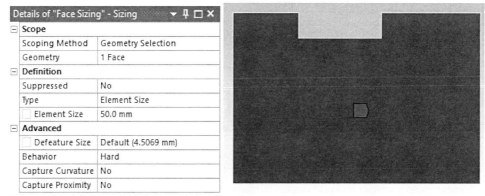

Figure 11.4d) Details of face sizing for the mesh

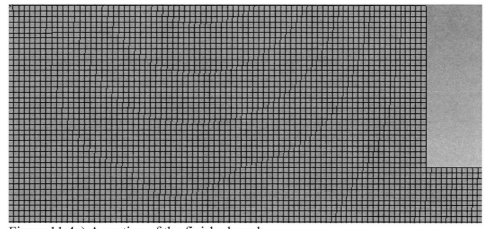

Figure 11.4e) A portion of the finished mesh

Select Geometry under Project and Model (A3) in the Outline. Select the Edge Selection Filer ⬚. Select the upper left horizontal edge, right click and select Create Named Selection. Name the edge "pressure-inlet" and click OK. Name the upper horizontal edge to the right "pressure-outlet" and control-select all the remaining six edges and enter the name "wall".

Select File>>Export…>>Mesh>>FLUENT Input File>>Export from the menu and save the mesh with the name *seepage-flow.msh*. Select File>>Save Project from the menu and save the project with the name *Dam-Seepage-Flow.wbpj*. Close the meshing window. Right click on Mesh and select Update under Project Schematic in ANSYS Workbench.

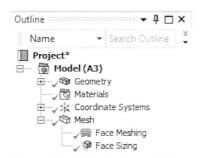

Figure 11.4f) Selection of Geometry

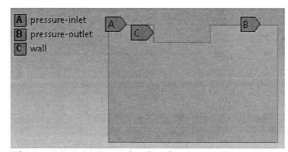

Figure 11.4g) Named selections

F. Launching ANSYS Fluent

5. Double click on Setup under Project Schematic in ANSYS Workbench. Check the Options box Double Precision. Select Parallel Processing Options. Move the cursor to the bottom of the computer monitor, right click and select Task Manager and click on the Performance tab. Click on Open Resource Monitor and select the number of Processes equal to the total number of CPUs. Click OK to launch Fluent.

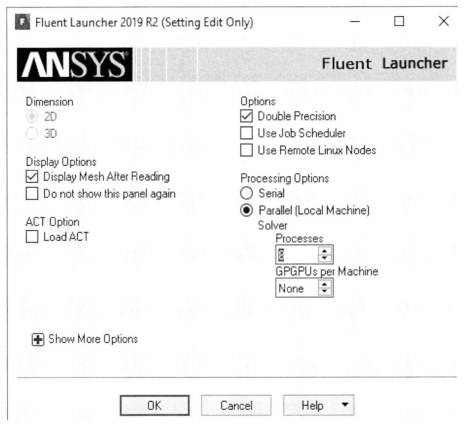

Figure 11.5 Launching ANSYS Fluent

6. Double click on Materials under Setup in the Outline View. Click on Create/Edit for Fluid under Materials on the Task Page. Click on Fluent Database in the Create/Edit Materials window. Select *water-liquid (h2o<l>)* as the Fluent Fluid Material. Click on Copy and Close. Set the Density to 992.2 (kg/m3) and the Viscosity to 0.00065 (kg/m-s). Click Change/Create and Close the window.

Figure 11.6a) Selection of Fluent Database

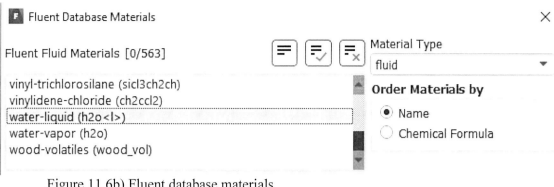

Figure 11.6b) Fluent database materials

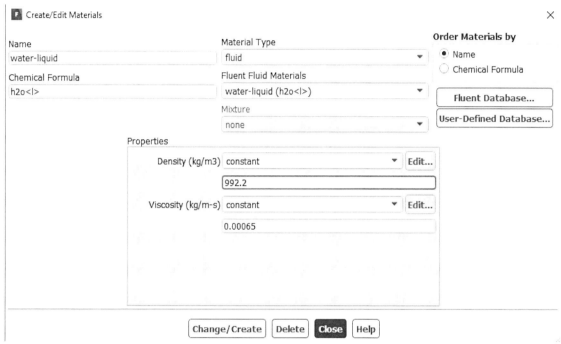

Figure 11.6c) Properties for water-liquid

7. Double click on Cell Zone Conditions and *surface_body* under Setup in the Outline View. Select *water-liquid* from the Material Name drop-down menu. Check the box for Porous Zone. Click on the Porous Zone tab and enter 1.98807e+06 (1/m2) for Viscous Resistance in both Direction-1 and Direction-2. Enter 1719.4 (1/m) for Inertial Resistance in both Direction-1 and Direction-2. Click on the OK button to close the Fluid window.

Figure 11.7 Fluid window

8. Double click on Boundary Conditions under Setup in the Outline View. Select the *pressure-inlet* Zone on the Task Page. Click on Edit. Enter 49050 (pascal) as the Gauge Total Pressure. Click on OK to close the window. Select the *pressure-outlet* Zone on the Task Page. Click on Edit. Enter 19620 (Pa) as the Gauge Pressure. Click OK to close the window.

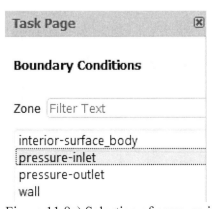

Figure 11.8a) Selection of pressure-inlet boundary condition

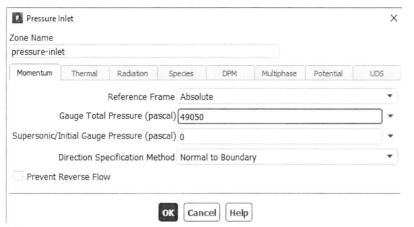

Figure 11.8b) Pressure inlet window

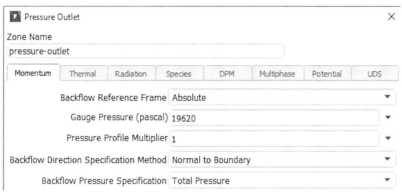

Figure 11.8c) Pressure outlet window

9. Double click on Initialization under Solution in the Outlet View. Check Standard Initialization as Initialization Method on the Task Page. Select Compute from *pressure-inlet* from the drop-down menu and click on Initialize.

Figure 11.9 Solution initialization

10. Double click on Monitors and Residual under Solution in the Outline View. Set the Absolute Criteria to 1e-12 for all Residuals and click on OK to exit the window.

    Double click on Run Calculation under Solution in the Outline View, enter 1000 for Number of Iterations on the Task Page and click on Calculate.

Figure 11.10a) Residual monitors window

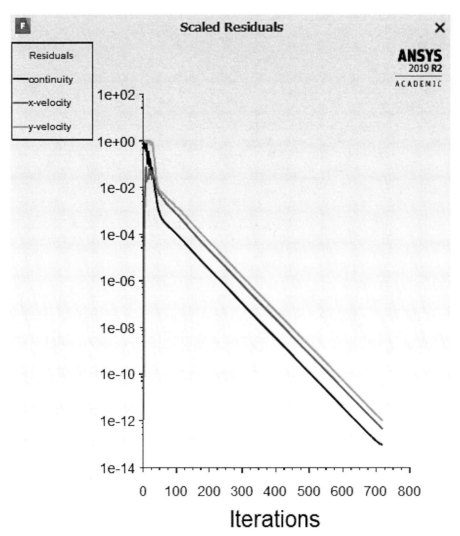

Figure 11.10b) Residual iterations

G. Post-Processing

11. Double click on Graphics and Contours under Results in the Outline View. Select Contours of Velocity and Velocity Magnitude from the drop-down menu. Deselect all Surfaces and click on Save/Display. Select Contours of Pressure and Static Pressure and click on Save/Display. Close the window.

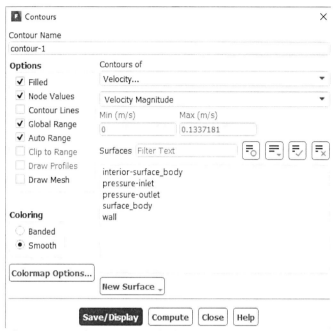

Figure 11.11a) Contours window

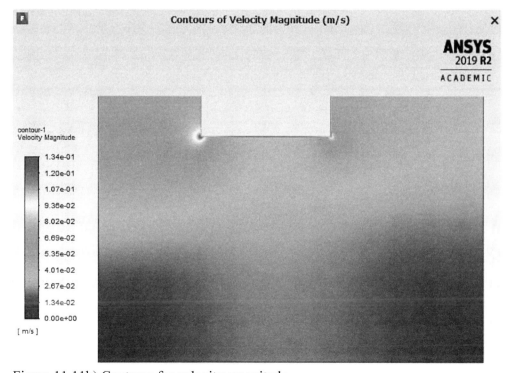

Figure 11.11b) Contours for velocity magnitude

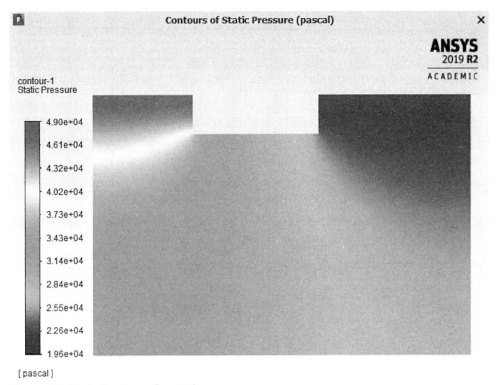

Figure 11.11c) Contours for static pressure

12. Double click on Plots and XY Plot under Results in the Outline View. Select Velocity and Velocity Magnitude for Y Axis Function and Direction Vector for X Axis Function. Select New Surface >> Line/Rake from the drop–down menu. Enter the following end points: x0 (m) = 9, y0 (m) = 10 and x1 (m) = 15, y1(m) = 10. Click on Create and Close the window. Click on Load File… and load the file with the name "*theory-flow-under-dam.dat*". This and other files are available for download at *sdcpublications.com*. Select *line-5* in the Surfaces section, select *Theory* under File Data. Click on Curves…, select Curve # 1, the pattern and no symbol as shown in Figure 11.12c). Click on Apply and Close the Curves-Solution XY Plot window. Click on Save/Plot in the Solution XY Plot window. Click on Axes… in the Solution XY Plot window. Select X Axis, Set Precision under Number Format to 0 and click on Apply. Select Y Axis, Set Precision under Number Format to 2 and click on Apply. Close the Axes – Solution XY Plot window.

Select New Surface >> Line/Rake from the drop–down menu. Enter the following end points: x0 (m) = 9, y0 (m) = 0 and x1 (m) = 9, y1 (m) = 8.5. Click on Create and Close the window. Select *line-6* in the Surfaces section, uncheck Position on X Axis under Options and select Mesh and Y-Coordinate as Y Axis Function. Select Pressure and Static Pressure as X Axis Function. Click on Axes… and uncheck Auto Range under Options for the X Axis. Set Minimum under Range to 25000 and Maximum to 30000. Set Precision under Number Format to 0. Select Y Axis and set the Precision to 0. Click on Apply and Close the Axes window. Click on Save/Plot.

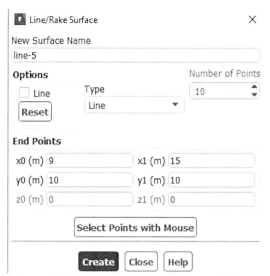

Figure 11.12a) Line/Rake Surface window

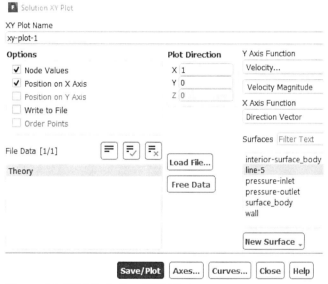

Figure 11.12b) Solution XY Plot

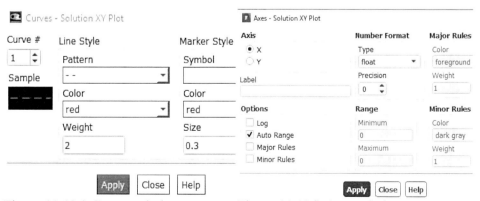

Figure 11.12c) Curves window   Figure 11.12d) Axes window

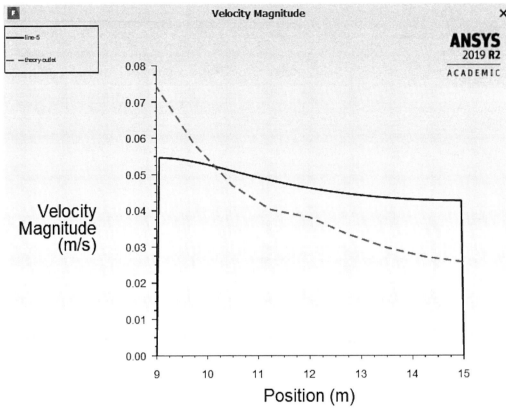

Figure 11.12e) Comparison of the variation for seepage velocity at the outlet from ANSYS Fluent simulations (full line) and finite element calculations (dashed line).

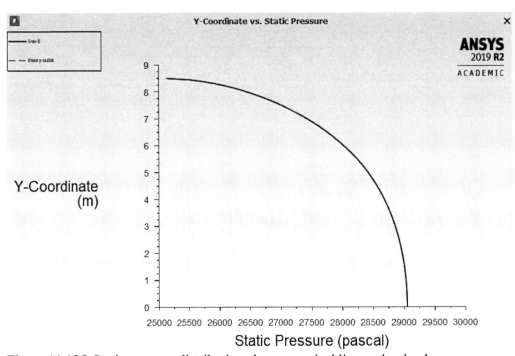

Figure 11.12f) Static pressure distribution along a vertical line under the dam

H. Theory

13. Groundwater seepage can frequently occur in soils and has many engineering applications. We can relate the mean fluid velocity v (m/s) through the porous medium to the pressure gradient dP/dx (Pa) using Darcy's law

$$v = -\frac{\kappa}{\mu}\frac{dP}{dx}$$
(11.1)

where κ (m^2) is permeability of the porous medium and μ (kg/m-s) is the dynamic viscosity of the fluid. Furthermore, we define the hydraulic conductivity or coefficient of permeability k (m/s) as

$$k = \kappa\frac{\rho g}{\mu}$$
(11.2)

Where g (m/s^2) is acceleration due to gravity and ρ (kg/m^3) is the density of the fluid. We will also use the following equation from the ANSYS Fluent user manual

$$\frac{dP}{dx} = -(\frac{\mu v}{\alpha} + \frac{C_2 \rho v^2}{2})$$
(11.3)

where $1/\alpha$ (1/m^2) is viscous resistance or inverse absolute permeability for the porous medium and C_2(1/m) is inertial resistance of the porous medium. When we combine the equations we get the following expression for the permeability coefficient

$$k = \frac{g}{\frac{v C_2}{2} + \frac{\mu}{\alpha \rho}}$$
(11.4)

The following values were used in or determined from the ANSYS Fluent simulations.

C_2 (1/m)	1719.4
$1/\alpha$ (1/m^2)	$1.98807 \cdot 10^6$
ρ (kg/m^3)	992.2
μ (kg/m-s)	0.00065
v (m/s)	0.05
g (m/s^2)	9.81
k (m/s)	0.221508
p_1 (Pa)	29046.9
p_2 (Pa)	25124.4

Table 11.1 Parameters & coefficients used or determined by ANSYS Fluent simulations

The 2D flow through a porous medium is governed by

$$k_x \frac{\partial^2 \phi}{\partial x^2} + k_y \frac{\partial^2 \phi}{\partial y^2} = 0$$
(11.5)

where ϕ is the hydraulic head and $k_x = k_y = k$ are coefficients of permeability in the x and y-directions. The seepage velocity components are related to the hydraulic head through

$$v_x = -k_x \frac{\partial \phi}{\partial x} \quad \text{and} \quad v_y = -k_y \frac{\partial \phi}{\partial y}$$
(11.6)

We follow the approach by Bhatti[3] using second order ($n = 2$) p-formulation. The equations for element **1**:

$$
\begin{pmatrix}
+0.2424 & -0.2021 & -0.1212 & +0.0809 & -0.0164 & +0.1320 & +0.0164 & -0.1320 \\
-0.2021 & +0.2424 & +0.0809 & -0.1212 & -0.0164 & -0.1320 & +0.0164 & +0.1320 \\
-0.1212 & +0.0809 & +0.2424 & -0.2021 & +0.0164 & -0.1320 & -0.0164 & +0.1320 \\
+0.0809 & -0.1212 & -0.2021 & +0.2424 & +0.0164 & +0.1320 & -0.0164 & -0.1320 \\
-0.0164 & -0.0164 & +0.0164 & +0.0164 & +0.4445 & 0 & +0.2021 & 0 \\
+0.1320 & -0.1320 & -0.1320 & +0.1320 & 0 & +0.1615 & 0 & -0.0809 \\
+0.0164 & +0.0164 & -0.0164 & -0.0164 & +0.2021 & 0 & +0.4445 & 0 \\
-0.1320 & +0.1320 & +0.1320 & -0.1320 & 0 & -0.0809 & 0 & +0.1615
\end{pmatrix}
\begin{pmatrix}
\phi_1 \\ \phi_4 \\ \phi_5 \\ \phi_2 \\ \delta_1^{(1,4)} \\ \delta_1^{(4,5)} \\ \delta_1^{(2,5)} \\ \delta_1^{(1,2)}
\end{pmatrix}
=
\begin{pmatrix}
0 \\ 0 \\ 0 \\ 0 \\ 0 \\ 0 \\ 0 \\ 0
\end{pmatrix}
$$

Equations for element **2**:

$$
\begin{pmatrix}
+0.1902 & +0.0380 & -0.0951 & -0.1331 & -0.0932 & +0.0233 & +0.0932 & -0.0233 \\
+0.0380 & +0.1902 & -0.1331 & -0.0951 & -0.0932 & -0.0233 & +0.0932 & +0.0233 \\
-0.0951 & -0.1331 & +0.1902 & +0.0380 & +0.0932 & -0.0233 & -0.0932 & +0.0233 \\
-0.1331 & -0.0951 & +0.0380 & +0.1902 & +0.0932 & +0.0233 & -0.0932 & -0.0233 \\
-0.0932 & -0.0932 & +0.0932 & +0.0932 & +0.1521 & 0 & -0.0380 & 0 \\
+0.0233 & -0.0233 & -0.0233 & +0.0233 & 0 & +0.3233 & 0 & +0.1331 \\
+0.0932 & +0.0932 & -0.0932 & -0.0932 & -0.0380 & 0 & +0.1521 & 0 \\
-0.0233 & +0.0233 & +0.0233 & -0.0233 & 0 & +0.1331 & 0 & +0.3233
\end{pmatrix}
\begin{pmatrix}
\phi_2 \\ \phi_5 \\ \phi_6 \\ \phi_3 \\ \delta_1^{(2,5)} \\ \delta_1^{(5,6)} \\ \delta_1^{(3,6)} \\ \delta_1^{(2,3)}
\end{pmatrix}
=
\begin{pmatrix}
0 \\ 0 \\ 0 \\ 0 \\ 0 \\ 0 \\ 0 \\ 0
\end{pmatrix}
$$

Equations for element **3**:

$$
\begin{pmatrix}
+0.2424 & -0.2021 & -0.1212 & +0.0809 & -0.0164 & +0.1320 & +0.0164 & -0.1320 \\
-0.2021 & +0.2424 & +0.0809 & -0.1212 & -0.0164 & -0.1320 & +0.0164 & +0.1320 \\
-0.1212 & +0.0809 & +0.2424 & -0.2021 & +0.0164 & -0.1320 & -0.0164 & +0.1320 \\
+0.0809 & -0.1212 & -0.2021 & +0.2424 & +0.0164 & +0.1320 & -0.0164 & -0.1320 \\
-0.0164 & -0.0164 & +0.0164 & +0.0164 & +0.4445 & 0 & +0.2021 & 0 \\
+0.1320 & -0.1320 & -0.1320 & +0.1320 & 0 & +0.1615 & 0 & -0.0809 \\
+0.0164 & +0.0164 & -0.0164 & -0.0164 & +0.2021 & 0 & +0.4445 & 0 \\
-0.1320 & +0.1320 & +0.1320 & -0.1320 & 0 & -0.0809 & 0 & +0.1615
\end{pmatrix}
\begin{pmatrix}
\phi_4 \\ \phi_7 \\ \phi_8 \\ \phi_5 \\ \delta_1^{(4,7)} \\ \delta_1^{(7,8)} \\ \delta_1^{(5,8)} \\ \delta_1^{(4,5)}
\end{pmatrix}
=
\begin{pmatrix}
0 \\ 0 \\ 0 \\ 0 \\ 0 \\ 0 \\ 0 \\ 0
\end{pmatrix}
$$

Equations for element **4**:

$$
\begin{pmatrix}
+0.1902 & +0.0380 & -0.0951 & -0.1331 & -0.0932 & +0.0233 & +0.0932 & -0.0233 \\
+0.0380 & +0.1902 & -0.1331 & -0.0951 & -0.0932 & -0.0233 & +0.0932 & +0.0233 \\
-0.0951 & -0.1331 & +0.1902 & +0.0380 & +0.0932 & -0.0233 & -0.0932 & +0.0233 \\
-0.1331 & -0.0951 & +0.0380 & +0.1902 & +0.0932 & +0.0233 & -0.0932 & -0.0233 \\
-0.0932 & -0.0932 & +0.0932 & +0.0932 & +0.1521 & 0 & -0.0380 & 0 \\
+0.0233 & -0.0233 & -0.0233 & +0.0233 & 0 & +0.3233 & 0 & +0.1331 \\
+0.0932 & +0.0932 & -0.0932 & -0.0932 & -0.0380 & 0 & +0.1521 & 0 \\
-0.0233 & +0.0233 & +0.0233 & -0.0233 & 0 & +0.1331 & 0 & +0.3233
\end{pmatrix}
\begin{pmatrix}
\phi_5 \\ \phi_8 \\ \phi_9 \\ \phi_6 \\ \delta_1^{(5,8)} \\ \delta_1^{(8,9)} \\ \delta_1^{(6,9)} \\ \delta_1^{(5,6)}
\end{pmatrix}
=
\begin{pmatrix}
0 \\ 0 \\ 0 \\ 0 \\ 0 \\ 0 \\ 0 \\ 0
\end{pmatrix}
$$

where $\phi_1 \ldots, \phi_9$ are hydraulic heads at the node points for the four elements and δ are the p-mode parameters, subscripts indicate mode number for the side modes and superscripts indicate node numbers on the corresponding line segments for an element. The boundary conditions are the following:

$$
(\phi_1, \phi_2, \phi_3, \phi_6, \phi_9, \delta_1^{(1,2)}, \delta_1^{(3,6)}, \delta_1^{(6,9)}) = (2.98422, 2.58123, 2, 2, 2, 0, 0, 0) \tag{11.7}
$$

The hydraulic head boundary conditions ϕ_1, ϕ_2 were determined from the static pressures

$$
p_1, p_2 = \rho g \phi_1, \rho g \phi_2 = 29046.9, 25124.4 \, Pa \tag{11.8}
$$

at nodes and 1 and 2, respectively. We can now assemble the global stiffness matrix.

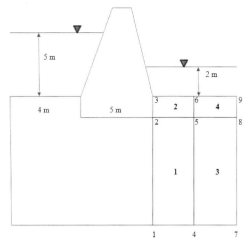

Figure 11.13a) Four element model for seepage flow

$$\begin{pmatrix} +0.485 & +0.162 & -0.202 & -0.121 & -0.016 & 0 & +0.016 & -0.264 & -0.016 & 0 & +0.016 & +0.132 & 0 \\ +0.162 & +0.865 & -0.121 & -0.164 & +0.016 & +0.023 & -0.110 & -0.264 & +0.016 & -0.047 & -0.110 & +0.132 & +0.023 \\ -0.202 & -0.121 & +0.242 & +0.081 & 0 & 0 & 0 & +0.132 & -0.016 & 0 & +0.016 & -0.132 & 0 \\ -0.121 & -0.164 & +0.081 & +0.433 & 0 & 0 & 0 & +0.132 & +0.016 & +0.023 & -0.110 & -0.132 & -0.023 \\ -0.016 & +0.016 & 0 & 0 & +0.445 & 0 & +0.202 & 0 & 0 & 0 & 0 & 0 & 0 \\ 0 & +0.023 & 0 & 0 & 0 & +0.323 & 0 & 0 & 0 & +0.133 & 0 & 0 & 0 \\ +0.016 & -0.110 & 0 & 0 & +0.202 & 0 & +0.597 & 0 & 0 & 0 & 0 & 0 & 0 \\ -0.264 & -0.264 & +0.132 & +0.132 & 0 & 0 & 0 & +0.323 & 0 & 0 & 0 & -0.081 & 0 \\ -0.016 & +0.016 & -0.016 & +0.016 & 0 & 0 & 0 & 0 & +0.445 & 0 & +0.202 & 0 & 0 \\ 0 & -0.047 & 0 & +0.023 & 0 & +0.133 & 0 & 0 & 0 & +0.647 & 0 & 0 & +0.133 \\ +0.016 & -0.110 & +0.016 & -0.110 & 0 & 0 & 0 & 0 & +0.202 & 0 & +0.597 & 0 & 0 \\ +0.132 & +0.132 & -0.132 & -0.132 & 0 & 0 & 0 & -0.081 & 0 & 0 & 0 & +0.161 & 0 \\ 0 & +0.023 & 0 & -0.023 & 0 & 0 & 0 & 0 & 0 & +0.133 & 0 & 0 & +0.323 \end{pmatrix} \begin{pmatrix} \phi_4 \\ \phi_5 \\ \phi_7 \\ \phi_8 \\ \delta_1^{(1,4)} \\ \delta_1^{(2,3)} \\ \delta_1^{(2,5)} \\ \delta_1^{(4,5)} \\ \delta_1^{(4,7)} \\ \delta_1^{(5,6)} \\ \delta_1^{(5,8)} \\ \delta_1^{(7,8)} \\ \delta_1^{(8,9)} \end{pmatrix} =$$

$$\begin{pmatrix} +0.916 \\ +1.698 \\ 0 \\ +0.456 \\ +0.007 \\ +0.060 \\ -0.139 \\ -0.735 \\ 0 \\ -0.060 \\ -0.373 \\ 0 \\ 0 \end{pmatrix}, \text{ with the solution } \begin{pmatrix} \phi_4 \\ \phi_5 \\ \phi_7 \\ \phi_8 \\ \delta_1^{(1,4)} \\ \delta_1^{(2,3)} \\ \delta_1^{(2,5)} \\ \delta_1^{(4,5)} \\ \delta_1^{(4,7)} \\ \delta_1^{(5,6)} \\ \delta_1^{(5,8)} \\ \delta_1^{(7,8)} \\ \delta_1^{(8,9)} \end{pmatrix} = \begin{pmatrix} +2.699 \\ +2.192 \\ +2.703 \\ +2.193 \\ -0.012 \\ +0.038 \\ +0.100 \\ -0.316 \\ +0.027 \\ -0.024 \\ +0.023 \\ -0.155 \\ +0.010 \end{pmatrix} \qquad (11.9)$$

We can summarize the solution at the outflow for elements 2 and 4 with the following table where v_y velocity component is compared with ANSYS Fluent in Figure 11.12e).

	x	y	φ	∂φ/∂x	∂φ/∂y	v_y
2	0	10	2.	0.	−0.32565825428980166	0.07432144875149277
2	0.75	10	2.	0.	−0.2555161785079309	0.05831368410289106
2	1.5	10	2.	0.	−0.2057152107246451	0.04694814975476898
2	2.25	10	2.	0.	−0.1762553509399443	0.04022484570712651
4	3	10	2.	0.	−0.16713659915382845	0.03814377195996365
4	3.75	10	2.	0.	−0.14647549864168652	0.03342851324124527
4	4.5	10	2.	0.	−0.13050473334316898	0.029783678820436723
4	5.25	10	2.	0.	−0.1192243032582763	0.027209268697538133
4	6	10	2.	0.	−0.11263420838700836	0.025705282872549466

Table 11.2 Solution summary at the outflow region

```
(*Seepage through soil, p=q=0,
2nd order p-formulation (n=2), wi = wj = 1, kx = ky = 0.2282191462137928` *)
Clear["Global`*"]; wi = 1; wj = 1; kx = 0.2282191462137928`; ky = 0.2282191462137928`;
NT = {(1 - s) * (1 - t) / 4, (1 + s) * (1 - t) / 4, (1 + s) * (1 + t) / 4, (1 - s) * (1 + t) / 4,
    (3*s^2/2 - 3/2) * (1 - t) / (2*Sqrt[6]), (3*t^2/2 - 3/2) * (1 + s) / (2*Sqrt[6]),
    (3*s^2/2 - 3/2) * (1 + t) / (2*Sqrt[6]), (3*t^2/2 - 3/2) * (1 - s) / (2*Sqrt[6])};
gcd[x0_, y0_] := Module[{x = x0, y = y0}, {J = {{D[x, s], D[x, t]}, {D[y, s], D[y, t]}};
    BT = Inverse[J] . {D[NT, s], D[NT, t]}; k = wi*wj*Transpose[BT] . {{kx, 0}, {0, ky}}.BT*Det[J];
    k1 = k //. {s -> -0.57735, t → -0.57735}; k2 = k //. {s -> -0.57735, t → 0.57735};
    k3 = k //. {s -> 0.57735, t → -0.57735}; k4 = k //. {s -> 0.57735, t → 0.57735}; kk = k1 + k2 + k3 + k4;}]


(*Element 1: 0<x<3, 0<y<8.5, -1<s<1, -1<t<1, Element 2: 0<x<3, 8.5<y<10, -1<s<1, -1<t<1,
Element 3: 3<x<6, 0<y<8.5, -1<s<1, -1<t<1, Element 4: 3<x<6, 8.5<y<10, -1<s<1, -1<t<1 *)
gcd[3*s/2 + 3/2, 8.5*t/2 + 8.5/2]; kk1 = kk; kk1 // MatrixForm;
gcd[3*s/2 + 3/2, 3*t/4 + 37/4]; kk2 = kk; kk2 // MatrixForm;
gcd[3*s/2 + 9/2, 8.5*t/2 + 8.5/2]; kk3 = kk; kk3 // MatrixForm;
gcd[3*s/2 + 9/2, y = 3*t/4 + 37/4]; kk4 = kk; kk4 // MatrixForm;


(*Global stiffness matrix and Boundary conditions *)
kG = SparseArray[{}, {21, 21}]; r1 = {1, 4, 5, 2, 11, 15, 13, 10}; kG[[r1, r1]] = kG[[r1, r1]] + kk1;
r2 = {2, 5, 6, 3, 13, 17, 14, 12};
kG[[r2, r2]] = kG[[r2, r2]] + kk2; r3 = {4, 7, 8, 5, 16, 20, 18, 15};
kG[[r3, r3]] = kG[[r3, r3]] + kk3; r4 = {5, 8, 9, 6, 18, 21, 19, 17}; kG[[r4, r4]] = kG[[r4, r4]] + kk4;
kG[[1]] = UnitVector[21, 1]; kG[[2]] = UnitVector[21, 2]; kG[[3]] = UnitVector[21, 3];
kG[[6]] = UnitVector[21, 6]; kG[[9]] = UnitVector[21, 9]; kG[[10]] = UnitVector[21, 10];
kG[[14]] = UnitVector[21, 14]; kG[[19]] = UnitVector[21, 19];


(*Global solution and element solutions) *)
RHS = {2.984224966974819`, 2.581234546896989`, 2, 0, 0, 2, 0, 0, 2, 0, 0, 0, 0, 0, 0, 0, 0, 0, 0, 0, 0};
ϕ = LinearSolve[kG, RHS]
gce[x0_, y0_, s0_, t0_] :=
  Module[{x = x0, y = y0}, {J = {{D[x, s], D[x, t]}, {D[y, s], D[y, t]}}; NT1 = NT //. {s → s0, t → t0};
    dNTds = D[NT, s] //. {s → s0, t → t0}; dNTdt = D[NT, t] //. {s → s0, t → t0};
    dNTdsodNTdt = {dNTds, dNTdt} //. {s → s0, t → t0}; BT = Inverse[J] . dNTdsodNTdt;
    B = Transpose[BT]; BTx = BT[[1]]; BTy = BT[[2]]; ϕxy = NT1.dT; dϕdx = BTx.dT; dϕdy = BTy.dT;}]


(*Solution for element 2 at location (x,y) = (0,10), (0.75,10), (1.5,10), (2.25,10) *)
dT = {ϕ[[2]], ϕ[[5]], ϕ[[6]], ϕ[[3]], ϕ[[13]], ϕ[[17]], ϕ[[14]], ϕ[[12]]};
gce[3*s/2 + 3/2, 3*t/4 + 37/4, -1, 1]; mxy1 = {0, 10, ϕxy, dϕdx, dϕdy, -ky*dϕdy};
gce[3*s/2 + 3/2, 3*t/4 + 37/4, -0.5, 1]; mxy2 = {0.75, 10, ϕxy, dϕdx, dϕdy, -ky*dϕdy};
gce[3*s/2 + 3/2, 3*t/4 + 37/4, 0, 1]; mxy3 = {1.5, 10, ϕxy, dϕdx, dϕdy, -ky*dϕdy};
gce[3*s/2 + 3/2, 3*t/4 + 37/4, 0.5, 1]; mxy4 = {2.25, 10, ϕxy, dϕdx, dϕdy, -ky*dϕdy};


(*Solution for element 4 at location (x,y) = (3,10), (3.75,10), (4.5,10), (5.25,10), (6,10) *)
dT = {ϕ[[5]], ϕ[[8]], ϕ[[9]], ϕ[[6]], ϕ[[18]], ϕ[[21]], ϕ[[19]], ϕ[[17]]};
gce[3*s/2 + 9/2, 3*t/4 + 37/4, -1, 1]; mxy5 = {3, 10, ϕxy, dϕdx, dϕdy, -ky*dϕdy};
gce[3*s/2 + 9/2, 3*t/4 + 37/4, -0.5, 1]; mxy6 = {3.75, 10, ϕxy, dϕdx, dϕdy, -ky*dϕdy};
gce[3*s/2 + 9/2, 3*t/4 + 37/4, 0, 1]; mxy7 = {4.5, 10, ϕxy, dϕdx, dϕdy, -ky*dϕdy};
gce[3*s/2 + 9/2, 3*t/4 + 37/4, 0.5, 1]; mxy8 = {5.25, 10, ϕxy, dϕdx, dϕdy, -ky*dϕdy};
gce[3*s/2 + 9/2, 3*t/4 + 37/4, 1, 1]; mxy9 = {6, 10, ϕxy, dϕdx, dϕdy, -ky*dϕdy};
```

```
(* Nodal solution summary and write to  file*)
mm = {mxy1, mxy2, mxy3, mxy4, mxy5, mxy6, mxy7, mxy8, mxy9}; MatrixForm[mm,
  TableHeadings → {{"2", "2", "2", "2", "4", "4", "4", "4", "4"}, {"x", "y", "ϕ", "∂ϕ/∂x", "∂ϕ/∂y", "vy"}}]
SetDirectory["C:\\Users\\jmatsson"]; mylist = Table[
    {{9, mxy1[[6]]}, {9.75, mxy2[[6]]}, {10.5, mxy3[[6]]}, {11.25, mxy4[[6]]}, {12, mxy5[[6]]},
     {12.75, mxy6[[6]]}, {13.5, mxy7[[6]]}, {14.25, mxy8[[6]]}, {15, mxy9[[6]]}}];
TableOfValues1 = Prepend[mylist, {"((xy/key/label \"theory-outlet\")"}];
TableOfValues1 = Prepend[TableOfValues1, {""}];
TableOfValues1 = Prepend[TableOfValues1, {"(labels \"X-Coordinate\" \"Velocity\")"}];
TableOfValues1 = Prepend[TableOfValues1, {"(title \"Theory\")"}];
TableOfValues1 = Append[TableOfValues1, {")"}]; Grid[TableOfValues1]
Export["theory.dat", TableOfValues1]
```

Figure 11.13b) Mathematica code for seepage flow under a dam

I. References

1. Ochs et al., "Soil-Water Pit Heat Store with Direct Charging System", Ecostock 2005 Conference Proceedings.
2. Moaveni S., "Finite Element Analysis: Theory and Applications with ANSYS", 3rd Ed., Prentice Hall, 2007.
3. Bhatti, M.A., "Fundamental Finite Element Analysis and Applications", John Wiley & Sons, Inc., 2005.

J. Exercise

11.1 Use ANSYS Fluent to study the seepage flow of water through the porous medium under the dam as shown in Figure 11.14. Include contour plots for velocity magnitude and static pressure together with an XY Plot of the velocity magnitude at the outlet. Use the same values for viscous and inertial resistance as was used in this chapter.

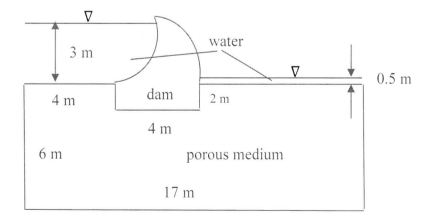

Figure 11.14 Geometry for Exercise 10.1

259

Notes:

CHAPTER 12. WATER FILTER FLOW

A. Objectives

- Using ANSYS Workbench to Model Flow Through Water Filter
- Inserting Boundary Conditions and Porous Medium Zone for Filter with Viscous and Inertial Resistance
- Using Volume of Fluid Model for Multiphase Flow with Surface Tension
- Running Laminar Transient 2D Axisymmetric ANSYS Fluent Simulations
- Using Volume Fraction Contour Plots for Visualizations and Movie
- Comparing ANSYS Fluent Results with Theory

B. Problem Description

We will study the flow through a ceramic gravity driven clay pot water filter using ANSYS Fluent. The dimensions and initial water levels are shown below. The thickness of the filter is $d = 20$ mm and the radius $R = 100$ mm while the initial height of water $h_0 = 200$ mm. The height $h(t)$ of the water in the filter will vary over time as the fluid seeps through the filter.

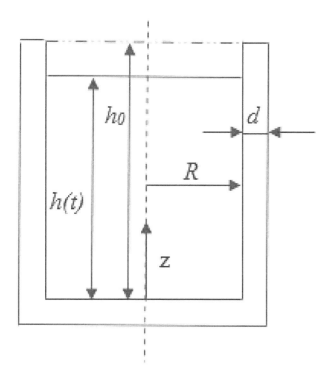

C. Launching ANSYS Workbench and Selecting Fluent

1. Start by launching ANSYS Workbench. Double click on Fluid Flow (Fluent) under Analysis Systems in the Toolbox.

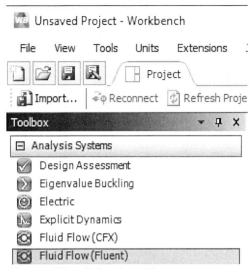

Figure 12.1 Selecting Fluent

D. Launching ANSYS DesignModeler

2. Right click Geometry under Project Schematic in ANSYS Workbench and select Properties. In Properties of Schematic A2: Geometry, select Analysis Type 2D under Advanced Geometry Options. Right click on Geometry in the Project Schematic window and select New DesignModeler Geometry.

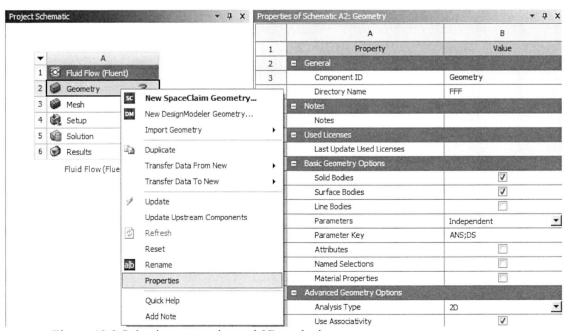

Figure 12.2 Selecting properties and 2D analysis type

3. Select Units>>Millimeter from the menu in DesignModeler. Select XY Plane in the Tree Outline and click on Look at Face/Plane/Sketch 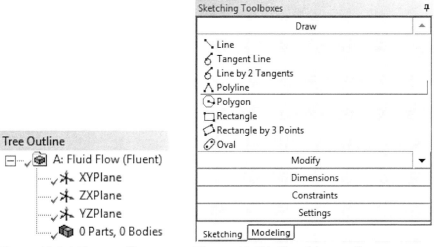. Select Sketching tab and Draw>>Polyline from Sketching Toolboxes. Start at origin and draw the Sketch with Dimensions as shown in Figure 12.3c).

Figure 12.3a) Tree outline   Figure 12.3b) Sketching toolboxes

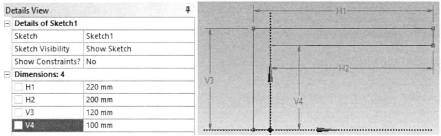

Figure 12.3c) Sketch of cylindrical water filter with dimensions

4. Select the Modeling tab and select Concepts>>Surfaces from Sketches from the menu. Select Sketch1 under XYPlane in the Tree Outline and Apply the sketch in Details View. Click on Generate.

    Select the XYPlane once again in the Tree Outline and click on New Sketch 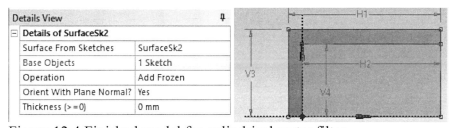. Select the new sketch (Sketch2) under XYPlane and click on the Sketching tab. Select Rectangle under Draw in Sketching Toolboxes and draw a rectangle inside the filter from the origin. Select Concepts>>Surfaces from Sketches from the menu and Apply the new sketch in Details View. Select Add Frozen as Operation in Details View. Click on Generate and Close DesignModeler.

Figure 12.4 Finished model for cylindrical water filter

263

E. Launching ANSYS Meshing

5. Double click on Mesh under Project Schematic in ANSYS Workbench. Select Mesh in the Outline. Set the Element Size to 2.0 mm under Defaults in Details of "Mesh". Select Yes for Capture Curvature under Sizing and set Smoothing to High under Quality. Right click on Mesh in the Outline and select Generate Mesh.

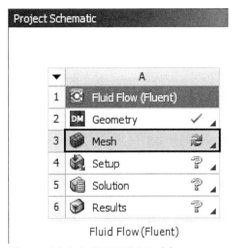

Figure 12.5a) ANSYS Meshing

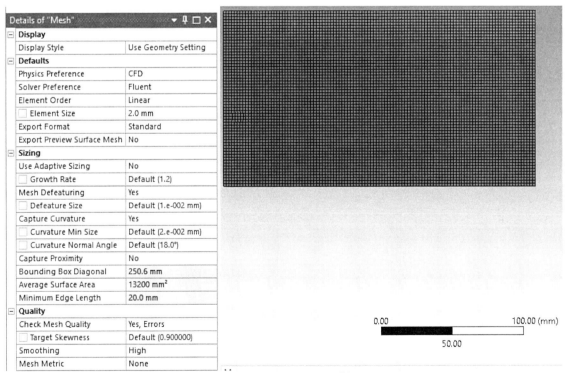

Figure 12.5b) Finished mesh for cylindrical water filter

6. Select Edge selection filter and control select the two edges on the right side of the computational domain. Right click on the edges and select Create Named Selection. Name the edges *outlet*.

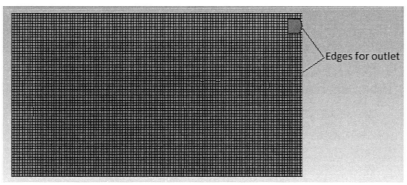

Figure 12.6a) Named selections for outlet

Control-select the upper horizontal edge and the left outer vertical edge, right click and select Create Named Selection. Name the edges *outlet-filter*.

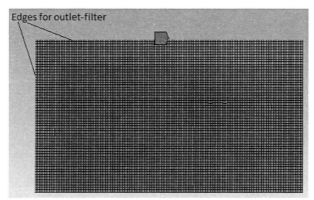

Figure 12.6b) Named selections for outlet-filter

Select Body and select the outer L-shaped filter region, right click and select Hide Body. Select Edge and control-select the upper horizontal edge and the left vertical edge, right click and select Create Named Selection. Name the edges *interface1*. Right click in the graphics window and select Show All Bodies.

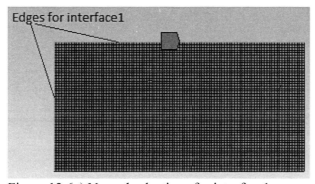

Figure 12.6c) Named selections for interface1

Select Body ![icon], left click on the inner fluid region, right click and select Hide Body.

Select Edge ![icon] and control-select the middle horizontal edge and the middle vertical edge, right click and select Create Named Selection. Name the edges *interface2*. Right click in the graphics window and select Show All Bodies.

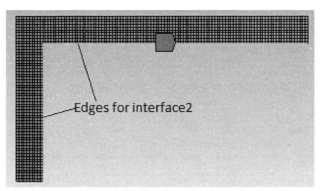

Figure 12.6d) Named selections for interface2

Control select the two lower horizontal edges and name them *symmetry*.

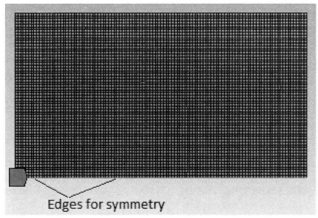

Figure 12.6e) Named selections for symmetry

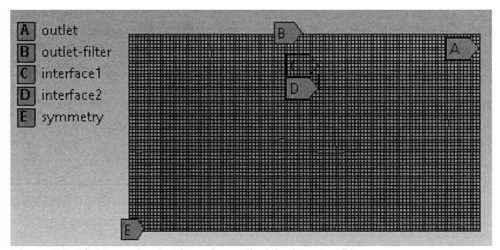

Figure 12.6f) Named selections for cylindrical water filter

Open Geometry in the Outline, select the first Surface Body, right click and select Rename. Name this body *Porous zone*. Rename the next Surface Body and call it *Inlet zone*.

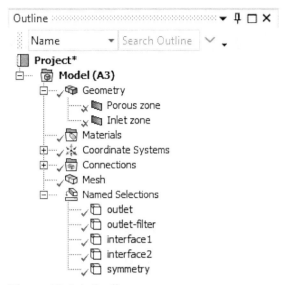

Figure 12.6g) Outline

Select File>>Export…>>Mesh>>FLUENT Input File>>Export from the menu and save the mesh with the name *cylindrical-water-filter.msh*. Select File>>Save Project from the menu and enter the name *Cylindrical Water Filter*. Right click on Mesh under Project Schematic in ANSYS Workbench and select Update.

F. Launching ANSYS Fluent

7. Double click on Setup under Project Schematic in ANSYS Workbench. Select Double Precision and Parallel Processing Options. Set the number of Processes equal to the number of processor cores and click on OK. Click on the plus sign next to Show More Options and take a note of the location for the *working directory*.

Select Transient Time and Axisymmetric 2D Space for the Solver on the Task Page. Check the box for Gravity and enter -9.81 as Gravitational Acceleration in the X direction. Double click on Models and Multiphase (Off) under Setup in the Outline View. Select Volume of Fluid model and check the box for Implicit Body Force. Click on OK to close the window.

Figure 12.7 Volume of Fluid Multiphase Model

267

8. Double click on Materials under Setup in the Tree. Select Create/Edit for Fluid under Materials on the Task Page. Select Fluent Database and scroll down to *water-liquid (h2o<l>)* and select this as Fluent Fluid Materials. Click on Copy and Close the window. Close the Create/Edit Materials window.

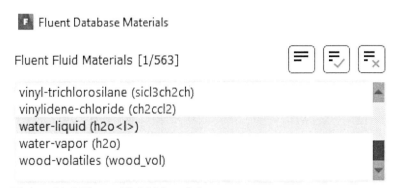

Figure 12.8 Fluent Fluid Materials

9. Double click on phase-1 – Primary Phase under Setup>>Models>>Multiphase>>Phases in the Outline View. Select *water-liquid* as the Primary Phase Material and enter *water* as the name. Click OK to close the Primary Phase window.

   Double click on phase-2 – Secondary Phase under Setup>>Models>>Multiphase>>Phases in the Outline View. Select *air* as the Secondary Phase Material and enter *air* as the name. Click OK to close the Secondary Phase window.

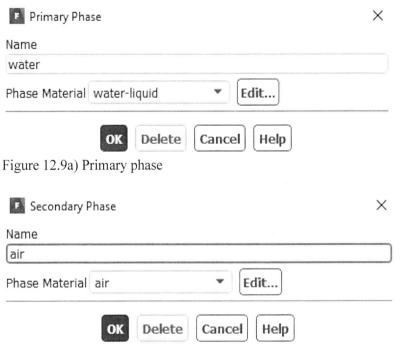

Figure 12.9a) Primary phase

Figure 12.9b) Secondary phase

Double click on Phase Interactions under Setup>>Models>>Multiphase in the Outline View. Select the Surface Tension tab and check the box for Surface Tension Force

Modeling. Select constant for the Surface Tension Coefficients and enter 0.07286 as the value. Click OK to close the Phase Interaction window.

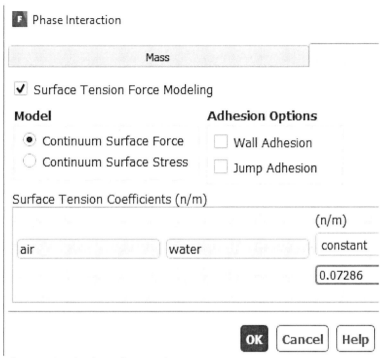

Figure 12.9c) Phase interaction

10. Double click on Cell Zone Conditions under Setup in the Outline View. Select the *porous_zone* under Cell Zone Conditions on the Task Page. Select *fluid* as Type and *mixture* as Phase and click on the Edit button on the Task Page. Check the Porous Zone box. Select the Porous Zone tab and make sure that Porosity is set to 1. Click OK to close the Fluid window.

Select water as the Phase for the *porous_zone* and click on Edit. Enter 9.76305e+08 as the Viscous Resistance in both directions. Click OK to close the Fluid window. Click on Operating Conditions on the Task Page under Cell Zone Conditions and check the box for Specified Operating Density. Enter Y (m) 0.2 as Reference Pressure Location. Click OK to close the Operating Conditions window.

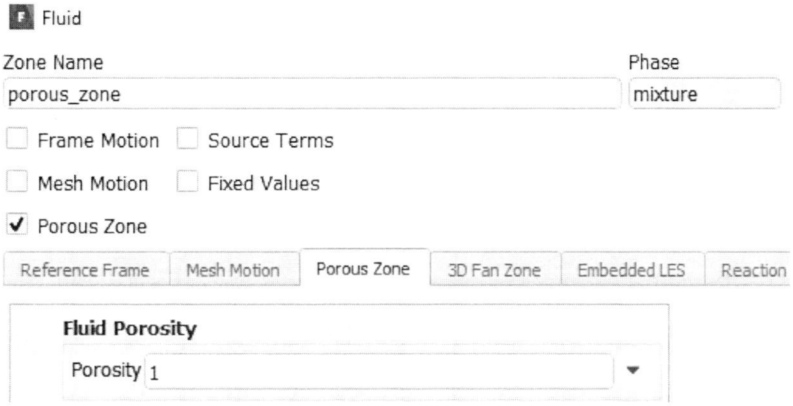

Figure 12.10a) Porous zone mixture phase

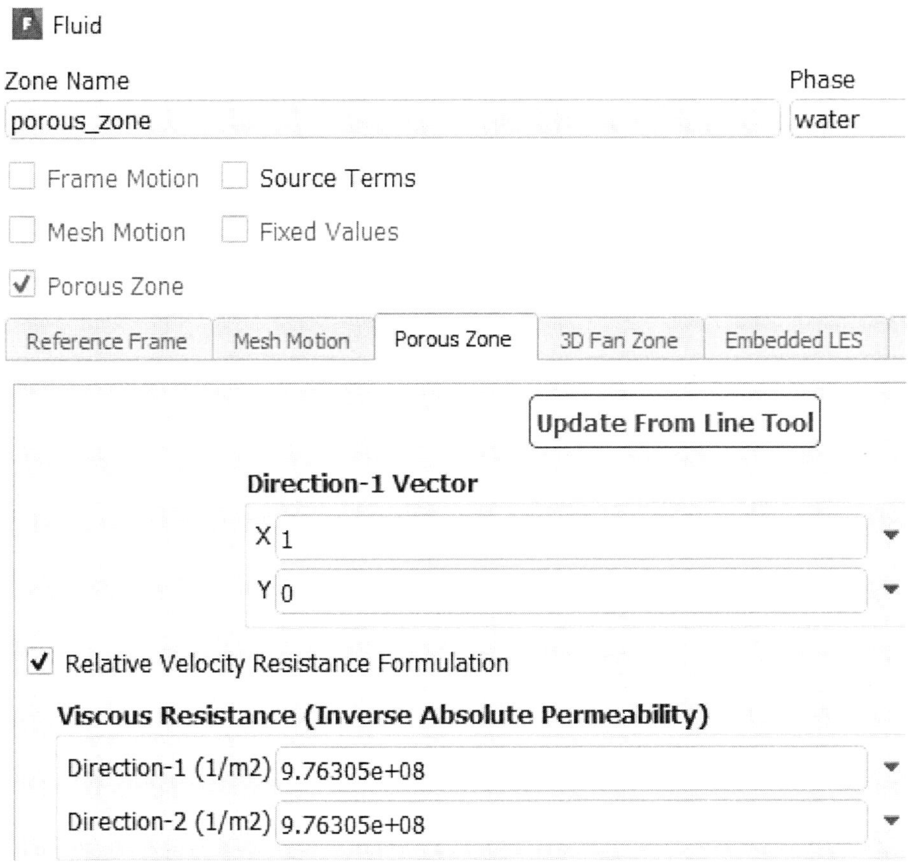

Figure 12.10b) Porous zone water phase

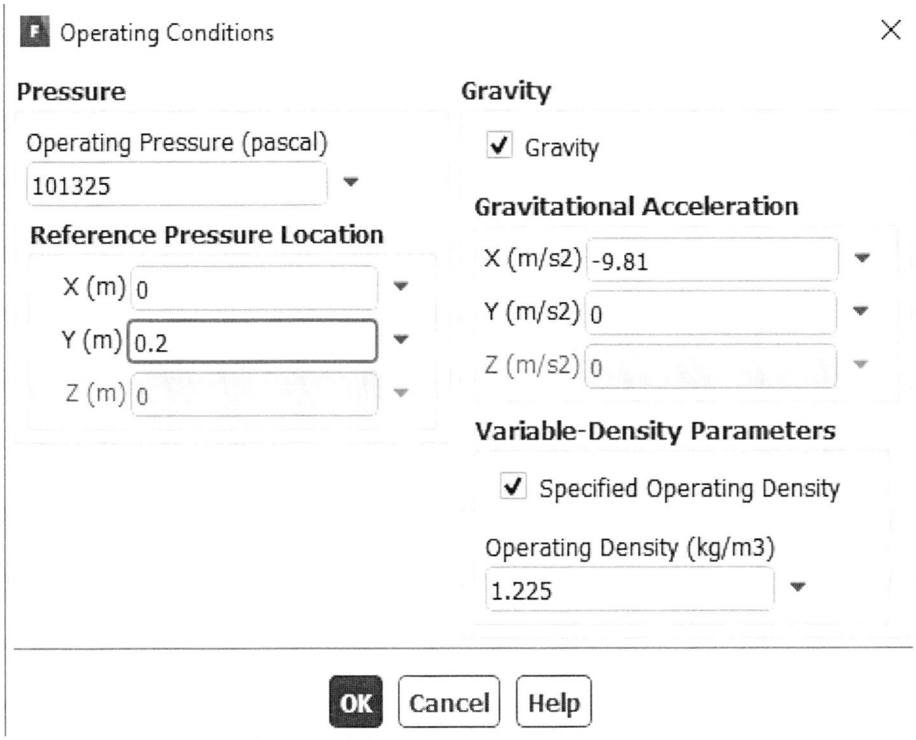

Figure 12.10c) Operating conditions

11. Double click on Boundary Conditions under Setup in the Outline View. Select the *outlet-inlet_zone* Boundary Condition on the Task Page and make sure that Type is set to pressure-outlet. Select *mixture* as Phase and click on Edit. Make sure that Gauge Pressure (pascal) is set to 0 and Backflow Pressure Specification as Total Pressure. Click OK to close the window. Select *air* as Phase and click on the Edit button on the Task Page under Boundary Conditions. Set the Backflow Volume Fraction to 1 and click OK to close the window. Repeat this step for the *outlet-porous_zone* Boundary Condition.

Furthermore, repeat this step for the *outlet-filter* Boundary Condition. Make sure that Type is set to pressure-outlet on the Task Page and select *mixture* as Phase and click on Edit. Gauge Pressure (pascal) is set to 0 and Backflow Pressure Specification as Total Pressure. Click OK to close the window. Select *air* as Phase and click on the Edit button. Select *From Neighboring Cell* as Volume Fraction Specification Method and click OK to close the window.

Figure 12.11a) Outlet-inlet_zone boundary condition for mixture phase

Figure 12.11b) Outlet-inlet_zone boundary condition for air phase

271

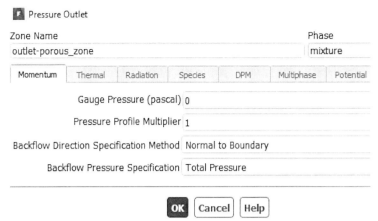

Figure 12.11c) Outlet-porous_zone boundary condition for mixture phase

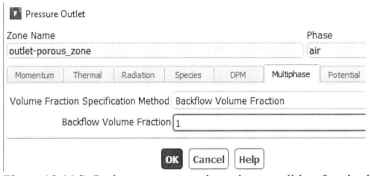

Figure 12.11d) Outlet-porous_zone boundary condition for air phase

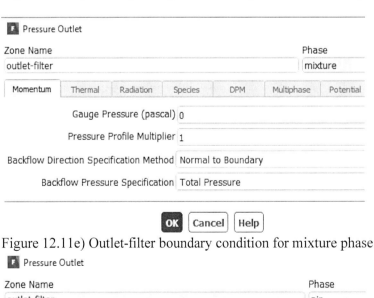

Figure 12.11e) Outlet-filter boundary condition for mixture phase

Figure 12.11f) Outlet-filter boundary condition for air phase

Double click on Boundary Conditions under Setup in the Outline View. Select *symmetry-inlet_zone* under Zone in Boundary Conditions on the Task Page. Select *mixture* as Phase and choose *axis* from the Type drop-down menu, change the zone name to *axis-inlet_zone* and click OK in the Axis window. Repeat this step for the *symmetry-porous_zone*.

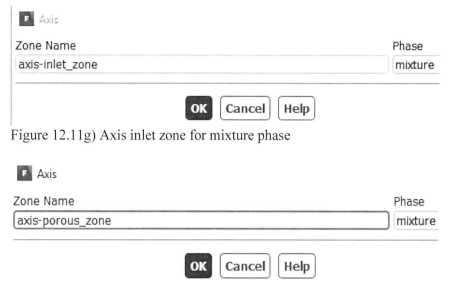

Figure 12.11g) Axis inlet zone for mixture phase

Figure 12.11h) Axis porous zone for mixture phase

12. Double click on Initialization under Solution in the Outline View. Select Hybrid Initialization Method on the Task Page and click on Initialize. Click on Patch on the Task Page under Solution Initialization. Select *air* as the Phase, select Volume Fraction as Variable, select *inlet_zone* and *porous_zone* as Zones to Patch, set the Value to 0 and click on Patch. Close the window.

Figure 12.12a) Initialization of solution

Figure 12.12b) Patch settings

13. Double click on Graphics and Contours under Results in the Outline View. Select Contours of Phases and Volume fraction for *water* as the Phase. Scroll down and deselect all Surfaces and uncheck Auto Range Options. Set Min to 0 and Max to 1. Click on Save/Display and Close the Contours window.

Figure 12.13a) Contours settings

Select the Viewing tab in the menu and click on Views…. Select *axis-porous_zone* and *axis-inlet_zone* as Mirror Planes and click on Apply. Click on the Camera… button in the Views window. Use your left mouse button to rotate the dial counter-clockwise 90 degrees until the bowl is upright. Close the Camera Parameters window. Click on the Save button under Actions in the Views window and Close the window.

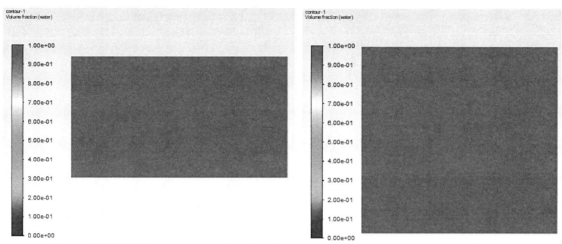

Figure 12.13b) Water volume fraction before and after rotation and mirroring

Double click on Calculation Activities and Solution Animations under Solution in the Outline View. Enter *water-filter* as the Name, enter Record after every 10 and select time-step. Set the Window ID to 2 and select *contour-1* as Animation Object. Click OK to close the Animation Definition window.

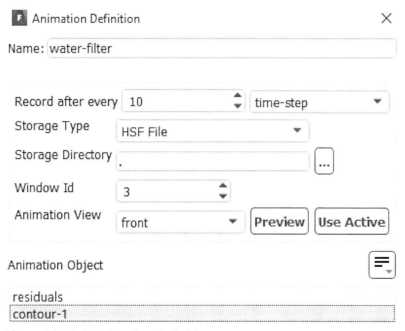

Figure 12.13c) Animation definition

275

14. Double click on Report Definitions under Solution in the Outline View. Select New>>Surface Report>>Volume Flow Rate. Enter *volume-flow-rate* as the name. Select *water* as the Phase and select *outlet-filter* under Surfaces. Check the boxes for Report File, Report Plot and Print to Console under Create. Click OK to close the window.

Select New>>Expression in the Report Definitions window. Select *volume-flow-rate* as Report Definition under Select Operand Field Functions from. Click on Select in Report Definitions and enter the Expression as shown in Figure 12.14b). Enter *absolute-volume-flow-rate* as Name and check boxes for Report File, Report Plot and Print to Console under Create. Click on Define and close the window.

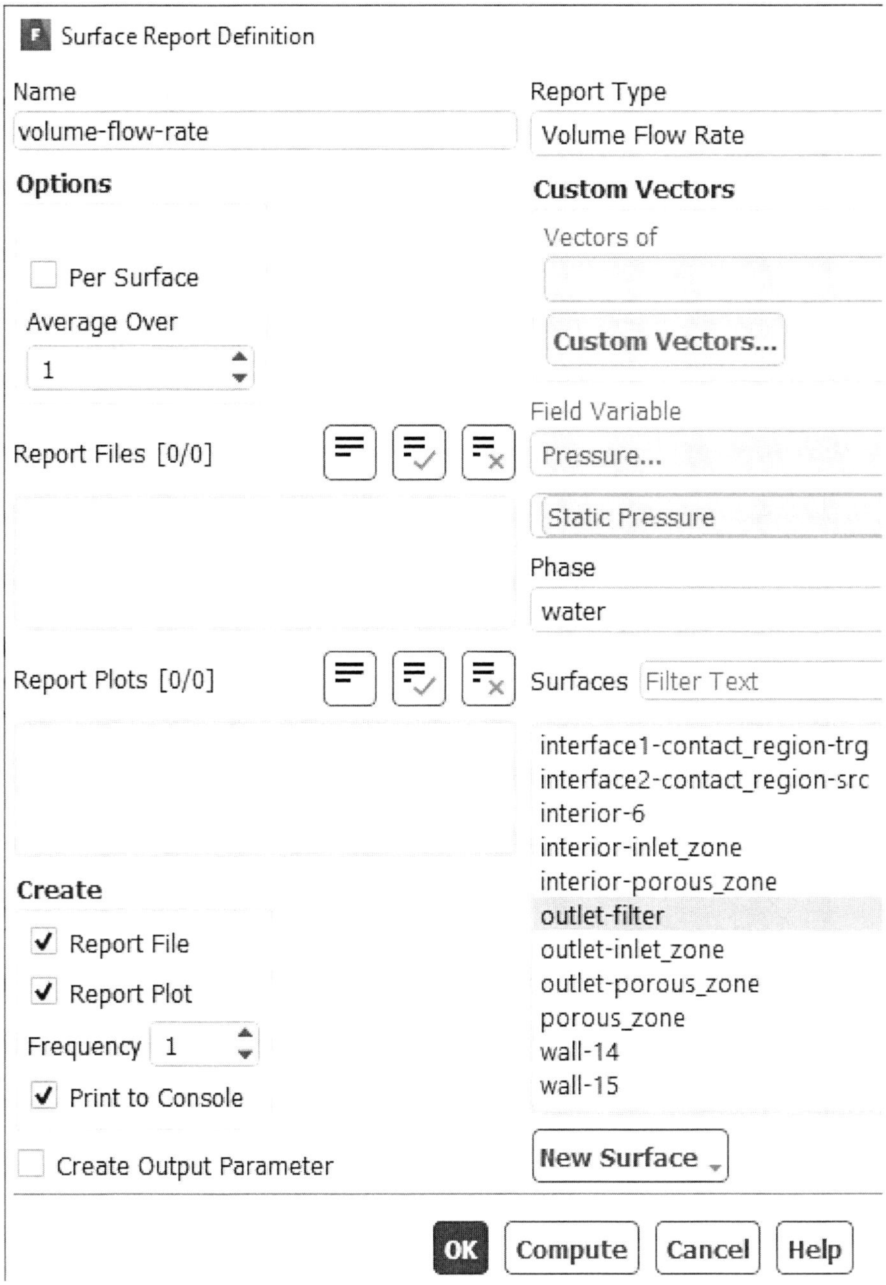

Figure 12.14a) Surface report definition for volume flow rate

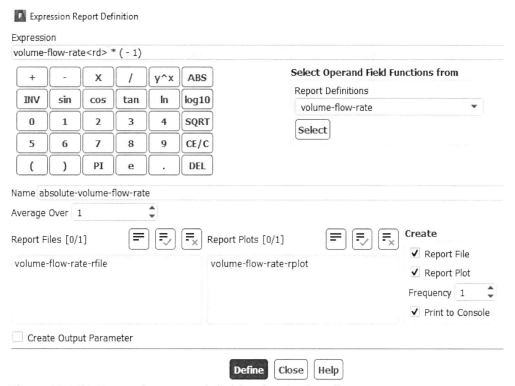

Figure 12.14b) Expression report definition for absolute flow rate

15. Double click on Run Calculation under Solution in the Outline View and set the Time Step Size (s) to 0.005. Set the Number of Time Steps to 50 and Max Iterations/Time Step to 30. Click on the Calculate button on the Task Page. Click OK in the window that appears. Click OK in the Information window when the calculation is complete.

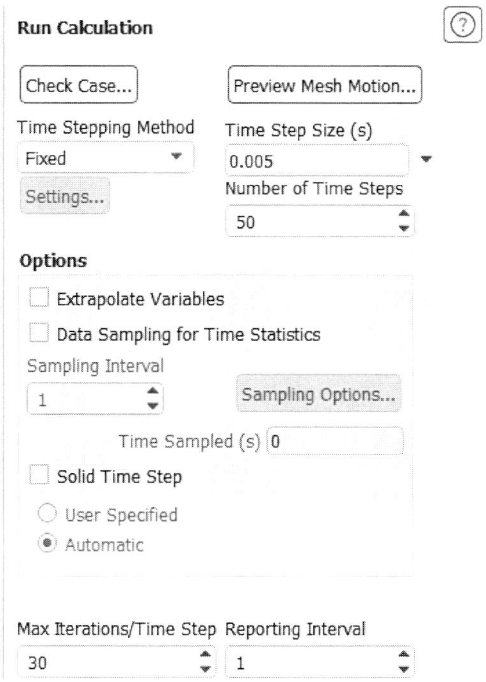

Figure 12.15a) Calculation settings

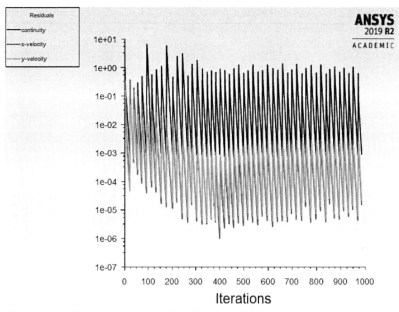

Figure 12.15b) Residuals during the first 0.25 s

G. Post-Processing and Continued Simulations

16. Select the tab Contours of Volume fraction (water) in the graphics window. Select the View tab in the menu and click on Views…. Select *view-0* in Views, click on Apply in the Views window and Close the window.

    Select the Results tab from the menu and select Surface>>Create>>Iso-Surface…. Select Surface of Constant Phases… and Volume Fraction. Select water as the Phase and set Iso-Values to 0.5. Select *inlet_zone* under Zones. Enter *free-surface -t=0.25s* as New Surface Name and click on Create. If you get a message that surface creation failed, do the following: select *air* and click on Create. Next, select *water* and click on Create. Close the window.

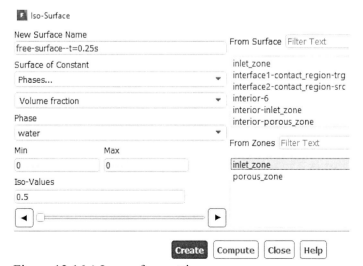

Figure 12.16a) Iso-surface settings

Select File>>Export>>Solution Data… from the menu. Select ASCII as File Type, Node under Location and Space as Delimiter. Select *inlet_zone* and *porous_zone* under Cell Zones and *Iso-surface>> free-surface-time-t=0.25s* under Surfaces. Select *Volume fraction (water)* under Quantities. Click on Write and save the ASCII File in the working directory with the name "free-surface-coordinates-t=0.25s". Close the Export window.

Figure 12.16b) Export settings

Open the saved file in Excel. Click on Next twice in the Text Import Wizard and click on Finish. Plot the free surface and take the average free surface height for the first 50 points. Repeat steps 15 – 16 seven more times for a total of 2 seconds.

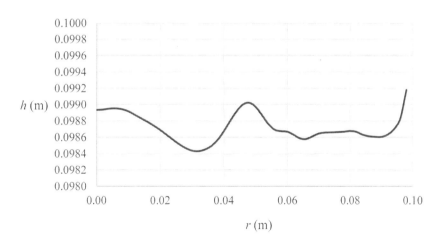

Figure 12.16c) Free surface height h (m) versus radius r (m) at $t = 0.5$ s

t (s)	Average h (m), ANSYS Fluent	h (m), Theory
0	0.2	0.2
0.25	0.139	0.1429
0.5	0.0987	0.1080
0.75	0.0729	0.08457
1	0.0549	0.06788
1.25	0.0416	0.05548
1.5	0.0318	0.04597
1.75	0.0242	0.03849
2	0.0178	0.03249

Table 12.1 Data for average free surface height over time

279

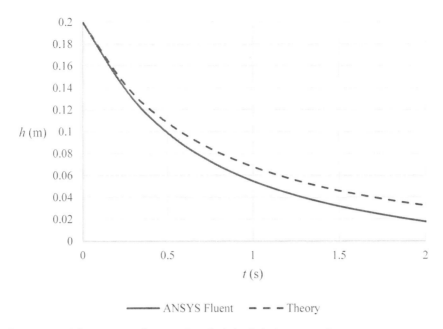

Figure 12.16d) Average free surface height h (m) versus time

Figure 12.16e) Water volume fraction at t = 0 – 2 s with an increment of 0.25 s

Double click on Animations and Solution Animation Playback under Results in the Tree. Uncheck the box for Use Stored View, set the Replay Speed to low and select Play Once as Playback Mode. Select MPEG as Write/Record Format. Click on the Write button for your chosen Animation Sequence. This will create the MPEG movie in your working directory. Close the Playback window. The movie can be viewed using, for example, VLC Media Player. In VLC Media Player select Media>>Open File… from the menu and open the movie. Select Playback>>Speed>>Slower from the menu in the VLC Media Player until you have a suitable speed for the movie.

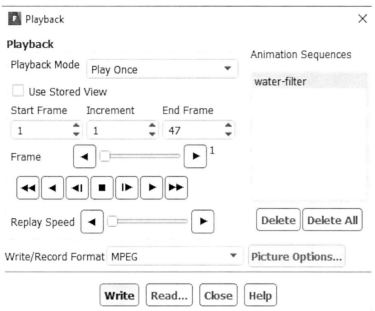

Figure 12.16f) Playback settings

Double click on File under Results and Plots in the Tree. Click on Load… under Files in the File XY Plot window and load the file "absolute-volume-flow-rate-rfile.out". Select *flow-time* as X Axis Variable and *absolute-volume-flow-rate* as Y Axis Variable.

Next, load the file "volume-flow-rate.dat". This and other files are available for download at *sdcpublications.com*. Select *Time(s)* as X Axis Variable and *Volume Flow Rate (m3/s)* as Y Axis Variable. Click on Axes… at the bottom of the File XY Plot window. Uncheck Auto Range under Options for X Axis. Set Minimum to 0 and Maximum to 2 under Range. Click on Apply and select Y Axis. Select float as Type under Number Format and set Precision to 3. Click on Apply and Close the Axes – File XY Plot window. Change the X Axis Label under Plot to "*t* (s)" and the Y Axis Label to "*dV/dt* (m3/s)". Delete the Title and Legend Label under Plot.

Click on Curves… and select the first available Pattern under Line Style for Curve # 0. Set the Color under Line Style to dark blue. Select no (blank) Symbol under Marker Style and click on Apply. Select Curve # 1, select the second available Pattern under Line Style and select dark blue Color. Select no (blank) Symbol under Marker Style and click on Apply. Close the Curves – File XY Plot window. Click on Plot at the bottom of the File XY Plot window.

Open the saved file "*absolute-volume-flow-rate-rfile*" in Excel. Select Delimited instead of Fixed width in Text Import Wizard – Step 1 of 3. Click on Next. Uncheck Tab as Delimiters and check Space as Delimiters in Text Import Wizard – Step 2 of 3. Click on Next. Click on Finish in Text Import Wizard – Step 3 of 3. Use the trapezoidal rule to find the area under the volume flow rate curve (2ⁿᵈ column in Excel file) for each time interval (3ʳᵈ column) and sum these areas in order to show the volume produced by the filter as seen in Figure 12.16i). Select File>>Export>>Data... from the menu in Fluent. Save the data file in the *working directory* folder with the name *water-filter-t=2s.dat*.

Figure 12.16g) File XY Plot settings

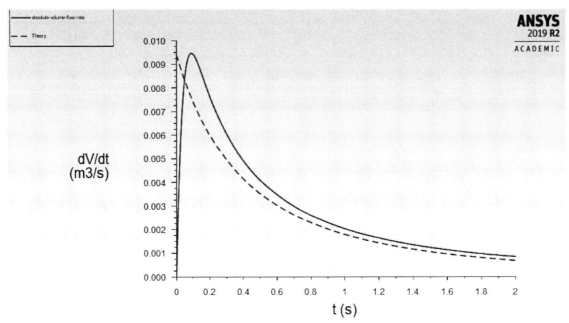

Figure 12.16h) Comparing ANSYS Fluent and theory-dashed curve for volume flow rate

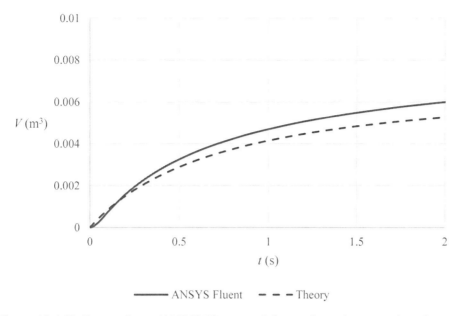

Figure 12.16i) Comparison ANSYS Fluent and theory for volume produced

H. Theory

17. We can relate the mean fluid velocity v (m/s) through the porous medium to the pressure gradient dP/dx (Pa) using Darcy's law in the same way as we did in the former chapter

$$v = -\frac{\kappa}{\mu}\frac{dP}{dx} \tag{12.1}$$

where κ (m^2) is permeability of the porous medium and μ (kg/m-s) is the dynamic viscosity of the fluid. Furthermore, we define the hydraulic conductivity or coefficient of permeability k (m/s) as

$$k = \kappa\frac{\rho g}{\mu} \tag{12.2}$$

Where g (m/s^2) is acceleration due to gravity and ρ (kg/m^3) is the density of the fluid. We will also use the following equation from the ANSYS Fluent user manual

$$\frac{dP}{dx} = -(\frac{\mu v}{\alpha} + \frac{C_2\rho v^2}{2}) \tag{12.3}$$

where $1/\alpha$ (1/m^2) is viscous resistance or inverse absolute permeability for the porous medium and C_2(1/m) is inertial resistance of the porous medium. When we combine these equations we get this expression for the permeability coefficient

$$k = \frac{g}{\frac{vC_2}{2} + \frac{\mu}{\alpha\rho}} \tag{12.4}$$

The following values were used in the ANSYS Fluent simulations in this chapter.

Parameter	Value
C_2 (1/m)	0
$1/\alpha$ (1/m²)	$9.76305 \cdot 10^8$
ρ (kg/m³)	998.2
μ (kg/m-s)	0.001003
g (m/s²)	9.81
k (m/s)	0.01
R (m)	0.1
h_0 (m)	0.2
d (m)	0.02
γ	2

Table 12.2 Parameters used in ANSYS Fluent simulations

For a cylindrical filter with a constant thickness d and constant radius R we have the schematic diagram as shown in Figure 12.17a).

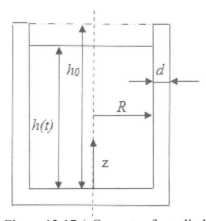

Figure 12.17a) Geometry for cylindrical ceramic water filter

The height of the free surface $h(t)$ will decrease over time as water is filtered through the filter. The volumetric flow rate through the filter can be described by

$$\dot{V}(t) = \frac{k}{d}\left[\pi R^2 h + R \int_0^{2\pi}\int_0^h (h-z)dzd\theta\right] = \frac{k\pi R h}{d}(R+h) \tag{12.5}$$

We can alternatively describe the volumetric flow rate as

$$\dot{V}(t) = -\pi R^2 \frac{dh}{dt} \tag{12.6}$$

Combining these two equations we get the following first order ordinary differential equation

$$\frac{dh}{dt} + \frac{kh}{d}\left(1 + \frac{h}{R}\right) = 0 \tag{12.7}$$

with the following solution where we have used the initial condition $h(0) = h_0$

$$h(t) = \frac{h_0 R}{e^{kt/d}(R+h_0)-h_0} \tag{12.8}$$

The volume flow rate using equation (12.6) will be

$$\dot{V}(t) = \frac{(R+h_0)\pi R^3 k h_0 e^{kt/d}}{d(e^{kt/d}(R+h_0)-h_0)^2} \tag{12.9}$$

The total water volume produced can be expressed as

$$V(t) = \pi R^2 (h_0 - h(t)) \tag{12.10}$$

and with the use of equation (12.8) we get

$$V(t) = \pi R^2 h_0 (1 - \frac{R}{e^{kt/d}(R+h_0)-h_0}) \tag{12.11}$$

We can alternatively make equation (12.7) non-dimensional using non-dimensional variables $h^* = \frac{h}{h_0}$ and $t^* = \frac{kt}{d}$ where h_0 is the initial height of fluid in the cylinder. This will transform equation (12.7) to the following equation after skipping[*]

$$\frac{dh}{dt} + h(1 + \gamma h) = 0 \tag{12.12}$$

where $\gamma = \frac{h_0}{R} = 2$ is the aspect-ratio.

Using initial condition $h(0) = 1$ we get the following solution

$$h(t) = \frac{1}{e^t (1+\gamma)-\gamma} = \frac{1}{3e^t - 2} \tag{12.13}$$

Now we can express the volumetric flow rate in non-dimensional form as (after introducing $V^* = \frac{V}{\pi R^2 h_0}$ and skipping[*])

$$\dot{V}(t) = -\frac{dh}{dt} = \frac{e^t(1+\gamma)}{[\gamma - e^t(1+\gamma)]^2} = \frac{3e^t}{(2-3e^t)^2} \tag{12.14}$$

The total water volume produced can be expressed as

$$V(t) = \pi R^2 (h_0 - h(t)) \tag{12.15}$$

and in non-dimensional form this expression will be the following after skipping[*]

$$V(t) = 1 - h(t) = 1 - \frac{1}{e^t(1+\gamma)-\gamma} = \frac{3e^t-3}{3e^t-2} \tag{12.16}$$

For a frustum filter with a constant thickness d and varying radius r we have the schematic diagram as shown in Figure 12.17b).

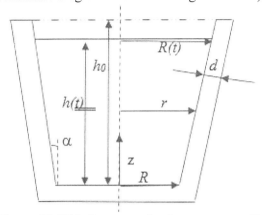

Figure 12.17b) Geometry for frustum water filter

The volumetric flow rate in this case can be described as

$$\dot{V}(t) = \frac{k}{d}\left[\pi R^2 h + \int_0^{2\pi}\int_0^h (h-z)r\,dz\,d\theta\right] \tag{12.17}$$

Using $r = R + z\,tan\alpha$, we can express equation (12.13) as

$$\dot{V}(t) = \frac{k\pi h}{d}\left(R^2 + hR + \frac{h^2 tan\alpha}{3}\right) \tag{12.18}$$

and equation (12.6) for a frustum shaped filter will be modified to

$$\dot{V}(t) = -\pi R(t)^2 \frac{dh}{dt} \tag{12.19}$$

where $R(t) = R + h(t)\,tan\alpha$. The differential equation for $h(t)$ will then be

$$\frac{dh}{dt} + \frac{kh}{d}\frac{\left(R^2 + hR + \frac{h^2 tan\alpha}{3}\right)}{(R + h tan\alpha)^2} = 0 \tag{12.20}$$

and in non-dimensional form after skipping* we have

$$\frac{dh}{dt} + \frac{h}{(1+\delta h)^2}\left(1 + \gamma h + \frac{1}{3}\delta\gamma h^2\right) = 0 \tag{12.21}$$

where $\delta = \gamma tan\alpha$. There is no analytical solution available except in the case $\delta = 0$ corresponding to the cylindrical geometry. Equation (11.17) can be solved numerically in the general case $\delta \neq 0$ using the initial condition $h(0) = 1$.

We express the volumetric flow rate in non-dimensional form after skipping*

$$\dot{V}(t) = -(1 + \delta h)^2 \frac{dh}{dt} \tag{12.22}$$

The total water volume produced can be expressed as

$$V(t) = \pi \left[R^2 + R(h_0 + h)\tan\alpha + \left(h_0{}^2 + h_0 h + h^2\right)\frac{\tan^2\alpha}{3} \right](h_0 - h) \tag{12.23}$$

and in non-dimensional form this expression will be the following after skipping[*]

$$V(t) = (1 - h) + \delta(1 - h^2) + \frac{\delta^2}{3}(1 - h^3) \tag{12.24}$$

I. References

1. Kelly, A.C., "Finite Element Modeling of Flow Through Ceramic Pot Filters.", *Master's Thesis in Civil and Environmental Engineering*, MIT, (2013).
2. Schweitzer, R.W., Cunningham, J.A., Mihelcic, J.R., "Hydraulic Modeling of Clay Ceramic Water Filters for Point-of-Use Water Treatment.", *Environ. Sci. Technol.*, **47**, 429-435, (2013).
3. Wald, I., "Modeling Flow Rate to Estimate Hydraulic Conductivity in a Parabolic Ceramic Water Filter.", *Undergraduate Journal of Mathematical Modeling*, **4**, 2, (2012).

J. Exercise

12.1 Complete ANSYS Fluent simulation of the flow through a frustum-shaped filter using the values listed in Table 11.3. Include graphs of your results showing a comparison between ANSYS Fluent and Theory for free surface height, volume flow rate and volume produced by the filter. Use a time step size of 0.005s and 1000 time-steps. Include contours of volume fraction for water at t = 1, 2, 3, 4, and 5 seconds.

Parameter	Value
C_2 (1/m)	0
$1/\alpha$ (1/m^2)	$9.76305 \cdot 10^8$
ρ (kg/m^3)	998.2
μ (kg/m-s)	0.001003
g (m/s^2)	9.81
k *(m/s)*	0.01
R *(m)*	0.1
h_0 *(m)*	0.3
d *(m)*	0.01
γ	3
α *(degrees)*	10

Table 12.3 Parameter values for frustum shaped filter

Notes:

CHAPTER 13. MODEL ROCKET FLOW

A. Objectives

- Model Geometry and Mesh
- Run Simulations for Turbulent Steady 3D Flow Past a Model Rocket in ANSYS Fluent
- Determine Drag Coefficient for Model Rocket
- Visualize Flow Around Model Rocket

B. Problem Description

We will study the flow past the model rocket Estes Firestreak SST with a free stream velocity of 30 m/s.

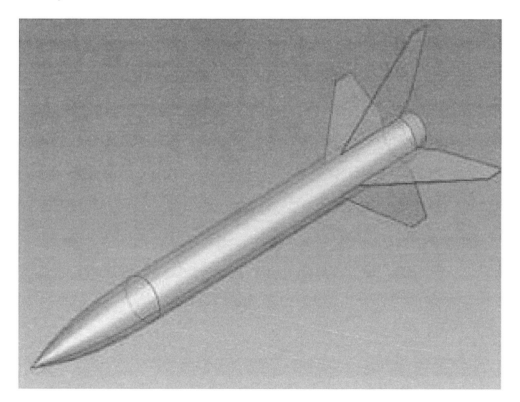

C. Launching ANSYS Workbench and Importing the Geometry

1. Start by launching ANSYS Workbench. Select File>>Import from the menu. Select Geometry File as format and open the file *Estes Model Rocket.IGS*. This and other files can be downloaded from *sdcpublications.com*.

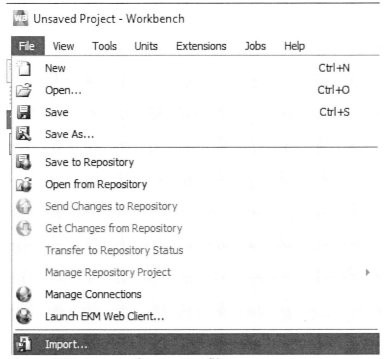

Figure 13.1 Import of geometry file

D. Launching ANSYS DesignModeler

2. Right click on the imported Geometry in ANSYS Workbench and select Edit DesignModeler Geometry. Click on Generate in DesignModeler.

    Select Tools>>Enclosure from the menu. Set the Number of Planes to 2 in Details View. Select ZXPlane from the Tree Outline as Symmetry Plane 1 and Apply the plane in Details View. Select YZPlane from the Tree Outline as Symmetry Plane 2 and Apply it in Details View. Click on Generate.

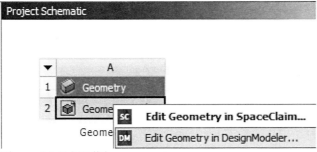

Figure 13.2a) Editing geometry

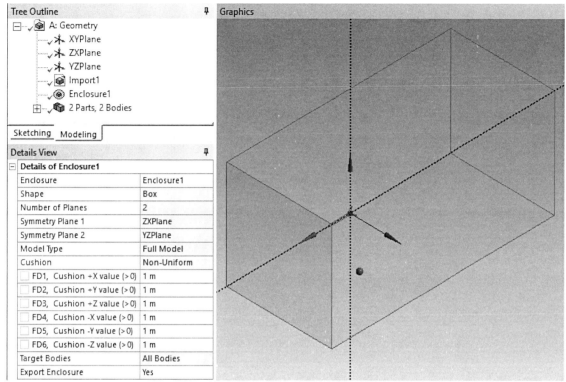

Figure 13.2b) Computational domain around the model rocket

3. Select Create>>Boolean from the menu. Select Subtract as Operation. Click on the plus sign next to 2 Parts, 2 Bodies in the Tree Outline. Select the second Solid and Apply it as Target Body in Details of Boolean1. Select the first Solid and Apply it as Tool Body in Details of Boolean1. Click on Generate. Right click on the Solid in the Tree Outline and Rename it to *Air*. Select File>>Save Project and name it "Model Rocket Flow Study" and close DesignModeler.

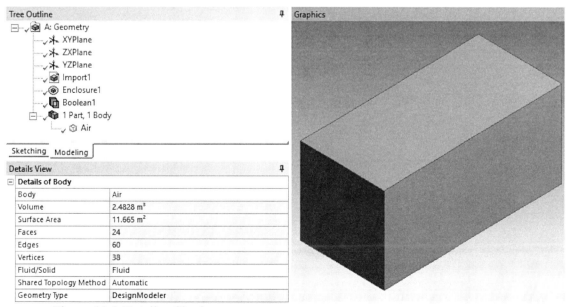

Figure 13.3 Details of body

E. Launching ANSYS Meshing

4. Double click on Fluid Flow (Fluent) under Analysis Systems in the Toolbox in ANSYS Workbench. Drag the Geometry to the Geometry under Fluid Flow (Fluent).

    Double click on Mesh under Fluid Flow (Fluent). In the Meshing window, right click on Mesh in the Outline and select Update. Click on the plus sign next to Sizing under Details of Mesh. Change Capture Proximity and Capture Curvature both to Yes. Click on the plus sign next to Quality under Details of Mesh. Set Smoothing to High. Update the mesh once again. Rotate the Mesh to see the details of the mesh around the model rocket.

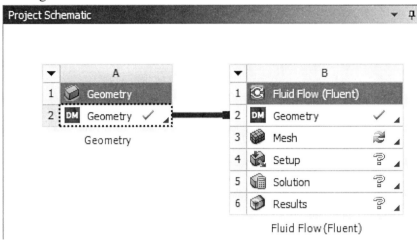

Figure 13.4a) Shared geometry with Fluent

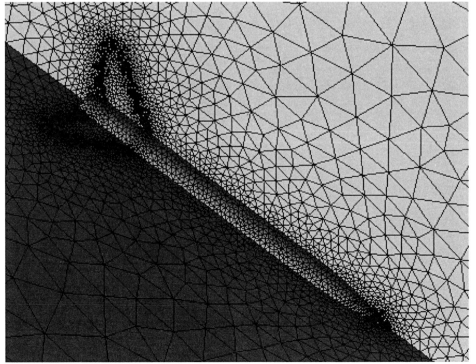

Figure 13.4b) Refined mesh around model rocket

5.   Right click on Mesh in the Outline, select Insert>> Sizing. Select Face 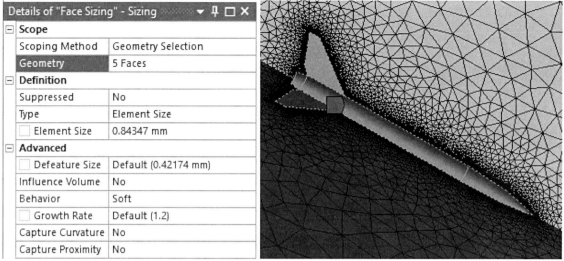 and control select the 5 faces of the model rocket as shown in figure 13.5a). Apply the faces as the Geometry under Scope in Details of "Face Sizing". Set the Element Size to 0.84347 mm. Update the mesh once again.

Figure 13.5a) Face sizing for the five faces of the model rocket

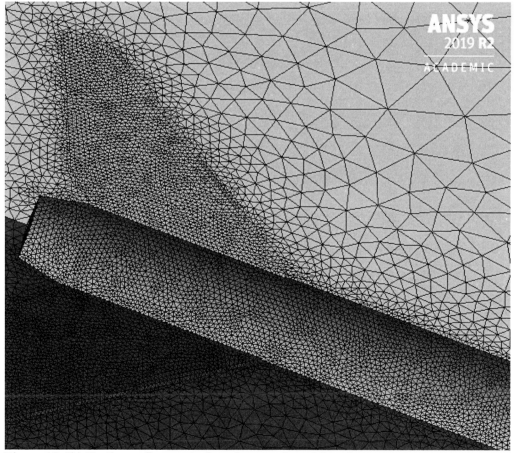

Figure 13.5b) Further refinement of mesh around model rocket

6. Click on the plus sign next to Inflation in Details of "Mesh". Set Use Automatic Inflation to Program Controlled. Update the mesh once again. Select Box Select from the menu of the graphics window, see Figure 13.6a). Select Face 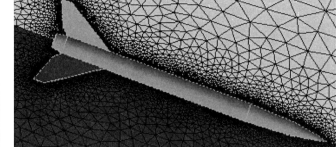 and make a Box Select around the model rocket. This will select all surfaces, see Figure 13.6b).

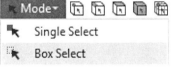

Figure 13.6a) Box Select   Figure 13.6b) Selection of surfaces

Right click in the graphics window and select Create Named Selection. Enter the name "model rocket' and click OK. Select *model rocket* under Named Selections and select Include from the drop-down menu for Program Controlled Inflation under Definition in Details of "model rocket". Update the mesh once again.

Details of "model rocket"	▼ ⊕ ☐ ✕
⊟ **Scope**	
Scoping Method	Geometry Selection
Geometry	18 Faces
⊟ **Definition**	
Send to Solver	Yes
Protected	Program Controlled
Visible	Yes
Program Controlled Inflation	Include
⊟ **Statistics**	
Type	Manual
☐ Total Selection	18 Faces
☐ Surface Area	5864.7 mm²
Suppressed	0
Used by Mesh Worksheet	No

Figure 13.6c) Details for model rocket named selection

Select Isometric View, select Single Select, see Figure 13.6a), and select the velocity-inlet face for the computational domain, see Figure 13.6d). Right click in the graphics window and select Create Named Selection. Enter the name "velocity-inlet' and click OK.

Select Face 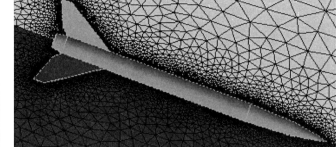 and select the opposite side of the computational domain. Right click in the graphics window and select Create Named Selection. Enter the name "pressure-outlet" and click OK.

Select one of the plane side surfaces (the one on the side) of the computational domain containing the model rocket and name it "symmetry1". Name the other face containing the model rocket (the bottom face) to "symmetry2". Name the remaining two surfaces "symmetry-top" and "symmetry-side". Update the mesh.

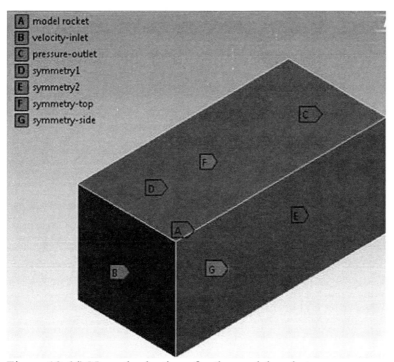

Figure 13.6d) Named selections for the model rocket

7. Go back to DesignModeler by double clicking on the first Geometry A under Project Schematic in ANSYS Workbench. Select Bottom view and select YZ Plane under Tree Outline in DesignModeler. Right click on YZ Plane and select Look At. Create a new sketch. Zoom in on the model rocket.

Click on the Sketching tab in the Tree Outline and select Rectangle. Draw a rectangle around the model rocket. Make sure you start drawing the rectangle on the vertical axis and that you get a *C* when you move the cursor on the vertical axis. This means that one of the sides will be positioned on the same vertical axis. Select Dimensions and click on the horizontal and vertical sides of the new rectangle. Enter 0.6375 m as the vertical height of the rectangle and 0.1275 m as the width. Select the Vertical dimensioning tool, click on the horizontal coordinate axis and the lower side of the rectangle and enter 0.275 m as this vertical dimension.

Select the Modeling tab in the Tree Outline and select Extrude. Select Sketch1 under YZ plane in the Tree Outline and Apply it as Geometry in Details of Extrude. Enter 0.1275 m as the FD1, Depth (>0) of the Extrusion. Click on Generate. Go to 2 Parts, 2 Bodies in the Tree Outline, right click on Solid and select Rename. Rename it to *ModelRocketBox*.

Go back to ANSYS Workbench, double click on Mesh and answer *Yes* to the question whether you would like to read upstream data.

295

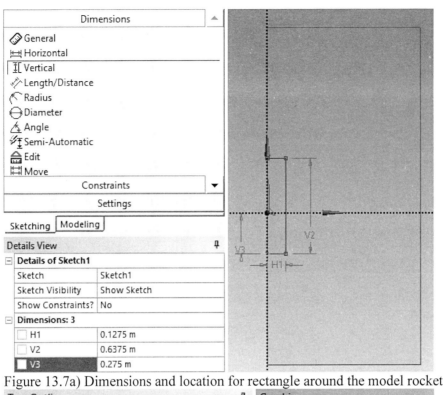

Figure 13.7a) Dimensions and location for rectangle around the model rocket

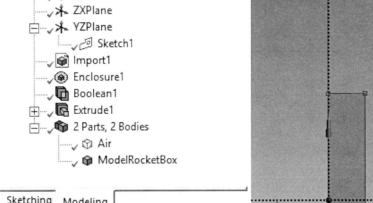

Figure 13.7b) Details of body

8. Right click Mesh under Project in Outline and select Update. Right click Mesh under Project in Outline, select Insert>>Sizing. Select Body 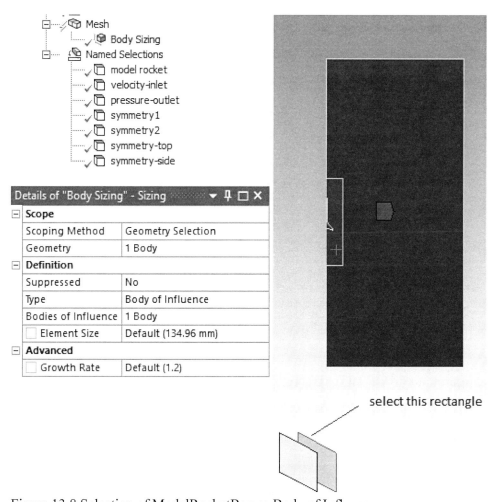 and select the larger computational domain in the graphics window. Apply the computational domain in Geometry under Scope for Details of Body Sizing. Select *Body of Influence* as Type under Definition.

Select Bottom view in the graphics window, zoom in on the model rocket, select the *ModelRocketBox* in the graphics window and Apply it as the Body of Influence. You will need to select the second blue small rectangle in the lower left corner of the graphics window in Figure 13.8 before you can select the ModelRocketBox that turns from green to red when you apply it as the *Body of Influence*. Update the Mesh.

Right click on *ModelRocketBox* under Geometry in Project Outline and select Hide Body. Select Mesh in the Outline and click on the plus sign next to Quality in Details of "Mesh". Select Skewness as Mesh Metric. The max skewness should not be above 0.9.

Delete any contact regions that you may have in the Outline and update the mesh. Select File>>Save Project. Select File>>Export...>>Mesh>>FLUENT Input File>>Export and save the mesh with the name "model-rocket-flow-mesh.msh". Close the Meshing window.

Figure 13.8 Selection of ModelRocketBox as Body of Influence

F. Launching ANSYS Fluent

9. Double click on Setup in ANSYS Workbench. Check Double Precision under Options and check Parallel under Processing Options. Select the number of Processes equal to the number of computer cores. Click on the plus sign next to Show More Options and take a note of the location of the *Working Directory*. Click OK to launch ANSYS Fluent.

Double click on Models under Setup in the Outline View and select Viscous – Laminar under Models on the Task Page. Click on the Edit button. Select the k-epsilon (2 eqn) turbulence model. Click OK to exit the Viscous Model window.

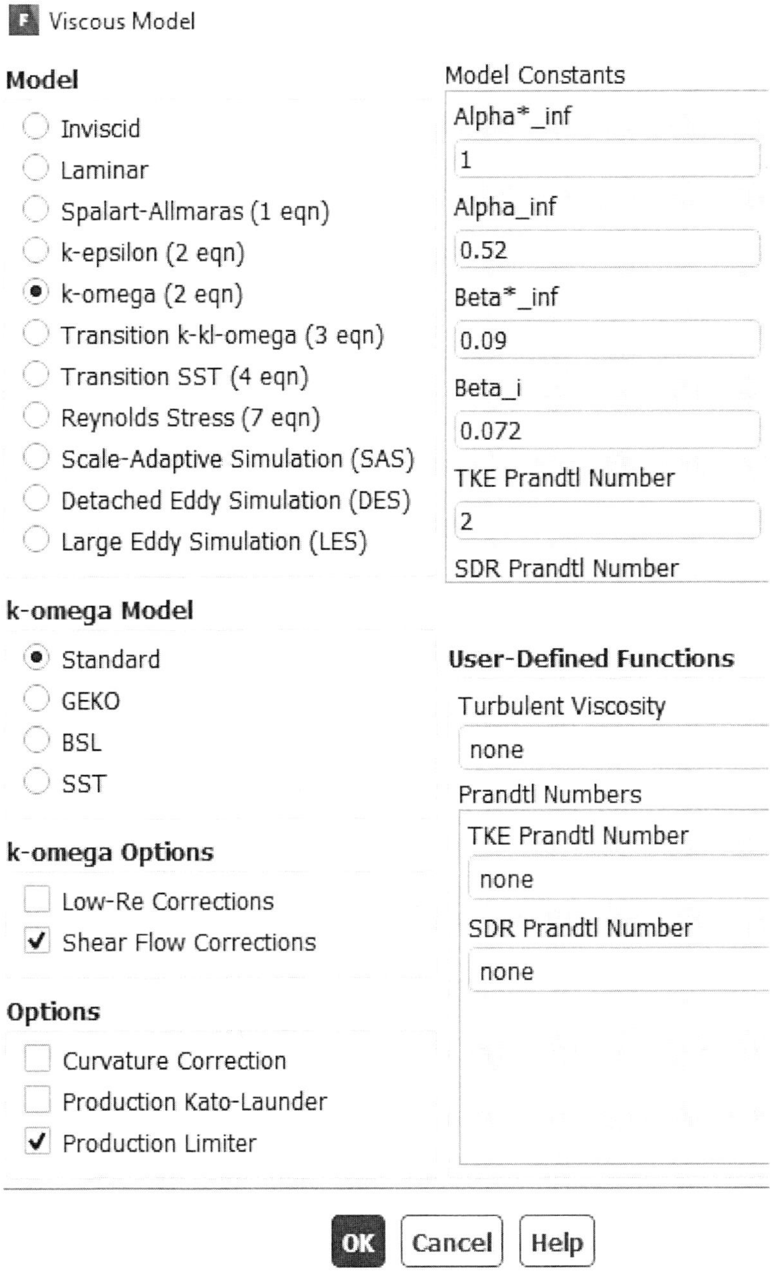

Figure 13.9 Details for the viscous model

10. Double click on Boundary Conditions under Setup in the Tree and select velocity-inlet under Zone for Boundary Conditions on the Task Page. Click on the Edit button. Select Components as Velocity Specification Method. Enter -30 as Z-Velocity (m/s). Set the Turbulent Intensity to 1%. Click OK to close the Velocity Inlet window.

Figure 13.10 Velocity inlet boundary condition

11. Double click Projected Areas under Results and Reports in the Outline View. Select *model_rocket* as the Surface, enter 0.0001 as Min Feature Size (m), select Z as Projection Direction and click on Compute. The computed frontal Area (m2) is 0.00012483. Close the window.

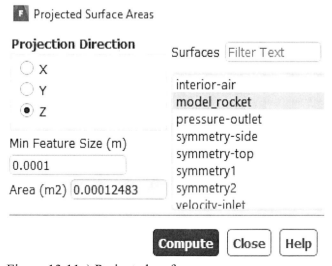

Figure 13.11a) Projected surface areas

Double click on Reference Values under Setup in the Outline View and change the Area (m2) to 0.00012483 and the Velocity (m/s) to 30. Select Compute from velocity-inlet and set Reference Zone to air.

Double click on Methods under Solution in the Outline View and set the Pressure-Velocity Coupling scheme to Coupled. Set the Spatial Discretization Gradient to Least Squares Cell Based, and Pressure to Standard. Set the remaining three (Momentum, Turbulent Kinetic Energy and Specific Dissipation Rate) to First Order Upwind.

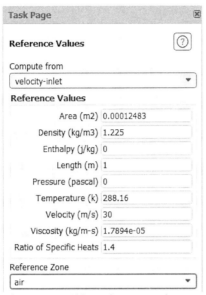
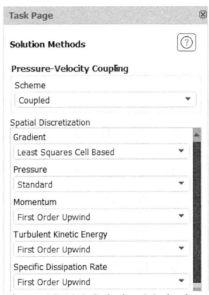

Figure 13.11b) Reference values   Figure 13.11c) Solution Methods

12. Double click on Controls under Solution in the Outline View and set the Pressure and Momentum Pseudo Transient Explicit Relaxation Factors to 0.25 and set the Turbulent Viscosity Explicit Relaxation Factor to 0.8. Click on Limits... and set the Maximum Turb. Viscosity Ratio to 10000000. Click on the OK button to close the Solution Limits window.

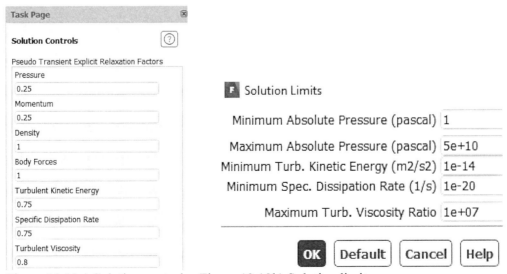

Figure 13.12a) Solution controls   Figure 13.12b) Solution limits

13. Double click on Monitors and Residual under Solution. Set the Convergence Criterion to none. Click on OK to close Residual Monitors.

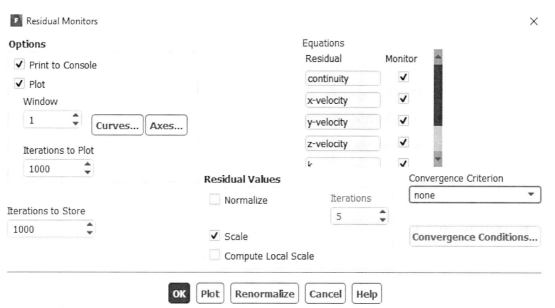

Figure 13.13 Settings for Residual Monitors

14. Double-click on Report Definitions under Solution in the Outline View. Select New>>Force Report>>Drag… from the drop-down menu. Select *model_rocket* as Wall Zone. Check the boxes for Report File, Report Plot and Print to Console under Create. Set the Force Vector to X = 0, Y = 0, and Z = -1. Click on the OK button to close the Drag Report Definition window. Close the Report Definitions window.

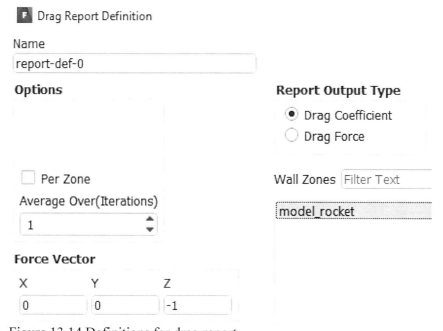

Figure 13.14 Definitions for drag report

15. Double click on Initialization under Solution in the Outline View and select *Hybrid Initializa*tion. Click on the Initialize button. Double click on Calculation Activities under Solution in the Outline View and click on Edit... for Autosave Every (Iterations). Set Save Data File Every (Iterations) to 100. Click OK to close the Autosave window.

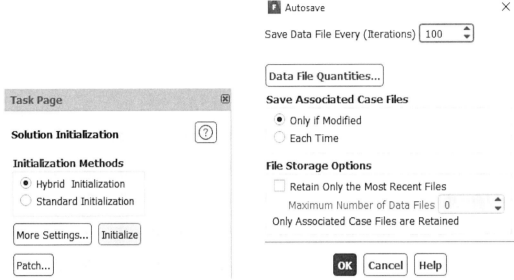

Figure 13.15a) Solution initialization   Figure 13.15b) Autosave window

Double click on Run Calculation under Solution in the Outline View. Set the Number of Iterations to 100. Click on Calculate.

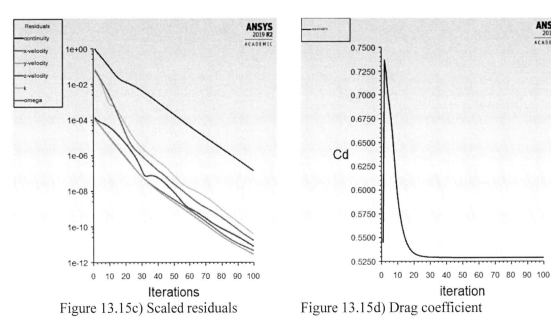

Figure 13.15c) Scaled residuals   Figure 13.15d) Drag coefficient

G. Post-Processing

16. Double click on Methods under Solution in the Outline View and replace First Order Upwind with Second Order Upwind for Momentum, Turbulent Kinetic Energy and Specific Dissipation Rate.

    Double click on Controls under Solution and set the Turbulent Viscosity value to 0.95. Double click on Run Calculation under Solution and set Number of Iterations to 300. Click on Calculate and Click OK in the window that appears.

    Double-click on Reports under Results in the Outline View and double-click on Forces under Reports. Set Direction Vector for X to 0, Y to 0, and Z to -1. Check the *model_rocket* Wall Zone and click on the Print button. The total drag coefficient is 0.4. Close the Force Reports window.

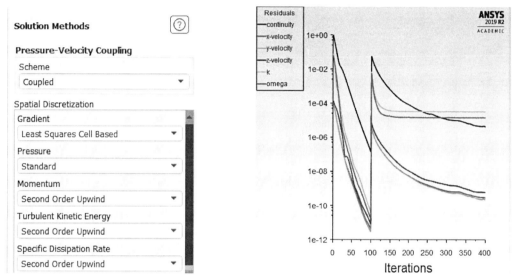

Figure 13.16a) Modified solution methods Figure 13.16b) Scaled residuals

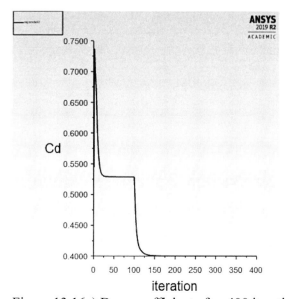

Figure 13.16c) Drag coefficient after 400 iterations

17. Double click on Graphics and Contours under Results. Select the settings as shown in Figure 13.17a) and Apply the Colormap settings as shown in Figure 13.17b). Click on Save/Display. Select the Y-Z plane view in the graphics window. Zoom in on the rocket. Close the Contours window.

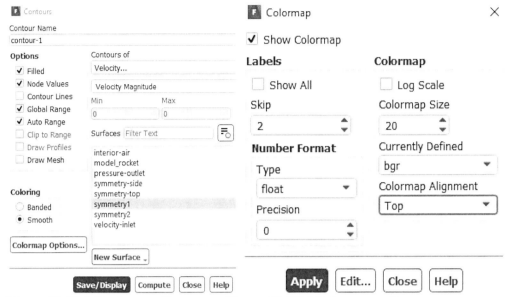

Figure 13.17a) Contours settings   Figure 13.17b) Colormap settings

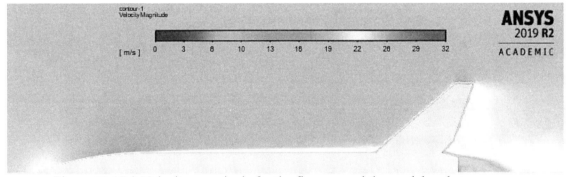

Figure 13.17c) Velocity magnitude for the flow around the model rocket

Double click on Pathlines under Results and Graphics in the Outline View. Select the settings and Apply the same Colormap Options and settings as shown in Figures 13.17b) and 13.17d). Click on Save/Display. Close the Pathlines window.

Figure 13.17d) Settings for pathlines

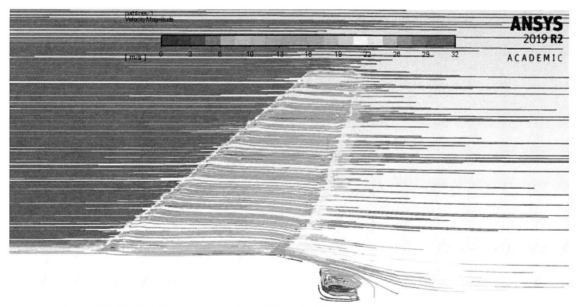

Figure 13.17e) Pathlines around model rocket fin

Double click on Contours under Results and Graphics in the Outline View. Select the settings as shown in Figure 13.17f) for static pressure. Apply the same Colormap settings as shown in Figures 13.17b). Click on Save/Display. Close the Contours window.

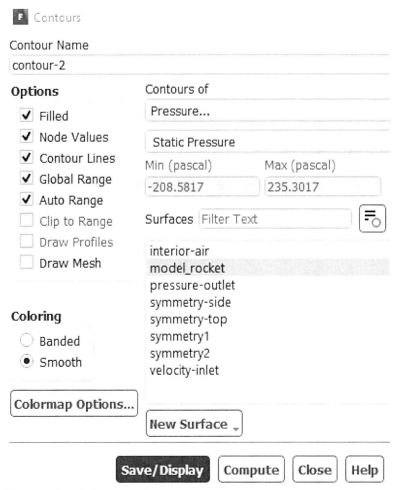

Figure 13.17f) Settings for static pressure

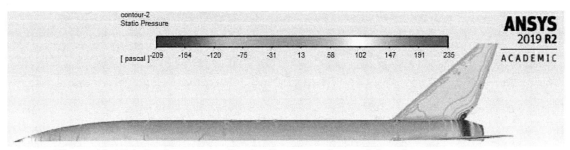

Figure 13.17g) Static pressure for the flow past the model rocket

H. Theory

18. The total drag coefficient for a model rocket[1,2] can be expressed using equation (13.1).

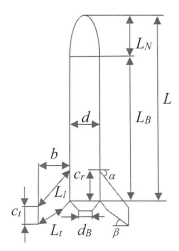

Figure 13.18 Geometry for model rocket

$$C_{D,T} = C_{D,NT} + C_{D,B} + C_{D,F} + C_{D,I} + C_{D,L} \tag{13.1}$$

, where

$$C_{D,NT} = 1.02 \frac{C_{f,turb} A_{w,NT}}{A_c} \left(1 + \frac{3}{2} \left(\frac{L}{d}\right)^{-3/2}\right) \tag{13.2}$$

$$C_{D,B} = \frac{0.029}{\sqrt{C_{D,NT}}} \left(\frac{d_b}{d}\right)^3 \tag{13.3}$$

$$C_{D,F} = \frac{2C_{f,lam} A_{w,F}}{A_c} \left(1 + 2\frac{t}{c_r}\right) \tag{13.4}$$

$$C_{D,I} = \frac{C_{f,lam} n d c_r}{A_c} \left(1 + 2\frac{t}{c_r}\right) \tag{13.5}$$

The different drag coefficients and parameters are explained in Table 13.1. We define the Reynolds number for the nose cone and body tube as

$$Re_{NT} = \frac{UL\rho}{\mu} = \frac{30*0.2365*1.225}{0.000017894} = 485,714 \tag{13.6}$$

, and the Reynolds number for the fin as

$$Re_F = \frac{U c_{ave} \rho}{\mu} = \frac{30*0.0271525*1.225}{0.000017894} = 55,765 \tag{13.7}$$

, where $c_{ave} = S/b$. The surface area for the fin can be determined from the geometry in Figure 13.19.

$$S = (c_t + L_l \, sin\alpha)L_l \, cos\alpha - \frac{1}{2}\{L_l^2 \, sin\alpha \, cos\alpha + L_t^2 \, sin\beta \, cos\beta + (L_l \, cos\alpha - L_t \, cos\beta)[(c_t - c_r + L_l \, sin\alpha - L_t \, sin\beta) + 2L_t \, sin\beta]\} \tag{13.8}$$

The skin friction coefficient can be approximated assuming fully turbulent flow on nose cone and body tube

$$C_{f,turb} = \frac{0.0315}{Re_{NT}^{1/7}} = \frac{0.0315}{485{,}714^{1/7}} = 0.00485255 \tag{13.9}$$

, and for a laminar boundary layer on the fin as

$$C_{f,lam} = \frac{1.328}{Re_F^{1/2}} = \frac{1.328}{55{,}765^{1/2}} = 0.00562365 \tag{13.10}$$

For an ogive nose cone we have the following relation

$$\frac{A_{w,NT}}{A_c} = \frac{8L_N + 12L_B}{3d} = 39.2012 \tag{13.11}$$

The different drag coefficient and the total value becomes

$$C_{D,NT} = 1.02 * 0.00485255 * 39.2012\left(1 + \frac{3}{2}(10.8986)^{-\frac{3}{2}}\right) = 0.2021 \tag{13.12}$$

$$C_{D,B} = \frac{0.029}{\sqrt{0.202}}\left(\frac{0.0164}{0.0217}\right)^3 = 0.0278 \tag{13.13}$$

$$C_{D,F} = \frac{2*0.00562*0.00419}{0.00037}\left(1 + 2\frac{0.0007}{0.0038}\right) = 0.1321 \tag{13.14}$$

$$C_{D,I} = \frac{0.00562*0.038*4*0.0217}{0.00037}\left(1 + 2\frac{0.0007}{0.0038}\right) = 0.0520 \tag{13.15}$$

$$C_{D,T} = 0.2021 + 0.0278 + 0.1321 + 0.0520 = 0.414 \tag{13.16}$$

The value for the total drag coefficient 0.414 according to the theory can be compared with the value 0.4 from ANSYS Fluent simulations, a difference of 3.4 %.

A_c (m^2): cross sectional area for body tube 0.000369836 m^2
$A_{w,F}$ (m^2): total wetted surface area for all fins 0.00418879 m^2
$A_{w,NT}$ (m^2): wetted surface area for nose and body tube 0.014498 m^2
α : fin leading edge sweep angle 50°
β : fin trailing edge angle 15°
b (m): span for the fin 0.0385673 m
c_{ave} (m): average fin chord length 0.0271525 m
c_r (m): root fin chord length 0.038 m
c_t (m): tip fin chord length 0.010 m
$C_{D,NT}$: nose and body tube drag coefficient 0.2021
$C_{D,B}$: base drag coefficient 0.0278
$C_{D,F}$: fin drag coefficient 0.1321
$C_{D,I}$: interference drag coefficient 0.0520
$C_{D,T}$: total drag coefficient 0.414
$C_{f,lam}$: skin friction coefficient for laminar boundary layer 0.00562365
$C_{f,turb}$: skin friction coefficient for turbulent boundary layer 0.00485255
d (m): body tube diameter 0.0217 m
d_b (m): base diameter 0.0164 m

L (m): length of nose and body 0.2365 m	
L_B (m): length of body tube 0.165 m	
L_l (m): length of leading edge of fin 0.060 m	
L_N (m): length of nose 0.0715 m	
L_t (m): length of trailing edge of fin 0.033 m	
n: number of fins 4	
Re_F: Reynolds number for the fin 55,765	
Re_{NT}: Reynolds number for nose cone and body tube 485,714	
S (m^2): area for fin 0.0010472 m^2	
t (m): thickness of fin 0.0007 m	
$U(m/s)$: free stream velocity 30 m/s	
$\rho(kg/m^3)$: density of air 1.225 kg/m^3	
$\mu(kg/ms)$: dynamic viscosity of air 0.000017894kg/m^3	

Table 13.1 Drag coefficients and parameters

I. References

1. DeMar, J.S.,"Model Rocket Drag Analysis Using a Computerized Wind Tunnel", NARAM-37, 1995.
2. Gregorek, G.M., "Aerodynamic Drag of Model Rockets.", Estes Industries, Penrose, CO, 1970.
3. Cannon, B.,"Model Rocket Simulation with Drag Analysis", BYU, 2004.
4. Milligan, T.V, "Determining the Drag Coefficient of a Model Rocket Using Accelerometer Based Payloads", NARAM-54, 2012.

J. Exercise

13.1 Rerun ANSYS Fluent simulations in this chapter at 10, 20, 40 and 50 m/s and compare the drag coefficient with values using the theory section. Include a plot of total drag coefficient versus Reynolds number Re$_{NT}$ corresponding to free stream velocities 10, 20, 30, 40 and 50 m/s and fill out Table 12.2 below.

U (m/s)	Re_{NT}	Re_F	$C_{D,NT}$	$C_{D,B}$	$C_{D,F}$	$C_{D,I}$	$C_{D,T}$	$C_{D,Fluent}$	% Diff.
10									
20									
30	485714	55765	0.2021	0.0278	0.1321	0.0520	0.414	0.54	30
40									
50									

Table 13.2 Drag coefficients at different Reynolds numbers

Notes:

CHAPTER 14. AHMED BODY

A. Objectives

- Model the Flow Past an Ahmed Body
- Run Simulations for Turbulent Steady 2D and 3D Flow Past Ahmed Body
- Determine the Drag Coefficient for Ahmed Body
- Visualize the Flow Around Ahmed Body using Streamlines, Pressure and Velocity

B. Problem Description

Studying the flow around the Ahmed body is a standard flow test case for CFD codes. The geometry in *mm* that is being used for the Ahmed body in this chapter is shown below.

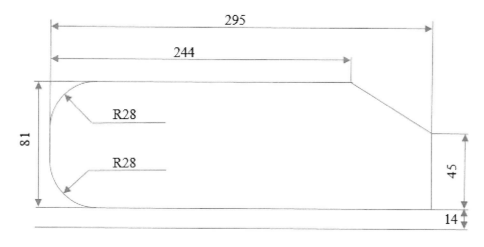

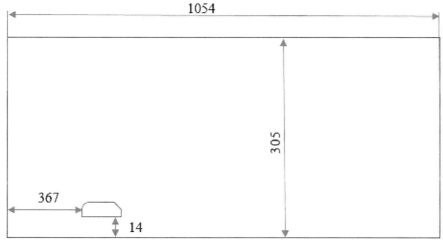

C. Launching ANSYS Workbench and Selecting Fluent

1. Start by launching ANSYS Workbench. Double click on Fluid Flow (Fluent) under Analysis Systems in the Toolbox.

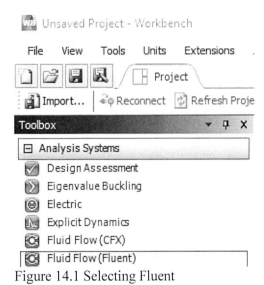

Figure 14.1 Selecting Fluent

D. Launching ANSYS DesignModeler

2. Right click on Geometry under Project Schematic and select Properties. In Properties of Schematic A2: Geometry, select Analysis Type 2D under Advanced Geometry Options. Right-click on Geometry in the Project Schematic window and select New DesignModeler Geometry. Select Units>>Millimeter from the menu as the desired length unit.

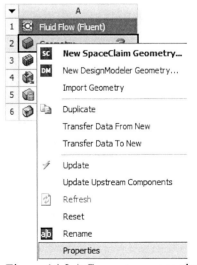

Figure 14.2a) Geometry properties   Figure 14.2b) 2D analysis type

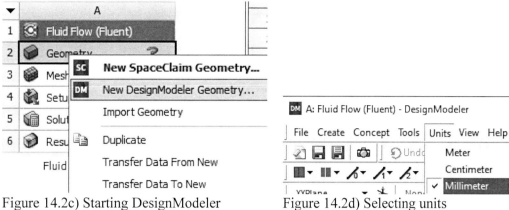

Figure 14.2c) Starting DesignModeler   Figure 14.2d) Selecting units

3.   Select Look At Face 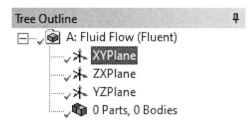. Select XY Plane in the Tree Outline and New Sketch. Select the Sketching tab in the Tree Outline, click on Draw and select Rectangle. Draw a rectangle from the origin in the first quadrant. Select Dimensions and set the height of the rectangle to 305 mm and the length to 1054 mm. Right click in the graphics window and select Zoom to Fit. Draw and dimension another rectangle inside the first rectangle. The second smaller rectangle will have the height 81 mm and the length 295 mm.

Tree Outline   ⏚
⊟ ✓ 🔷 A: Fluid Flow (Fluent)
    ✓ ⚓ XYPlane
    ✓ ⚓ ZXPlane
    ✓ ⚓ YZPlane
    ✓ 🔷 0 Parts, 0 Bodies

Figure 14.3a) Selection of XY Plane

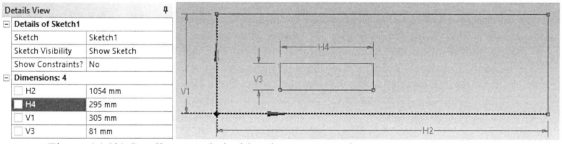

Details View		⏚
⊟ Details of Sketch1		
Sketch	Sketch1	
Sketch Visibility	Show Sketch	
Show Constraints?	No	
⊟ Dimensions: 4		
☐ H2	1054 mm	
☐ H4	295 mm	
☐ V1	305 mm	
☐ V3	81 mm	

Figure 14.3b) Small rectangle inside a larger rectangle

4. Select Modify and Fillet under Sketching Toolboxes. Set the Radius of the Fillet to 28 mm. Click on the two left corners of the smaller rectangle.

Click on Chamfer under Modify. Set the Length of the Chamfer to 63 mm. Click on the upper right corner of the smaller rectangle.

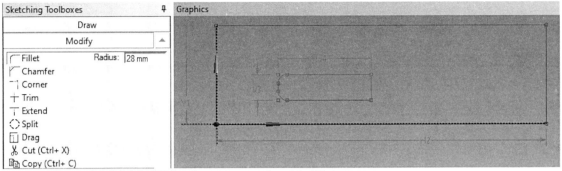
Figure 14.4a) Modifying inner rectangle with fillets

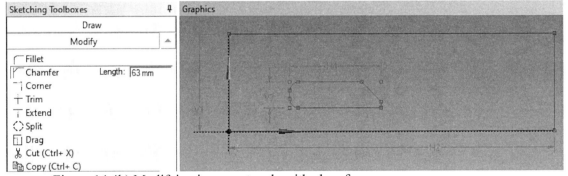
Figure 14.4b) Modifying inner rectangle with chamfer

5. Complete all the remaining dimensions as shown in Figure 14.5. The vertical distance between the bottom of the Ahmed body and the lower horizontal edge of the larger rectangle is 14 mm. The horizontal length of the chamfer is 51 mm. The angle between the upper horizontal edge of the Ahmed body and the chamfer is 35 degrees. Use Angle under Dimensions, click on the two lines, right click and select Alternate Angle. The horizontal distance between the front edge of the Ahmed body and the left vertical edge of the larger rectangle is 367 mm.

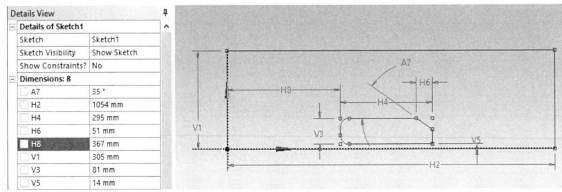
Figure 14.5 Dimensions for Ahmed body and mesh region

314

6. Select Concepts>>Surfaces from Sketches from the menu. Select Sketch1 under XYPlane in Tree Outline and click on Apply as Base Object in Details View. Click on Generate.

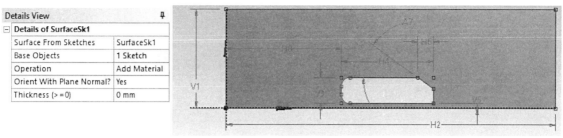

Figure 14.6 Surface for Ahmed body

7. Create another sketch in the XYPlane. Draw 2 vertical lines from top to bottom through the whole mesh region, one line to the right of the Ahmed body and the other vertical line to the left of the body. Finally, draw a horizontal line above the body from left to right. Position the rightmost vertical line 265 mm behind the Ahmed body and the other vertical line is positioned 45 mm in front of the front end of the Ahmed body. The horizontal line is positioned 120 mm above the roof of the Ahmed body.

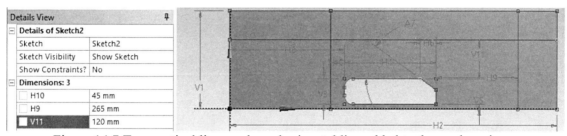

Figure 14.7 Two vertical lines and one horizontal line added to the mesh region

8. Select Tools>>Face Split from the menu. Select the mesh region as the Target Face and Apply it in the Details View. Click on the yellow region next to Tool Geometry in Details View. Control-select the two endpoints of the vertical line to the right of the Ahmed body as the Tool Geometry and Apply it in Details View.

Click on the white region to the right of the Tool Geometry highlighted in blue. Control-select the two endpoints of the other vertical line to the left of the Ahmed body as the Tool Geometry and Apply it in Details View. Repeat this step once again for the horizontal line. Click on Generate.

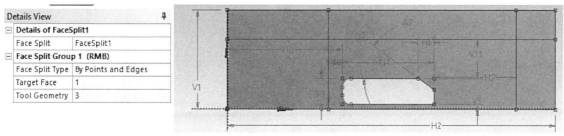

Figure 14.8a) Details of face split

315

Select Tools>>Merge from the menu. Select Faces as Merge Type in Details View.

Select Selection Filter: Faces ⬚ . Control-select the three upper faces and Apply them as Faces in Details View. Click on Generate. Select File>>Save Project from the menu, name it "Ahmed body study" and close DesignModeler.

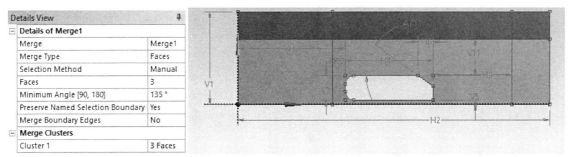

Figure 14.8b) Details of merge

E. Launching ANSYS Meshing

9. Double-click on Mesh under Project Schematic in ANSYS Workbench. Right click on Mesh in the Outline and select Insert>>Inflation. Select Selection Filter: Faces ⬚ . Select the surface surrounding the Ahmed body as the face and Apply it as Geometry under Scope in Details of Inflation.

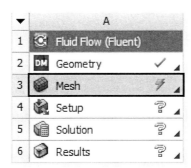

Figure 14.9a) Starting the Mesh

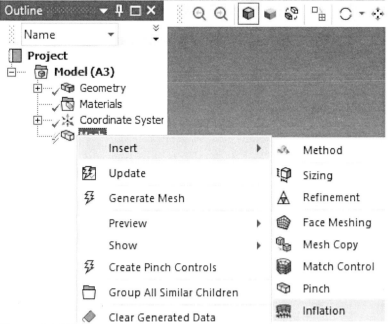

Figure 14.9b) Inserting Inflation

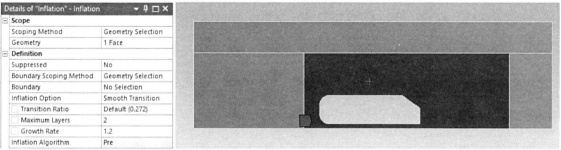

Figure 14.9c) Details for inflation around Ahmed body

10. Select Selection Filter: Edges ⬚ . Control-select the seven edges of the Ahmed body. Apply the edges as the Boundary under Definition in the Details of Inflation.

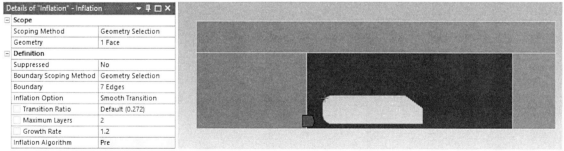

Figure 14.10 Selection of Ahmed body edges for inflation

11. Right click on Mesh in the Outline and select Insert>>Method. Select the whole mesh region in the graphics window and Apply it as Geometry under Scope in Details of Method. Select Triangles as Method under Definition in Details of Method.

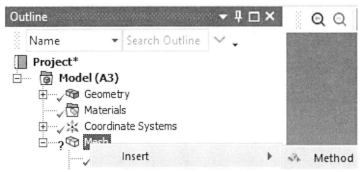

Figure 14.11a) Selection of meshing method

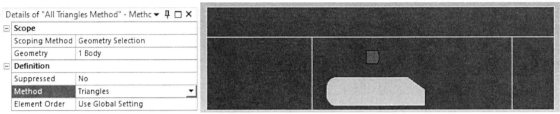

Figure 14.11b) Details of triangles method

12. Right click on Mesh in the Outline and select Insert>>Sizing. Select Selection Filter: Edges ⬛, control select the seven edges of the Ahmed body. Apply the seven edges as Geometry under Scope in Details of Sizing. Set the Element Size to *0.001 m* under Definition in Details of Sizing. Select the Mesh in the Outline and set the Element Size to *0.005 m*.

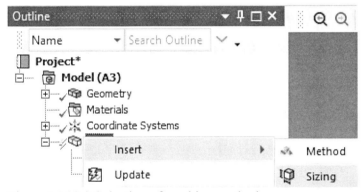

Figure 14.12a) Selection of meshing method

Details of "Edge Sizing" - Sizing ▼ ⧰ ☐ ✕	
⊟ **Scope**	
Scoping Method	Geometry Selection
Geometry	7 Edges
⊟ **Definition**	
Suppressed	No
Type	Element Size
☐ Element Size	1.e-003 m

Figure 14.12b) Setting the Element Size for the edges of the Ahmed body

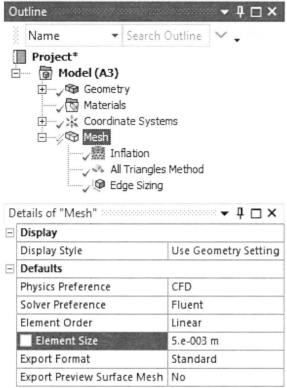

Details of "Mesh" ▼ ⧰ ☐ ✕	
⊟ **Display**	
Display Style	Use Geometry Setting
⊟ **Defaults**	
Physics Preference	CFD
Solver Preference	Fluent
Element Order	Linear
☐ Element Size	5.e-003 m
Export Format	Standard
Export Preview Surface Mesh	No

Figure 14.12c) Setting the Element Size in Details of Mesh

Right click on Mesh in the Outline and select Generate Mesh. Open Statistics under Details of "Mesh". The number of Elements is 32133 and the number of Nodes is 17403.

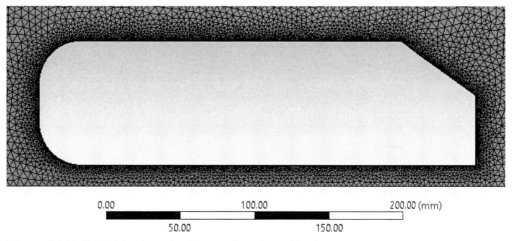

0.00	100.00	200.00 (mm)
	50.00	150.00

Figure 14.12d) Finished mesh close to the Ahmed body

319

Figure 14.12e) Finished mesh for the whole mesh region around the Ahmed body

13. Control-select the three upper edges of the rectangle surrounding the mesh region. Right click and select Create Named Selection. Enter *symmetry* as the name and click OK.

Repeat this step with the three lower edges and name them *street*.

Control-select the two left edges of the rectangle surrounding the mesh region. Right click and select Create Named Selection. Enter *inlet* as the name and click OK.

Repeat this step with the two rightmost edges and name them *outlet*.

Control-select the seven edges of the Ahmed body. Right click and select Create Named Selection. Enter *ahmed body* as the name and click OK.

Select File>>Export>>Mesh>>FLUENT Input File>>Export from the menu and save the mesh with the name *ahmed-body-mesh.msh*. Select File>>Save Project from the menu and close the meshing window by selecting File>>Close Meshing from the menu. Right-click on Mesh under Project Schematic in ANSYS Workbench and select Update.

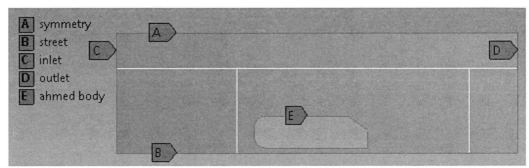

Figure 14.13a) Named selections

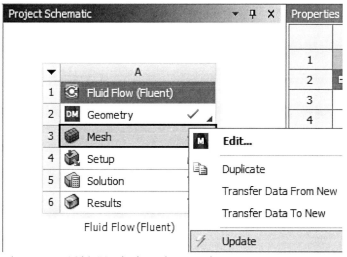

Figure 14.13b) Updating the Mesh

F. Launching ANSYS Fluent

14. Double-click on Setup under Project Schematic in ANSYS Workbench. Check the Options box for Double Precision. Select Parallel Processing Options and set the number of processes equal to the number of processor cores on your computer. Click on OK to launch Fluent.

Select Transient Time under Solver under General on the Task Page. Double-click on Models under Setup in the Outline View and select the Viscous - Laminar model on the Task Page. Click on the Edit… button. Select the k-epsilon (2 eqn) turbulence model. Click OK to exit the Viscous Model window.

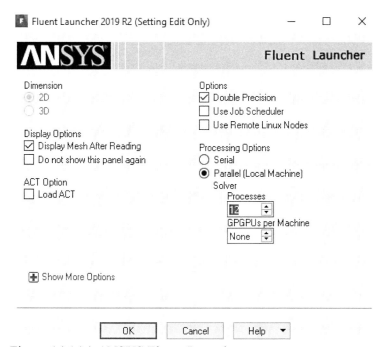

Figure 14.14a) ANSYS Fluent Launcher

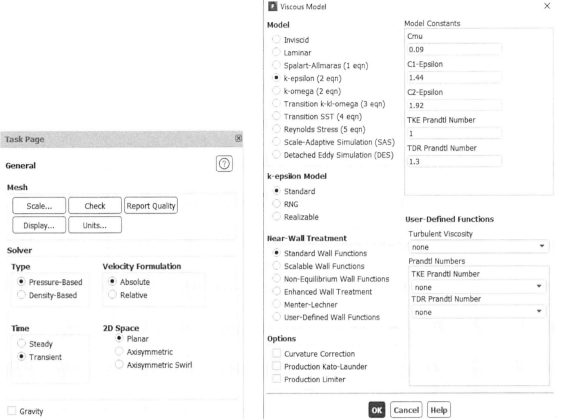

Figure 14.14b) Transient setting   Figure 14.14c) Details for the viscous model

15. Double-click on Boundary Conditions under Setup in the Outline View and select *inlet* under Zone for Boundary Conditions. Click on the Edit… button. Select Components as Velocity Specification Method. Enter 30 as X-Velocity (m/s). Click OK to close the Velocity Inlet window.

Double-click on Reference Values under Setup in the Outline View and change the Area (m2) to 0.00891, the Depth (m) to 0.11, the Length (m) to 0.295 and the Velocity (m/s) to 30. Select *solid-surface_body* as Reference Zone.

Double-click on Methods under Solution in the Tree and select PISO as the Scheme for Pressure-Velocity Coupling under Solution Methods on the Task Page. Select Green-Gauss Cell Based Gradient for Spatial Discretization. Select Presto! as Spatial Discretization for Pressure and QUICK for Momentum, Turbulent Kinetic Energy and Turbulent Dissipation Rate.

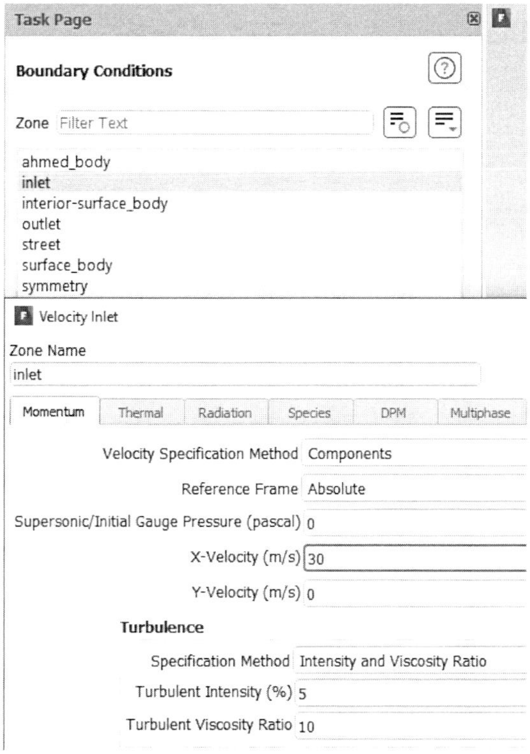

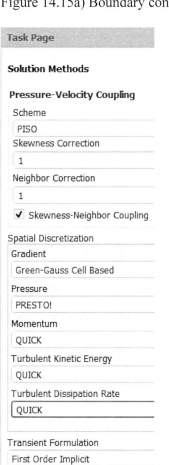

Figure 14.15a) Boundary condition

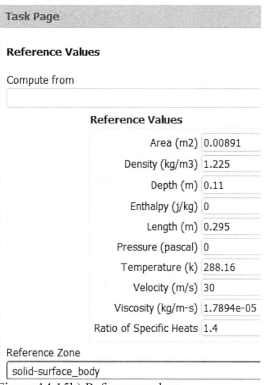

Figure 14.15b) Reference values

Figure 14.15c) Solution Methods

16. Double-click on Report Definitions under Solution in the Outline View. Select New>>Force Report>>Drag from the drop-down menu. Select *ahmed_body* as Wall Zone. Check the boxes for Report File, Report Plot and Print to Console under Create. Click on the OK button to close the window. Close the Report Definitions window.

Double click on *report-def-0-rplot* that is located under Solution, Monitors and Report Plots in the Outline View. Click on Axes in the Edit Report Plot window. Select Y Axis and uncheck the box for Auto Range. Set the Maximum value to 1.6 under Range, click on Apply and Close the windows.

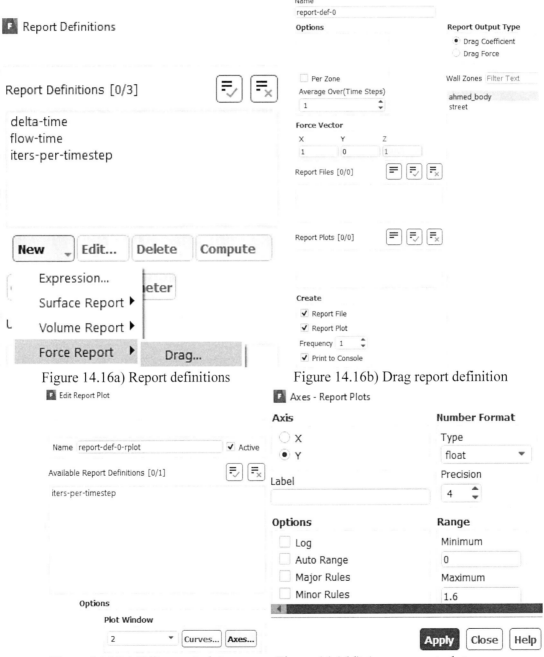

Figure 14.16a) Report definitions

Figure 14.16b) Drag report definition

Figure 14.16c) Edit report plot

Figure 14.16d) Axes - report plots

17. Double-click on Initialization under Solution in the Outline View and set the X Velocity (m/s) to 30. Select Compute from inlet. Click on the Initialize button.

Double-click on Run Calculation under Solution in the Outline View. Set the Time Step to 0.0002 s and the number of time steps to 250. Check Max Iterations/Time Step to 60. Click on Calculate. Click OK when you get the Information window saying Calculation complete.

Figure 14.17a) Solution initialization   Figure 14.17b) Running the calculations

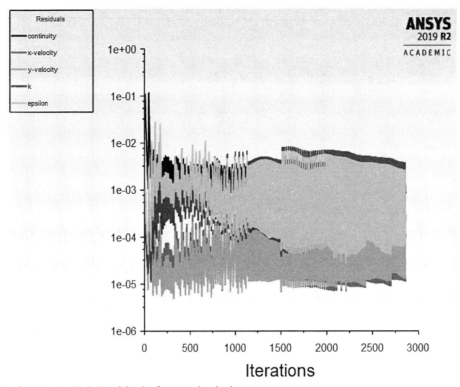

Figure 14.17c) Residuals from calculations

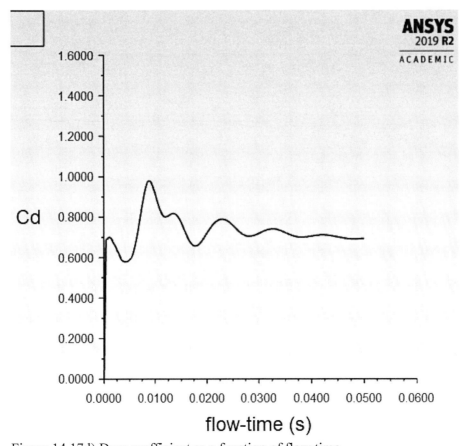

Figure 14.17d) Drag coefficient as a function of flow time

G. Post-Processing

18. Double-click on Reports under Results in the Outline View and double-click on Forces under Reports. Deselect the *street* Wall Zone and click on the Print button. The total drag coefficient is approximately 0.694. Close the Force Reports window.

Figure 14.18 Force reports window

19. Double-click on Graphics under Results in the Outline View. Select Contours under Graphics on the Task Page and click on Set Up…. Select Contours of Velocity… and X Velocity. Deselect all Surfaces and click on Save/Display.

Repeat this step for the Static Pressure field. Finally, select Velocity and Stream Function and create another plot. Check the Banded Coloring option for the Stream Function.

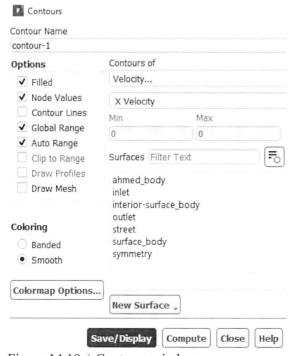

Figure 14.19a) Contours window

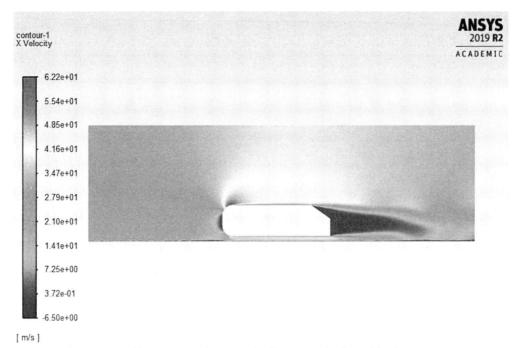
Figure 14.19b) Contours for X Velocity around Ahmed body

Figure 14.19c) Contours for static pressure around Ahmed body

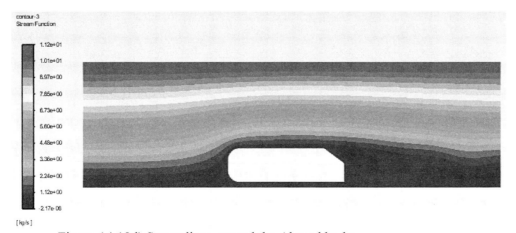
Figure 14.19d) Streamlines around the Ahmed body

H. 3D Ahmed Body Design

20. Start by repeating step 1 in this chapter by launching ANSYS Workbench. Double click on Fluid Flow (Fluent) under Analysis Systems in the Toolbox.

    Right-click on Geometry in the Project Schematic window and select New DesignModeler Geometry. Select Units>>Millimeter from the menu as the desired length unit, see step 2.

    Select Look At Face ⬛. Select XY Plane in the Tree Outline and New Sketch ⬛. Select the Sketching tab, click on Draw and select Rectangle. Draw a rectangle from the origin in the first quadrant. Select Dimensions and set the height of the rectangle to 288 mm and the length to 1044 mm. Right click in the graphics window and select Zoom to Fit.

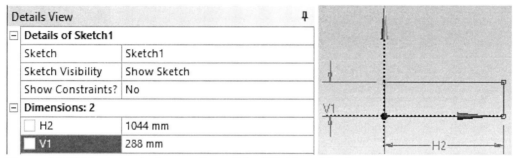

Figure 14.20 First step in the creation of the 3D Ahmed body

21. Select Modify and Fillet under Sketching Toolboxes. Set the Radius of the Fillet to 100 mm. Click on the two left hand side corners of the rectangle.

    Click on Chamfer under Modify. Set the Length of the Chamfer to 201.2 mm. Click on the upper right corner of the rectangle. The rear slant angle is 25 degrees. Select Dimensions and set the Angle to 25 degrees. You may need to right-click and select alternate angle when you define the angle. Select General under Dimensions and select the chamfer to set the length to 201.2 mm, see Figure 14.21a).

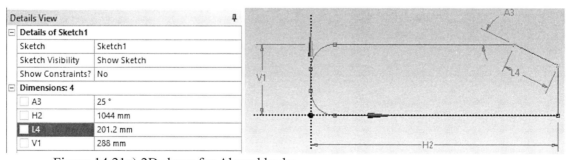

Figure 14.21a) 2D shape for Ahmed body

Click on ⬛ Extrude and select Sketch 1 in the Tree Outline under XYPlane. Apply the sketch in Details View next to Geometry. Set the Direction for the Extrude to Both-

Symmetric in Details View and set the depth of the extrusion to 194.5 mm. Click on Generate.

Select Blend>>Fixed Radius from under menu. Set the Radius to 100 mm. Control select the two vertical edges at the front of the Ahmed body and Apply the edges next to Geometry in Details View. Click on Generate.

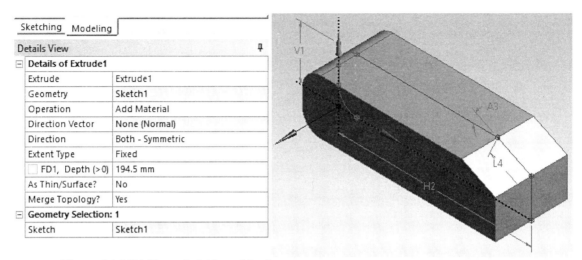

Figure 14.21b) Extruded Ahmed body

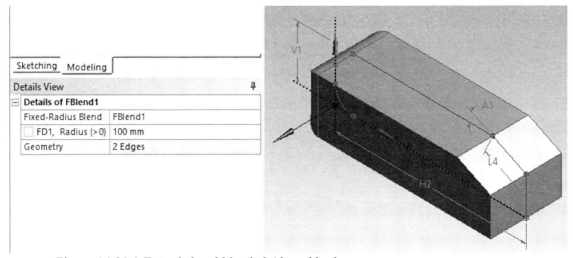

Figure 14.21c) Extruded and blended Ahmed body

22. Select ZXPlane in the Tree Outline. Right click in the graphics window and select View>>Bottom View. Select the Sketching tab in Tree Outline and select Circle. Draw a circle and use General under Dimensions to define a 30 mm diameter circle that you position 202 mm from the front of the Ahmed body and 163.5 mm from the center plane. Create three more circles with the same diameter and position them according to Figure 14.22a).

Click on ⌐ 🔳 Extrude and select Sketch 2 in the Tree Outline under ZXPlane. Apply the sketch in Details View next to Geometry. Set the Direction under Details View to Reversed and set the depth of the extrusion to 50 mm. Click on Generate.

Select Create>> New Plane from the menu. Select in Details View From Plane as Type, ZXPlane as the Base Plane and Offset Z as Transform 1 (RMB). Set the Offset Z value to – 50 mm. Click on Generate. Select Tools>>Enclosure from the menu. Select Box as the Shape in Details View and set the Number of Planes to 2. Select XYPlane as Symmetry Plane 1, Plane4 as Symmetry Plane 2 and Apply them in Details View. Set the Model Type to Full Model and the Cushion to Non-Uniform. Set the different Cushion values FD1 – FD4 as listed in Figure 14.22c). Click on Generate.

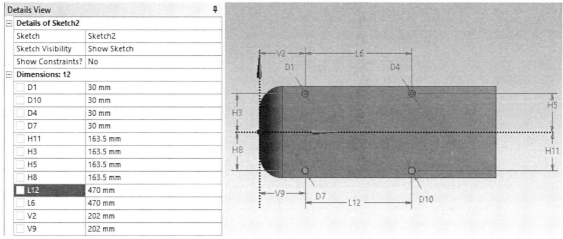

Figure 14.22a) Locations for the four cylindrical supports

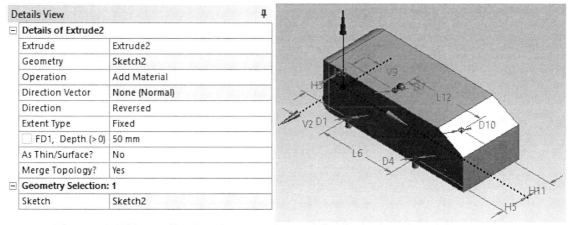

Figure 14.22b) Details view for extrusion and finished Ahmed model

331

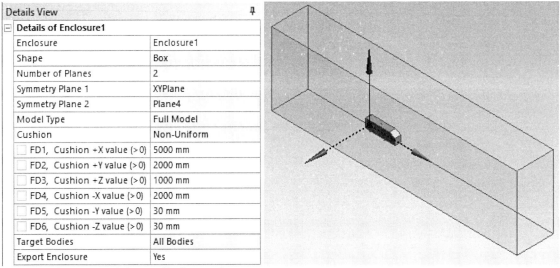

Details View	卓
Details of Enclosure1	
Enclosure	Enclosure1
Shape	Box
Number of Planes	2
Symmetry Plane 1	XYPlane
Symmetry Plane 2	Plane4
Model Type	Full Model
Cushion	Non-Uniform
FD1, Cushion +X value (>0)	5000 mm
FD2, Cushion +Y value (>0)	2000 mm
FD3, Cushion +Z value (>0)	1000 mm
FD4, Cushion -X value (>0)	2000 mm
FD5, Cushion -Y value (>0)	30 mm
FD6, Cushion -Z value (>0)	30 mm
Target Bodies	All Bodies
Export Enclosure	Yes

Figure 14.22c) Details for enclosure

23. Select Create>>Boolean from the menu. Select Subtract as Operation. Click on the plus sign next to 2 Parts, 2 Bodies in the Tree Outline. Select the second Solid and Apply it as Target Body in Details of Boolean1. Select the first Solid and Apply it as Tool Body in Details of Boolean1. Click on Generate. Right click on the Solid in the Tree Outline and Rename it to Air. Select File>>Save Project and name it "3D Ahmed Body Study" and close DesignModeler.

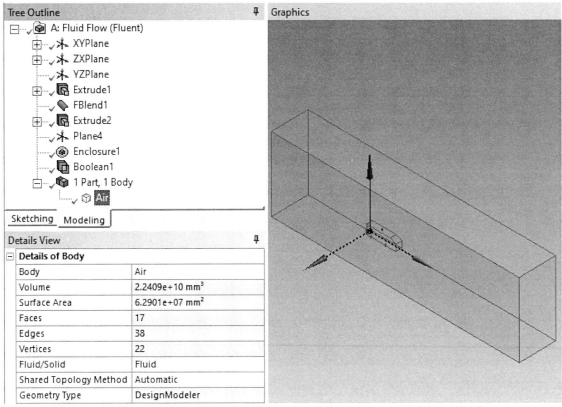

Tree Outline 卓

- A: Fluid Flow (Fluent)
  - XYPlane
  - ZXPlane
  - YZPlane
  - Extrude1
  - FBlend1
  - Extrude2
  - Plane4
  - Enclosure1
  - Boolean1
  - 1 Part, 1 Body
    - Air

Sketching Modeling

Details View	卓
Details of Body	
Body	Air
Volume	2.2409e+10 mm³
Surface Area	6.2901e+07 mm²
Faces	17
Edges	38
Vertices	22
Fluid/Solid	Fluid
Shared Topology Method	Automatic
Geometry Type	DesignModeler

Figure 14.23 Finished model and computational domain around Ahmed body

I. 3D Ahmed Body Mesh

24. Double click on Mesh under Project Schematic in ANSYS Workbench. In the Meshing window, right click on Mesh in the Outline and select Update. Select the Home tab in the menu. Select Layout>>Reset Layout under the Home tab.

    Click on the plus sign next to Sizing under Details of "Mesh". Change Capture Proximity and Capture Curvature both to Yes. Click on the plus sign next to Quality under Details of "Mesh". Set Smoothing to High. Update the mesh once again. Right click in the graphics window and select View>>Back.

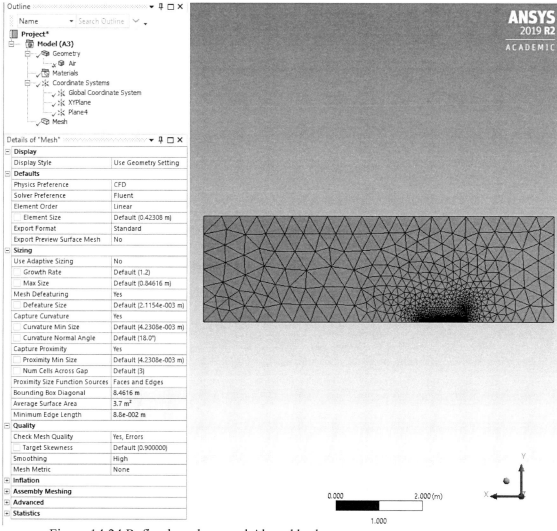

Figure 14.24 Refined mesh around Ahmed body

25. Right click on Mesh in the Outline, select Insert>> Sizing. Right click in the graphics window and select Cursor Mode>>Face. Select all 11 faces of the Ahmed body as shown in figure 14.25a). You will need to rotate and zoom in on the model in order to select all faces. Apply the faces as the Geometry under Scope in Details of "Face Sizing". Set the Element Size to 0.0075 m. Update the mesh once again.

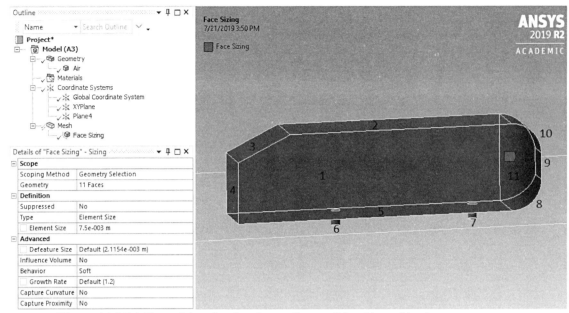

Figure 14.25a) Face sizing for the eleven faces of the Ahmed body

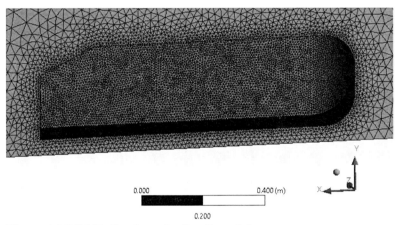

Figure 14.25b) Refined mesh after face sizing

26. Click on the plus sign next to Inflation in Details of Mesh. Set Use Automatic Inflation to Program Controlled. Right click in the graphics window and select Cursor Mode>>Vertex. Control select the 14 vertices as shown in Figure 14.26a).

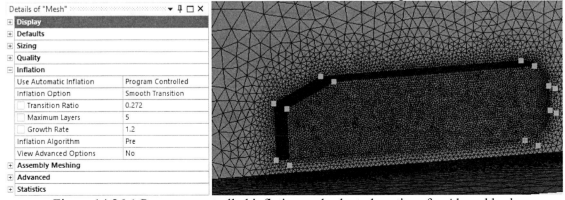

Figure 14.26a) Program controlled inflation and selected vertices for Ahmed body

Right click in the graphics window and select Create Named Selection. Enter the name "ahmed body" and click OK. Select *ahmed body* under Named Selections and select Include from the drop-down menu for Program Controlled Inflation under Definition in Details of "ahmed body", see Figure 14.26b).

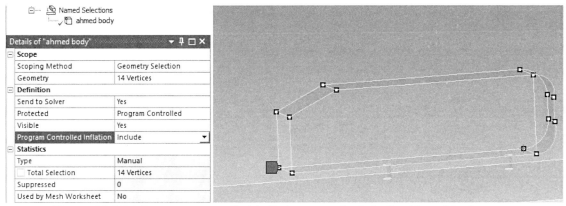

Figure 14.26b) Program controlled inflation set to include for Ahmed body

27. Right click in the graphics window and select View>>Left. Right click in the graphics window and select Cursor Mode>>Face. Select the face for the computational domain that is available from the Left View. Right click in the graphics window and select Create Named Selection. Enter the name "velocity-inlet" and click OK.

Right click in the graphics window and select View>>Right. Select the face for the computational domain that is available from the Right View. Right click in the graphics window and select Create Named Selection. Enter the name "pressure-outlet" and click OK.

Right click in the graphics window and select View>>Back. Select the face for the computational domain that is available from the Back View. Right click in the graphics window and select Create Named Selection. Enter the name "symmetry1" and click OK.

Right click in the graphics window and select View>>Bottom. Select the face for the computational domain that is available from the Bottom View. Right click in the graphics window and select Create Named Selection. Enter the name "street" and click OK.

Right click in the graphics window and select View>>Top. Select the face for the computational domain that is available from the Top View. Right click in the graphics window and select Create Named Selection. Enter the name "symmetry-top" and click OK.

Right click in the graphics window and select View>>Front. Select the face for the computational domain that is available from the Front View. Right click in the graphics window and select Create Named Selection. Enter the name "symmetry-side" and click OK. Update the mesh.

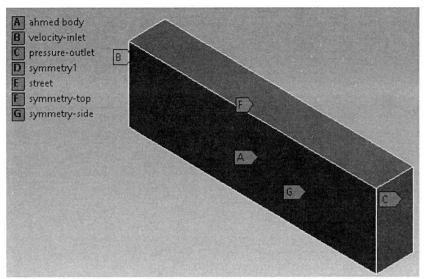

Figure 14.27 Named selections for the Ahmed body

28. Go back to DesignModeler by double clicking on Geometry under Project Schematic in ANSYS Workbench. Select Back View. Select XYPlane in the Tree Outline and create a new Sketch 🗔.

Click on the Sketching tab in the Tree Outline and select Rectangle. Draw a rectangle around the Ahmed body from the bottom of the computational domain. Select Dimensions and click on the vertical and horizontal sides of the new rectangle. Enter 900 mm as the vertical height of the rectangle and 2700 mm as the width. Set the horizontal distance from the front of the Ahmed body to the right-hand side vertical edge of the rectangle to 552 mm. Set the vertical distance between the lower horizontal edge of the rectangle and the bottom of the Ahmed body to 50 mm.

Select the Modeling tab in the Tree Outline and select Extrude. Select the new Sketch3 under XYPlane in the Tree Outline and Apply it as Geometry in Details of Extrude3. Enter 450 mm as the FD1, Depth (>0) of the Extrusion. Click on Generate. Click on plus sign next to 2 Parts, 2 Bodies in the Tree Outline, right click on Solid and select Rename. Rename it to "AhmedBodyBox". Close the DesignModeler window.

Go back to ANSYS Workbench, double click on Mesh and answer *Yes* to the question whether you would like to read upstream data.

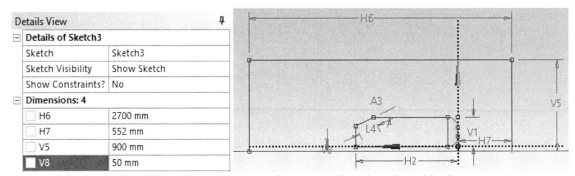

Figure 14.28a) Dimensions for rectangle surrounding the Ahmed body

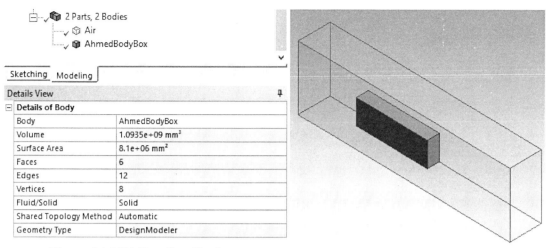

Figure 14.28b) Details of body

29. Right click Mesh under Project in Outline, select Insert>>Sizing. Right click in the graphics window and select Cursor Mode>>Body. Select the computational domain in the graphics window. Apply the computational domain in Geometry under Scope in Details of "Sizing". Select Body of Influence as Type under Definition.

Select Back view in the graphics window, zoom in on the Ahmed body, select the AhmedBodyBox and Apply it as the Body of Influence. You will need to select the second small rectangle in the lower left corner of Figure 14.29a) before you can select the AhmedRocketBox that turns from green to red when you apply it as the body of influence. Update the Mesh. If you click on the plus sign next to Statistics in Details of Mesh you will find that the number of Elements for the mesh is 482846 and the number of Nodes is 139354.

Right click on AhmedBodyBox under Geometry in Outline and select Hide Body. Select Mesh in the Outline and click on the plus sign next to Quality in Details of Mesh. Select Skewness as Mesh Metric. The max skewness should not be above 0.9. Select File>>Save Project. Select File>>Export>>Mesh>>FLUENT Input File>>Export and save the mesh with the name "ahmed-body-flow-mesh.msh". Close the Meshing window.

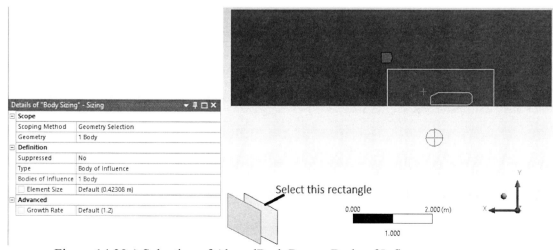

Figure 14.29a) Selection of AhmedBodyBox as Body of Influence

337

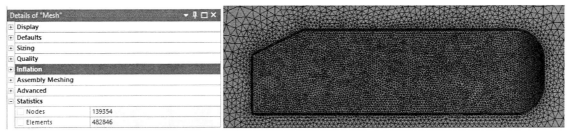

Figure 14.29b) Finished mesh for Ahmed body

J. Launching ANSYS Fluent for 3D Ahmed Body

30. Double click on Setup in ANSYS Workbench. Check Double Precision under Options and check Parallel under Processing Options. Select the number of Processes equal to the number of cores for the computer. Click OK to launch Fluent.

    Double click on Models under Setup in the Outline View and select Viscous – Laminar under Models on the Task Page. Click on the Edit… button. Select the k-epsilon (2 eqn) turbulence model. Select Realizable as the k-epsilon model and check Non-Equilibrium Wall Functions as Near-Wall Treatment. Click OK to exit the Viscous Model window.

    Double click on Boundary Conditions under Setup in the Outline View and select *velocity-inlet* under Zone for Boundary Conditions on the Task Page. Click on the Edit… button. Select Components as Velocity Specification Method. Enter 30 as X-Velocity (m/s). Click OK to close the Velocity Inlet window.

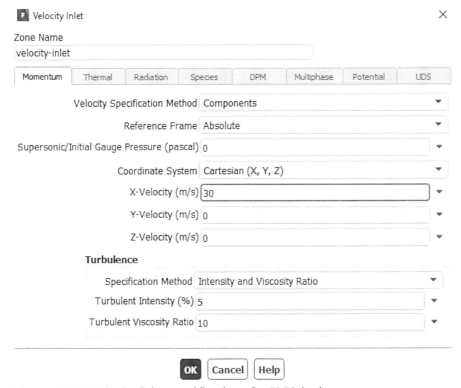

Figure 14.30 Velocity inlet specifications for X-Velocity

31. Double click Projected Areas under Results and Reports in the Outline View. Select *wall-air* as the Surface, enter 0.030 as Min Feature Size (m), select X as Projection Direction and click on Compute. The computed frontal area is 0.06175669 m2. Close the window.

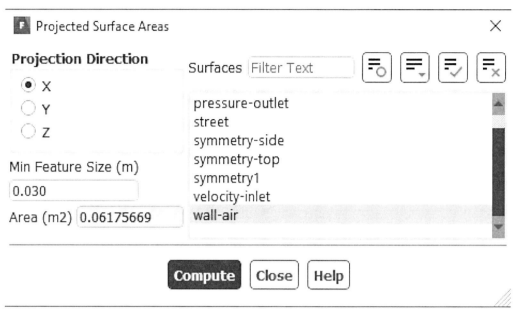

Figure 14.31a) Projected surface area

Double click on Reference Values under Setup in the Outline View and change the Area (m2) to 0.06175669 and the Velocity (m/s) to 30. Select Compute from velocity-inlet and set Reference Zone to air.

Double click on Methods under Solution in the Outline View and set the Pressure-Velocity Coupling scheme to Coupled. Set the Spatial Discretization Gradient to Least Squares Cell Based, and Pressure to Standard. Set the remaining three for Momentum, Turbulent Kinetic Energy and Turbulent Dissipation Rate to First Order Upwind. Uncheck the box for Pseudo Transient.

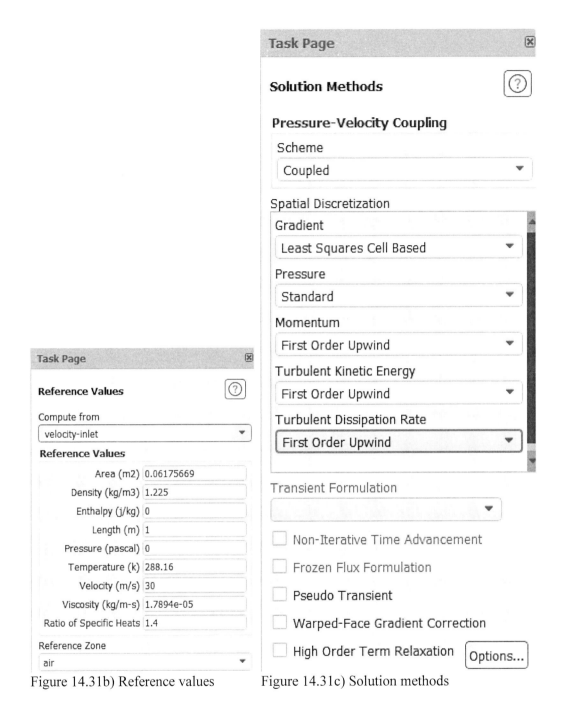

Figure 14.31b) Reference values   Figure 14.31c) Solution methods

32. Double click on Controls under Solution in the Outline View, set the Flow Courant Number to 50, set the Momentum and Pressure Explicit Relaxation Factors to 0.25 and set the Turbulent Viscosity Under-Relaxation Factor to 0.8. Click on Limits… and set the Maximum Turb. Viscosity Ratio to 10000000. Click on the OK button to close the window.

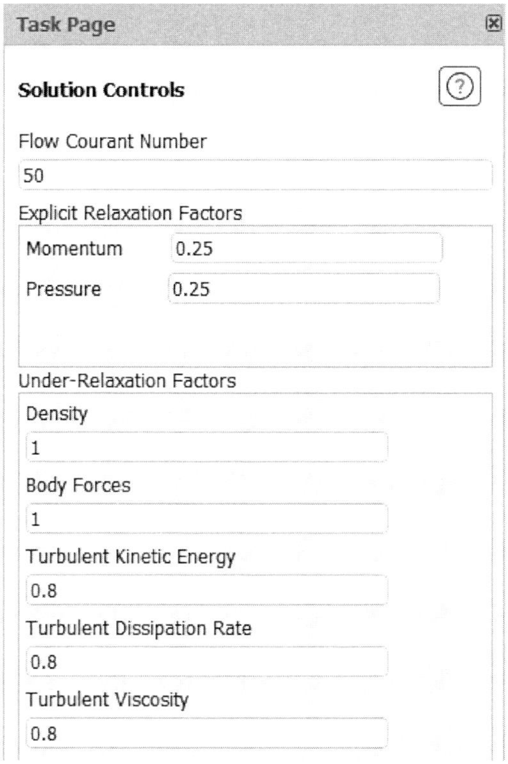

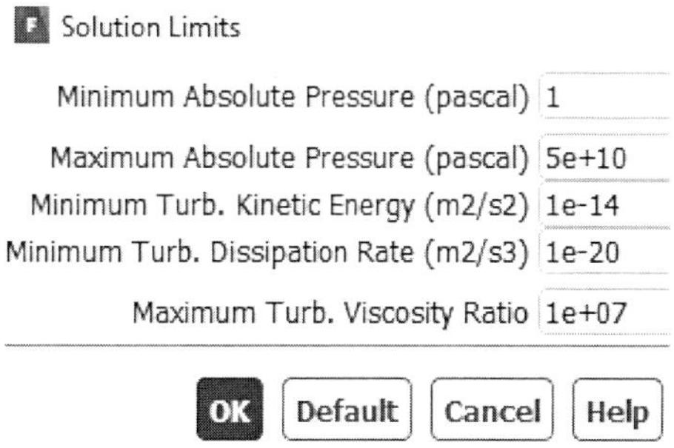

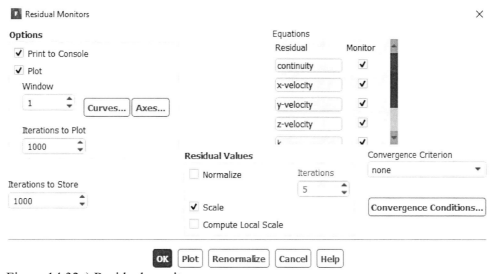

Figure 14.32a) Solution controls   Figure 14.32b) Solution limits

Double click on Monitors and Residual under Solution in the Outline View. Set the Convergence Criterion to none. Click on OK to close Residual Monitors.

Figure 14.32c) Residual monitors

Double-click on Report Definitions on the left-hand side under Solution in the Tree. Select New>>Force Report>>Drag… from the drop-down menu. Select *wall-air* as Wall Zone. Check the boxes for Report File, Report Plot and Print to Console under Create. Set the Force Vector to X = 1, Y = 0, and Z = 0. Click on the OK button to close the window. Close the Report Definitions window.

Drag Report Definition

Name

report-def-0

Options   **Report Output Type**

                                                    ● Drag Coefficient
                                                    ○ Drag Force

☐ Per Zone   Wall Zones Filter Text

Average Over(Iterations)

1   street
                                                    wall-air

Force Vector

X   Y   Z

1   0   0

Report Files [0/0]

Report Plots [0/0]

Create

☑ Report File

☑ Report Plot

Frequency 1

☑ Print to Console

☐ Create Output Parameter   ☐ Highlight Zones

OK   Compute   Cancel   Help

Figure 14.32d) Drag report definition

33. Double click on Initialization under Solution in the Outline View and select *Hybrid Initializa*tion. Click on the Initialize button. Double click on Calculation Activities under Solution in the Outline View and click on Edit… for Autosave Every (Iterations). Set Save Data File Every (Iterations) to 100. Click OK to close the Autosave window. Double click on Run Calculation under Solution in the Outline View. Set the Number of Iterations to 200. Click on Calculate.

Double click on Methods under Solution in the Outline View and replace First Order Upwind with Second Order Upwind for Momentum, Turbulent Kinetic Energy and Turbulent Dissipation Rate. Double click on Controls under Solution and set the Turbulent Viscosity value to 0.95. Double click on Run Calculation under Solution and set Number of Iterations to 500. Click on Calculate and Click OK in the window that appears.

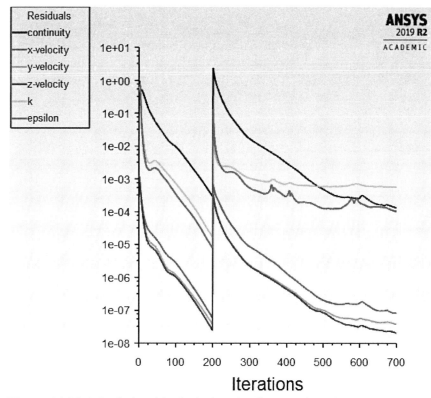

Figure 14.33a) Scaled residuals during the first 700 iterations

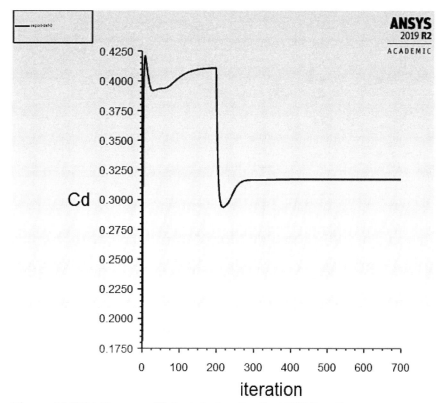

Figure 14.33b) Drag coefficient during the first 700 iterations

K. Post-Processing for 3D Ahmed Body

34. Double-click on Reports under Results in the Outline View and double-click on Forces under Reports. Set Direction Vector for X to 1, Y to 0, and Z to 0. Select the *wall-air* Wall Zone, deselect *street* Wall Zone and click on the Print button. The total drag coefficient is 0.31715. Close the Force Reports window.

Double-click on Graphics and Contours under Results in the Outline View. Select Contours of Pressure… and Static Pressure. Select *Symmetry1* as Surfaces and click on Save/Display.

Figure 14.34a) Static pressure for Ahmed body at 30 m/s.

Double-click on Graphics and Contours under Results in the Outline View. Select Contours of Velocity… and Velocity Magnitude. Select *Symmetry1* as the Surface and click on Save/Display.

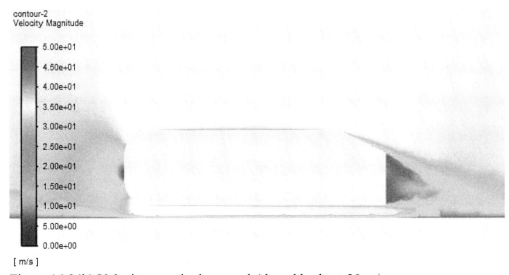

Figure 14.34b) Velocity magnitude around Ahmed body at 30 m/s.

344

35. Set the inlet velocity in the boundary condition to 40 m/s. Double click on Methods under Solution in the Outline View and replace Second Order Upwind with First Order Upwind for Momentum, Turbulent Kinetic Energy and Turbulent Dissipation Rate. Double click on Controls under Solution and set the Turbulent Viscosity value to 0.8. Double click on Reference Values under Setup in the Outline View and set the Velocity (m/s) to 40. Repeat steps 33-35.

U (m/s)	Re	Cd, Fluent	Cd, Meile et al.	Percent difference
3	214,413	0.40217	0.36001	11.71
4	285,884	0.37498	0.35684	5.083
5	357,354	0.35878	0.35380	1.408
6	428,825	0.34623	0.35088	1.324
7.5	536,032	0.33697	0.34670	2.807
10	714,709	0.33075	0.34027	2.799
15	1,072,063	0.32431	0.32919	1.482
20	1,429,418	0.32072	0.32010	0.193
30	2,144,127	0.31715	0.30655	3.458
40	2,858835	0.31486	0.29744	5.855
50	3,573,544	0.31371	0.29133	7.683
60	4,288,253	0.31273	0.28722	8.883
70	5,002,962	0.31193	0.28445	9.659
80	5,717,671	0.31126	0.28260	10.14

Table 14.1 Comparison between ANSYS Fluent and established data

Repeat step 35 for all inlet velocities as listed in Table 14.1.

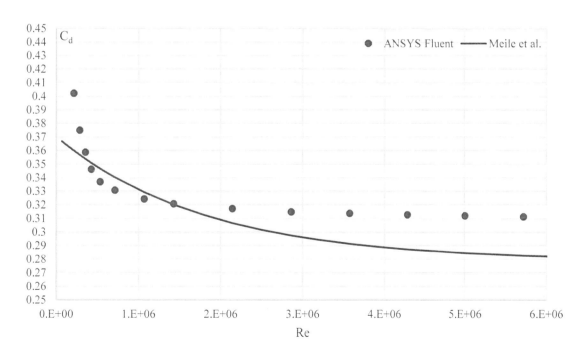

Figure 14.35 Drag coefficient versus Reynolds number for Ahmed body

L. Theory

We start by defining the Reynolds number for the 3D case outlined in this chapter

$$Re = \frac{UL\rho}{\mu} \tag{14.1}$$

where U (m/s) is inlet velocity, L (m) is the length of the Ahmed body, ρ (kg/m^3) is the density of the fluid and μ (m^2/s) is dynamic viscosity of the fluid.
Next, we define the drag coefficient C_d as

$$C_d = \frac{F_d}{\frac{1}{2}\rho U^2 A} \tag{14.2}$$

where F_d(N) is the drag force and A (m^2) is the frontal area of the Ahmed body. Meile *et al.*[6] determined the following relationship between the drag coefficient and the Reynolds number for the Ahmed body.

$$C_d = 0.2788 + 0.0915e^{-Re/1797100} \tag{14.3}$$

M. References

1. Ahmed, S.R., Ramm, G.,"Some Salient Features of the Time-Averaged Ground Vehicle Wake", *SAE-Paper 840300*, 1984.
2. Dogan, T., Conger, M., Kim, D-H., Mousaviraad, M., Xing, T., Stern, F.,"Simulation of Turbulent Flow over the Ahmed Body", *ME: 5160 Intermediate Mechanics of Fluids CFD Lab 4*, (2016).
3. Kalyan, D.K., Paul, A.R., "Computational Study of Flow around a Simplified 2D Ahmed Body", *International Journal of Engineering Science and Innovative Technology (IJESIT)*, **2**, 3, (2013).
4. Khan, R.S, Umale, S.,"CFD Aerodynamic Analysis of Ahmed Body", *International Journal of Engineering Trends and Technology (IJETT)*, **18**, 7, (2014).
5. Lienhart, H., Stoots, C. and Becker, S.,"Flow and Turbulence Structures in the Wake of a Simplified Car Model (Ahmed Model), *Notes on Numerical Fluid Mechanics*, **77**, 6, (2002).
6. Meile, W., Brenn, G., Reppenhagen, A., Lechner, B., Fuchs, A.,"Experiments and numerical simulations on the aerodynamics of the Ahmed body", *CFD Letters*, **3**, 1, (2011).

N. Exercise

14.1 Model the 2D flow past the Ahmed body with the dimensions as shown and units in mm from Figure 14.37. Use an element size of 0.006 m. Use a free stream velocity 40 m/s and the k-epsilon (2 eqn) turbulence model. Use a time step of 0.0002 s and 1500 time steps. Set the Max Iterations/Time Step to 60.

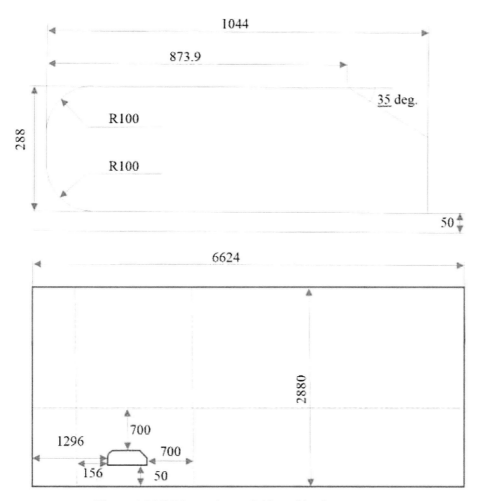

Figure 14.37 Dimensions of Ahmed body

Notes:

CHAPTER 15. HOURGLASS

A. Objectives

- Using ANSYS Workbench to Create Geometry and Mesh for the Hourglass
- Inserting Boundary Conditions
- Running the Calculations
- Using Contour Plots for Volume Fractions and a Movie for Visualizations

B. Problem Description

We will study the flow in the hourglass and will analyze the problem using ANSYS Fluent.

C. Launching ANSYS Workbench and Selecting Fluent

1. Start by launching ANSYS Workbench. Double click on Fluid Flow (Fluent) under Analysis Systems in the Toolbox.

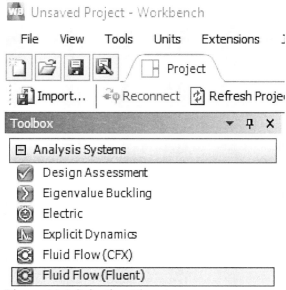

Figure 15.1 Selecting Fluent

D. Launching ANSYS DesignModeler

2. Right click Geometry under Project Schematic in ANSYS Workbench and select
   Properties. In Properties of Schematic A2: Geometry, select Analysis Type 2D under
   Advanced Geometry Options. Right click on Geometry in the Project Schematic window
   and select New DesignModeler Geometry.

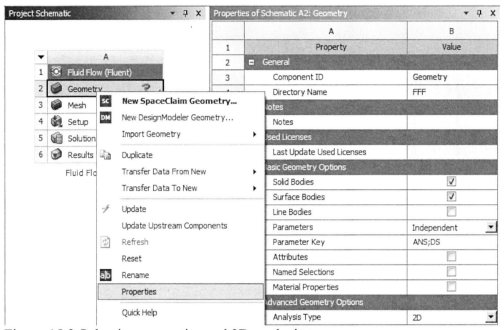

Figure 15.2 Selecting properties and 2D analysis type

3. Select Units>>Millimeter from the menu in DesignModeler. Select the XY Plane in the

   Tree Outline and click on Look at Face/Plane/Sketch ![icon]. Select the Sketching tab and
   select Line under Draw from Sketching Toolboxes. Start at the origin and draw the sketch
   with the dimensions as shown in Figure 15.3a).

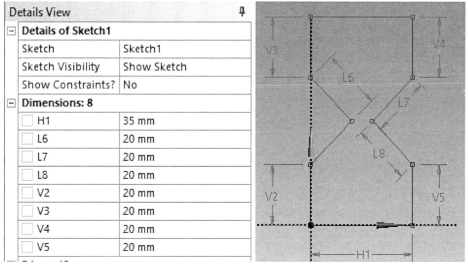

Figure 15.3a) Dimensions for hourglass

Select Concept>>Surfaces from Sketches from the menu. Select Sketch1 under XYPlane in Tree Outline and apply the sketch as the Base Object in Details View. Click on Generate and close DesignModeler.

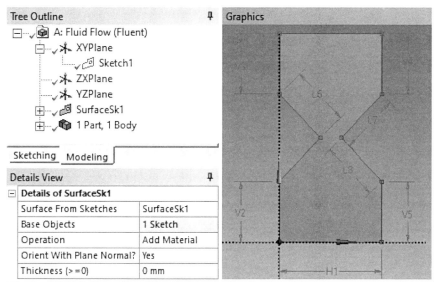

Figure 15.3b) Completed hourglass in DesignModeler

E. Launching ANSYS Meshing

4. Double click on Mesh under Project Schematic in ANSYS Workbench. Set the Element Size under Defaults in Details of Mesh to 0.0005 m. Right click on Mesh under Project in Outline and select Generate Mesh.

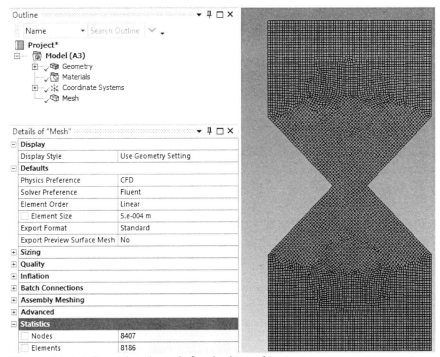

Figure 15.4a) Completed mesh for the hourglass

Right click in the graphics window and select Cursor Mode>> Edge and select the upper horizontal edge for the mesh. The edge turns green. Right click on the edge and select Create Named Selection. Enter *outlet* as the name and click Ok to close the Selection Name window. Control select the remaining nine edge of the mesh, right click and select Create Named Selection. Name these edges *wall*.

Select File>>Export>>Mesh>>FLUENT Input File>>Export from the menu and save the mesh with the name *hourglass.msh*. Select File>>Save Project from the menu and save the project with the name *Hour-Glass.wbpj*. Close the Meshing window and right-click on Mesh under Project Schematic in ANSYS Workbench and select Update.

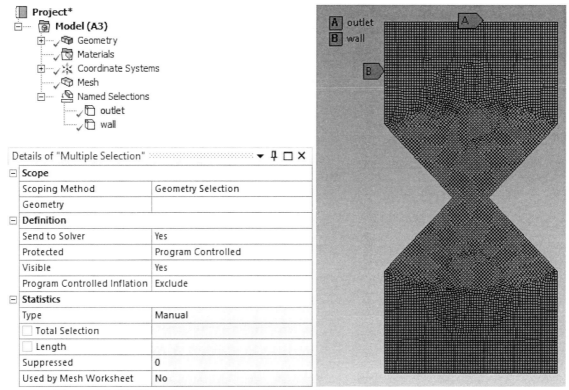

Figure 15.4b) Named selections for the hourglass

F. Launching ANSYS Fluent

5. Double click on Setup under Project Schematic in ANSYS Workbench. Check the box for Double Precision under Options in the ANSYS Fluent Launcher and select Parallel Processing Options. Set the number of Processes equal to the number of core processors for your computer. Click on OK to launch Fluent.

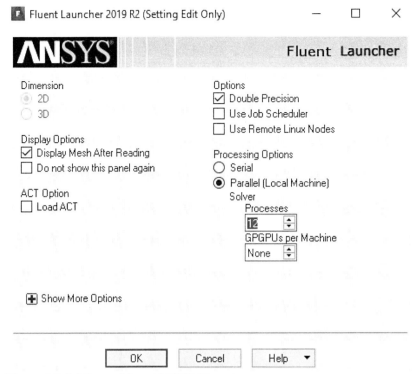

Figure 15.5a) Launching ANSYS Fluent

Select Transient under Time on the Task Page. Check the box for Gravity and enter -9.81 as the value for Y (m/s2).

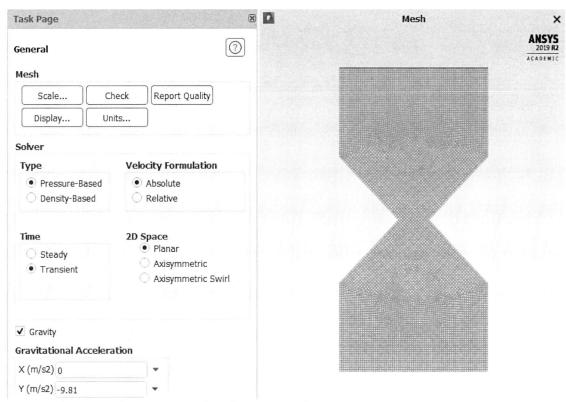

Figure 15.5b) General settings in ANSYS Fluent

6. Double click on Models and Multiphase under Setup in the Outline View and select Eulerian Model. Set the Number of Eulerian Phases to 2 and Implicit Formulation for Volume Fraction Parameters. Click OK to close the Multiphase Model window.

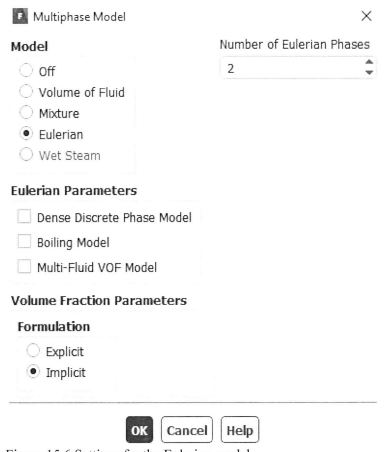

Figure 15.6 Settings for the Eulerian model

7. Open Materials and Fluid under Setup in the Outline View and select *air*. Right click on *air* and select copy. Enter the name *wood* and set the Density (kg/m3) to 850. Click on Change/Create and answer Yes to the question that appears. Close the Create/Edit Materials window.

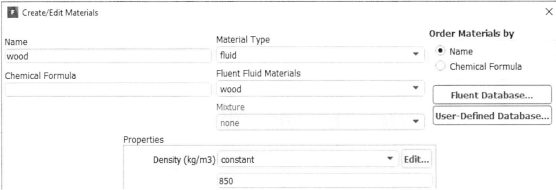

Figure 15.7 Settings for wood

8. Open Multiphase and Phases under Models in the Setup and select phase- 1 – Primary Phase. Right click phase-1 and select Edit…. Select *air* as Phase Material and enter *air* as the Name for the Primary Phase. Click OK to close the Primary Phase window.

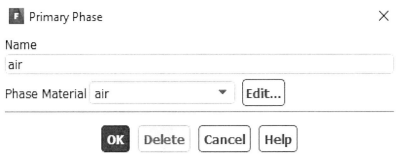

Figure 15.8a) Primary phase

Right click phase-2 and select Edit…. Select *wood* as Phase Material and enter *wood* as the Name for the Secondary Phase. Check the box for Granular and enter the settings as shown in Table 15.1. Click OK to close the Secondary Phase window.

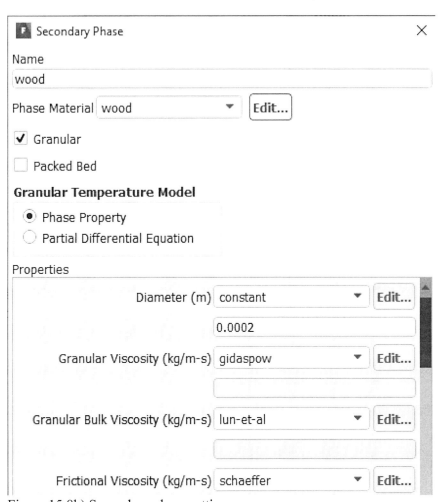

Figure 15.8b) Secondary phase settings

Diameter (m)	0.0002
Granular Viscosity (kg/m-s)	gidaspow
Granular Bulk Viscosity (kg/m-s)	lun-et-al
Frictional Viscosity (kg/m-s)	schaeffer

357

Angle Of Internal Friction (deg)	45
Frictional Pressure (pascal)	Based-ktgf
Frictional Modulus (pascal)	derived
Friction Packing Limit	0.45
Granular Temperature (m2/s2)	algebraic
Solids Pressure (pascal)	lun-et-al
Radial Distribution	lun-et-al
Elasticity Modulus (pascal)	derived
Packing Limit	0.63

Table 15.1 Properties for secondary phase

9. Double-click on Phase Interactions under Multiphase (Eulerian) and Models in Setup. Set Virtual Mass Coefficient, Drag Coefficient and Lift Coefficient to *none*. Set the Restitutions Coefficient on the Collisions tab to 0.001. Click OK to close the Phase Interactions window.

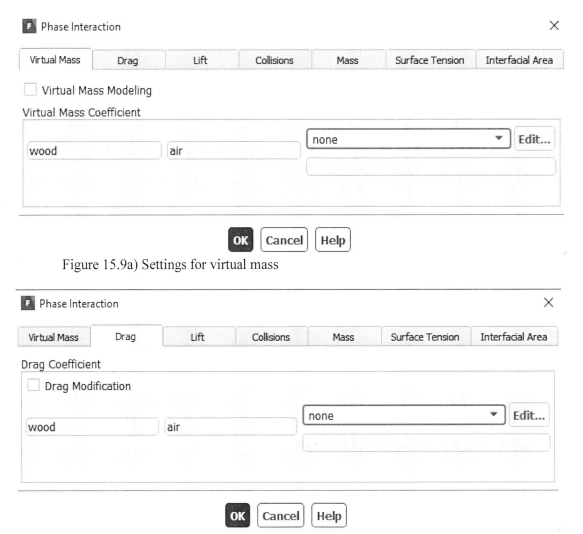

Figure 15.9a) Settings for virtual mass

Figure 15.9b) Settings for drag

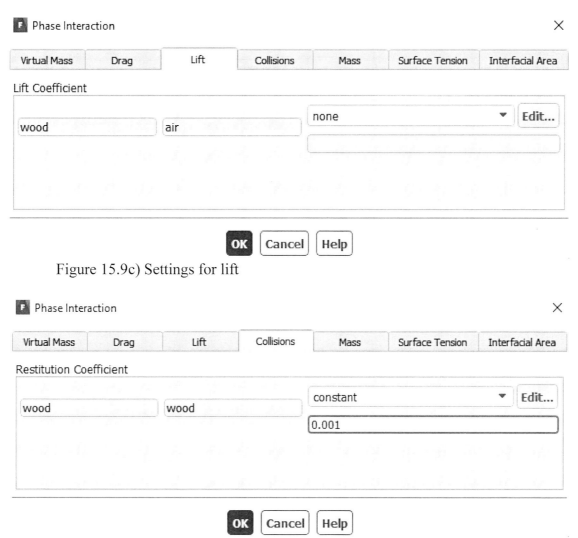

Figure 15.9c) Settings for lift

Figure 15.9d) Settings for phase interaction

10. Double-click on Boundary Conditions under Setup and click on Operating Conditions under Boundary Conditions on the Task Page. Check the box for Specified Operating Density and enter Reference Pressure Location X (m) 0.0175 and Y (m) 0.06828427.

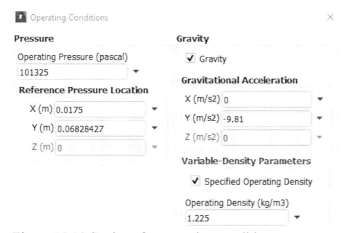

Figure 15.10 Settings for operating conditions

11. Double-click on Methods under Solution and set the Spatial Discretization for Momentum to Second Order Upwind. Double-click on Controls under Solution and set the Under-Relaxation Factor for Momentum to 0.3. Double click on Residual under Monitors and Solution. Set all Absolute Criteria for continuity, u-air and v-air to 1e-05. Set the other Absolute Criteria to 0.001 and click OK to close the Residual Monitors window.

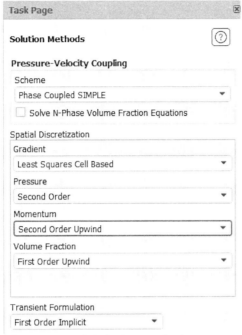

Figure 15.11a) Solution methods

Figure 15.11b) Under-relaxation

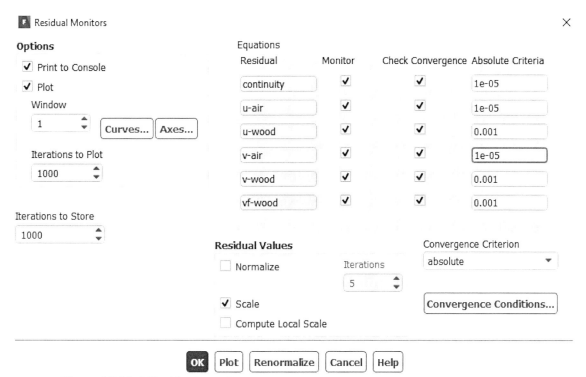

Figure 15.11c) Residual monitors

12. Double-click on Initialization under Solution and set Initializations Method to Hybrid Initialization. Click on Initialize.

Figure 15.12a) Hybrid initialization

Select Adapt>>Refine / Coarsen… from the Domain tab in the menu. Select Cell Registers>>New>>Field Variable… in the Adaption Controls window.

Select Gradient as Derivative Option, *wood* as Phase and Gradients of Phases… and Volume Fraction. Select Cells in Range as Type and set the Gradient-Min to 0.001 and Gradient-Max to 0.01. Click on Save and Close the Field Variable Register window. Check Dynamic Adaption in the Adaption Controls window and set the Frequency (time-step) to 1.

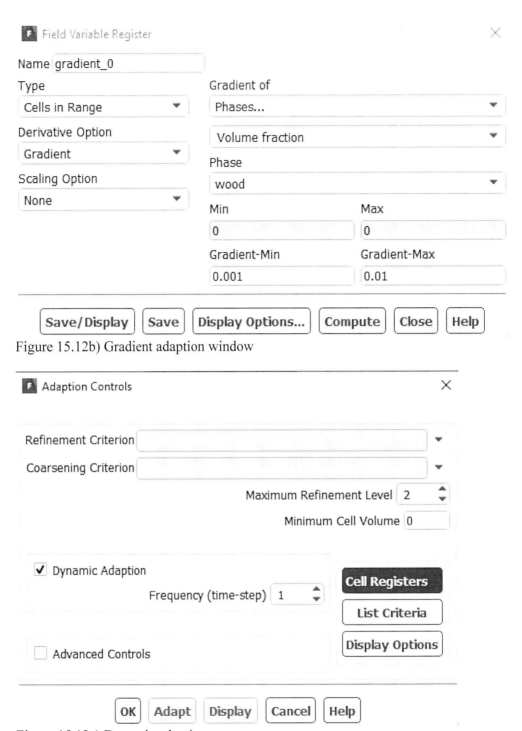

Figure 15.12b) Gradient adaption window

Figure 15.12c) Dynamic adaption

Select Cell Registers>>New>>Region… in the Adaption Controls window.

Set the X Max (m) value to 0.035 and Y Min (m) value to 0.034 and Y Max (m) value to 0.04. Click on Save and Close the Region Register window. Click OK to close the Adaption Controls window.

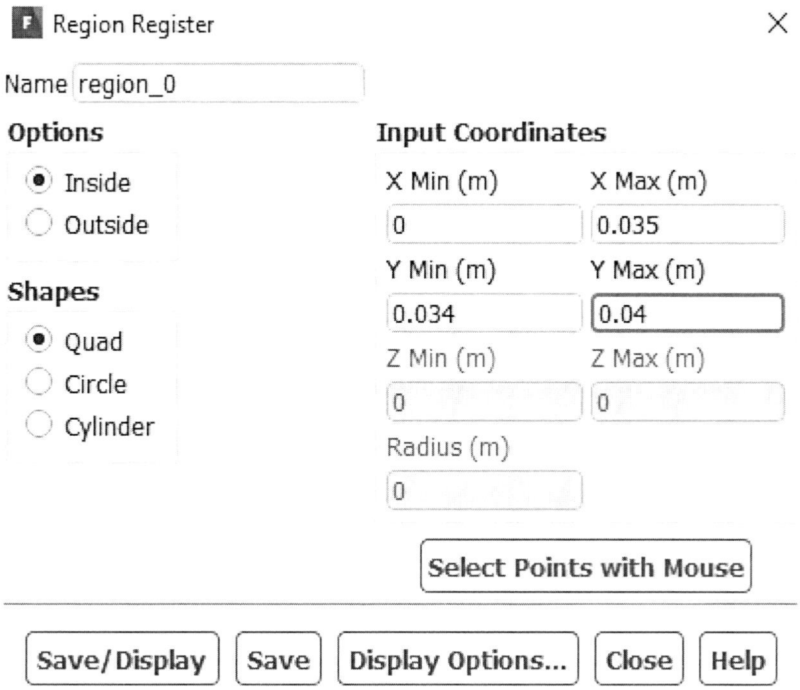

Figure 15.12d) Region register

Click on Patch... under Solution Initialization on the Task Page. Select wood as the Phase, select Volume Fraction as Variable, region_0 as Registers to Patch and Value to 0.63. Click on Patch and Close the Patch window.

Figure 15.12e) Patch window

13. Double-click on Contours under Graphics and Results in the Outline View. Select wood as Phase and select Contours of Phases... and Volume fraction. Click on Save/Display and Close the Contours window.

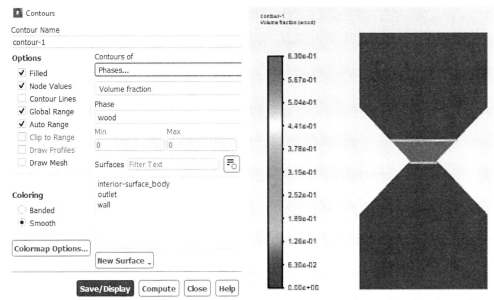

Figure 15.13a) Contours window   Figure 15.13b) Volume fraction (wood)

14. Double-click on Solution Animations under Solution and Calculation Activities in the Outline View. Select Record after every 1 time-step. Select HSF File as Storage Type and select your *working directory* as Storage Directory. Set Window Id to 2 and select contour-1 as Animation Object. Enter *hour-glass* as Name and click OK to close the Animation Definition window.

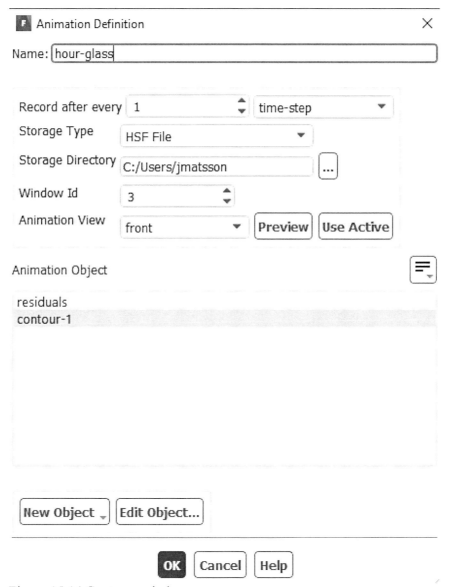

Figure 15.14 Contours window

15. Double-click on Run Calculation under Solution in the Outline View. Enter 0.001 as Time Step Size (s). Enter 40 as Number of Time Steps Max Iterations/Time Step to 30, see Figure 15.15a). Select File>>Export>>Case & Data… from the menu and save the Case/Data File with the name *hour-glass.cas*. Click on Calculate under Run Calculation on the Task Page. Continue running the calculations as shown on the contour plots of volume fraction, see Figure 15.15b).

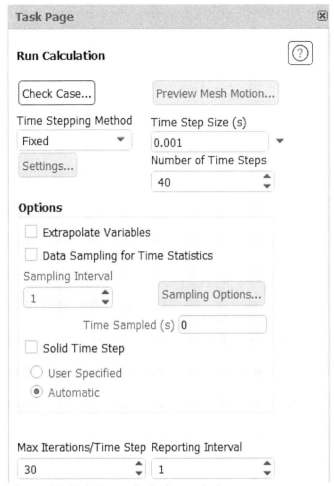

Figure 15.15a) Run calculations window

G. Post-Processing

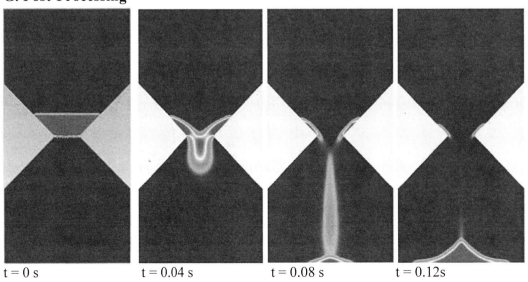

t = 0 s   t = 0.04 s   t = 0.08 s   t = 0.12s

Figure 15.15b) Volume fraction (wood) at different times

H. Theory

16. We start with continuity, momentum and energy equations.

$$\frac{\partial}{\partial t}(\alpha_s \rho_s) + \nabla \cdot (\alpha_s \rho_s \bar{u}_s) = \dot{m}_{fs} \tag{15.1}$$

$$\frac{\partial}{\partial t}(\alpha_s \rho_s \bar{u}_s) + \nabla \cdot (\alpha_s \rho_s \bar{u}_s \bar{u}_s) = -\alpha_s \nabla p_f + \nabla \cdot \tau_s + \sum_{s=1}^{n}(\bar{R}_{fs} + \dot{m}_{fs}\bar{u}_{fs}) + \bar{F}_s \tag{15.2}$$

$$\frac{3}{2}\left[\frac{\partial}{\partial t}(\alpha_s \rho_s \theta_s) + \nabla \cdot (\alpha_s \rho_s \bar{u}_s \theta_s)\right] = \tau_s : \nabla \bar{u}_s + \nabla \cdot (\kappa_\theta \nabla \theta_s) - \gamma_s + \phi_{lm} + \phi_{fs} \tag{15.3}$$

where

$$\tau_s = -P_s \bar{I} + 2\alpha_s \mu_s \bar{S} + \alpha_s(\lambda_s - \frac{2}{3}\mu_s)\nabla \cdot \bar{u}_s \bar{I} \tag{15.4}$$

$$\bar{S} = \frac{1}{2}[\nabla \cdot \bar{u}_s + (\nabla \cdot \bar{u}_s)^T] \tag{15.5}$$

The total granular solids phase pressure is the sum of kinetic and frictional pressures

$$P_s = P_{s,friction} + P_{s,kinetic} \tag{15.6}$$

The Frictional Pressure (pascal) in ANSYS Fluent is the frictional part of equation (15.6). The following expression was given by Johnson and Jackson[4].

$$P_{s,friction} = \frac{\alpha_s}{10}\frac{(\alpha_s - \alpha_{s,min})^2}{(\alpha_{s,max} - \alpha_s)^5} \tag{15.7}$$

Alternatively, we have the expression by Syamlal et al[7].

$$P_{s,friction} = 2\alpha_s^2 \rho_s g_0 \theta_s (1 + e_s) \tag{15.8}$$

where the radial distribution function

$$g_0 = \frac{1}{1 - (\frac{\alpha_s}{\alpha_{s,max}})^{1/3}} \tag{15.9}$$

The Solids Pressure (pascal) in ANSYS Fluent is the kinetic portion of granular solids phase pressure and can be described using the following relation by Lun et al[5].

$$P_{s,kinetic} = \alpha_s \rho_s \theta_s[1 + 2\alpha_s g_0(1 + e_s)] \tag{15.10}$$

The granular phase shear viscosity can be described as the sum of the collisional, kinetic and frictional parts.

$$\mu_s = \mu_{s,collision} + \mu_{s,kinetic} + \mu_{s,friction} \tag{15.11}$$

The collisional part of the solids phase shear viscosity was modeled by Gidaspow et al.[1] and Syamlal et al[7].

$$\mu_{s,collision} = \frac{4}{5}\alpha_s^2 \rho_s d_s g_0 (1 + e_s)\sqrt{\frac{\theta_s}{\pi}} \qquad (15.12)$$

The Granular Viscosity (kg/m-s) in ANSYS Fluent is the kinetic part of equation (15.11). The following expression was given by Gidaspow et al[1].

$$\mu_{s,kinetic} = \frac{10\sqrt{\pi\theta_s}\rho_s d_s}{96(1+e_s)g_0}\left[1 + \frac{4}{5}(1 + e_s)g_0 \alpha_s\right]^2 \qquad (15.13)$$

Alternatively, we have the expression by Syamlal et al[7].

$$\mu_{s,kinetic} = \frac{\alpha_s\sqrt{\pi\theta_s}\rho_s d_s}{6(3-e_s)}\left[1 + \frac{2}{5}(1 + e_s)(3e_s - 1)g_0 \alpha_s\right] \qquad (15.14)$$

The Frictional Viscosity (kg/m-s) in ANSYS Fluent is the frictional part of equation (15.11). The equation is given by Schaeffer[6]

$$\mu_{s,friction} = \frac{P_{s,friction}sin\varphi}{2\sqrt{I_2}} \qquad (15.15)$$

The Granular Bulk Viscosity (kg/m-s) in ANSYS Fluent accounts for resistance of the granular material to compression and expansion. The equation is given by Lun et al[5].

$$\lambda_s = \frac{4}{3}\alpha_s^2 \rho_s d_s g_0 (1 + e_s)\sqrt{\frac{\theta_s}{\pi}} \qquad (15.16)$$

α_s	volume fraction for granular material
$\alpha_{s,min}$	friction packing limit
$\alpha_{s,max}$	packing limit
φ	internal angle of friction
γ_s	energy dissipation
κ_θ	granular temperature conductivity
λ_s	bulk viscosity
μ_s	granular shear viscosity
$\mu_{s,collision}$	collisional viscosity
$\mu_{s,friction}$	frictional viscosity
$\mu_{s,kinetic}$	kinetic viscosity
ϕ_{fs}	energy exchange between fluid and granular phase
ϕ_{lm}	energy exchange between granular phases
ρ_s	density
θ_s	temperature
τ_s	stress tensor
d_s	particle diameter
e_s	coefficient of restitution
g_0	radial distribution function
I_2	second invariant of the deviatoric stress tensor
$\dot{m}_{fs}$	unidirectional mass transfer

p_f	fluid pressure
P_s	granular pressure
$P_{s,friction}$	frictional pressure
$P_{s,kinetic}$	kinetic pressure
$\bar{S}$	strain rate
t	time
$\bar{u}_s$	granular velocity vector

Table 15.2 Parameters used in theory section

I. References

1. Gidaspow, D., Bezburuah, R., Ding, J. "Hydrodynamics of Circulating Fluidized Beds: Kinetic Theory Approach", *7th Fluidization Conference*, May 3, (1992).
2. Hirt, C.W.," A Flow-3D Continuum Model for Granular Media.", Flow Science Report 02-13, (2013).
3. Jansson, M., "CFD Simulations of Silos Content, An Investigation of Flow Patterns and Segregation Mechanisms.", *Master's Thesis within the Innovative and Sustainable Chemical Engineering Programme*, Chalmers, (2014).
4. Johnson, P.C., Jackson. R., "Frictional-Collisional Constitutive Relations for Granular Materials, with Application to Plane Shearing". *J. Fluid Mech.* **176**. (1987).
5. Lun, C.K.K., Savage, S.B., Jeffrey, D.J., Chepurniy, N., "Kinetic Theories for Granular Flow: Inelastic Particles in Couette Flow and Slightly Inelastic Particles in a General Flow Field". *J. Fluid Mech.* **140**, (1984).
6. Schaeffer, D.G., "Instability in the Evolution Equations Describing Incompressible Granular Flow.", *Journal of Differential Equations*, **66**, (1987).
7. Syamlal, M., Rogers, W., O'Brien, T.J. "MFIX Documentation Theory Guide", DOE/METC-94/1004 (1993).

J. Exercises

15.1 Use ANSYS Fluent to simulate an axisymmetric cylindrical heap of sand that deforms due to gravity into a conical pile. Use an initial 100 mm in diameter and 100 mm high heap of sand resting on a horizontal surface with a volume fraction packing limit of 0.63, see Hirt[2]. Use the density 1638 kg/m3 for the sand, a grain diameter of 0.45 mm and an internal angle of friction of 34 degrees. Determine the angle of repose for the conical pile of sand and show contours for the volume fraction of sand over time as it slumps.

15.2 Use ANSYS Fluent to simulate a 2-D hourglass. The shape of the hourglass is 200 mm wide at the top and the bottom, a total height of 500 mm and sides with a slope of 40.5 degrees. The opening at the waist of the hourglass is 10 mm. Start the simulation with sand (1638 kg/m3) and a grain diameter of 0.45 mm in the upper half of the hourglass with a packing limit of 0.63 for the volume fraction of sand. Use an internal angle of friction of 34 degrees. Determine the angle of repose for the final conical pile of sand in the bottom half of the hourglass and show contours for the volume fraction of sand over time as it moves due to gravity from the upper half to the lower half of the hourglass. See Hirt[2] for a similar simulation using Flow-3D.

15.3 Use ANSYS Fluent to simulate the flow of wood when filling a 2-D axisymmetric silo, see Jansson[3]. The shape of the silo is shown in Figure 15.16 with the following dimensions: *v1* = 9 m, *h1* = 10 m, *v2* = 17 m, *h2* = 0.5 m, *v3* = 0.5 m, *v4* = 1.5 m, *h3* =

0.5 m. Use an inlet volume fraction for wood of 0.4 and other values as listed in Table 15.2.

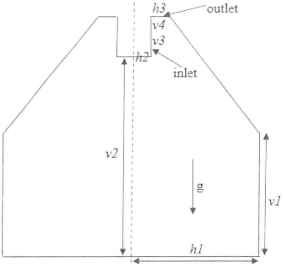

Figure 15.16 Geometry for silo

$\alpha_{s,min} = 0.45$	friction packing limit
$\alpha_{s,max} = 0.63$	packing limit
$\varphi = 45°$	internal angle of friction
$\rho_s = 850\ kg/m3$	wood density
$d_s = 0.02\ m$	particle diameter
$e_s = 0.001$	coefficient of restitution

Table 15.3 Parameters used in Exercise 15.3

CHAPTER 16. BOUNCING SPHERES

A. Objectives

- Use the Macroscopic Particle Model
- Create a Movie of the Resulting Motion of the Spheres

B. Problem Description

In this tutorial we will be simulating a number of spheres falling through an hourglass shaped geometry. We will let the balls bounce with each other and they will bounce with the walls.

C. Launching ANSYS Workbench and Selecting Fluent

1. Start by launching ANSYS Workbench. Double click on Fluid Flow (Fluent) under Analysis Systems in the Toolbox.

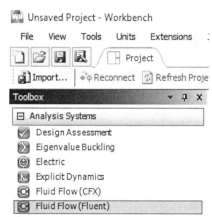

Figure 16.1 Selecting Fluent

D. Launching ANSYS DesignModeler

2. Right click on Geometry in the Project Schematic window in ANSYS Workbench and select New DesignModeler Geometry. Select Units>>Millimeter from the menu in DesignModeler. Select the XY Plane in the Tree Outline and click on Look at Face/Plane/Sketch ⬚. Select the Sketching tab and select Polyline under Draw from Sketching Toolboxes. Start at the origin and draw the sketch, right click and select *closed end* and enter the dimensions as shown in Figure 16.2a). Select ⬚Revolve and apply

Sketch1 as Geometry in Details View. Select the left vertical side of the sketch and apply it as the Axis in Details View. Click on Generate and close DesignModeler.

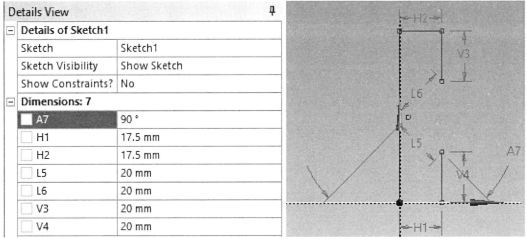

Figure 16.2a) Dimensions for sketch

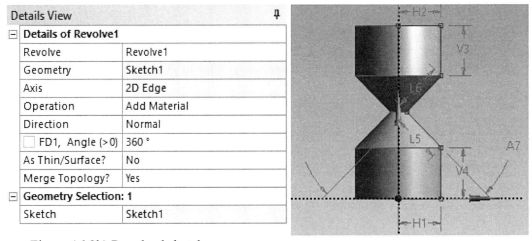

Figure 16.2b) Revolved sketch

E. Launching ANSYS Meshing

3. Double click on Mesh under Project Schematic in ANSYS Workbench. Set the Element Size under Defaults in Details of Mesh to 0.001 m. Right click on Mesh under Project in Outline and select Generate Mesh. Under Statistics in Details of Mesh we can see that this mesh has 111,860 Nodes and 107,352 Elements. Right click in the graphics window and select Cursor Mode>>Face. Control select all the 6 faces for the mesh, right click and select Create Named Selection. Enter the name *wall* and click on OK to close the Selection Name window.

   Select File>>Export...>>Mesh>>FLUENT Input File>>Export from the menu and save the mesh with the name *3d-enclosure.msh*. Select File>>Save Project from the menu and save the project with the name *3D-Enclosure.wbpj*. Close the Meshing window, right-click on Mesh under Project Schematic in ANSYS Workbench and select Update.

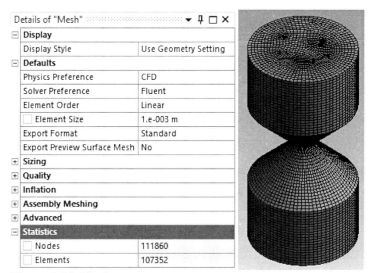

Figure 16.3 Mesh

F. Launching ANSYS Fluent

4. Double click on Setup under Project Schematic in ANSYS Workbench. Check the box for Double Precision under Options in the ANSYS Fluent Launcher and select Parallel Processing Options. Set the number of Processes equal to the number of core processors for your computer. Click on the plus sign next to Show More Options and take a note of the location of your *working directory* under General Options tab as you will need this information later in this chapter in step 9. Click on OK to launch Fluent.

Figure 16.4a) Launching ANSYS Fluent

Enter the following commands on the Console to load the Macroscopic Particle Model (MPM).

>**define**
/define> **models**
/define/models/> **addon**
Enter Module Number: [0] **10**

```
Console
> define

/define> models

/define/models> addon
Fluent Addon Modules:
     0. None
     1. MHD Model
     2. Fiber Model
     3. Fuel Cell and Electrolysis Model
     4. SOFC Model with Unresolved Electrolyte
     5. Population Balance Model
     6. Adjoint Solver
     7. Single-Potential Battery Model
     8. Dual-Potential MSMD Battery Model
     9. PEM Fuel Cell Model
    10. Macroscopic Particle Model
    11. Reduced Order Model
Enter Module Number: [0] 10
```

Figure 16.4b) Console commands to load MPM module

5. Double click on General under Setup in the Outline View and select Transient under Time on the Task Page. Check the box for Gravity and enter -9.81 as the value for Y (m/s2). Click on Scale... under Mesh in General on the Task Page.

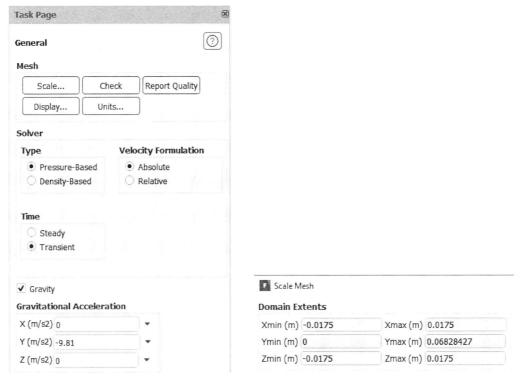

Figure 16.5a) General settings   Figure 16.5b) Scale mesh

6. Double click on Models and Macroscopic Particles under Setup in the Outline View and check the box to Enable Macroscopic Particle Model. Select the Drag tab and select Disable Drag Calculations under Drag Law Options. Select the Injections tab and click on Create. Select plane as Injection Type. Set the Diameter (m) to 0.003. Set the Plane Shape to Circular and select Y as Axis Direction. Enter Y (m) 0.06828427 and Radius (m) 0.0175 under Center Location/Radius of Circular Plane. Click on Create/Modify.

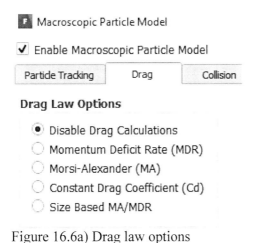

Figure 16.6a) Drag law options

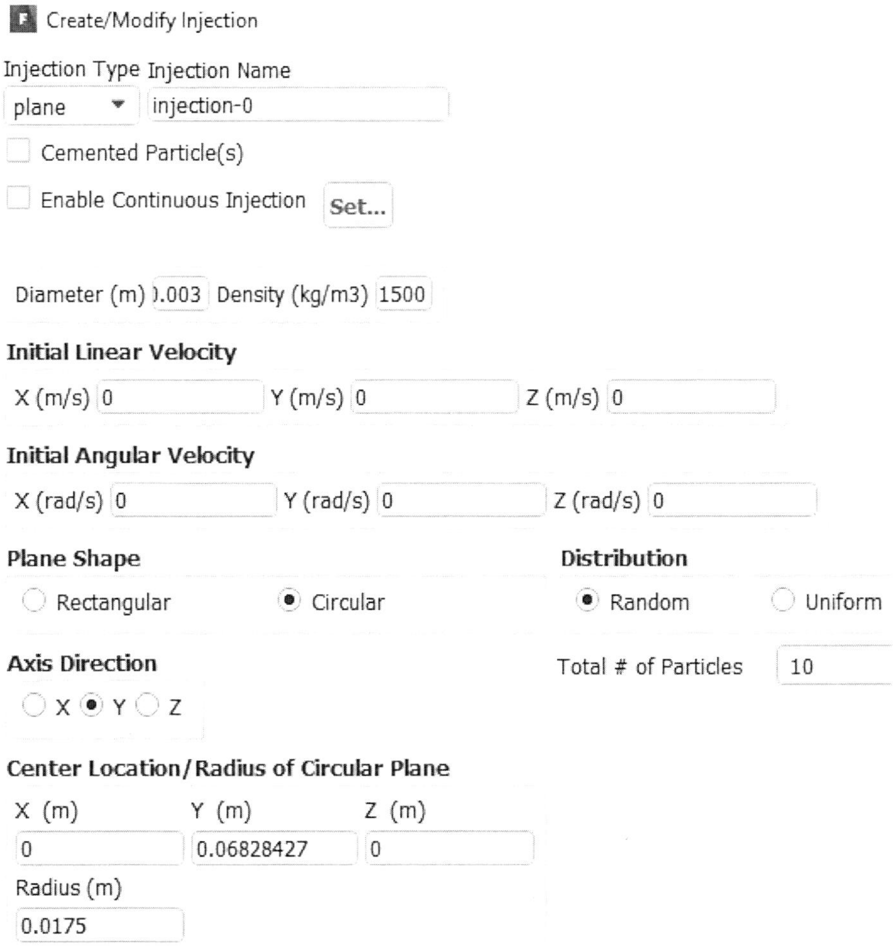

Create/Modify Injection

Injection Type Injection Name

plane   ▼   injection-0

☐ Cemented Particle(s)

☐ Enable Continuous Injection   Set...

Diameter (m)).003 Density (kg/m3) 1500

Initial Linear Velocity

X (m/s) 0   Y (m/s) 0   Z (m/s) 0

Initial Angular Velocity

X (rad/s) 0   Y (rad/s) 0   Z (rad/s) 0

Plane Shape   **Distribution**

○ Rectangular   ● Circular   ● Random   ○ Uniform

Axis Direction   Total # of Particles   10

○ X ● Y ○ Z

Center Location/Radius of Circular Plane

X (m)   Y (m)   Z (m)

0   0.06828427   0

Radius (m)

0.0175

Figure 16.6b) Injection options

Select the Initialize MPM tab in the MPM window. Check the box for ASCII File under Write Particle Data and save the file with the name *bouncing-spheres*. Check the box for Print Warning Messages and click on Initialize MPM Functions. Click on Initialize Particles.

Select ⬡ at the bottom of the graphics window. Select *wall* under Surfaces. Only have the box for Edges checked under Options and select Outline as Edge Type, see Figure 16.6d). Click on Display and close the window.

Click on Display Injections. Select Particle ID under Display Particles Colored by, click on Display, select isometric view and Close the Display Particles window. Click on Apply in the MPM window and Close the same window.

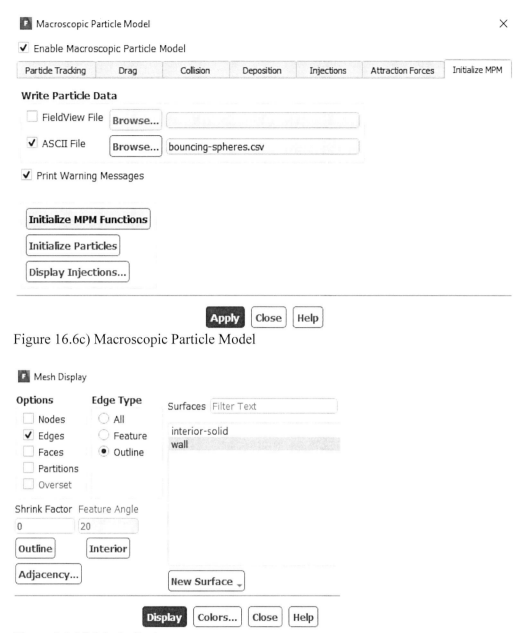

Figure 16.6c) Macroscopic Particle Model

Figure 16.6d) Mesh display

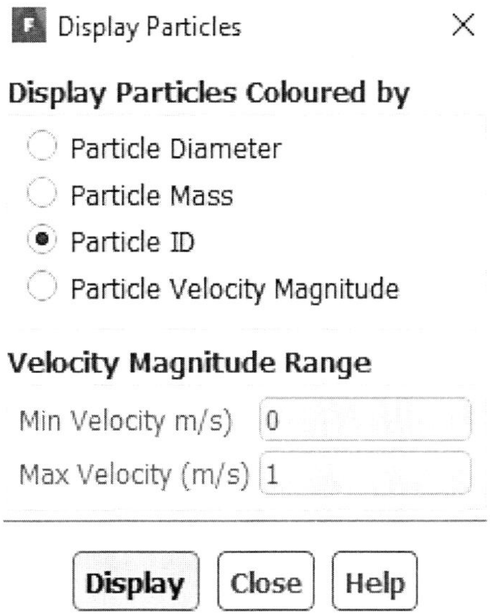

Display Particles   ✕

Display Particles Coloured by

○ Particle Diameter

○ Particle Mass

● Particle ID

○ Particle Velocity Magnitude

Velocity Magnitude Range

Min Velocity m/s)   0

Max Velocity (m/s)   1

Display   Close   Help

Figure 16.6e) Display particles settings

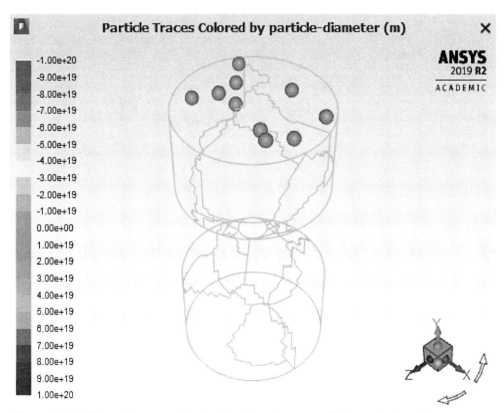

Figure 16.6f) Ten spheres randomly distributed on top of the mesh domain

7. Double click on Methods under Solution in the Outline View and select Second Order Implicit as Transient Formulation under Solution Methods on the Task Page.

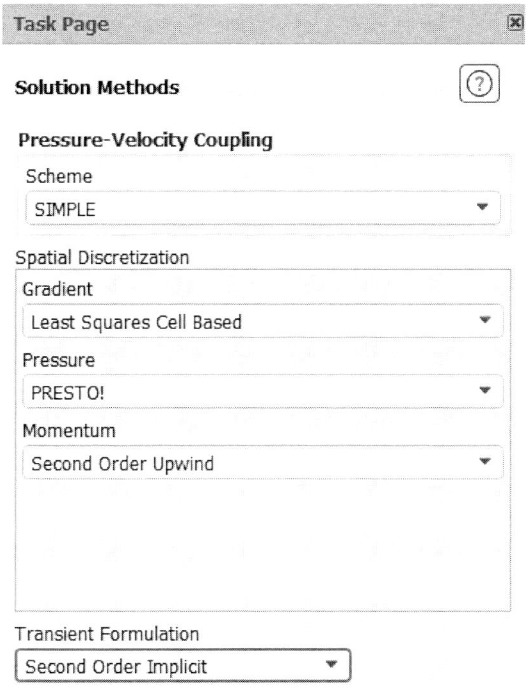

Figure 16.7a) Solution methods settings

Double click on Cell Zone Conditions and solid (fluid, id=2) under Setup in the Outline View and uncheck the box for Source Terms in the Fluid window. Click on OK to close the Fluid window.

Double click on Monitors and Residual under Setup in the Outline View and uncheck the box for Plot under Options. Select none as Convergence Criterion and click on OK to close the Residual Monitors window.

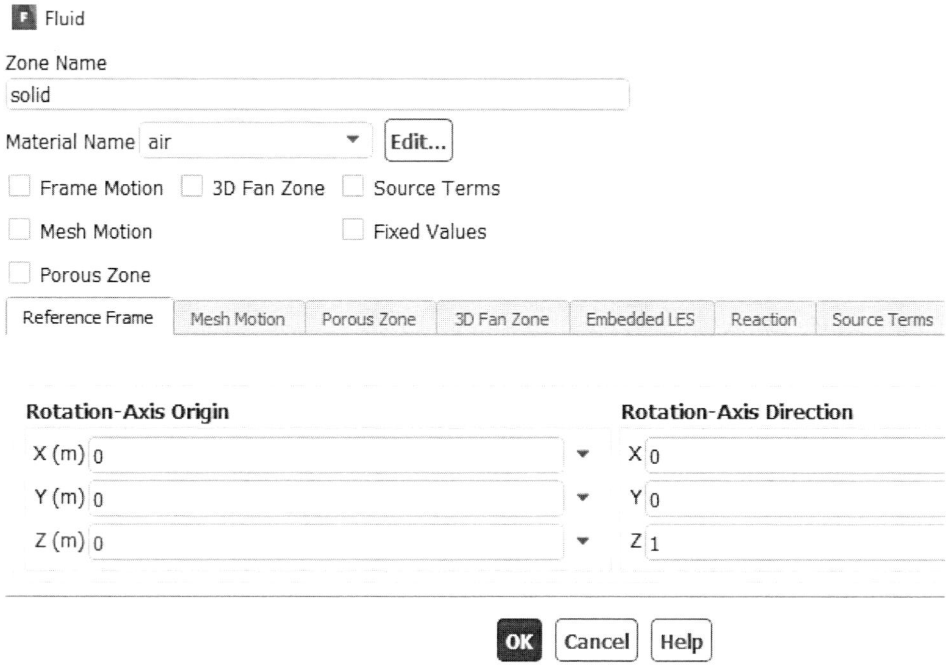

Figure 16.7b) Fluid window

Figure 16.7c) Residual monitors window

8. Double click on Initialization under Solution in the Outline View and select Hybrid Initialization. Click on Initialize. Answer OK if you get a question.

Figure 16.8 Solution initialization

9. Create a new folder in your *working directory* called *jpg-files*. Double click on Calculation Activities and Execute Commands under Solution in the Outline View. Enter the commands listed below and as shown with settings in Figure 16.9. You will need to change the second command so that it is in line with the name and location of your *working directory*. Click OK to close the window.

(display-mpm-injections 'particle-id 0 10)
dis hard C:/Users/jmatsson/jpg-files/mpm-%t.jpg

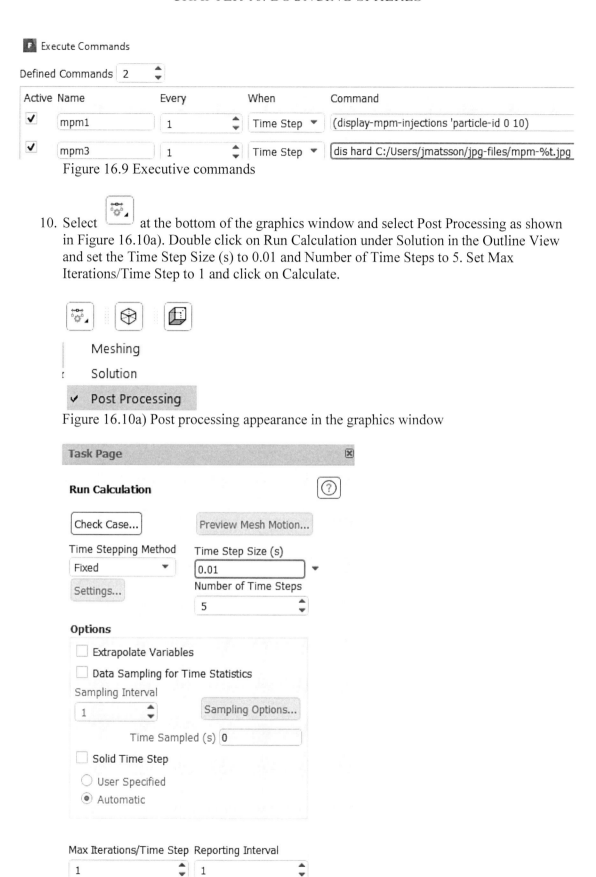

Figure 16.9 Executive commands

10. Select ⬡ at the bottom of the graphics window and select Post Processing as shown in Figure 16.10a). Double click on Run Calculation under Solution in the Outline View and set the Time Step Size (s) to 0.01 and Number of Time Steps to 5. Set Max Iterations/Time Step to 1 and click on Calculate.

Figure 16.10a) Post processing appearance in the graphics window

Figure 16.10b) Running the calculations

G. Post-Processing

11. Select the *YZ* plane by clicking on the red *X* axis of the coordinate system in the lower right corner of the graphics window as shown in Figure 16.11a). Continue running the calculations two more times. Next, change the Number of Time Steps to 10 and run the calculations once again. Answer OK to the question that you may get. Next, change the Number of Time Steps to 25 and run the calculations once again. Answer OK to the question that you may get. Next, change the Number of Time Steps to 50 and run the calculations once again. Answer OK to the question that you may get. Next, change the Number of Time Steps to 100 and run the calculations twice. Answer OK to the question that you may get.

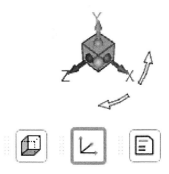

Figure 16.11a) Coordinate system in the graphics window

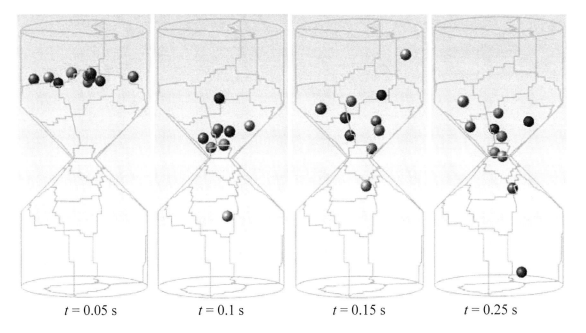

| $t = 0.05$ s | $t = 0.1$ s | $t = 0.15$ s | $t = 0.25$ s |

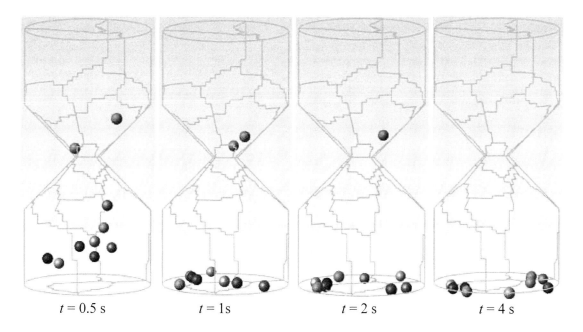

$t = 0.5$ s $t = 1$s $t = 2$ s $t = 4$ s

Figure 16.11b) Distribution of spheres at different times

H. Reference

1. Agrawal, M., Bakker, A., Prinkey, M.T. "Macroscopic Particle Model Tracking Big Particles in CFD", *AIChE Annual Meeting, Particle Technology Forum, Paper 268b, November 7-12, Austin, TX*, (2004).

I. Exercise

1. Use ANSYS Fluent and the macroscopic particle model to perform a billiard table simulation of the first shot to break the balls including the collision of the cue ball with the 15 object balls initially racked together in a triangular pattern on a 50 inch x 100 inch billiard table. The diameter of the billiard balls is 57 mm.

Notes:

CHAPTER 17. FALLING SPHERE

A. Objectives

- Using the Macroscopic Particle Model Module
- Determine the Terminal Velocity for a Falling Sphere

B. Problem Description

A 2 mm diameter sphere with a density of 1695 kg/m^3 is falling in a tube with a diameter of 20 mm and a length of 60 mm.

C. Launching ANSYS Workbench and Selecting Fluent

1. Start by launching ANSYS Workbench. Double click on Fluid Flow (Fluent) under Analysis Systems in the Toolbox. Select Units>>Metric (tonne, mm, s, …) from the menu.

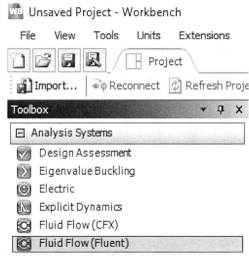

Figure 17.1 Selecting Fluent

D. Launching ANSYS DesignModeler

2. Right click on Geometry in the Project Schematic window in ANSYS Workbench and select New DesignModeler Geometry. Select Units>>Millimeter from the menu in DesignModeler. Select the XY Plane in the Tree Outline and click on Look at Face/Plane/Sketch ⬛. Select the Sketching tab and select Rectangle under Draw from

Sketching Toolboxes. Start at the origin (make sure you see a P when the cursor is at the origin and you are about to start drawing) and draw the rectangle in the first quadrant. Click on Dimensions and click on the lower horizontal edge of the rectangle. Enter a length of 10 mm for the edge. Click on the right vertical edge of the rectangle. Enter a length of 60 mm for the edge.

Select 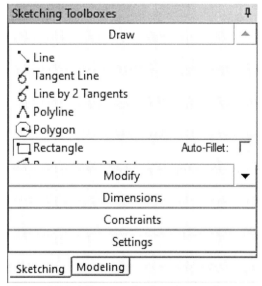 Revolve and apply Sketch1 under XYPlane as Geometry in Details View. Select the left vertical side of the rectangle sketch and apply it as the Axis in Details View. Click on Generate and close DesignModeler.

Figure 17.2a) Rectangle drawing tool

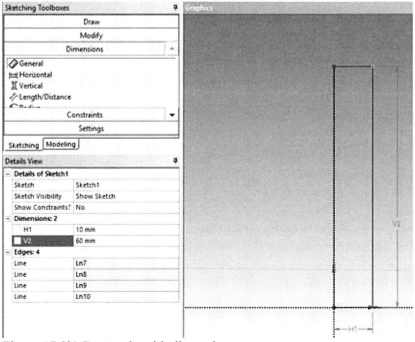

Figure 17.2b) Rectangle with dimensions

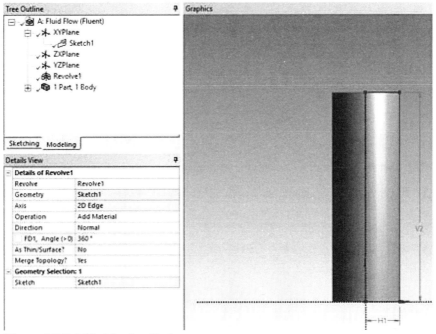

Figure 17.2c) Finished cylinder

E. Launching ANSYS Meshing

3. Double click on Mesh under Project Schematic in ANSYS Workbench. Click on Mesh in the Outline under Project. Select Home>>Tools>>Units>>Metric (mm, kg, N, …) from the menu. Right click on Mesh under Project in Outline and select Generate Mesh. A coarse mesh is generated.

   Set the Element Size under Defaults in Details of Mesh to 0.4 mm. Right click on Mesh under Project in Outline and select Generate Mesh. Under Statistics in Details of Mesh we can see that this mesh has 524,423 Nodes and 510,300 Elements.

   Right click in the graphics window and select Cursor Mode>>Face. Control select the 3 faces of the mesh, right click and select Create Named Selection. Enter the name *wall* and click on OK to close the Selection Name window.

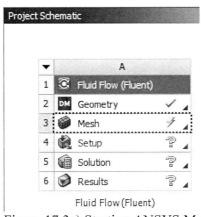

Figure 17.3a) Starting ANSYS Meshing

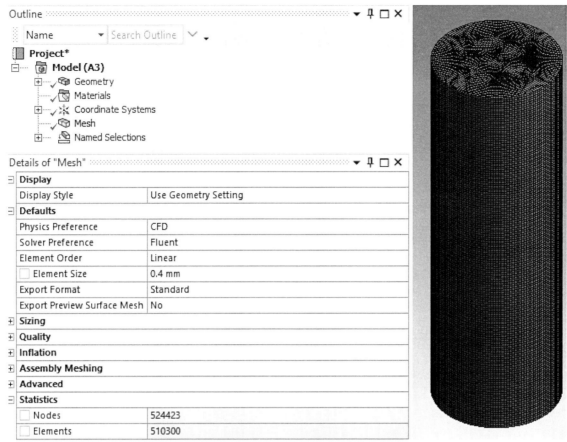

Figure 17.3b) Mesh for cylinder

Select File>>Export...>>Mesh>>FLUENT Input File>>Export from the menu and save the mesh in the *working directory* with the name *cylinder-mesh-lambda-0.1.msh*. Select File>>Save Project from the menu and save the project with the name *Cylinder Mesh Falling Sphere Lambda = 0.1.wbpj*. Close the Meshing window and right-click on Mesh under Project Schematic in ANSYS Workbench and select Update.

F. Launching ANSYS Fluent

4. Double click on Setup under Project Schematic in ANSYS Workbench. Check the box for Double Precision under Options in the ANSYS Fluent Launcher and select Parallel Processing Options. Set the number of Processes equal to the number of cores of your computer. Take a note of the location of your *working directory* under General Options as you will need this information later in this chapter. Click on OK to launch Fluent.

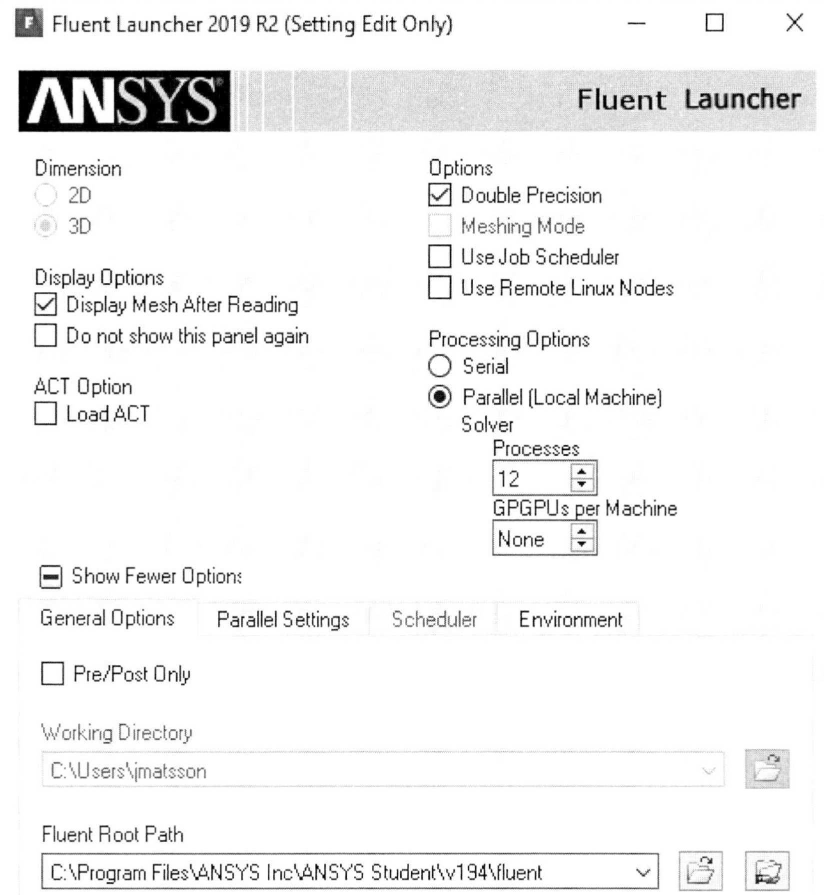

Figure 17.4a) ANSYS Fluent launcher

Enter the following commands on the Console to load the Macroscopic Particle Model (MPM).

>**define**
/define> **models**
/define/models/> **addon**
Enter Module Number: [0] **10**

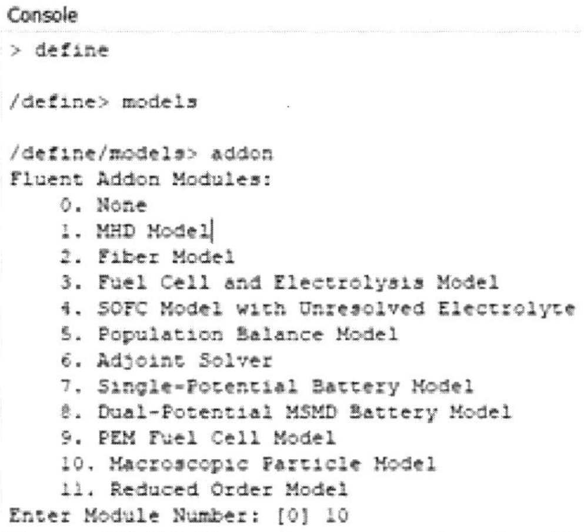

Figure 17.4b) Console commands to load MPM module

389

5. Double click on General under Setup in the Outline View and select Transient under Time on the Task Page. Check the box for Gravity and enter -9.8 as the value for Y (m/s2). Click on Scale… under Mesh in General on the Task Page.

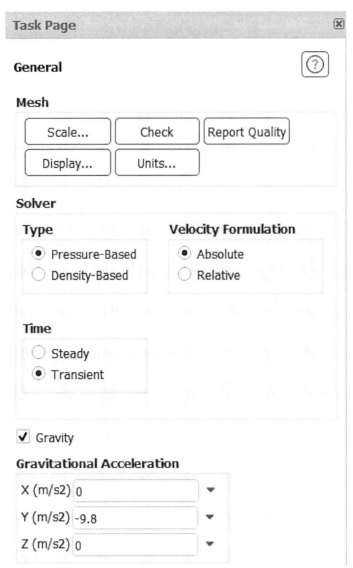

Figure 17.5a) General settings

Figure 17.5b) Scale mesh

6. Double click on Materials under Setup in the Outline View. Click on Create/Edit for Fluid under Materials on the Task Page. Click on Fluent Database in the Create/Edit Materials window. Scroll down and select *water-liquid (h2o<l>)* as the Fluent Fluid Material. Click on Copy and Close the Fluent Database Materials window. Set the Density (kg/m3) to 1020 and Viscosity (kg/m-s) to 0.49. Click on Change/Create and Close the Create/Edit Materials window.

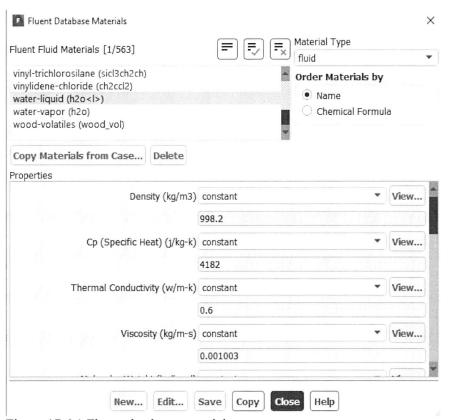

Figure 17.6a) Fluent database materials

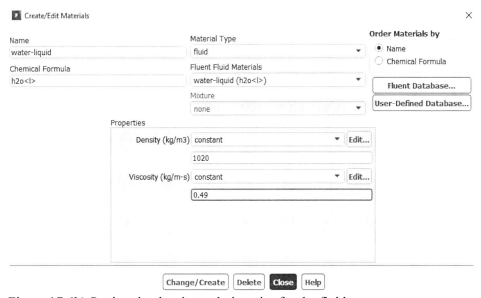

Figure 17.6b) Setting the density and viscosity for the fluid

Open Cell Zone Conditions under Setup in the Outline View. Double click on *solid (fluid, id=2)* under Cell Zone Conditions in the Outline View. Select *water-liquid* as Material Name and enter *water-liquid* as Zone Name. Check the box for Source Terms and click on the Source Terms tab. Click on Edit for X Momentum. Set Number of X Momentum Sources to 1, select *udf x_mom::mpm* and click OK. Repeat this for Y Momentum and Z Momentum and Mass. Click OK to close the Fluid window.

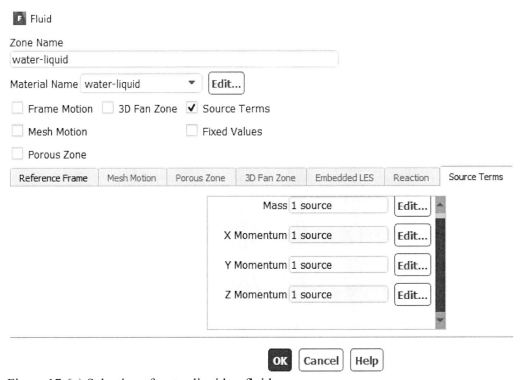

Figure 17.6c) Selection of water-liquid as fluid

Double click on Models and Macroscopic Particles under Setup in the Outline View and check the box to Enable Macroscopic Particle Model. Select the Particle Tracking tab and check the box for Enable Interaction with Continuous Phase. Set the Particle Sub-Timesteps within each Flow Timestep to 10 and Under-Relaxation Factor to Velocities in Touched Cells to 1.

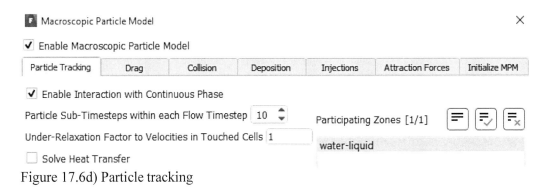

Figure 17.6d) Particle tracking

Select the Drag tab and select Momentum Deficit Rate (MDR) under Drag Law Options. Click on Apply.

392

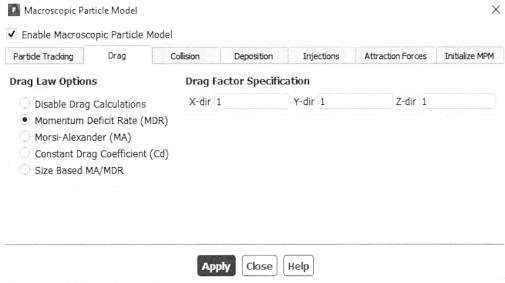

Figure 17.6e) Drag law options

Select the Collision tab and uncheck Enable Particle-Particle Collision and uncheck Enable Particle-Wall Collision. Click on Apply.

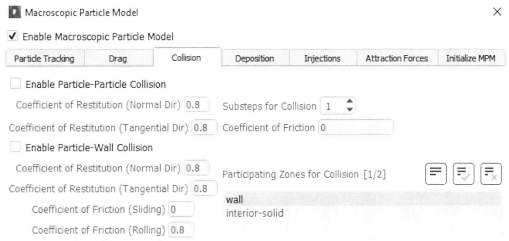

Figure 17.6f) Collision options

Select the Injections tab and click on Create. Select *point* as Injection Type. Set the Diameter (m) to 0.002 and set the Density (kg/m3) to 1695. Check the box for Cylindrical Coordinates and select Y as Axis Direction. Enter Axial (m) 0.03 under Initial Location. Click on Create/Modify.

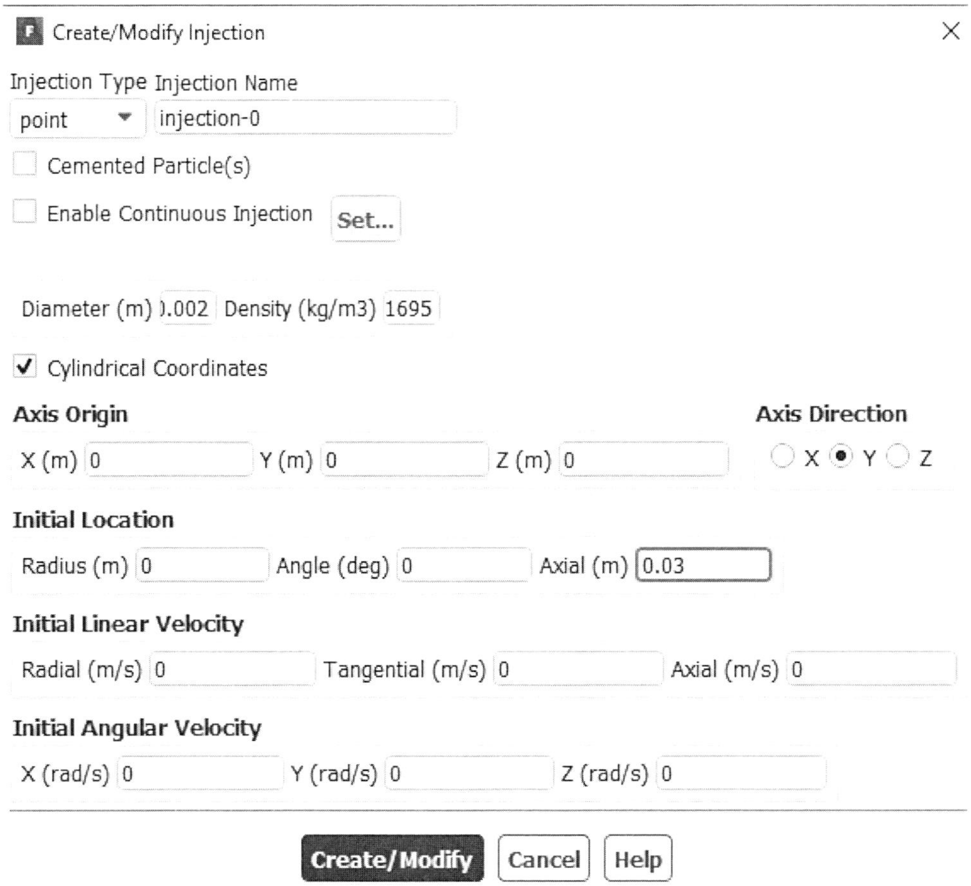

Figure 17.6g) Injection options

Select the Initialize MPM tab and check the box for ASCII File under Write Particle Data. Click on Browse, enter the file name *sphere-falling-lambda-0p1.csv*, save the file in the *working directory* and click on OK. Check the box for Print Warning Messages. Click on Initialize MPM Functions. Click on Initialize Particles.

Select ⬡ at the bottom of the graphics window. Select *wall* under Surfaces. Only have the box for Edges checked under Options and select Outline as Edge Type, see Figure 17.6i). Click on Display and Close the Mesh Display window.

Click on Display Injections. Select Display Particles Colored by Particle Diameter. Click on Display and Close the Display Particles window. Click on Apply and close the Macroscopic Particle Model window.

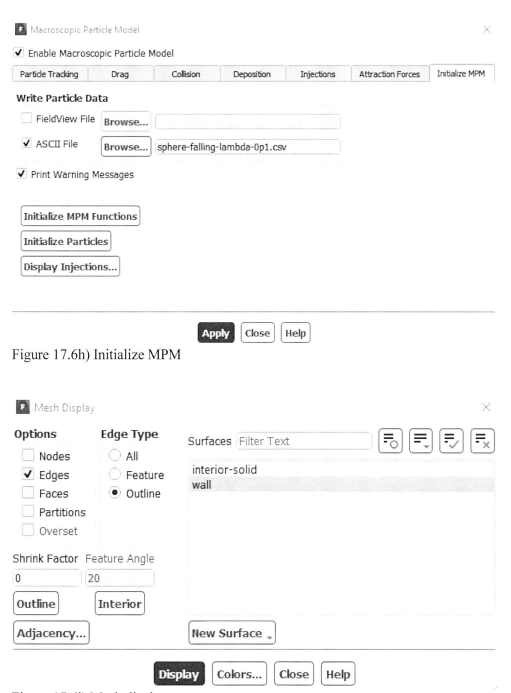

Figure 17.6h) Initialize MPM

Figure 17.6i) Mesh display

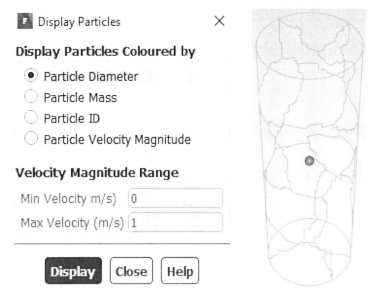

Figure 17.6j) Display particles

Figure 17.6k) Sphere in the cylinder

7. Double click on Methods under Solution in the Outline View and select Second Order Implicit as Transient Formulation under Solution Methods on the Task Page. Click on Options. Select Flow Variables Only and set the Relaxation Factor to 0.75. Click OK to close the window.

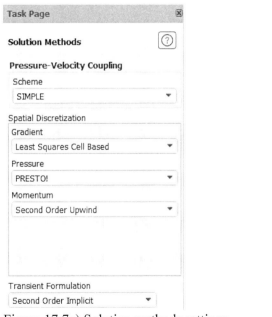

Figure 17.7a) Solution methods settings

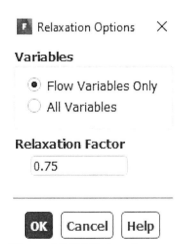

Figure 17.7b) Relaxations

Double click on Monitors and Residual under Setup in the Outline View and check the boxes for Print to Console and Plot under Options. Click on OK to close the Residual Monitors window.

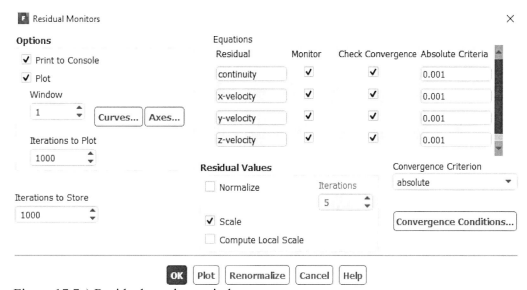

Figure 17.7c) Residual monitors window

8. Double click on Initialization under Solution in the Tree and select Hybrid Initialization. Click on Initialize. Answer OK to the question that you may get.

Figure 17.8 Solution initialization

9. Create a folder in your working directory called *falling-sphere-lambda-0.1-jpg-files*. Double click on Calculation Activities and Execute Commands under Solution in the Outline View. Enter the commands listed below and as shown with settings in Figure 17.9a). You will need to change the second command so that it is in line with the name and location of your *working directory*. Click OK to close the window.

(display-mpm-injections 'particle-id 0 20)
dis hard C:/Users/jmatsson/falling-sphere-lambda-0.1-jpg-files/mpm-%t.jpg

Figure 17.9a) Executive commands

397

Double click on Results>>Graphics>>Particle Tracks in the Outline View. Set the Track Style to *sphere* and Color by Particle Variables… and Particle Diameter. Select *injection-0* under Release from Injections. Click on Attributes under Track Style. Check the Constant box under Options and set the Diameter to 0.002. Click on Apply and Close the window. Check the box for Draw Mesh under Options. Select *wall* as Surfaces. Click on Display and Close the Mesh Display window. Click on Save/Display and Close the Particle Tracks window.

Figure 17.9b) Particle sphere style attributes

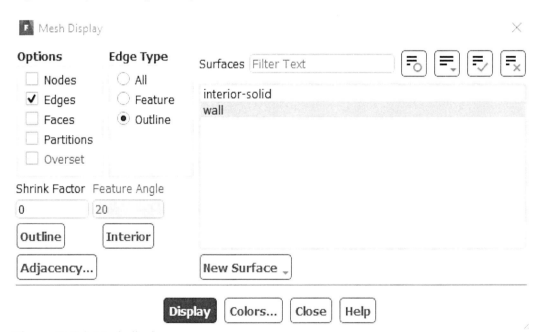

Figure 17.9c) Mesh display

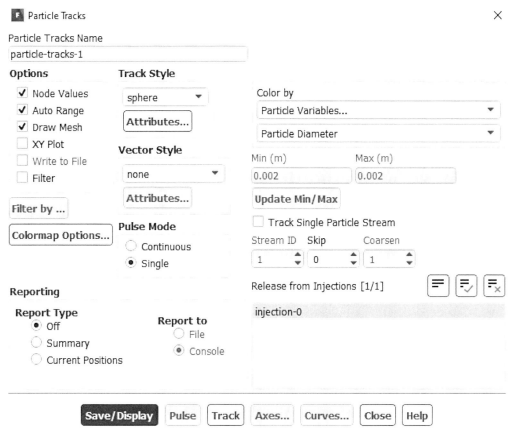

Figure 17.9d) Particle tracks

10. Select  at the bottom of the graphics window and select Post Processing as shown in Figure 17.10a). Select File>>Save Project from the menu. Select File>>Export>>Case & Data from the menu. Save the Case/Data File in the *working directory* with the name *falling-sphere-lambda-0.1.cas.gz*.

Double click on Run Calculation under Solution in the Outline View and set the Time Step Size (s) to 2e-5 and Number of Time Steps to 2000. Set Max Iterations/Time Step to 20 and click on Calculate.

Figure 17.10a) Post processing appearance in the graphics window

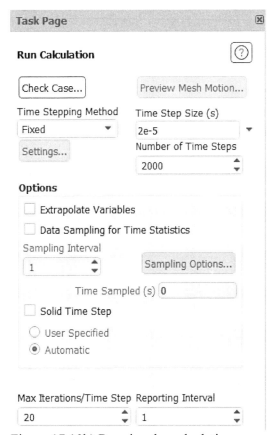

Figure 17.10b) Running the calculations

G. Post-Processing

11. Open Excel and open the file *sphere-falling-lambda-0.1.csv.* Copy the first column to column *O*. In position P3, enter =ABS(G3) and drag the column downwards to get the absolute *y*-velocity component. Select the data values in columns *O* and *P*. Select from the Excel menu Insert>>Charts>>Scatter with Smooth Lines, see Figures 17.11a) – c).

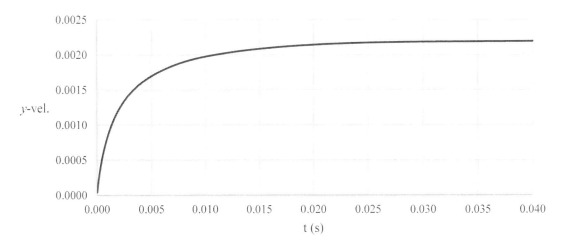

Figure 17.11a) Sphere velocity over time

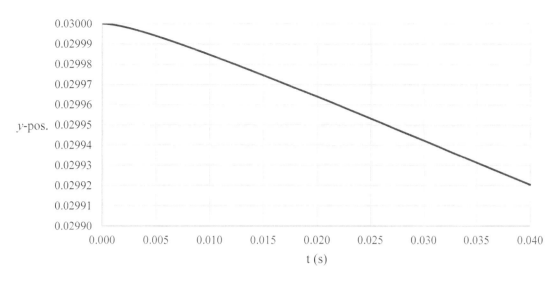

Figure 17.11b) Sphere position over time

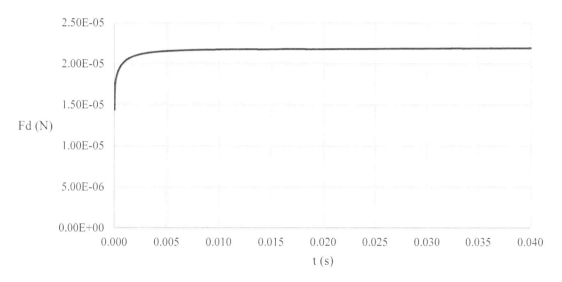

Figure 17.11c) Drag force over time

diameter of sphere	d (m)	0.002
diameter of mesh	D (m)	0.02
diameter ratio	$\lambda = d/D$	0.1
height of mesh	H (m)	0.06
wall factor	f	0.791576
density of sphere	ρ_s (kg/m3)	1695
density of fluid	ρ_f (kg/m3)	1020
dynamic viscosity of fluid	μ (Pa-s)	0.49
terminal velocity	U_∞ (m/s)	0.003

modified terminal velocity	$U = f U_\infty$ (m/s)	0.0023747
Reynolds number	Re	0.0098866
upper limit for Reynolds number	Re_{max}	0.027
relaxation time	τ_∞ (s)	0.001
upper limit for time step size	Δt (s)	0.00002
element size used to create mesh	Element Size (mm)	0.4
number of nodes for mesh	#Nodes	524,423
number of elements for mesh	#Elements	510,300
mesh count	N	510,300
volume of sphere	V_s (m^3)	4.1888E-09
total volume of mesh	V_{mesh} (m^3)	1.8850E-05
number of cells per particle volume	N_{CPV} (m^{-3})	113.4
number of cells per particle diameter	N_{CPD} (m^{-1})	6.0
modified terminal velocity from ANSYS Fluent	$f U_\infty$ (m/s), Fluent	0.0021923
percent different between ANSYS Fluent and theory	% Difference	7.7
wall factor from ANSYS Fluent	f, Fluent	0.731
drag force on sphere	F_d (N)	2.1919E-05
drag coefficient for sphere	C_d	0.008943

Table 17.1 Parameter values for ANSYS Fluent simulation.

H. Theory

12. For Stokes flow or creeping flow with Reynolds number $\ll 1$ we can define the terminal velocity U_∞ for a sphere falling in an infinite quiescent Newtonian fluid under the influence of gravity as

$$U_\infty = \frac{(\rho_s - \rho_f) d^2 g}{18\mu} \tag{17.1}$$

, where $d\,(m)$ is the diameter of the sphere, ρ_s (kg/m^3) is the density of the sphere, ρ_f (kg/m^3) is the density of the fluid, μ (kg/m-s) is the dynamic viscosity of the fluid, and g (m/s^2) is acceleration due to gravity. The relaxation time for an infinite fluid is defined by

$$\tau_\infty = \frac{\left(\rho_s + \frac{\rho_f}{2}\right) d^2}{18\mu} \tag{17.2}$$

The terminal velocity will be reduced by the presence of a surrounding cylindrical wall. The wall factor for very low Reynolds numbers is according to Haberman and Sayre (1958)

$$f = \frac{1 - 2.105\lambda + 2.0865\lambda^3 - 1.7068\lambda^5 + 0.72603\lambda^6}{1 - 0.75857\lambda^5} \tag{17.3}$$

, where $\lambda = d/D$ and D is the mesh diameter or inner diameter of the clear glass graduated cylinder. The modified terminal velocity is defined as $U = fU_\infty$. The upper level of the Reynolds number for the Stokes regime and the wall factor is shown versus λ in Table 17.2 and Figure 17.12, see Chhabra *et al.* (2003).

λ	f	Re_{max}
0.1	0.792	0.027
0.2	0.595	0.040
0.3	0.422	0.050
0.4	0.279	0.083
0.5	0.170	0.18
0.6	0.094	0.52
0.7	0.047	2.10
0.8	0.020	8.40
0.9	0.008	25.17

Table 17.2 Values of wall factor and max Re for different λ

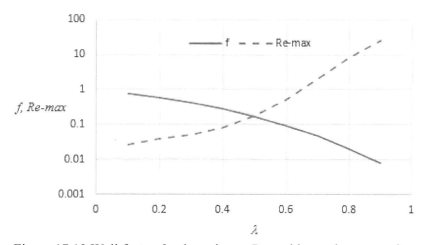

Figure 17.12 Wall factor f and maximum Reynolds number versus λ

The Reynolds number is defined as

$$Re = \frac{Ud\rho_f}{\mu} = \frac{fU_\infty d\rho_f}{\mu} \qquad (17.4)$$

The time step size used in ANSYS Fluent simulations is described by the following

$$\Delta t = \frac{2\tau_\infty}{100} \qquad (17.5)$$

The volume for the spherical particle is given by

$$V_s = \frac{\pi d^3}{6} \qquad (17.6)$$

The total volume of the mesh including the volume of the sphere used in ANSYS Fluent simulations

$$V_{mesh} = \frac{\pi H D^2}{4} \tag{17.7}$$

, where H is the height of the mesh. This height needs to be a minimum of $H = 3D$ in the ANSYS Fluent simulations. We can now determine the number of cells per particle volume

$$N_{CPV} = \frac{N V_s}{V_{mesh}} \tag{17.8}$$

, where N is the mesh count or number of elements for the mesh. The number of cells per particle diameter is defined as

$$N_{CPD} = \left(\frac{6 N_{CPV}}{\pi}\right)^{\frac{1}{3}} = \left(\frac{6 N V_s}{\pi V_{mesh}}\right)^{\frac{1}{3}} \tag{17.9}$$

, and was chosen to be at least 5 in the ANSYS Fluent simulations. The modified terminal velocity will depend on this parameter in simulations. Finally, we can find the drag coefficient for the sphere

$$C_d = \frac{F_d}{\frac{1}{2}\rho_f (f U_\infty)^2} \tag{17.10}$$

, where F_d is the drag force on the sphere.

I. References

1. Agrawal M., Bakker A. and Prinkey M.T. "Macroscopic particle model – tracking big particles in CFD", *Proceedings of AIChE 2004 Annual Meeting, Austin, TX.*
2. Chhabra R.P., Agarwal S. and Chaudhary K. "A note on wall effect on the terminal falling velocity of a sphere in quiescent Newtonian media in cylindrical tubes", *Powder Technology*, **129**, 53 - 58, (2003).
3. Haberman W.L and Sayre R.M. "David Taylor Model Basin Report No. 1143", *Department of Navy, Washington, DC* (1958).

J. Exercises

17.1 Run ANSYS Fluent Simulations for $\lambda = 0.2 - 0.9$ as shown in Table 17.3. Fill out the missing results in the table based on your simulations. Use the element size as listed in the table when you create the mesh for each λ. Change the #Nodes, #Elements and Mesh Count in the table to the values that you get when creating the mesh for each λ. The value for Mesh Count is equal to the value for #Elements. #Cells/Particle Volume and #Cells/Particle Diameter will need to be recalculated based on your actual values. Plot the modified terminal velocity versus λ from ANSYS Fluent simulations and compare with Haberman and Sayre (1958).

d (m)	0.002	0.004	0.006	0.008	0.01	0.012	0.014	0.016	0.018
D (m)	0.02	0.02	0.02	0.02	0.02	0.02	0.02	0.02	0.02
$\lambda = d / D$	0.1	0.2	0.3	0.4	0.5	0.6	0.7	0.8	0.9
H (m)	0.06	0.06	0.06	0.06	0.06	0.06	0.06	0.06	0.06
f	0.79157616	0.595336803	0.421995126	0.279200952	0.170357599	0.09440553	0.046675065	0.020398637	0.008245803
ρ_s(kg/m3)	1695	1695	1695	1695	1695	1695	1695	1695	1695
ρ_f(kg/m3)	1020	1020	1020	1020	1020	1020	1020	1020	1020
μ(Pa-s)	0.49	1.96	4.41	7.84	12.25	17.64	24.01	31.36	39.69
U_∞(m/s)	0.003	0.003	0.003	0.003	0.003	0.003	0.003	0.003	0.003
fU_∞(m/s)	0.00237473	0.00178601	0.001265985	0.000837603	0.000511073	0.000283217	0.000140025	6.11959E-05	2.47374E-05
Re	0.00988662	0.003717818	0.001756878	0.000871791	0.000425546	0.000196518	8.32803E-05	3.18469E-05	1.14432E-05
Re_{max}	0.027	0.04	0.05	0.083	0.18	0.52	2.1	8.4	25.17
τ_∞ (s)	0.001	0.001	0.001	0.001	0.001	0.001	0.001	0.001	0.001
Time Step Size (s)	0.00002	0.00002	0.00002	0.00002	0.00002	0.00002	0.00002	0.00002	0.00002
#Nodes	346,060	47,141	13,720	6,450	3,059	1,890	1,092	980	624
#Elements	335,787	44,776	12,753	5,829	2,684	1,600	840	741	465
Element Size(mm)	0.465	1.045	1.555	2.065	2.705	3.16	317	320	420
Mesh Count	335,787	44,776	12,753	5,829	2,684	1,600	840	741	465
Particle Volume (m^3)	4.1888E-09	3.3510E-08	1.1310E-07	2.6808E-07	5.2360E-07	9.0478E-07	1.4368E-06	2.1447E-06	3.0536E-06
Total Volume (m^3)	1.8850E-05	1.8850E-05	1.8850E-05	1.8850E-05	1.8850E-05	1.8850E-05	1.8850E-05	1.8850E-05	1.8850E-05
#Cells/Particle Volume	74.62	79.60	76.52	82.90	74.56	76.80	64.03	84.31	75.33
#Cells/Particle Diameter	5.2	5.3	5.3	5.4	5.2	5.3	5.0	5.4	5.2
fU_∞ (m/s), Fluent	0.0024186								
% Diff	1.85								
f, Fluent	0.8062								

Table 17.3 Data for $\lambda = 0.1 - 0.9$

17.2 Run ANSYS Fluent Simulations for $\lambda = 0.5$ as shown in Table 17.3 for different values of #Cells/Particle Diameter from 1 – 20. Include a plot of f versus #Cells/Particle Diameter.

Notes:

CHAPTER 18. FLOW PAST A SPHERE

A. Objectives

- Using ANSYS DesignModeler to Model the Sphere
- Inserting Boundary Conditions and Free Stream Velocity
- Running the Calculations
- Using Velocity and Pressure Plots for Visualizations
- Determining the Drag Coefficient

B. Problem Description

We will study the axisymmetric flow past a sphere and we will analyze the problem using ANSYS Fluent. A 50 mm diameter sphere will be used and the Reynolds number will be set to $Re = 100$.

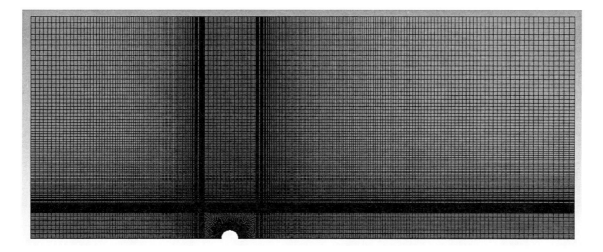

C. Launching ANSYS Workbench and Selecting Fluent

1. Start by launching ANSYS Workbench. Double click on Fluid Flow (Fluent) under Analysis Systems in the Toolbox. Select Units>>Metric (tonne, mm, s, …) from the menu.

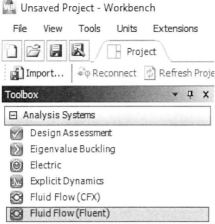

Figure 18.1 Selecting Fluent

D. Launching ANSYS DesignModeler

2. Right click Geometry and select Properties. In Properties of Schematic A2: Geometry, select Analysis Type 2D under Advanced Geometry Options. Right click on Geometry in the Project Schematic window and select New DesignModeler Geometry. Select millimeter as the desired length unit from the menu (Units>>Millimeter).

    Select the Sketching tab and click on Arc by Center. Click on Look at Face/Plane/Sketch

    . Draw in the upper two quadrants a half-circle centered at the origin of the coordinate system in the graphics window. Click on the Dimensions tab and select Radius. Click on the half-circle in the graphics window and enter 25 mm for the radius. Draw a line between the two end points of the half-circle.

    Select Concepts>>Surfaces from Sketches from the menu. Control select the half-circle and the line in the graphics window, and select Apply for Base Objects in Details View. Click on Generate.

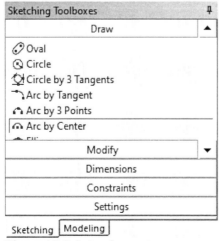

Figure 18.2a) Arc by center

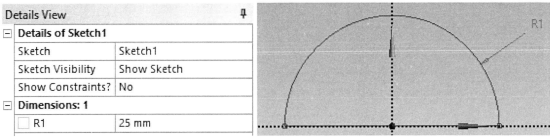

Figure 18.2b) Half-circle and line

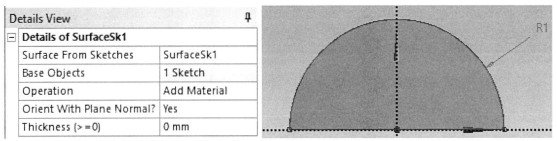

Figure 18.2c) Finished half-circle

Next, we will be creating the 2D axisymmetric mesh region around the half-sphere. Click on the modeling tab and select the XYPlane in the Tree Outline. Click on ⬚ to generate a new sketch. Select Rectangle by 3 Points from the sketching tools. Click anywhere at the upper left corner of the graphics window, followed by clicking anywhere on the left hand plane on the horizontal axis, and finally click on the right hand plane on the horizontal axis. Select Dimensions, click on Horizontal and click on the vertical edges of the rectangle. Enter 1575 mm as the horizontal length of the rectangle. Click on the vertical axis and the vertical edge of the rectangle on the left hand side. Enter 575 mm as the length. Click on the Vertical dimensioning tool and click on the horizontal edges of the rectangle. Enter 625 mm as the vertical height of the rectangle.

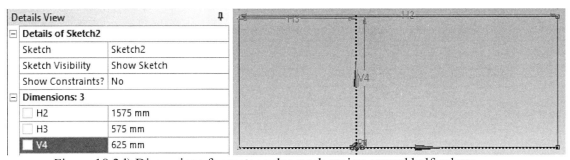

Figure 18.2d) Dimensions for rectangular mesh region around half-sphere

3. Select Concept>>Surface from Sketches. Click on Sketch2 in the Tree Outline and select Apply for Base Objects in Details View. Select Operation>>Add Frozen in Details View followed by Generate.

Select Create>>Boolean from the menu. Select Subtract Operation from the Details View. Click on the mesh region in the graphics window and click on Apply for Target Body. Select the Sphere as the Tool Body and click on Generate.

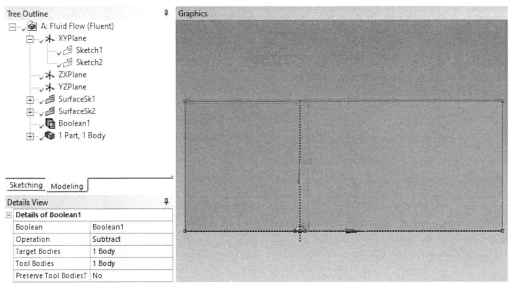

Figure 18.3 Mesh region around sphere

4. Select XYPlane in the tree outline and create a new sketch . Select the Sketching tab and select Line. Draw a vertical line from top to bottom and to the left of the sphere. The vertical line will intersect the entire mesh region. Position the line 75 mm from the vertical axis. Select Concepts>>Lines from Sketches from the menu. Select the newly created vertical line and Apply it as a Base Object in the Details View. Click on Generate.

Create another sketch in the XYPlane with a vertical line 75 mm to the right of the vertical axis and repeat all the different steps as listed above. Repeat these steps one more time with a horizontal line from left to right intersecting the mesh region and positioned 75 mm above the half-sphere centerline.

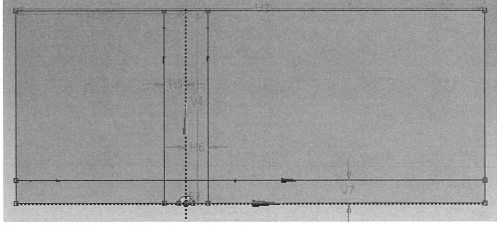

Figure 18.4a) Lines added to the mesh region

410

Create another sketch in the XYPlane with a vertical line towards the half-sphere as shown in Figure 18.4b). Finally, create the last sketch with two diagonal lines at 45 degrees towards the half-sphere as shown in Figure 18.4b).

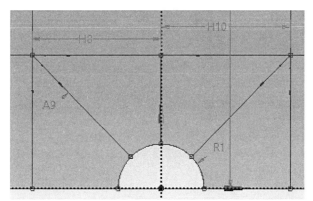

Figure 18.4b) Lines added to the mesh region close to the half-sphere

5. Select Tools>>Projection from the menu. Select Edges on Face as type in Details View. Control-select all 11 line-segments for the 6 lines that you have created and Apply as the Edges in the Details View. Select the mesh region and Apply it as the Target under Details View. Click Generate.

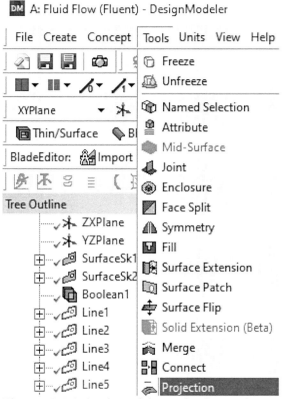

Figure 18.5 Selection of the projection tool

You should now have 9 different regions for meshing. Select File>>Save Project from the menu and save the project with the name "Axisymmetric Sphere Flow Study.wbpj". Close DesignModeler.

E. Launching ANSYS Meshing

6. Double click on Mesh under Project Schematic in ANSYS Workbench. Click on Mesh in the Outline under Project. Select Home>>Tools>>Units>>Metric (mm, kg, N, …) from the menu. Right click on Mesh under Project in Outline and select Generate Mesh. A coarse mesh is generated.

Select Mesh under Model (A3) in Project under Outline on the left-hand side. Select the Mesh tab in the menu and Controls>>Face Meshing. Control-select all 9 faces of the mesh. Apply the Geometry under Details of "Face Meshing".

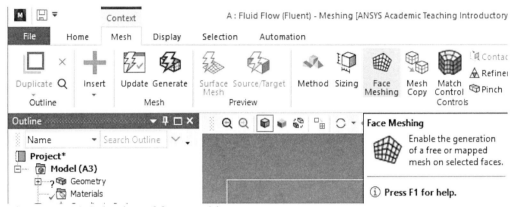

Figure 18.6a) Selection of face meshing

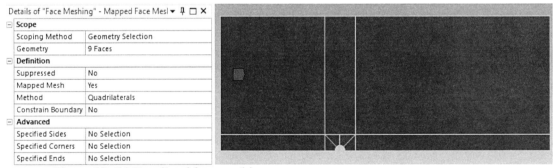

Figure 18.6b) Details of face meshing

Select Mesh>>Controls>>Sizing from the menu, right-click in the graphics window and select Cursor Mode>>Edge. Control-select the two edges 8 and 19 as shown in Figure 18.6c).

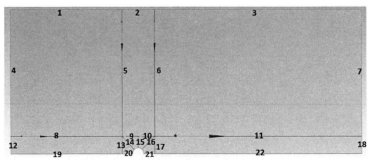

Figure 18.6c) Numbered edges for mesh sizing

Apply the Geometry under Details of "Sizing". Select Number of Divisions as Type under Details of "Sizing". Set the number of Divisions to 100. Set the Behavior to Hard. Select the first Bias Type from the drop down menu. Enter a Bias Factor of 10.

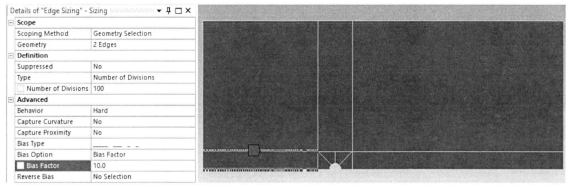

Figure 18.6d) Details for 1st mesh sizing

Select Mesh Control>>Sizing from the menu. Control-select edges 11 and 22. Apply the Geometry under Details of "Sizing". Select Number of Divisions as Type under Details of "Sizing". Set the number of Divisions to 150. Set the Behavior to Hard. Select the second Bias Type from the drop down menu. Enter a Bias Factor of 10.

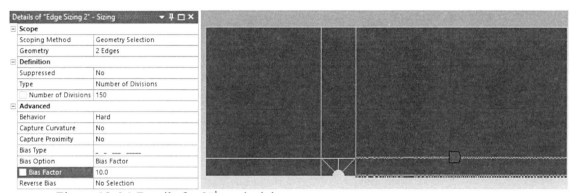

Figure 18.6e) Details for 2nd mesh sizing

Select Mesh Control>>Sizing from the menu. Select edge 1. Apply the Geometry under Details of "Sizing". Select Number of Divisions as Type under Details of "Sizing". Set the number of Divisions to 100. Set the Behavior to Hard. Select the second Bias Type from the drop down menu. Enter a Bias Factor of 10.

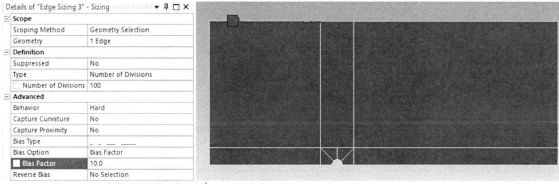

Figure 18.6f) Details for 3rd mesh sizing

413

Select Mesh Control>>Sizing from the menu. Select edge 3. Apply the Geometry under Details of "Sizing". Select Number of Divisions as Type under Details of "Sizing". Set the number of Divisions to 150. Set the Behavior to Hard. Select the first Bias Type from the drop down menu. Enter a Bias Factor of 10.

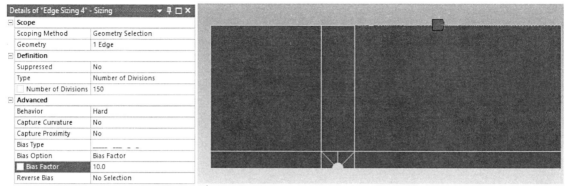

Figure 18.6g) Details for 4th mesh sizing

Select Mesh Control>>Sizing from the menu. Select edge 2. Apply the Geometry under Details of "Sizing". Select Number of Divisions as Type under Details of "Sizing". Set the number of Divisions to 54. Set the Behavior to Hard.

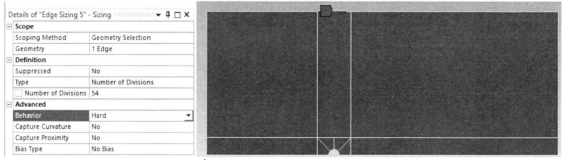

Figure 18.6h) Details for 5th mesh sizing

Select Mesh Control>>Sizing from the menu. Control-select edges 9, 10, 12, 13, 17, 18, and the four parts of the half-circle. Apply the Geometry under Details of "Sizing". Select Number of Divisions as Type under Details of "Sizing". Set the number of Divisions to 27. Set the Behavior to Hard.

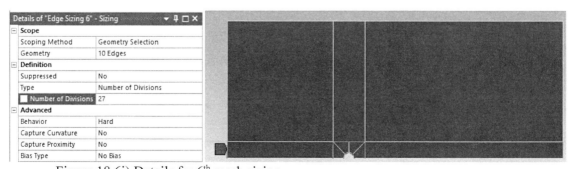

Figure 18.6i) Details for 6th mesh sizing

Select Mesh Control>>Sizing from the menu. Control-select the three edges 4, 5, and 6. Apply the Geometry under Details of "Sizing". Select Number of Divisions as Type under Details of "Sizing". Set the number of Divisions to 100. Set the Behavior to Hard. Select the first Bias Type from the drop down menu. Enter a Bias Factor of 20.

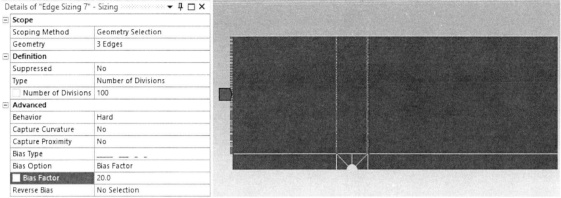

Figure 18.6j) Details for 7th mesh sizing

Select Mesh Control>>Sizing from the menu. Select edge 7. Apply the Geometry under Details of "Sizing". Select Number of Divisions as Type under Details of "Sizing". Set the number of Divisions to 100. Set the Behavior to Hard. Select the second Bias Type from the drop down menu. Enter a Bias Factor of 20.

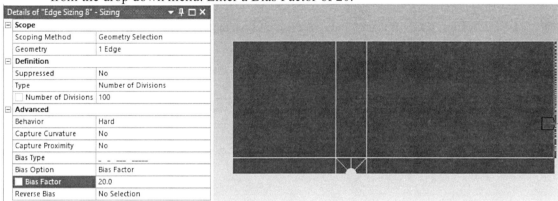

Figure 18.6k) Details for 8th mesh sizing

Select Mesh Control>>Sizing from the menu. Select edges 14, 15, 16, 20, and 21. Apply the Geometry under Details of "Sizing". Select Number of Divisions as Type under Details of "Sizing". Set the number of Divisions to 18. Set the Behavior to Hard.

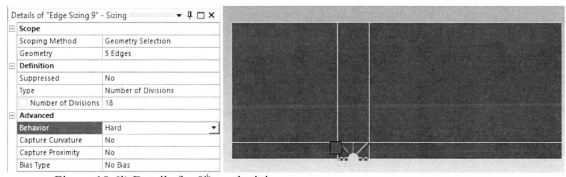

Figure 18.6l) Details for 9th mesh sizing

415

Right click on Mesh in the tree outline and select Generate Mesh.

Figure 18.6m) Details of mesh around half-sphere

7. Select geometry in the Outline. Right-click in the graphics window and select Cursor Mode>>Edge. Control select the two vertical edges on the right hand side, right click and select Create Named Selection. Name the edges "outlet" and click OK. Name the two vertical edges to the left "inlet" and the four edges of the sphere with the name "sphere". Name the three horizontal edges at the top "symmetry" and name the four horizontal edges at the bottom "axisymmetry". Close the meshing window. Right click on Mesh under Project Schematic in ANSYS Workbench and select Update.

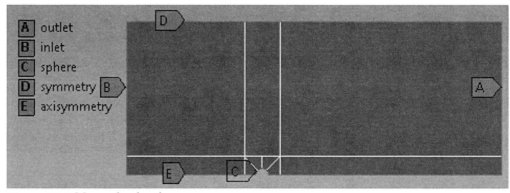

Figure 18.7 Named selections

F. Launching ANSYS Fluent

8. Double click on Setup under Project Schematic in ANSYS Workbench. Check the Options box Double Precision. Select Parallel Processing Options and increase the Number of Processes to the same number as computer cores. Click on OK. Select 2D Space Axisymmetric under General on the Task Page.

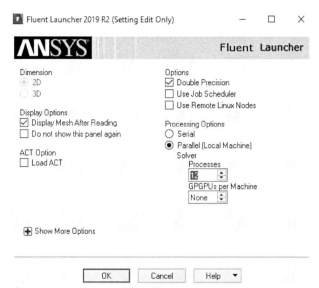

Figure 18.8a) Launching Fluent

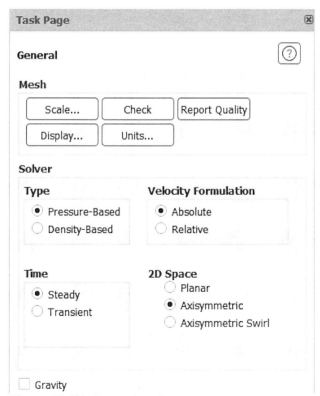

Figure 18.8b) General settings

9. Double click on Boundary Conditions under Setup in the Outline View. Select the inlet Zone under Boundary Conditions on the Task Page. Click on Edit…. Select Components as Velocity Specification Method. Enter 0.02921469 as Axial-Velocity (m/s). This is corresponding to Reynolds number $Re = 100$. Select OK to close the Velocity Inlet window.

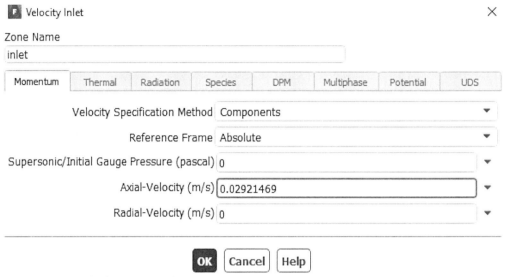

Figure 18.9 Velocity inlet settings

10. Double click on Initialization under Solution in the Outline View. Select Standard Initialization. Enter 0.02921469 for Axial Velocity (m/s). Click on Initialize. Double click on Reference Values under Setup in the Outline View. Set the reference values as shown in Figure 18.10b).

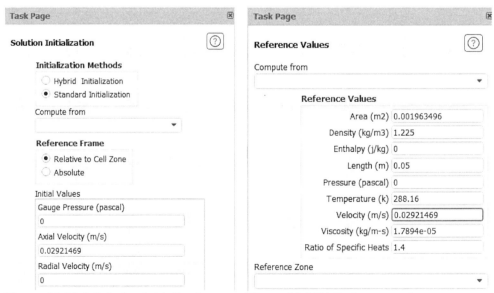

Figure 18.10a) Solution initialization   Figure 18.10b) Reference values

Double-click on Report Definitions under Solution in the Outline View. Select New>>Force Report>>Lift… from the drop-down menu. Select *sphere* as Wall Zones. Check the boxes for Report File, Report Plot and Print to Console under Create. Click on the OK button to close the Lift Report Definition window. Repeat this step for the Drag. Close the Report Definitions window.

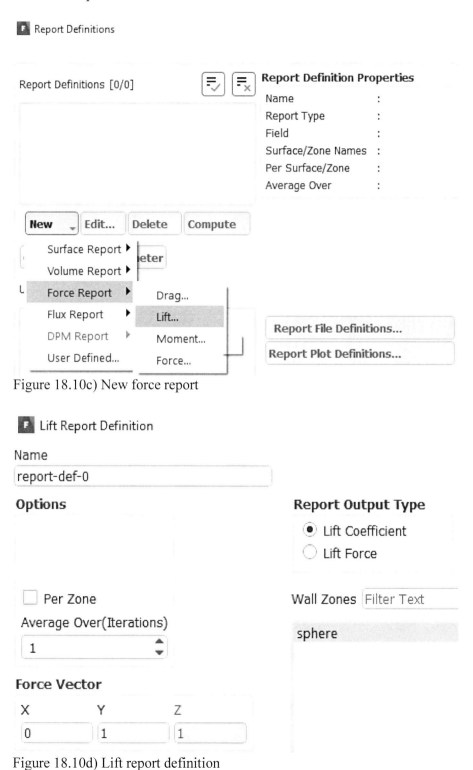

Figure 18.10c) New force report

Figure 18.10d) Lift report definition

11. Double click on Monitors and Residual under Solution in the Outline View. Check the boxes for Print to Console and Plot. Set all three Absolute Criteria to 1e-12. Click on OK to exit the Residual Monitors window.

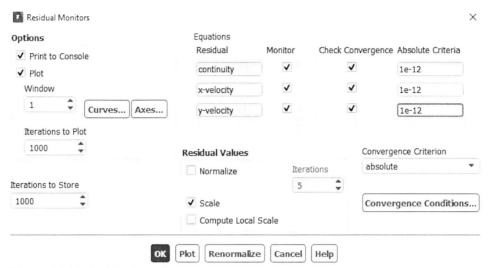

Figure 18.11 Residual monitors

Double click on Run Calculation under Solution in the Outline View. Enter 300 for the Number of Iterations and click on Calculate.

G. Post-Processing

12. The value for the drag coefficient at $Re = 100$ for the first coarse mesh is $C_d = 1.08846$.

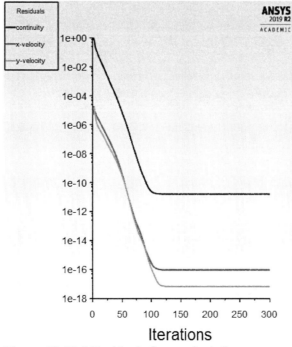

Figure 18.12a) Residuals from calculations

Double-click on Contours in Graphics under Results in the Outline View. Enter *static-pressure* as Contour Name in the Contours window. Select Contours of Pressure… and Static Pressure. Check the box Filled under Options. Deselect all Surfaces and click on Save/Display.

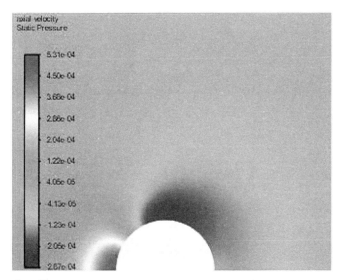

Figure 18.12b) Contours plot for static pressure

Select Contours of Velocity and Axial Velocity. Enter *axial-velocity* as Contour Name in the Contours window. Check the box Filled under Options. Deselect all surfaces and click on Save/Display.

Figure 18.12c) Contours plot for axial velocity

Find the coefficient of drag by double-clicking on Reports under Results in the Outline View. Double-click on Forces under Reports. Click Print and write down the value for the total drag coefficient that you have calculated: 1.08846.

13. Select the Domain tab in the menu. Select Adapt>>Refine / Coarsen under the Domain tab from the menu. Select Cell Registers>>New>>Region in the Adaption Controls window and enter -0.575 for X Min (m), 1 for X Max (m), 0 for Y Min (m), and 0.625 for Y Max (m). Select Save to close the Region Register window. Select *region_0* as Refinement Criterion in the Adaption Controls window and click on Adapt. This increases the number of cells by a factor of 4 from 39,094 to 156,376 cells. Select OK to close the Adaption Controls window. Select File>>Export>>Case & Data… from the menu. Save the file in the *working directory* with the name "Axisymmetric Coarse Mesh Flow Past a Sphere at Re = 100.cas".

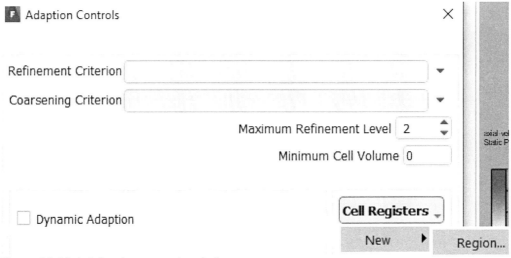

Figure 18.13a) Adaption controls window

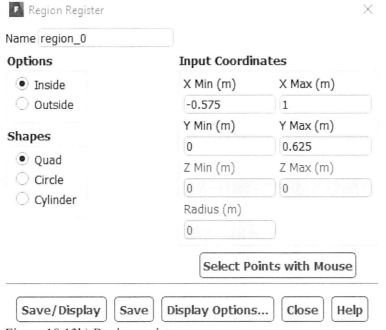

Figure 18.13b) Region register

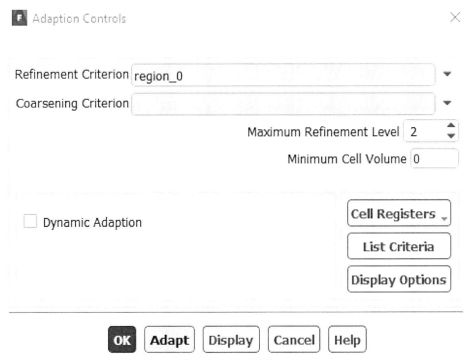

Figure 18.13c) Region_0 as refinement criterion

Initialize the flow and run the calculations once again for this new medium mesh. Enter 300 for the Number of Iterations and click on Calculate. The value of the drag coefficient at $Re = 100$ for the medium mesh is $C_d = 1.0954523$.

Number of Cells	C_d
39,094	1.0885
156,376	1.0955

Table 18.1 Drag coefficient before and after refinement of mesh

H. Theory

14. The drag coefficient from experiments for a smooth sphere is found using the following curve-fit formula:

$$C_{D,Exp} = \frac{24}{Re} + \frac{6}{1+Re^{1/2}} + 0.4 \qquad 0 \le Re \le 200,000 \qquad (18.1)$$

We determine the Reynolds number for the flow around the sphere that is defined as

$$Re = Ud/v = 0.02921469 * 0.05 / 1.46 * 10^{-5} = 100 \qquad (18.2)$$

, where U is the magnitude of the free stream velocity, d is the diameter of the sphere, and v is the kinematic viscosity of air at room temperature. The difference between ANSYS Fluent and experiments for the drag coefficient is 7.6%.

I. References

1. Clift, R., Grace, J.R. and Weber, M.E. "Bubbles, Drops and Particles", Academic Press, New York, (1978).
2. Jones, D.A. and Clarke, D.B. "Simulation of Flow Past a Sphere using the Fluent Code", Australian Government Department of Defence, Defence Science and Technology Organisation, Maritime Platforms Division, DSTO-TR-2232, (2008).
3. Roos, F.W. and Willmarth, W.W. "Some Experimental Results on Sphere and Disk Drag", AIAA Journal, **9**(2), 285-291, (1971).
4. Tabata, M. and Itakura, K., "A Precise Computation of Drag Coefficients of a Sphere", Int. J. Comput. Fluid Dynam. **9**, 303, (1998).

J. Exercises

18.1 Run ANSYS Fluent Simulations for $Re = 20, 40, 60, 80, 100, 120, 140, 160, 180$ and 200 and compare your results with equation (18.1). Include a plot of drag coefficient versus Reynolds number in this range.

CHAPTER 19. TAYLOR-COUETTE FLOW

A. Objectives

- Using ANSYS Meshing to Create the Mesh for 3D Taylor-Couette Flow
- Inserting Wall Boundary Conditions for Rotating Inner Wall
- Running Laminar Steady 3D ANSYS Fluent Simulations
- Using Contour Plots for Visualizations
- Compare Results with Neutral Stability Theory

B. Problem Description

We will study the flow between two vertical cylinders where the inner wall is rotating at 1.5 rad/s. The inner and outer cylinders have radii of 30 mm and 35 mm, respectively. The height of both cylinders is 100 mm. The centrifugal instability will cause the appearance of counter-rotating vortices at low rotation speeds for the inner wall with a fixed outer wall.

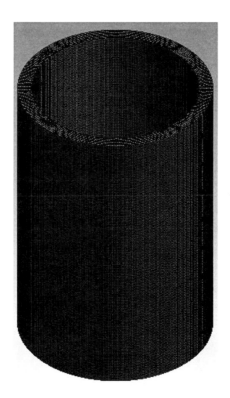

C. Launching ANSYS Workbench and Selecting Fluent

1. Start by launching ANSYS Workbench. Double click on Fluid Flow (Fluent) under Analysis Systems in the Toolbox. Select Units>>Metric (tonne, mm, s, …) from the menu.

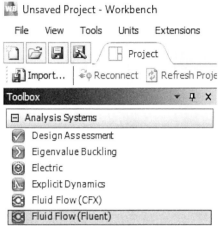

Figure 19.1 Selecting Fluent

D. Launching ANSYS DesignModeler

2. Right click on Geometry in the Project Schematic window and select New DesignModeler Geometry. Select millimeter as the desired length unit from the menu (Units>>Millimeter) in DesignModeler. Select the ZX Plane in the Tree Outline and select Look at Face/Plane/Sketch. Select the Sketching tab and click on Circle. Draw two circles centered at the origin. Click on the Dimensions tab and select Radius. Click on the circles in the graphics window and enter 30 mm and 35 mm for the radii of the circles in Details View.

    Select Concepts>>Surfaces from Sketches from the menu. Control select the two circles in the graphics window, and select Apply for Base Objects in Details View. Click on Generate.

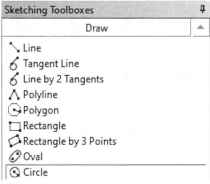

Figure 19.2a) Circle sketch tool

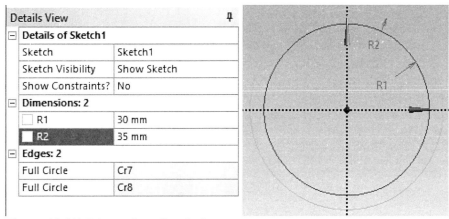

Figure 19.2b) Dimensions for circles

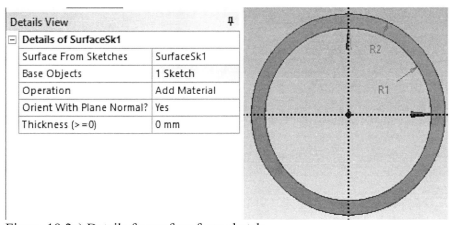

Figure 19.2c) Details for surface from sketch

Select 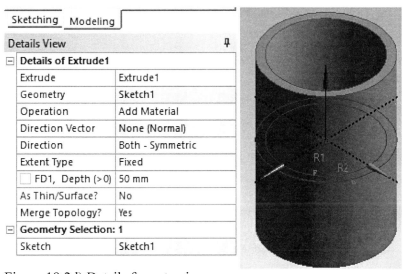 Extrude and apply Sketch1 under ZXPlane in the Tree Outline as Geometry in Details View. Select Direction Both – Symmetric from the drop down menu in Details View. Enter 50 mm as the FD1, Depth (>0) of the extrusion. Click on Generate and select isometric view in the graphics window. Close the DesignModeler.

Figure 19.2d) Details for extrusion

E. Launching ANSYS Meshing

3. Double click on Mesh under Project Schematic in ANSYS Workbench. Click on Mesh in the Outline under Project. Select Home>>Tools>>Units>>Metric (mm, kg, N, …) from the menu. Right click on Mesh under Project in Outline and select Generate Mesh. A coarse mesh is generated.

   Set the Element Size under Defaults in Details of Mesh to 0.65 mm. Right click on Mesh under Project in Outline and select Generate Mesh. Under Statistics in Details of Mesh we can see that this mesh has 452,124 Nodes and 400,574 Elements.

   Right click in the graphics window and select Cursor Mode>>Face. Select the outer cylindrical face, right click and select Create Named Selection. Enter the name *wall_outer* and click on OK to close the Selection Name window. Repeat this for the inner cylindrical face with the name *wall_inner*, the bottom face named *wall_bottom* and the top face named *wall_top*.

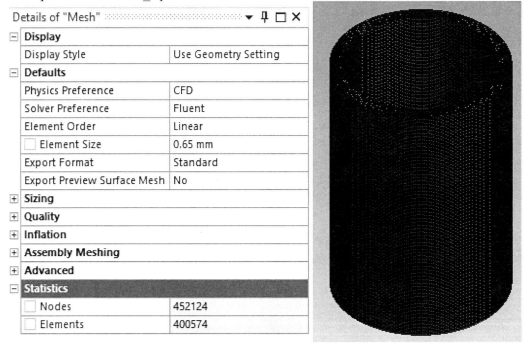

Details of "Mesh"	
Display	
Display Style	Use Geometry Setting
Defaults	
Physics Preference	CFD
Solver Preference	Fluent
Element Order	Linear
Element Size	0.65 mm
Export Format	Standard
Export Preview Surface Mesh	No
Sizing	
Quality	
Inflation	
Assembly Meshing	
Advanced	
Statistics	
Nodes	452124
Elements	400574

Figure 19.3a) Details for Taylor-Couette mesh

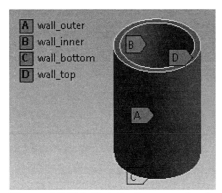

Figure 19.3b) Details for named selections

Select File>>Export...>>Mesh>>FLUENT Input File>>Export from the menu and save the mesh in the *working directory* with the name *cylinder-mesh-taylor-couette-flow.msh*. Select File>>Save Project from the menu and save the project with the name *Taylor-Couette.wbpj*. Close the Meshing window and right-click on Mesh under Project Schematic in ANSYS Workbench and select Update.

F. Launching ANSYS Fluent

4. Double click on Setup under Project Schematic in ANSYS Workbench. Check the Options box Double Precision. Select Parallel Processing Options and increase the Number of Processes to the same number as computer cores. Click on OK.

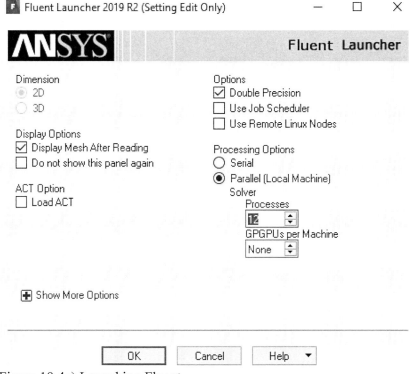

Figure 19.4a) Launching Fluent

Click on Check and Scale... under Mesh in General on the Task Page to verify the Domain Extents. Close the Scale Mesh window. Select Relative Velocity Formulation. Check the box for Gravity. Enter -9.81 as Gravitational Acceleration in the Y direction.

Figure 19.4b) Domain extents for Taylor-Couette flow mesh

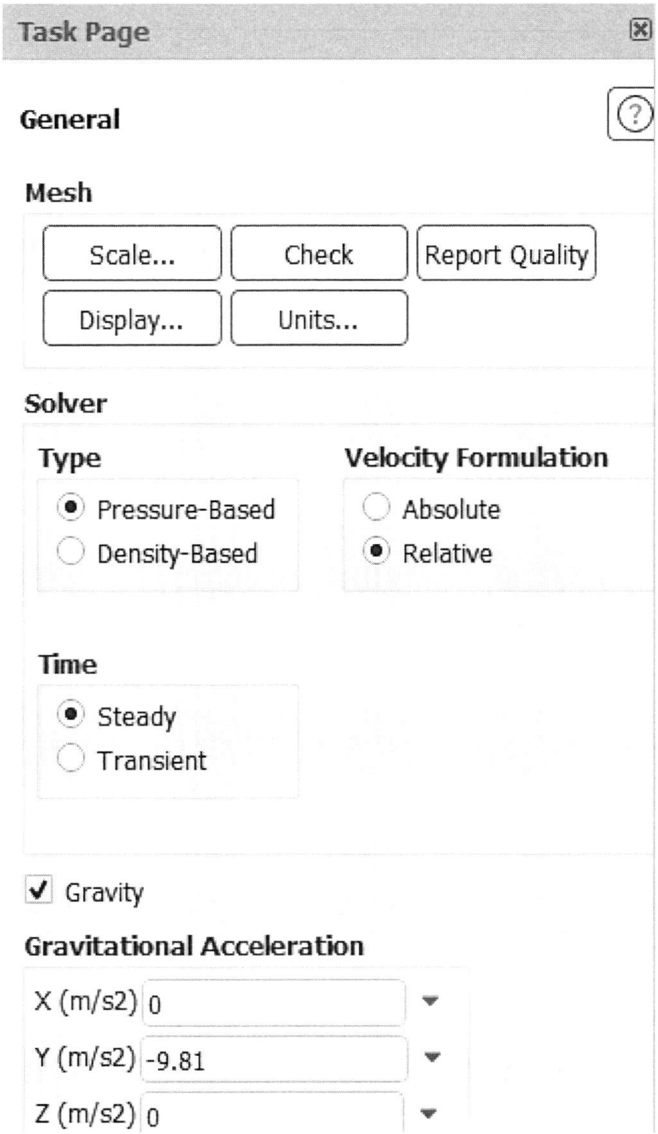

Figure 19.4c) General settings

Double click on Materials under Setup in the Outline View. Click on Create/Edit for Fluid under Materials on the Task Page. Click on Fluent Database in the Create/Edit Materials window. Scroll down and select *water-liquid (h2o<l>)* as the Fluent Fluid Material. Click on Copy and Close the Fluent Database Materials window. Click on Change/Create and Close the Create/Edit Materials window.

Figure 19.4d) Selection of water-liquid as fluid

5.   Open Cell Zone Conditions under Setup in the Outline View. Double click on *solid (fluid, id=2)* under Cell Zone Conditions. Select *water-liquid* as Material Name and enter *water-liquid* as the Zone Name. Check the box for Frame Motion and enter Speed (rad/s) -1.5 as Rotational Velocity. Set the Rotation-Axis Direction as X 0, Y 1, Z 0. Click OK to close the Fluid window.

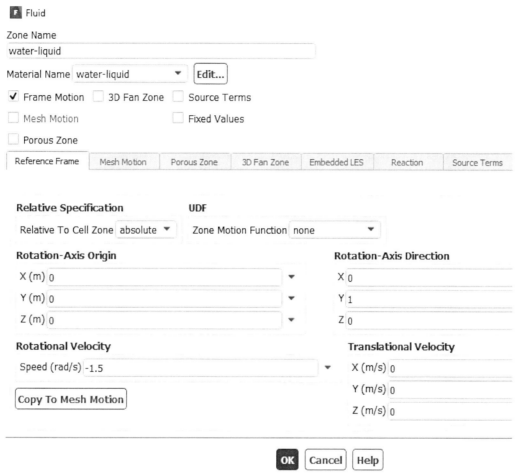

Figure 19.5a) Selection of water-liquid as fluid and setting for rotational velocity

Double click on Boundary Conditions. Select *wall_inner* under Zone in Boundary Conditions on the Task Page. Click on the Edit… button for wall Type. Select *Moving Wall* under Wall Motion. Check Absolute and Rotational under Motion and enter 1.5 as Speed (rad/s). Set the Rotation-Axis Direction as X 0, Y 1, Z 0, see Figure 19.5b). Click OK to close the window. Repeat this step for the *wall_outer* Zone, use Absolute and Rotational Motion, enter 0 as Speed (rad/s) and set the Rotation-Axis Direction as X 0, Y 1, Z 0, see Figure 19.5b). Do the same for the top and bottom walls, see Figure 19.5b).

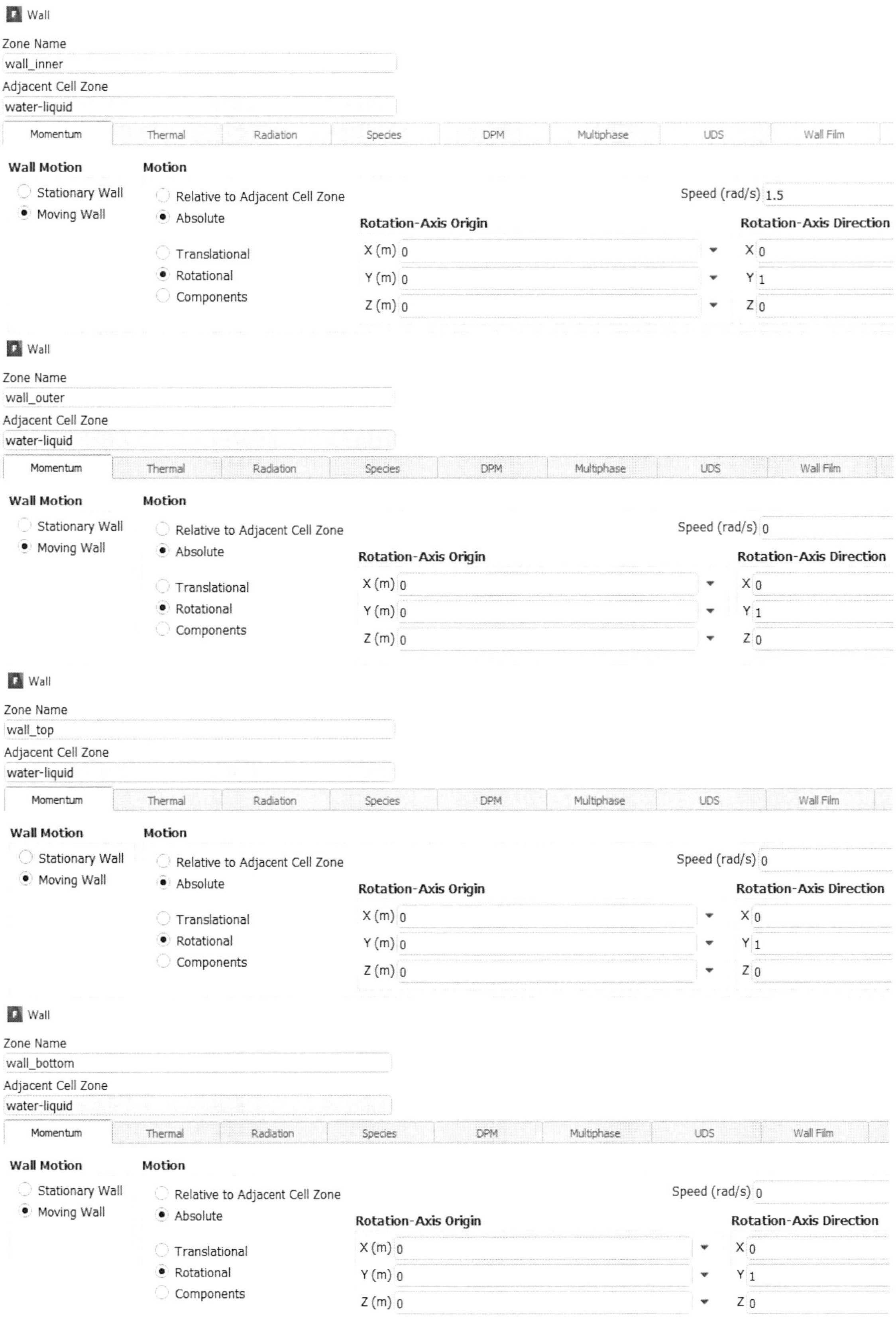

Wall

Zone Name
wall_inner

Adjacent Cell Zone
water-liquid

| Momentum | Thermal | Radiation | Species | DPM | Multiphase | UDS | Wall Film |

Wall Motion

○ Stationary Wall
● Moving Wall

Motion

○ Relative to Adjacent Cell Zone
● Absolute

○ Translational
● Rotational
○ Components

Speed (rad/s) 1.5

Rotation-Axis Origin

X (m) 0
Y (m) 0
Z (m) 0

Rotation-Axis Direction

X 0
Y 1
Z 0

Wall

Zone Name
wall_outer

Adjacent Cell Zone
water-liquid

| Momentum | Thermal | Radiation | Species | DPM | Multiphase | UDS | Wall Film |

Wall Motion

○ Stationary Wall
● Moving Wall

Motion

○ Relative to Adjacent Cell Zone
● Absolute

○ Translational
● Rotational
○ Components

Speed (rad/s) 0

Rotation-Axis Origin

X (m) 0
Y (m) 0
Z (m) 0

Rotation-Axis Direction

X 0
Y 1
Z 0

Wall

Zone Name
wall_top

Adjacent Cell Zone
water-liquid

| Momentum | Thermal | Radiation | Species | DPM | Multiphase | UDS | Wall Film |

Wall Motion

○ Stationary Wall
● Moving Wall

Motion

○ Relative to Adjacent Cell Zone
● Absolute

○ Translational
● Rotational
○ Components

Speed (rad/s) 0

Rotation-Axis Origin

X (m) 0
Y (m) 0
Z (m) 0

Rotation-Axis Direction

X 0
Y 1
Z 0

Wall

Zone Name
wall_bottom

Adjacent Cell Zone
water-liquid

| Momentum | Thermal | Radiation | Species | DPM | Multiphase | UDS | Wall Film |

Wall Motion

○ Stationary Wall
● Moving Wall

Motion

○ Relative to Adjacent Cell Zone
● Absolute

○ Translational
● Rotational
○ Components

Speed (rad/s) 0

Rotation-Axis Origin

X (m) 0
Y (m) 0
Z (m) 0

Rotation-Axis Direction

X 0
Y 1
Z 0

Figure 19.5b) Details of wall motion for inner wall, outer wall, top wall and bottom wall

6. Double click on Initialization under Solution in the Outline View and select Hybrid Initialization. Click on Initialize. Double click on Run Calculation under Solution in the Outline View. Enter 1000 for the Number of Iterations and click on Calculate.

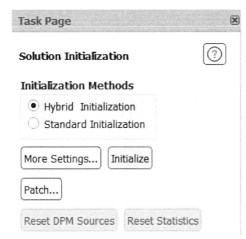

Figure 19.6 Solution initialization

G. Post-Processing

7. The residuals are shown in Figure 19.7a). Double-click on Contours in Graphics under Results in the Outline View. Enter *y-velocity* as Contour Name in the Contours window. Select Contours of Velocity… and Y Velocity. Check the box Filled under Options. Uncheck Node Values under Options. Select *interior-solid* under Surfaces and click on Save/Display. Select the red X coordinate axis in the graphics window.

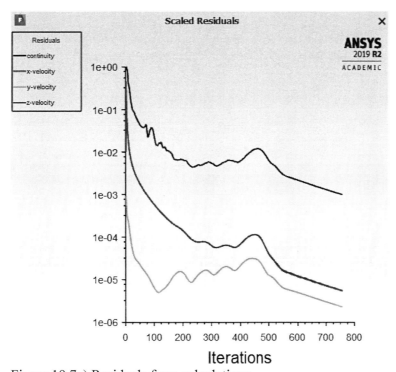

Figure 19.7a) Residuals from calculations

433

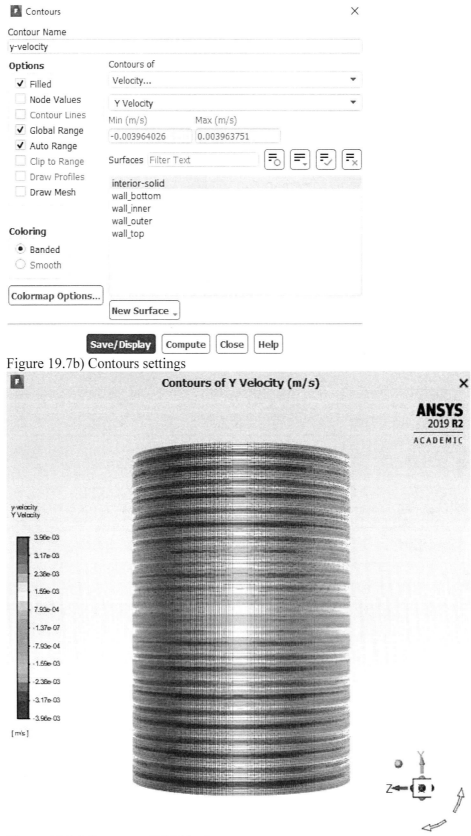

Figure 19.7b) Contours settings

Figure 19.7c) Contours of Y Velocity

H. Theory

8. The instability of the flow between two vertical rotating cylinders is governed by the so called Taylor number Ta.

$$Ta = \frac{4\Omega_i^2 d^4}{\nu^2} \tag{19.1}$$

where Ω_i is the rotation rate of the inner cylinder, d is the distance between the cylinders and ν is the kinematic viscosity of the fluid. Below the critical $Ta_{crit} = 3430$ for a non-rotating outer cylinder, the flow is stable but instabilities will develop above this Taylor number. The non-dimensional wave number α of the centrifugal instability is determined by

$$\alpha = \frac{2\pi d}{\lambda} \tag{19.2}$$

where λ is the spanwise wave length of the instability. The critical wave numbers $\alpha_{crit} = 3.12$ in the narrow gap limit: $\eta \to 1$. The radius ratio is defined as $\eta = r_i/r_o$ where r_i and r_o is the radius of the inner and outer cylinders, respectively. From figure 19.7c), the wave number can be determined to be

$$\alpha = \frac{2\pi \cdot 0.005}{0.00753} = 4.17 \tag{19.3}$$

In order to determine the wave length that is used to determine the wave number in equation (19.3), you can measure the total length in the vertical spanwise direction for twelve red or twelve blue successive bands in figure 19.7c). Next, you take this vertical length and divide by twelve to get the average wave length in the vertical spanwise direction. To get the scale for figure 19.7c), use the total height of the cylinder in the vertical direction in figure 19.7c) that corresponds to the 100 mm height of the cylinder.

The Taylor number in the calculations is

$$Ta = \frac{4 \cdot 1.5^2 \cdot 0.005^4}{(1.004 \cdot 10^{-6})^2} = 5580 \tag{19.4}$$

The neutral stability curve can be given to the first approximation, see figure 19.8.

$$Ta = \frac{2(\pi^2 + \alpha^2)^3}{(1+\mu)\alpha^2 \left\{ 1 - 16\alpha\pi^2 \cosh^2(\frac{\alpha}{2})/[(\pi^2+\alpha^2)^2(\sinh\alpha + \alpha)] \right\}} \tag{19.5}$$

where $\mu = \Omega_o/\Omega_i$ and Ω_o is the rotation rate of the outer cylinder.

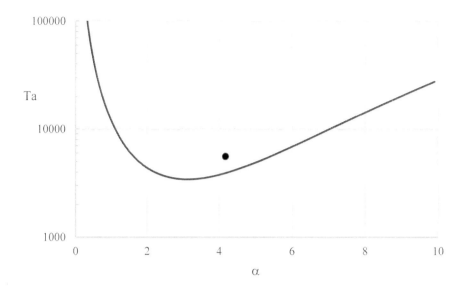

Figure 19.8 Neutral stability curve for Taylor-Couette flow with a stationary outer cylinder $\mu = 0$. The filled circle represents result from ANSYS Fluent. The radius ratio is $\eta = 6/7$ in ANSYS Fluent and $\eta = 1$ for the stability curve.

I. References

1. Chandrasekhar, S., Hydrodynamic and Hydromagnetic Stability, Dover, 1981.
2. Koschmieder, E.L., Benard Cells and Taylor Vortices, Cambridge, 1993.
3. Matsson, J.E, On the Integration of Fluid Flows and Fabrication, *Proceedings of the 2002 American Society for Engineering Education Annual Conference & Exposition.*, Montreal, Canada, (2002).
4. Taylor, G.I., Stability of a Viscous Liquid Contained between Two Rotating Cylinders, *Phil. Trans. Roy. Soc.* London Ser. A, Vol. **223**, (1923).

J. Exercises

19.1 Run the calculations for the flow in the Taylor-Couette apparatus with only the inner cylinder rotating $\mu = 0$ for Taylor numbers $Ta = 10000$, 20000 and 30000 and compare the spanwise wave numbers with the one determined in this chapter for $Ta = 5580$. Include your results in figure 19.8 for comparison with the neutral stability curve.

19.2 Run the calculations for the flow in the Taylor-Couette apparatus with both cylinders rotating $\mu = 1$ and for Taylor numbers $Ta = 3000$, 5000 and 10000 and determine the spanwise wave numbers. Include your results in a graph and compare with the neutral stability curve corresponding to $\mu = -1/2$, see equation (19.5).

19.3 Run the calculations for the flow in a Rayleigh-Bénard cell for Rayleigh numbers $Ra = 5000$, 10000 and 20000 and compare the wave numbers with the one determined in this chapter for $Ra = 2953$. Include your results in figure 19.8 for comparison with the neutral stability curve.

CHAPTER 20. DEAN FLOW IN A CURVED CHANNEL

A. Objectives

- Using ANSYS Meshing to Create the Mesh for 3D Dean Flow in a Curved Channel
- Inserting Wall Boundary Conditions
- Running Laminar Steady 3D ANSYS Fluent Simulations
- Using Contour Plots for Visualizations
- Compare Results with Neutral Stability Theory

B. Problem Description

Dean flow appears in a curved tube but can also be realized in a narrow gap curved channel. We will therefore study the flow between two narrow curved walls where the inner wall has a radius of 395 mm and the radius of the outer wall is 405 mm. The height of both walls is 100 mm. The centrifugal instability will cause the appearance of counter-rotating vortices at low flow rates.

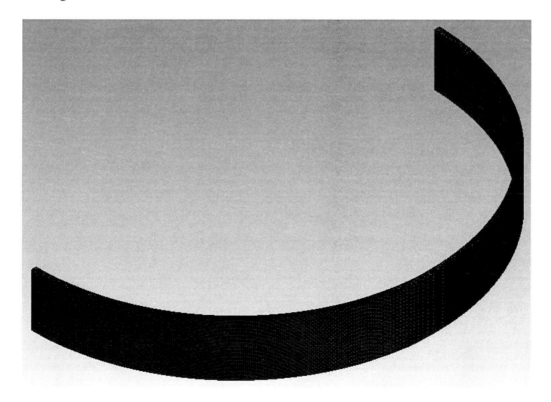

C. Launching ANSYS Workbench and Selecting Fluent

1. Start by launching ANSYS Workbench. Double click on Fluid Flow (Fluent) under Analysis Systems in the Toolbox. Select Units>>Metric (tonne, mm, s, …) from the menu.

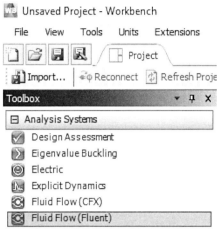

Figure 20.1 Selecting Fluent

D. Launching ANSYS DesignModeler

2. Right click on Geometry in the Project Schematic window and select New DesignModeler Geometry. Select millimeter as the desired length unit from the menu (Units>>Millimeter) in DesignModeler. Select the ZX Plane in the Tree Outline and select Look at Face/Plane/Sketch ⬚. Select the Sketching tab and click on Arc by Center. Draw two 180 degrees half-circle arcs centered at the origin. Click on the Dimensions tab and select Radius. Click on the arcs in the graphics window and enter 395 mm and 405 mm for the radii of the circles in Details View. Select the Line sketch tool and draw two horizontal lines that connect the ends of the arcs.

    Select Concepts>>Surfaces from Sketches from the menu. Control select the two arcs in the graphics window, and select Apply for Base Objects in Details View. Click on Generate.

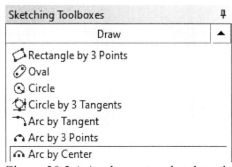

Figure 20.2a) Arc by center sketch tool

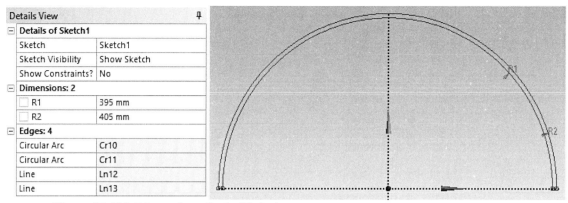

Figure 20.2b) Dimensions for half-circles

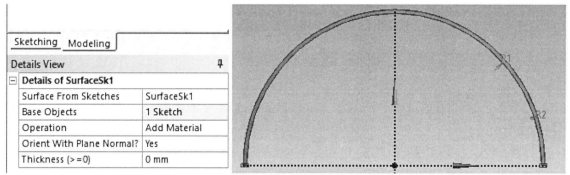

Figure 20.2c) Details for surface from sketch

Select  and apply Sketch1 under ZXPlane in the Tree Outline as Geometry in Details View. Select Direction Both – Symmetric from the drop down menu in Details View. Enter 50 mm as the FD1, Depth (>0) of the extrusion. Click on Generate and select isometric view in the graphics window. Close the DesignModeler.

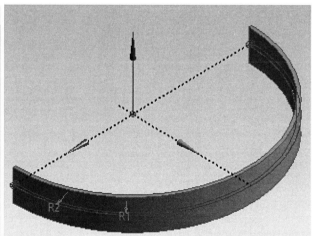

Figure 20.2d) Details for extrusion

E. Launching ANSYS Meshing

3. Double click on Mesh under Project Schematic in ANSYS Workbench. Click on Mesh in the Outline under Project. Select Home>>Tools>>Units>>Metric (mm, kg, N, …) from the menu. Right click on Mesh under Project in Outline and select Generate Mesh. A coarse mesh is generated.

    Set the Element Size under Defaults in Details of Mesh to 1.4 mm. Right click on Mesh under Project in Outline and select Generate Mesh. Under Statistics in Details of Mesh we can see that this mesh has 525,044 Nodes and 452,631 Elements.

    Right click in the graphics window and select Cursor Mode>>Face. Control select the outer cylindrical face, inner cylindrical face, top curved face and bottom curved face, right click and select Create Named Selection. Enter the name *wall* and click on OK to close the Selection Name window. Select the flat inlet face and name it *inlet* and select the flat outlet face and name it *outlet*.

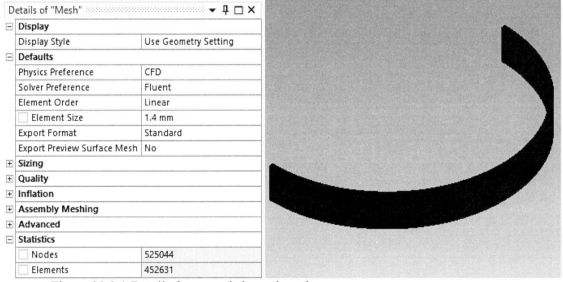

Figure 20.3a) Details for curved channel mesh

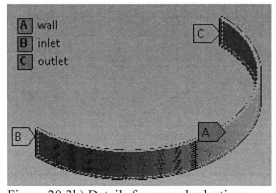

Figure 20.3b) Details for named selections

Select File>>Export…>>Mesh>>FLUENT Input File>>Export from the menu and save the mesh in the *working directory* with the name *curved-channel-mesh-dean-flow.msh*. Select File>>Save Project from the menu and save the project with the name *Dean Flow in Curved Narrow Channel.wbpj*. Close the Meshing window and right-click on Mesh under Project Schematic in ANSYS Workbench and select Update.

F. Launching ANSYS Fluent

4. Double click on Setup under Project Schematic in ANSYS Workbench. Check the Options box Double Precision. Select Parallel Processing Options and increase the Number of Processes to the same number as computer cores. Click on OK.

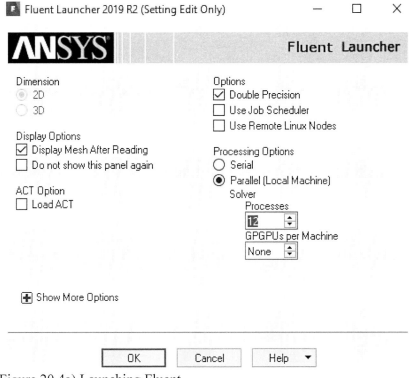

Figure 20.4a) Launching Fluent

Click on Check and Scale… under Mesh in General on the Task Page to verify the Domain Extents. Close the Scale Mesh window. Check the box for Gravity. Enter -9.81 as Gravitational Acceleration in the Y direction.

Scale Mesh

Domain Extents

Xmin (m)	0	Xmax (m)	0.405
Ymin (m)	-0.05	Ymax (m)	0.05
Zmin (m)	-0.405	Zmax (m)	0.405

Figure 20.4b) Domain extents for curved channel flow mesh

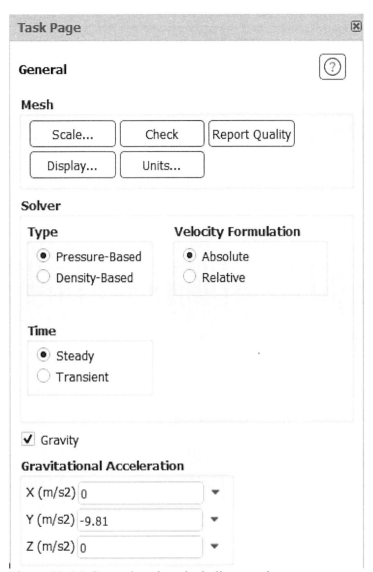

Figure 20.4c) General settings including gravity

Double click on Materials under Setup in the Outline View. Click on Create/Edit for Fluid under Materials on the Task Page. Click on Fluent Database in the Create/Edit Materials window. Scroll down and select *water-liquid (h2o<l>)* as the Fluent Fluid Material. Click on Copy and Close the Fluent Database Materials window. Click on Change/Create and Close the Create/Edit Materials window.

Figure 20.4d) Selection of water-liquid as fluid

5. Open Cell Zone Conditions under Setup in the Outline View. Double click on *solid (fluid, id=2)* under Cell Zone Conditions. Select *water-liquid* as Material Name and enter *water-liquid* as the Zone Name. Click OK to close the Fluid window.

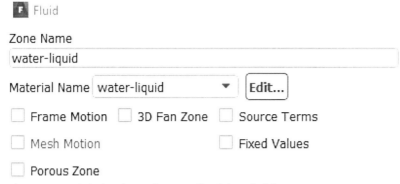

Figure 20.5a) Selection of water-liquid as fluid

Double click on Boundary Conditions. Select *inlet* under Zone in Boundary Conditions on the Task Page. Click on the Edit… button for velocity-inlet Type. Select *Components* as Velocity Specification Method. Select Local Cylindrical (Radial, Tangential, Axial) as Coordinate System. Enter 0.05 as Tangential-Velocity (m/s). Enter X 0, Y 1 and Z 0 as Axis Direction, see figure 20.5b). Select OK to close the Velocity Inlet window.

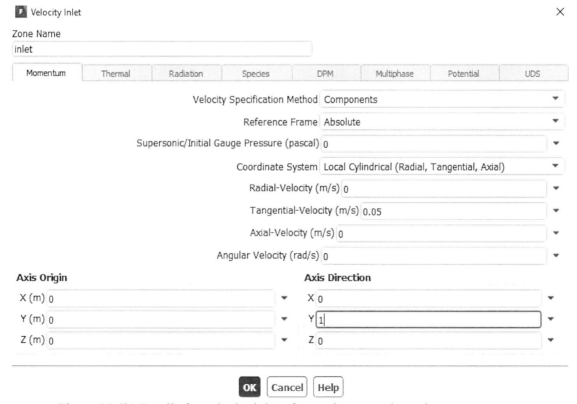

Figure 20.5b) Details for velocity inlet of curved narrow channel

6. Double click on Initialization under Solution in the Outline View and select Hybrid Initialization. Click on Initialize. Double click on Run Calculation under Solution in the Outline View. Enter 500 for the Number of Iterations and click on Calculate.

Figure 20.6 Solution initialization

G. Post-Processing

7. The residuals are shown in Figure 20.7a). Double-click on Contours in Graphics under Results in the Outline View. Enter *y-velocity* as Contour Name in the Contours window. Select Contours of Velocity… and Y Velocity. Check the box Filled under Options. Uncheck Node Values under Options. Select *interior-solid* under Surfaces and click on Save/Display. Select the red X coordinate axis in the graphics window.

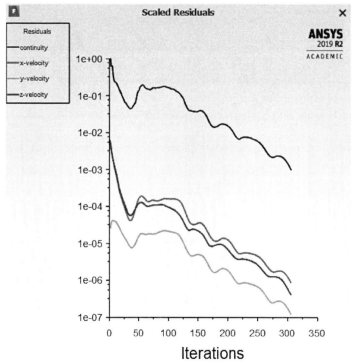

Figure 20.7a) Residuals from calculations

444

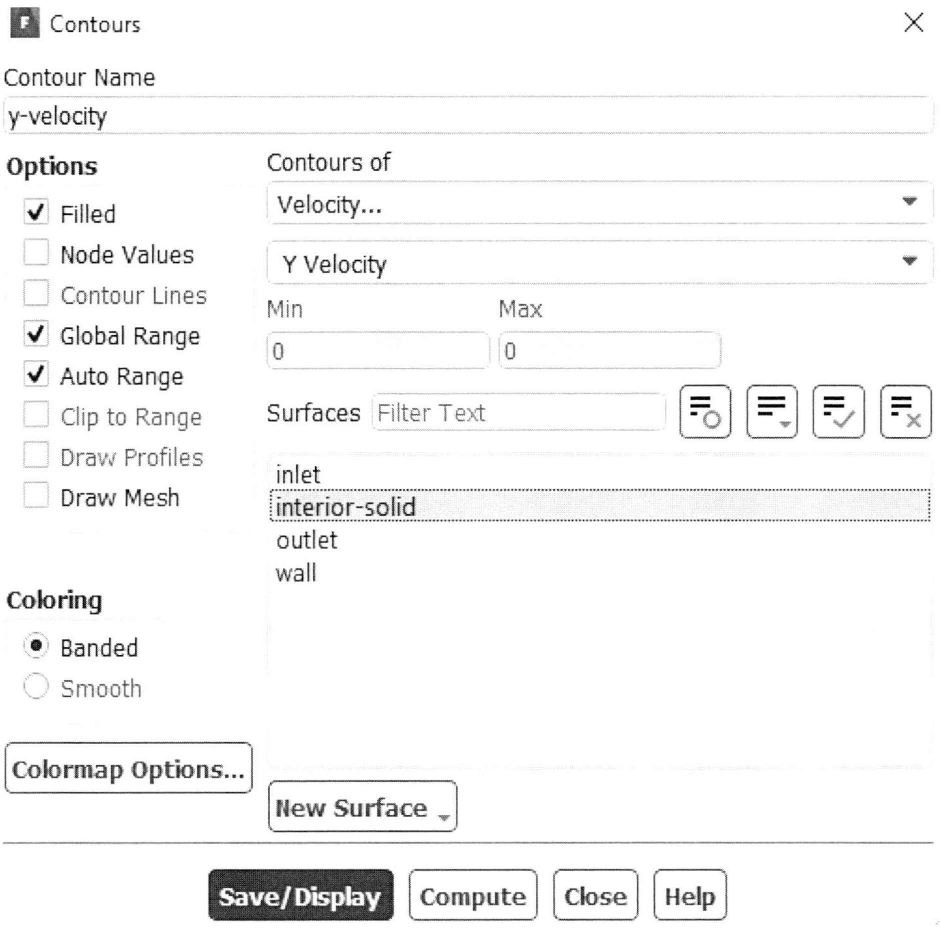

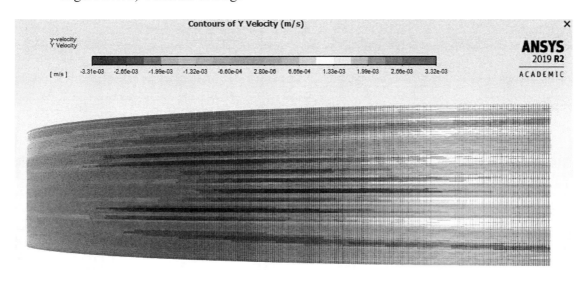

Figure 20.7b) Contours settings

Figure 20.7c) Contours of Y Velocity

H. Theory

8. The centrifugal instability for the flow in a curved channel is governed by the so called Dean number De.

$$De = Re\sqrt{\gamma} = \frac{U_b d}{v}\sqrt{\frac{d}{R}} \tag{20.1}$$

where U_b is the bulk flow velocity in the curved channel, d is the channel width, R its radius of curvature at the channel centerline and v is the kinematic viscosity of the fluid. Below the critical $De_{crit} = 36.27$, the flow is stable but instabilities will develop above this Dean number. The non-dimensional wave number α of the centrifugal instability is determined by

$$\alpha = \frac{2\pi d}{\lambda} \tag{20.2}$$

where λ is the spanwise wave length of the instability. The critical wave numbers $\alpha_{crit} = 3.96$ for $\gamma = 0.025$. From figure 20.7c), the wave number can be determined to be

$$\alpha = \frac{2\pi \cdot 0.010}{0.0105} = 5.98 \tag{20.3}$$

In order to determine the wave length that is used to determine the wave number in equation (20.3), you can measure the total length in the vertical spanwise direction for three red or three blue successive bands in figure 20.7c). Next, you take this vertical length and divide by three to get the average wave length in the vertical spanwise direction. To get the scale for figure 20.7c), use the total height of the curved channel in the vertical direction in figure 20.7c) that corresponds to 100 mm height.

The Dean number in the calculations is

$$De = Re\sqrt{\gamma} = \frac{0.05*0.010}{10^{-6}}\sqrt{\frac{0.010}{0.4}} = 79 \tag{20.4}$$

I. References

1. Dean, W.R., Fluid motion in a curved channel. *Proc. Roy. Soc.* **A121**, 402, 1928.
2. Matsson, J.E. and Alfredsson, P.H., Curvature- and rotation induced instabilities in channel flow. *J. Fluid Mech.* **210**, 537, (1990).

J. Exercises

20.1 Run the calculations for the flow in the curved channel but use the following tangential velocities: 0.03, 0.06, 0.09 and 0.12 m/s and determine the Dean number and the spanwise wave number for each tangential velocity.

20.2 Run the calculations for the flow in the curved channel as shown in this chapter for different mesh sizes using Element Size 1.6, 1.8, 2.0 and 2.2 mm. Determine the spanwise wave number for each case and compare with the critical value.

INDEX

Notes: